STUDIES ON FERMENTATION

THE DISEASES OF BEER

THEIR CAUSES, AND THE MEANS OF PREVENTING THEM

BY

L. PASTEUR

MEMBER OF INSTITUTE OF FRANCE, THE ROYAL SOCIETY OF LONDON, ETC.

A TRANSLATION, MADE WITH THE AUTHOR'S SANCTION, OF "ÉTUDES SUR LA BIÈRE," WITH NOTES, INDEX, AND ORIGINAL ILLUSTRATIONS

BY

FRANK FAULKNER
AUTHOR OF "THE ART OF BREWING," ETC.

AND

D. CONSTABLE ROBB, B.A.
LATE SCHOLAR OF WORCESTER COLL., OXFORD

London

MACMILLAN & CO

1879

KRAUS REPRINT CO.
New York
1969

Reprinted from the original edition in the
Wesleyan University Library

LC 4-21883

KRAUS REPRINT CO.
A U.S. Division of Kraus-Thomson Organization Limited

Printed in U.S.A.

TO

THE MEMORY OF

MY FATHER,

FORMERLY A SOLDIER UNDER THE FIRST EMPIRE,

AND

KNIGHT OF THE LEGION OF HONOUR.

THE LONGER I LIVE, THE BETTER DO I UNDERSTAND THE KINDNESS OF THY HEART AND THE EXCELLENCE OF THY MIND.

TO THY EXAMPLE AND COUNSELS DO I OWE THE EFFORTS THAT HAVE BEEN DEVOTED TO THESE STUDIES, AS WELL AS TO ALL THE WORK I HAVE EVER DONE. AND NOW, HOW CAN I BETTER HONOUR THESE FILIAL REMEMBRANCES THAN BY DEDICATING MY BOOK TO THY MEMORY?

L. PASTEUR.

AUTHOR'S PREFACE.

Our misfortunes inspired me with the idea of these researches. I undertook them immediately after the war of 1870, and have since continued them without interruption, with the determination of perfecting them, and thereby benefiting a branch of industry wherein we are undoubtedly surpassed by Germany.

I am convinced that I have found a precise, practical solution of the arduous problem which I proposed to myself—that of a process of manufacture, independent of season and locality, which should obviate the necessity of having recourse to the costly methods of cooling employed in existing processes, and at the same time secure the preservation of its products for any length of time.

These new studies are based on the same principles which guided me in my researches on wine, vinegar, and the silkworm disease—principles, the applications of which are practically unlimited. The etiology of contagious diseases may, perhaps, receive from them an unexpected light.

I need not hazard any prediction concerning the advantages likely to accrue to the brewing industry from the adoption of such a process of brewing as my study of the subject has enabled me to devise, and from an application of the novel facts upon which this process is founded. Time is the best appraiser of scientific work, and I am not unaware that an industrial discovery rarely produces all its fruit in the hands of its first inventor.

I began my researches at Clermont-Ferrand, in the laboratory, and with the help, of my friend M. Duclaux, professor of chemistry at the Faculty of Sciences of that town. I continued them in Paris, and afterwards at the great brewery of Tourtel Brothers, of Tantonville, which is admitted to be the first in France. I heartily thank these gentlemen for their extreme kindness. I owe also a public tribute of gratitude to M. Kuhn, a clever brewer of Chamalières, near Clermont-Ferrand, as well as to M. Velten, of Marseilles, and to MM. de Tassigny, of Reims, who have placed at my disposal their establishments and their products, with the most praiseworthy willingness.

L. PASTEUR.

PARIS, *June* 1, 1876.

PREFACE TO ENGLISH EDITION.

My first idea of placing before English brewers a translation of "Études sur la Bière" was meagre in the extreme, compared with the final realization of it as it appears in the following pages.

Seeing the vast importance of Pasteur's work from a practical point of view, after writing a review of it for the *Brewers' Journal*, I determined to procure, at any rate for the use of my pupils, a literal translation, illustrated by photo-lithographic copies of the original plates, the thankless task of executing this preliminary translation for so limited a number of readers being most kindly and generously carried out for me by my friend Mr. Frank U. Waite, who, being engaged with me at the time in practical brewing operations, shared my views as to the value of the original work.

It was on the completion of this translation that my views and desires expanded. The more I studied the work, the more I was convinced of its immense value to the brewer as affording him an intelligent knowledge of the processes and materials with which he deals, but over and above all this, it was impossible not to feel that the researches of such a devoted and accomplished *savant* as Pasteur, possessed a scientific interest much wider than their mere relation to the art of brewing would imply. As the work of a skilful chemist and a laborious and accurate observer, such a protracted and careful study of the lowest and simplest forms of life, must necessarily be of first importance to the biologist—to the beginner as an admirable introduction to the study of practical physiology in general, as well as to the more advanced student, from the suggestive light which it throws on the nature of analogous phenomena in more complex organisms.

I determined accordingly *to publish* the work if I could secure the consent of its distinguished author, but at the same time I felt that the publication of M. Pasteur's "Studies" in the form in which Mr. Waite had, at my request, translated it, and illustrated only with inferior copies of the original plates, would not be either advisable or just; but that I was bound rather to put the book before the English public in as satisfactory and complete a form as lay within my power. Under these circumstances I was induced to seek the aid of Mr. D. Constable Robb, B.A., of The Oxford University Museum, who, in taking Mr. Waite's version as a basis, has so elaborated, annotated, and recast it, that I feel bound to say that much of the value of "Studies on Fermentation," as it now appears, is due to the care that Mr. Robb has bestowed upon the revision that he so kindly undertook; a revision the result of which has created a feeling of confidence in the success of the translation as it now stands, which I could not have had in any mere literal version.

To the practical worker the original illustrations alone, which appear in this version, cannot but be of immense value in the microscopical study of the changes in the liquids with which he deals; whilst the many notes and additions, which are a feature peculiar to the English edition, more particularly the rendering into the equivalents, with which, unfortunately, practical men on this side of the channel are still most at home, of the metric weights and measures and centigrade temperatures, as well as the Index which Mr. Robb has compiled, will, I trust, render the book of still greater service than it otherwise would have been to many of those who may favour it with their attention.

The debt which we English brewers owe to M. Pasteur can hardly be over-estimated, and I must be allowed here to express my personal obligations to that distinguished worker for the permission which allows this translation; and to the French publishers for their help with regard to the interleaved illustrations.

The author's preface and dedication are, of course, reproduced, the former making it unnecessary for me to refer more in detail to the contents of the translation.

FRANK FAULKNER.

THE BREWERY, ST. HELEN'S, LANCASHIRE,
 September, 1879.

ERRATA.

Page 80, line 18 from top, insert * after unsubmerged.
,, 181, ,, 13 ,, ,, ,, " after *pullulans*.
,, 301, place * before footnote.

TABLE OF CONTENTS.

	PAGE
AUTHOR'S DEDICATION	v
,, PREFACE	vii
TRANSLATOR'S PREFACE	ix

CHAPTER I.

ON THE INTIMATE RELATION EXISTING BETWEEN THE DETERIORATION OF BEER, OR THE WORT FROM WHICH IT IS MADE, AND THE PROCESS OF BREWING 1

CHAPTER II.

ON THE CAUSES OF THE DISEASES WHICH AFFECT BEER AND WORT.

§ I. Every unhealthy change in the quality of beer coincides with a development of microscopic germs which are alien to the pure ferment of beer 19

§ II. The absence of change in wort and beer coincides with the absence of foreign organisms 25

CHAPTER III.

ON THE ORIGIN OF FERMENTS PROPERLY SO CALLED.

§ I. On the conditions which cause variations in the nature of the organized products existing in infusions 33

§ II. Experiments on blood and urine taken in their normal state, and exposed to contact with air that has been deprived of the particles of dust which it generally holds in suspension . 40
§ III. Experiments on the juice contained in grapes 54
§ IV. Wort and must exposed to common air 59
§ V. New comparative studies on the germs held in suspension by the air of different places which are near each other, but subjected to different conditions affecting the production and diffusion of the particles of dust found in them . . . 72
§ VI. Yeast may become dry and be reduced to dust without losing its faculty of reproduction 81

CHAPTER IV.

THE GROWTH OF DIFFERENT ORGANISMS IN A STATE OF PURITY: THEIR AUTONOMY.

§ I. Growth of *Penicillium glaucum* and *Aspergillus glaucus* in a state of purity.—Proofs that these fungoid growths do not become transformed into the alcoholic ferments of beer or wine.—Preliminary inquiry into the cause of fermentation . 86
§ II. Growth of *Mycoderma vini* in a state of purity.—Confirmation of our original conjectures as to the cause of fermentation.— *Mycoderma vini* does not change into yeast, although it may give rise to fermentation 108
§ III. Growth of *Mycoderma aceti* in a state of purity . . . 121
§ IV. Growth of *Mucor racemosus* in a state of purity.—Example of life more active and lasting when removed from the influence of air 127

CHAPTER V.

THE ALCOHOLIC FERMENTS.

§ I. On the origin of ferment 143
§ II. On "spontaneous" ferment 182
§ III. On "high" and "low" ferments 186
§ IV. On the existence and production of other species of ferment . 196
§ V. On a new race of alcoholic ferments: Aërobian ferments . 205
§ VI. The purification of commercial yeasts 219

CHAPTER VI.

THE PHYSIOLOGICAL THEORY OF FERMENTATION.

		PAGE
§ I.	On the relations existing between oxygen and yeast	235
§ II.	Fermentation in saccharine fruits immersed in carbonic acid gas	266
§ III.	Reply to certain critical observations of the German naturalists, Oscar Brefeld and Moritz Traube.	279
§ IV.	Fermentation of dextro-tartrate of lime	284
§ V.	Another example of life without air.—Fermentation of lactate of lime	292
§ VI.	Reply to the critical observations of Liebig, published in 1870	316

CHAPTER VII.

NEW PROCESS FOR THE MANUFACTURE OF BEER.

§ I.	Preliminary experiments.	338
§ II.	Method of estimating the oxygen held in solution in wort	353
§ III.	On the quantity of oxygen existing in a state of solution in brewers' worts	364
§ IV.	On the combination of oxygen with wort.	371
§ V.	On the influence of oxygen in combination on the clarification of wort	381
§ VI.	Application of the principles of the new process of brewing with the use of limited quantities of air	387

APPENDIX 396

INDEX 403

INDEX TO PLATES.

		TO FACE PAGE
I.	Principal disease-ferments met with in wort and beer	6
II.	Appearance under the microscope of the deposit from "turned" beer	20
III.	*Torulæ* in process of development	72
IV.	*Mycoderma vini* functioning as an alcoholic ferment.—Right half, showing appearance of spores just sown; left half, their appearance after an interval of submerged life	116
V.	*Mucor*, vegetating submerged, in deficit of air	136
VI.	Ferment of *mucor*	138
VII.	Yeast-cells—worn out and dissociated (left), after revival in a sweet wort (right)	148
VIII.	Fertile mould-cells from the outer surface of grapes	152
IX.	Various examples of the mode of growth of mould-cells from the outer surface of grapes	154
X.	One of the ferments of acid fruits at the commencement of fermentation in its natural *medium*	166
XI.	*Saccharomyces pastorianus*, in course of regular growth	168
XII.	Ferment-cells from a spontaneous fermentation just starting	184

STUDIES ON FERMENTATION.

CHAPTER I.

ON THE INTIMATE RELATION EXISTING BETWEEN THE DETERIO-
RATION OF BEER, OR THE WORT FROM WHICH IT IS MADE,
AND THE PROCESS OF BREWING.

At the outset of these "Studies," let us briefly consider the nature of beer and the methods of its manufacture.

Beer is a beverage which has been known from the earliest times. It may be described as an infusion of germinated barley and hops, which has been caused to ferment after having been cooled, and which, by means of "settling" and racking, has ultimately been brought to a high state of clarification. It is an alcoholic beverage, vegetable in its origin—a *barley wine*, as it is sometimes rightly termed.*

Beer and wine, however, differ widely in their composition. Beer is less acid and less alcoholic than wine; it holds more ingredients in solution, and the nature of these ingredients is by no means similar to that of those which are found in wine.

These differences in the component parts of wine and beer give rise to corresponding differences in the keeping qualities of the

---

* This expression is found for the first time, it would appear, in Theophrastus, B.C. 371. [See, however, Herodotus, Bk. II., chap. 77. Speaking of some Egyptians he says, "They drink a kind of wine made from barley (οἴνῳ δ' ἐκ κριθέων πεποιημένῳ), for the grape does not grow in that part of the country." Herodotus wrote about 450 B.C. Æschylus (480 B.C.) has a similar expression, Suppl. 953.—D. C. R.]

two liquids. The small amount of acidity in beer, its poverty in alcohol, and the presence of matter that is saccharine, or liable to become so, all operate in imparting to beer a tendency to change, which wine does not possess. That this unequal resistance to the aggression of diseases is due to such differences, may be proved by the fact that wine could be made much more liable to change than it actually is, by a diminution of its acidity and its usual proportion of alcohol, or by increasing the proportion of viscid or saccharine matters,* modifications which would tend to assimilate its composition to that of beer.

We have remarked elsewhere that the pains devoted to the rearing of vines, and to the ordinary operations of vinification, such as *ouillage*,† sulphuring, and repeated rackings, as well as the use of cellars and vessels hermetically closed, are entailed by the necessity of counteracting and preventing the diseases to which wine is liable. The same may be said, *a fortiori*, of beer, inasmuch as it is more liable to change than wine. Manufacturers and retailers of this beverage have to strive constantly with the difficulty of preserving it, or the wort used in its manufacture. We may readily be convinced of this by reviewing the usual processes of the art of brewing.

When the infusion of malt and hops, which is termed wort, is completed, it is left to cool. It is next put into one or more casks or vats, in which it is made to undergo alcoholic fermentation— the most important of all the processes in brewing.

The cooling must be as rapid as possible. This is a condition of success; otherwise, the wort may deteriorate, which will necessarily lead to deterioration in the quality of the beer. As long as the wort is at a high temperature it will remain sound;

* One of these modifications is a real source of serious danger to the preservation of wine; for instance, during rainy years, at the time of vintage, the grapes may happen to be covered with earthy matter, consisting principally of carbonate of lime; this will dissolve in wine and partly neutralize its acidity, and the wine will thus become more liable to disease.

† Transferring from one cask to another for the purpose of clarifying the wine.

when under 70° C. (158° F.), and particularly when at a temperature of from 25° C. to 35° C. (77° F. to 95° F), it will be quickly invaded by lactic and butyric ferments. Rapidity in cooling is so essential that to secure it recourse is had to special apparatus.* Even in the preparation of wort, especially when it is effected by successive mashings, in summer, deterioration is imminent: in fact, it is not rare to see the wort becoming acid during the *mashes*, if these are not accomplished with all possible celerity.

After the wort has been cooled, it is mixed with yeast. This is obtained from a previous fermentation, and, after being thoroughly pressed, is added at the rate of from one to two thousandth parts of the weight of the wort, that is, from 100 to 200 grammes per hectolitre (about 4 oz. to 8 oz. average for every 25 gallons). At first sight, this yeast seems free from the possible diseases of the wort and beer; but this is by no means the case.

Now, why do we add yeast to our wort? This practice is unknown in the art of vinification. The must is always left to spontaneous fermentation. Why should we not leave the wort to operate in the same manner?

It would be a mistake to suppose that in the brewing of beer yeast is added with the sole object of accelerating fermentation, and making it more rapid. Rapidity in fermentation is a very questionable advantage, and one which is not desired by brewers, who rather agree in pronouncing it injurious to the quality of beer. It is in the easy deterioration of the wort, or what is tantamount to it, in the facility it affords to various spontaneous fermentations, that we find an answer to these questions. The must, through its acidity, due to the presence of bitartrate of potash—which seems to promote alcoholic fermentation—through its proportion of sugar, and perhaps in consequence of some other peculiarity of its composition, always undergoes regular alcoholic fermentation. The

* We shall hereafter revert to this rapidity in cooling, to show that it is also of use in the subsequent clarification of beer.

diseases of wine, at the commencement of its manufacture, show themselves, so to say, in a latent state only. Therefore a vintage can be left, without inconvenience, to spontaneous fermentation.

With wort the case is quite different. Under certain accidental circumstances it is possible that alcoholic fermentation alone may take place in a wort left to ferment spontaneously, and the quality of the beer remain unimpaired, but such an event would be exceptional, and of very rare occurrence. In most cases we should obtain an acid or putrid liquid resulting from the production and multiplication of alien ferments.

The addition of yeast is made in consequence of the necessity of exciting through the whole bulk of wort, as soon as it is cold, a single fermentation—viz., the alcoholic, the only one that can produce beer properly so called.

The alcoholic ferments concerned in the production of beer will be found represented in several of the engravings in this work. Other ferments we may term "diseased"; these include all those that may occur spontaneously—that is, whose germs have not been directly and intentionally introduced—amongst the actual alcoholic ferments.

The expression, "diseased ferments," is justified by the circumstance that the propagation of these ferments is always accompanied by the production of substances which are acid, putrid, viscous, bitter, or otherwise unpalatable, a consideration of commercial rather than scientific importance. From a physiological point of view, all these ferments are of equal interest and importance. The botanist, as a man of science, in contemplating nature, must give equal attention to all plants, whether useful or noxious, since they are all governed by the same natural laws, among which no order of merit could be established. The exigencies of industry and health require, however, wide distinctions.

The first engraving (Plate I.) represents the different diseased ferments, together with some cells of alcoholic yeast, to show the relative size of these organisms.

No. 1 of the engraving represents the ferments of *turned* beer, as it is called. These are filaments, simple or articulated into chains of different size, and having a diameter of about the thousandth part of a millimetre (about $\frac{1}{25000}$ inch). Under a very high power they are seen to be composed of many series of shorter filaments, immovable in their articulations, which are scarcely visible.

In No. 2 are given the lactic ferments of wort and beer. These are small, fine and contracted in their middle. They are generally detached, but sometimes occur in chains of two or three. Their diameter is a little greater than that of No. 1.

In No. 3 are given the ferments of putrid wort and beer. These are mobile filaments whose movements are more or less rapid, according to the temperature. Their diameter varies, but is for the most part greater than that of the filaments of Nos. 1 and 2. They generally appear at the commencement of fermentation, when it is slow, and are almost invariably the result of very defective working.

In No. 4 are given the ferments of viscous wort, and those of ropy beer, which the French call *filante*. They form chaplets of nearly spherical grains. These ferments rarely occur in wort, and still less frequently in beer.

No. 5 represents the ferments of pungent, sour beer, which possesses an acetic odour. These ferments occur in the shape of chaplets, and consist of the *mycoderma aceti*, which bears a close resemblance to lactic ferments (No. 2), especially in the early stages of development. Their physiological functions are widely different, in spite of this similarity.

The ferments given in No. 7 characterize beer of a peculiar acidity, which reminds one more or less of unripe, acid fruit, with an odour *sui generis*. These ferments occur in the form of grains which resemble little spherical points, placed two together, or forming squares. They are generally found with the filaments of No. 1, and are more to be feared than the latter, which cause no very great deterioration in the quality of beer, when alone. When No. 7 is present, by itself or with No. 1, the beer acquires a sour taste and smell that render it detestable. We have met with this ferment existing in beer, unaccompanied by other ferments, and have been convinced of its fatal effects.

No. 6 represents one of the deposits belonging to wort. This must not be confounded with the deposits of diseased ferments. The latter are always visibly organized, whilst the former is shapeless, although it would not always be easy to decide between the two characters, if several samples of both descriptions were not present. This shapeless deposit interferes with wort during its cooling. It is generally absent from beer, because it remains in the backs, or on the coolers; or it may get entangled in the yeast during fermentation and disappear with it.

Among the shapeless granulations of No. 6 may be discerned little spheres of different sizes and perfect regularity. These are balls of resinous and colouring matter that are frequently found in old beer, at the bottom of bottles or casks; sometimes they occur in wort preserved after Appert's method. They resemble organized products, but are nothing of the kind. We have remarked before, in "Studies on Wine," that the colouring matter of wine would settle, in course of time, in that form.

It is evident that the different ferments delineated in Plate I. are worthy of thorough study, in consequence of the fermentations to which they may give rise. Care must be taken to isolate the action of each of them in fermentations which we may call pure—a condition of some difficulty, but one that may be carried out by an adoption of the methods explained in this work.

All these diseased ferments have a common origin. Their germs, infinitesimal and hardly perceptible as they are, even with the aid of the microscope, form a part of the dust conveyed through the air. This dust the air is continually taking from or depositing upon all objects in nature, so that the dust that clings to the ingredients from which our beer is manufactured, may teem with the germs of diseased ferments.

During the process of fermentation, the occult power of diseased ferments, although it may escape the observation of the brewer, is manifested in a high degree.

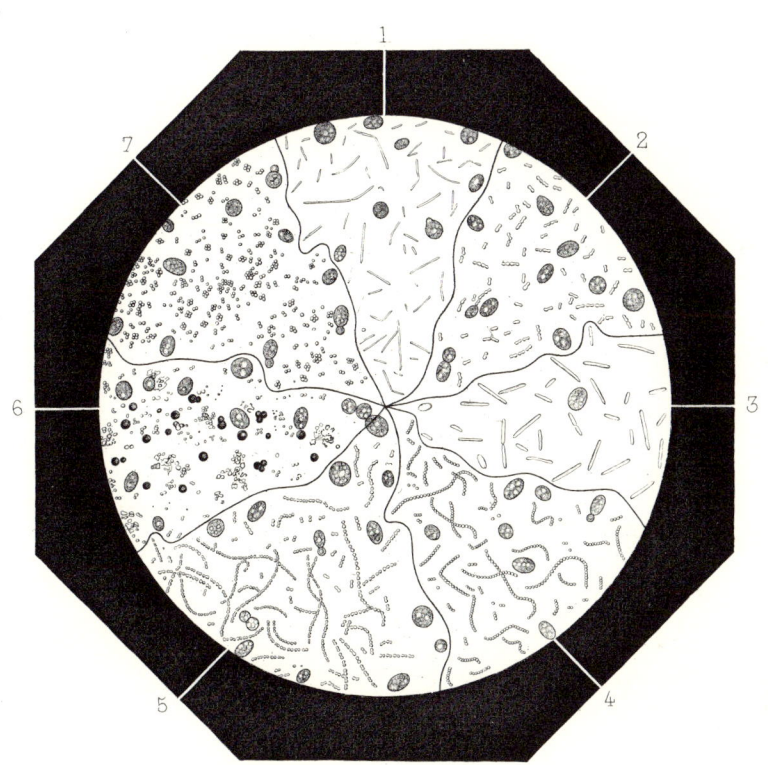

During the last thirty years, or so, the art of brewing has undergone a radical change, at least in Europe. This change has been effected by a partial abandonment of the process of fermentation formerly used. Thirty years ago only one kind of beer was known; there are nowadays two distinct kinds—beer fermented at a high temperature, and beer fermented at a low temperature. Each of these is subdivided into many varieties, to which different names are given, according to their strength or colour. This is the case in England, where we find porter, ale, pale ale, stout, bitter beer, and other varieties of beer, although, as a matter of fact, the English have but one kind of beer, all the English beers being fermented at a high temperature.

Let us briefly examine the differences existing between the two kinds of beer.

Formerly all beer was fermented at a high temperature. The wort, after having been cooled in the backs, was run into a large vat, at a temperature of about 20° C. (68° F.). Yeast was then added to it, and when the fermentation began to show itself, in the formation of a light, white froth, upon the surface of the liquid, the wort was run into casks, having a capacity of from 50 to 100 litres (11 to 22 gallons)—75 litres being the commonest size. These casks were placed in cellars, having a temperature of from 18° C. to 20° C. (64° F. to 68° F.). The activity of fermentation soon produced a froth that grew thicker and more and more viscous in proportion to the quantity of yeast it contained. The yeast worked out of the bung-holes and dropped into a vessel placed under the casks; there it was gathered for subsequent operations. It always exceeded the quantity used in the first instance, the ferment increasing greatly during the process of fermentation. The increase in its weight varied with the weight of yeast used and the composition of the wort. Under the ordinary conditions of brewing, where the weight of the pitching yeast was about one thousandth part of the weight of the wort, the increase is said to have been from five to seven times the weight of the yeast;

but such increase must naturally have been determined by the quality of the wort, the quantity of hops used, the action of oxygen, and the proportion of barm employed. The process of fermentation lasted from three to four days. By that time the beer was finished, and had become limpid, the fermentation having been completed. The bungs could then be placed in the casks, and the beer be delivered to the customer.* A certain amount of yeast still remained in the casks, and caused the beer to become thick, in transit; but a few days' rest sufficed to restore its brilliancy, and render it fit for drinking or bottling.

Here we have an explanation of the term "*high* fermentation," which has been applied to the foregoing process. This process is conducted at a high temperature, which, commencing at 19° C. or 20° C. (66° F. or 68° F.), is raised to 20° C. or 21° C. (68° or 70° F.) by the action of fermentation, which is always accompanied by an increase of heat.†

* In some breweries (at Lyons especially) fermentation at a high temperature is practised in large vats at about 15° C. (59° F.). The yeast which covers the surface of the liquid is skimmed off and stored in flat tubs.

† The initial temperature of the wort must be regulated by the quantity of wort subjected to fermentation. In English breweries, where large quantities are brewed at a time, the heat created by the action of fermentation would produce a temperature sufficiently high to affect the quality of the beer, if the yeast were added at 19° C. or 20° C.

The following are the temperatures at which the worts are pitched, in the principal London breweries:—For common ale, 60° F. or 15·5° C.; for pale ale, 58° F. or 14·4° C.; for porter, 64° F. or 17·8° C. The fermentation is commenced in large vats; from these the beer is run into vessels of a much smaller capacity, in which it completes its fermentation by working off the yeast and cleansing itself.

For white beer of superior quality, the temperature during fermentation must not rise beyond 72° F. or 22·2° C.; some brewers never allow it to exceed 18° C. (65° F.). The temperature is lowered by means of a current of cold water, which circulates through a coil fixed in the vats or other fermenting vessels.

In the case of porter, the initial heat of which is 64° F. or 17·8° C., the temperature in the vats sometimes rises to 78° F. or 25·5° C.; but such an increase in temperature excites considerable apprehension.

We have seen a tun for pale ale, containing 200 barrels of 36 gallons,

This is not, however, the only reason for the use of the term "*high* fermentation." We have just seen that the fermenting casks were so arranged that most of the yeast produced during the process of fermentation would rise to the upper part of the casks and work out of the bung-holes. In this practical fact we have the actual origin of the expressions "*high fermentation*" and "*high beer*," which are used to distinguish this peculiar fermentation and the quality of beer derived from it.

As we have already observed, all beer was formerly produced by this mode of fermentation, which even at the present time is still practised in the breweries of Great Britain, where beer fermented at a low temperature is absolutely unknown.

"Low fermentation" is a slow process, effected at a low temperature, during which the yeast sinks to the bottom of the vats or casks. The wort, after cooling, is run into open wooden vats. In cooling, the wort is brought to as low a temperature as 8° C. (47° F.), or even 6° C. (43° F.), at which point it is maintained by cones or cylinders (styled *nageurs*, i.e., floats, by the French) floating in the fermenting vats. These floats may be filled with ice if the outside temperature requires it, as is invariably the case in summer.

pitched with 600 lbs. of fairly solid yeast. In forty-six hours the attenuation was considered sufficient, and the beer, which from an initial heat of 58·1° F. or 14·5° C., had risen to 72° F. or 22·2° C., was cleansed to working casks. The large vats in which the fermentation is started may be considered as equivalent to the *cuves guilloires* of French breweries, the casks in which it is completed and the yeast thrown off representing their 75-litre vessels, improperly called *quarts*. Notwithstanding the enormous English beer manufacture, and although the fermenting vat, as in making porter, for instance, sometimes attains the capacity of 2,000 to 3,000 litres (400 to 600 gallons), the casks into which it is run are never larger than 15 to 20 hectolitres (300 to 400 gallons); and even at Burton, in the celebrated breweries of Allsopp and Bass, the pale ale is finished in casks of a capacity less than 10 hectolitres, and yet the average turn-out of these immense works reaches 3,000 to 4,000 hectolitres (60,000 to 80,000 gallons) of beer per day.

The duration of this fermentation is ten, fifteen, or even twenty days. The yeast, which is produced less abundantly than in the case of beer fermented at a high temperature, is gathered after the beer has been drawn off, and is partly used in subsequent fermentations.

The term "*low* fermentation" is derived partly from the lowness of the temperature during the fermenting process, and partly from the fact that the yeast is gathered at the bottom, and not at the upper part of the fermenting vessels.*

Beer fermented at a low temperature, of which there are several varieties, differing in colour and quality, is of Bavarian origin.† The preference of the public for this kind of beer, and the increased facilities that such a beer affords the trade, are the two reasons why its manufacture has so greatly increased. In Austria, Bavaria, Prussia, and other Continental countries this new method of brewing is almost exclusively adopted.

In the *Moniteur de la Brasserie* of the 23rd April, 1871, may be found the following significant remarks on the increase in the production of beer fermented at a low temperature on the Continent: "The number of breweries manufacturing *high* beer is rapidly decreasing, whilst the number of those producing *low* beer is still more rapidly increasing. There were in Bohemia; in 1860, 281 breweries in which high fermentation was practised; in 1865, only 81 of these remained; in 1870, the number had declined to 18. On the other hand, the number of breweries practising *low* fermentation increased from 135 in 1860 to 459 in 1865, and in 1870 had risen to 831. In 1860 there were 620 breweries in which the two methods were employed; in 1865 there were 486; in 1870 only 119 remained. The number of breweries at present existing in Bohemia amounts to 968."

* [The expressions "high" and "low" fermentation or beer strictly refer to temperature, whereas the other expressions used ("top" or "bottom") refer to the behaviour of the yeast. The French words *haute* and *basse* seem to look both ways.—D. C. R.]

† It is said that the floating cones or cylinders filled with ice, which enable brewers to manufacture beer at a low temperature, even in summer, were first used in Alsace.

In France, we are still in a period of transition; but year by year the manufacture of "low beer" is increasing, to the evident detriment of its competitor.

It is unnecessary to dwell upon certain differences existing between the two kinds of beer, such as may be traced to the preparation and composition of their respective worts. The brewing of "high beer," by hand or machinery, is effected in one operation; the brewing of "low beer" is accomplished by successive mashings, the temperatures of which are gradually raised. These differences, and others that result from the longer boiling of the wort, in the "high fermentation" process, give rise to diversities in the composition and colour of the worts, from which circumstance "low beers" are sometimes termed *white beers*, in contradistinction to the others, which have a deeper colour, and are known as *dark beers* (*bruns*). The name of Strasburg is generally given to "low beer" in France, but sometimes it is called German beer.

It is easy to account for the changes introduced into the construction and working of breweries by the new process of "low fermentation." A low temperature is essential not only to the manufacture but also to the preservation of "low beer," and must be secured by the use of ice-cellars in which the temperature may be maintained at 5° R. or 6° R. (43° F. or 45°F.), and even at 1°, 2°, or 3° R. (35° to 39 °F.) throughout the year. This necessitates an accumulation of ice and the construction of cellars of enormous extent, for the storage of the beer. "Low beer" is essentially a stock beer, especially if brewed in winter, when due advantage is taken of the low temperature of the season. It is kept in cold cellars until the spring or summer, when beer is consumed in larger quantities. It is calculated that 100 kilos. (1·96 cwt.) of ice is the average quantity used per hectolitre (22 gallons) of good beer, between the cooling of the wort and the day of sale.*

* 45 million kilos. of ice are annually consumed in the brewery of M. Dreher, in Vienna. The brewery of Sedlmayer, at Munich, uses about 10 million kilos. (*Journal des Brasseurs*, 22nd June, 1873.)

In the manufacture of "high beer" we find none of these complications, nor have we in that manufacture any similar difficulty of working or expense of construction to contend against. The whole process of brewing, including the delivery of the beer, does not take more than eight days. Why should a mode of brewing so simple, so rapid, and comparatively so inexpensive, have been abandoned by the greater part of Europe in favour of a system disadvantageous to the brewer in so many respects? It would be a mistake to suppose that the sole reason for such a change might be found in the superior quality of "low beer." That such a superiority does exist is admitted as a fact by the majority of beer drinkers; but taken by itself, this fact is not sufficient to account for the radical transformation that has taken place in the manufacture of beer, as is proved by the example of England, which, we believe, does not possess as yet one single "low beer" brewery, from which circumstance we may fairly suppose that the English have a decided preference for "high beer."

The principal advantage of working at a low temperature lies in the fact that "low beer" is less liable to deterioration, and is less prone to contract diseases than "high beer," especially whilst it remains in the brewery—a circumstance that places the brewer in a position vastly superior to that which he occupied in former times. With the help of ice the brewer can manufacture beer during winter and the early part of spring, for consumption in summer.* "High beer," on the

* It should, however, be borne in mind that these remarks on the relative preservative powers of the two beers hold true on account of three things—differences in the respective modes of brewing, artificial cooling during the process of fermentation, and the storing of the "low beer" in ice-cellars. In itself, perhaps, "low beer" is more liable to change than "high beer;" that this does not actually take place, is due to the employment of artificial cooling. A brewery which has an average annual production of 10,000 hect. will use 8,000 cwt. of ice. If we add to this the ice used during the retail of the beer, which is best drunk at 12° C. (54° F.), we shall arrive at the total of 100 kilos. per hectolitre.

other hand, must be consumed within a short time of its production. The brewer is thus compelled to manufacture it as it is wanted, and as orders are sent in, the demand for it being in a great measure dependent upon the state of the weather.

Conditions so unfavourable as these must necessarily operate prejudicially against trade. Industry requires more stability and uniformity, both in the production and the sale of its goods. "Low beer" can be brewed in large quantities at any time to be delivered at any other time, according to requirements; its manufacture, therefore, is unattended by the inconveniences which we have just noticed.*

How is it that the use of ice and yeast operating at a low temperature so greatly facilitates the preservation of our beer

* [In connection with the comparison here instituted by M. Pasteur between the drinking and keeping qualities of the two kinds of beer, it may be useful to draw the reader's attention to a review by Dr. Charles Graham of the French edition of this work, published in *Nature* for January 11th, 1877, page 216. At the same time we must remark that Dr. Graham appears to have overlooked M. Pasteur's footnote, page 12, English edition:—"His assertion, that by bottom fermentation store beers can be produced, whereas those produced by top fermentation must be consumed at once and cannot be transported, are certainly strange to an Englishman. So far from these unfavourable comparisons being true in all cases, the exact opposite is generally the case. Bavarian and other bottom fermentation beers are in fact those which can neither be preserved nor transported without the liberal employment of ice; even that sent from Vienna to London must be kept cold artificially, in order to avoid rapid destruction. As regards flavour, there are many who think a glass of Burton pale ale, or of good old College rent ale, to be superior to any Bavarian beer. The chief cause of the decline in the production of top fermentation beers on the Continent has been the want of attention in the fermentation process; whereas the English brewer, especially the brewer of high-class ales, has been unremitting in his attention to the temperature in fermentation and to the perfect cleansing of the ale. Now, where such attention is given, it is not difficult to obtain ales which will keep a few years. While objecting to our English produce being so hastily depreciated by M. Pasteur, our brewers will be the first to avail themselves of his biological researches, in order to render their produce more stable and better flavoured, without having recourse to the general adoption of the vastly more costly system of bottom fermentation."—D. C. R.]

and enables us to secure such striking advantages? The explanation is simple: the diseased ferments, which we have pointed out, rarely appear at a lower temperature than 10° C. (50° F.), and at that temperature their germs cease to be active. The adoption of low temperatures by brewers is mainly due to this physiological fact. On one occasion only have we met with active *vibrios* (No. 3, Plate I.), at a very low temperature; these were forming with great difficulty in wort fermenting at 5° C. (41° F.),

From this we see that the changes which the manufacture of beer has undergone during the present century have been based mainly on the diseases to which beer is liable, either during or after the process of brewing. The fact that English brewers have not as yet adopted "low fermentation" may be accounted for, in a great measure, by the difficulty of enlarging existing breweries, in cities like London, to the extent required for the new method of manufacture. Even in the event of public taste demanding a "low beer," English brewers will hesitate a long time before converting their breweries. Such conversion would impose upon them expenses and difficulties of a very serious nature. If ever such a change should take place, it will probably be inaugurated out of London. It is, however, worthy of remark that English brewers, without adopting "low fermentation," have introduced considerable improvements in brewing, especially in the management of the temperature during fermentation; this must be preserved within narrow and exact limits, for fear of injury to the product. It might easily be shown that these improvements have resulted from the liability of the beer to contract diseases, although this fact may not have been recognized by the brewers who have introduced them.

Besides the yeasts which belong to the two principal kinds of fermentation, there exist many varieties of alcoholic ferment that produce, each of them, a special kind of beer. Among these special beers some are deficient in taste, others in aroma, others in brilliancy. Let us suppose that in the manufacture of a beer with one of these yeasts, from which a peculiar flavour is derived, a different and inferior variety is accidentally mixed with that which we intend to use; in such a case, the inferior variety, the product of which will possess an inferior quality, will exercise such an influence on the brewing as to induce the belief that disease must be present. The microscope, if consulted, will reveal no special organism, nor any of those diseased ferments of which we have given specimens. It is in the study of yeast that we must endeavour to find the cause of the results we observe. This point, which is of the greatest importance to brewers, will become clearer as we proceed.

If we examine the practices of the beer trade, in its retail as well as in its export branches, we shall find that many of them afford evidence of the liability of the beer to deteriorate. We may cite some of these. When taken out of the ice-cellars, the beer is kept in casks of small capacity, that it may be the sooner consumed; when exposed to a high temperature, the beer will not keep sound for any length of time, but will speedily effloresce with *mycoderma vini* or *mycoderma aceti*.

Beer which is intended for bottling should not be kept for more than a month or six weeks. Even in bottling we may perceive the tendency of the liquid to deteriorate.* It is necessary that the bottles, immediately after being filled, should be laid on their sides for twenty-four or forty-eight hours; they may then be placed upright; the reason for this is that the air

* To preserve bottled beer from deterioration, some bottlers employ, at the moment of filling, a small quantity of bisulphite of lime. Others heat the bottles to a temperature of 55° C. (131° F.) In the north of Germany and in Bavaria, this practice has been widely adopted since the publication of the author's "Studies on Wine," and some of M. Velten's writings. The process has been termed *pasteurization* in recognition of the author's discovery of the causes of deterioration in fermented liquors, and of the means of preserving such liquors by the application of heat. Unfortunately this process is less successful in the case of beer than in that of wine, for the delicacy of flavour which distinguishes beer is affected by heat, especially when the beer has been manufactured by the ordinary process. This effect would be less felt in beer manufactured by the process which is advocated in this work.

left between the cork and the beer might give rise to the production of efflorescence. If we lay the bottles down on their sides, the oxygen of this air will be absorbed by the oxidizable substances in the liquid, and there will be little fear of germs developing themselves when the bottles are placed upright. The bottles should not, however, be left on their sides longer than forty-eight hours; otherwise the supplementary fermentation may force the corks out. Moreover, when the bottles stand upright the products of fermentation collect at the bottom, and not at the sides.

Beer which is intended for keeping, if exported or conveyed some distance off, must be surrounded with ice. Without this precaution it will ferment too much or contract some disease.

"High beer" cannot stand travelling. This kind of beer should not be exported unless the ordinary proportion of hops has been greatly increased—hop oil acting in some respects as an antiseptic, and preventing the beer from contracting diseases.[*] The export of English beer to India and the Continent has fallen off of late years, or rather, has not increased to the extent that was anticipated; in fact, this trade has entailed great losses upon those engaged in it. It is said that an English firm lost as much as £48,000 on one consignment, which on its arrival in India was found to be all turned.

There are no breweries in hot countries, where beer would command a very large sale. It is a well-known fact that beer is a remarkably pleasant drink in tropical climates, provided its temperature be a few degrees below that of the atmosphere, but the expenses of its production would be enormous, on account of the immense quantity of ice that would be required in its manufacture and for its preservation. It is in hot countries that beer is most liable to deterioration.

Beer is said to be the beverage of northern regions, which

---

[*] A convincing proof of the influence of hops on the ferment organisms is contained in the fact that beer, even after being raised to 60° C. or 70° C. (140° or 160° F.), will, if unhopped, readily take on the butyric fermentation, from which, if hopped, it would remain perfectly free.

are deprived of the vine, by the rigour of their climate. In these regions man has sought in the abundance of grain-fruit a substitute for grapes. To a certain extent this is true; nevertheless, it is an undoubted fact that beer was first brewed in Egypt, a very hot country, whence its manufacture has spread over Europe. It was called Pelusian wine, from Pelusium, a city on the banks of the Nile, which produced a beer that was held in high esteem.*

Beyond a doubt, hot countries, even those in which the vine is cultivated, would consume much beer, could it but stand their high temperature.† A considerable quantity of beer is now brewed in British India, but its manufacture entails an enormous outlay for ice.

The complications which result from the tendency of wort and beer to deteriorate, underlie almost all the details of the process of brewing and the sale of beer, and have been the cause of most of the changes and improvements that have been effected in brewing, during the present century.

* For historical details, see *l'Encyclopédie*, Art. *Bière*.

† As a wine-producing country France has been highly favoured by nature, but the consumption of beer in France is increasing every year. In 1873 the quantity of beer, paying excise duties, amounted to 7,413,190 hect., which yielded to the Treasury the sum of 20,165,136 fr. These figures are taken from a report published in 1875 by M. Jacquème, inspector of finances, who remarks that the quantity of beer upon which excise duties are paid represents, probably, not more than one-third of the total production: two-thirds of the quantity brewed evades the duties.

CHAPTER II.

ON THE CAUSES OF THE DISEASES WHICH AFFECT BEER AND WORT.

FROM our preceding observations it will be evident that the manufacture of beer, the arrangement of breweries, and all the processes practised by the brewer immediately depend upon this fact, that beer and wort are fluids essentially liable to change. Thus it becomes a matter of extreme importance that we should have an exact knowledge of the causes and nature of the changes which affect our produce, and it may be that this knowledge will lead us to regard the conditions of the brewing industry from a novel point of view, and bring about important modifications in the practices of the trade. We might vainly search the numerous works which have been written on brewing for information respecting the proposed subject of these studies. At the most we should find the diseases to which beer is liable in the course of its manufacture, or afterwards, vaguely hinted at; perhaps we might be favoured with certain empirical recipes for disguising the evil effects of those diseases.

It will be our endeavour to demonstrate the truth of the proposition we have already laid down, that every change to which wort and beer are liable is brought about solely by the development of organic ferments, whose germs are being perpetually wafted to and fro in the dust floating through the air, or distributed over the surface of the different materials and utensils used in brewing, such as malt, yeast, water, coolers, vats, tubs, casks, shovels, workmen's clothes, and innumerable other things.

It is evident that this proposition bears a marked resemblance to the one which we have demonstrated concerning the diseases of wine.*

By the expression *diseases* of wort and beer, we mean radical changes which so affect the nature of those liquids as to make them unpalatable, especially if they are kept; such changes produce beer which is sharp, sour, turned, oily, putrid, and otherwise bad. It would be unreasonable to apply the term *disease* to certain modifications in the quality of beer, which may be produced by practices more or less commendable. Such modifications, too, may result from want of skill in the brewer, from the composition of the wort, from the specific nature of the yeast, or from the inferior quality of ingredients. It is a well-known fact that "low beer," if manufactured according to the ordinary process, has not that same delicacy of flavour which characterizes beer fermented at a lower temperature than 10° C. (50° F.). Fermented at 10° C. (50° F.), or 12° C. (53° F.) or at a higher temperature, it loses the peculiar properties which consumers prize. Nevertheless, in point of soundness it may be as good a beer as one which has been fermented at 6° C. (43° F.), or 8° C. (46° F.). One might say of the former beer that it is inferior to the latter in estimation; but we could not rightly call it diseased, for we are supposing a case in which disease does not actually exist.

§ I.—Every Unhealthy Change in the Quality of Beer coincides with a Development of Microscopic Germs which are alien to the Pure Ferment of Beer.

Our proposition concerning the causes of the diseases of wort and beer might be demonstrated in several ways. The following is one of the simplest:—Take a few bottles of sound beer,

* A statement of this proposition, as far as it concerns beer, appeared first in outline in the author's *Etudes sur le vin*, published in 1866.

say, for instance, that which is known in Paris as Tourtel's, Grüber's, or Dreher's, from the name of the brewer who manufactures it. Place some of these bottles in a hot-water bath and raise the temperature to about 60° C. (140° F.). Permit them to cool, and then place them by the side of the other bottles that have not been heated. In every case, especially if we conduct this experiment in summer, we shall find that in the course of a few weeks—the length of time varying according to the temperature and the quality of the beer—all the bottles which have not been heated will have become diseased, in some cases even to the extent of being undrinkable. Let us next examine, by way of comparison, the deposits in the heated and non-heated bottles. We shall find associated with the pure alcoholic ferment other organisms, filiform and for the most part very slender, and either simple or articulated, as represented in Plate II., the design of which is taken from actual deposits occurring in beer that had been kept for some time at the ordinary temperature. A number of bottles of beer which had been heated on October 8th, 1871, were compared with those of an equal number of bottles of the same beer which had not been heated. The examination took place on July 27th, 1872. The beer, which had been heated to 55° C. (131° F.), was remarkably sound, well flavoured, and still in a state of fermentation. As a matter of fact, we have proved by exact experiments that alcoholic ferments, heated in beer, can endure a temperature of 55° C. (131° F.), without losing the power of germination; but the action is rendered somewhat more difficult and slower. Diseased ferments, however, existing in the same medium, perish at this temperature, as they do in the case of wine. The beer which had not been heated, had undergone changes which rendered it quite undrinkable. Its acidity, due to volatile acids, was higher than that of the other beer in the proportion of 5 to 1. The beer which had been heated contained ½ per cent. of alcohol more than the other.

The deposits in the heated bottles also showed filaments of disease, but in such minute quantity that it was necessary to

Pl. II

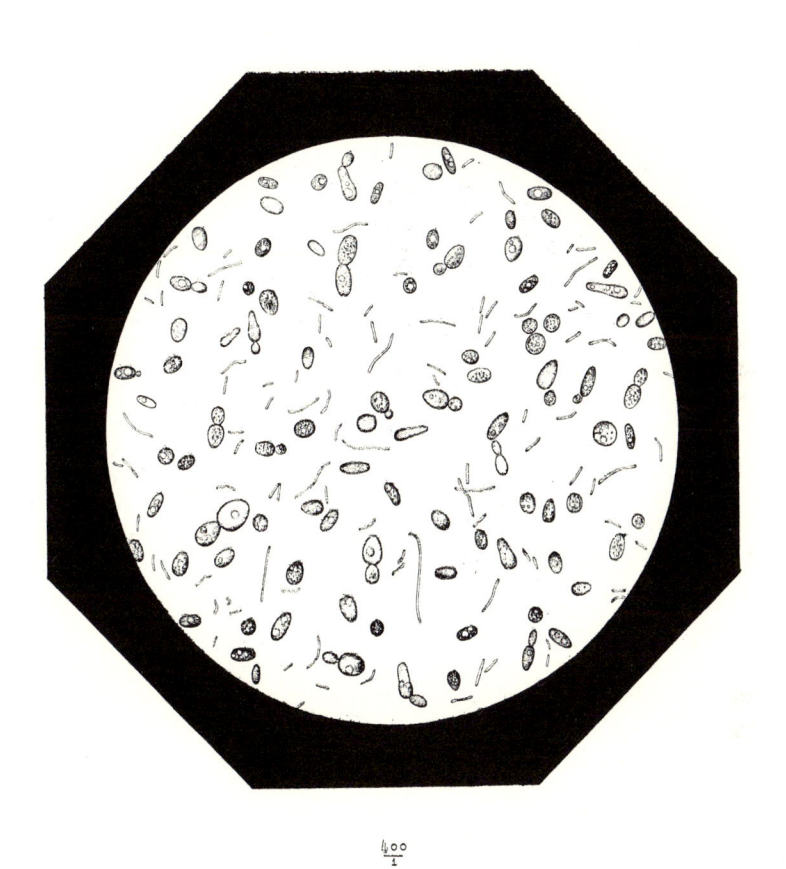

$\frac{400}{1}$

Deyrolle del

Picart sc

Imp. Gany Gros. Paris.

search many fields of the microscope to discover their existence. Those which we found after the heating must have existed in the beer before that operation; the heat had destroyed them, without sensibly altering their shape or size; they could neither multiply nor continue to exert any influence upon the components of the beer.*

From these experiments we may easily perceive, on the one hand, that beers apparently sound to the taste do not contain these or any other filiform ferments, save in a scarcely appreciable quantity; and, on the other hand, that these same ferments appear with the first unfavourable change in the quality of the beers, and that they exist more or less abundantly in proportion to the intensity of disease.

In certain extremely rare cases it may happen—so, at least, we have been assured, but we have not proved the fact ourselves —that beer may keep sound in bottle, even without the preliminary heating. This exception can only occur in the case of certain beers of a peculiar composition, which are highly hopped, and are made during the favourable months of November or December, out of the choicest materials, and fermented with yeast that happens to be pure. In the deposit of such beer, even after a lapse of several months or several years, we should find only the ordinary alcoholic ferment, the slow action of which would merely cause a gradual increase in the quantity of alcohol existing in the beer, and a diminution in the proportion of dextrine. This beer might grow old, as wine does, and remain perfectly sound.

Very often the whole work of the brewer is jeopardized by the unsuspected presence of diseased ferments, a remedy for

---

* As the deposit in the heated bottles is, as a rule, inconsiderable, it is necessary to exercise some precaution in collecting it. The bottles are taken up; after some days' rest they are decanted very carefully, with as little shaking as possible, until not more than one or two cubic centimetres (about a tea-spoonful) of the liquid remains at the bottom. The bottles are then shaken vigorously, with the object of collecting the whole of the deposit from the bottom and the sides into this small quantity of liquid; a drop of this is then examined under the microscope.

which is only devised after the evil has evoked the complaints of customers. In such a case the brewer avails himself of the kindness of some other brewer to obtain a change of yeast—a custom which is recognized and valued in the trade, since all managers of breweries have an interest in keeping it up. The brewer whose produce is most satisfactory recognizes the fact that unforeseen circumstances may compel him at any moment to change his yeast.

We have frequently had occasion to show that this necessity for a change of yeast depends, in most cases, on some change brought about by the presence of diseased ferments, the multiplication of which has resulted fortuitously from some unconscious neglect during the process of brewing, or from climatic influences. When we reflect that yeast is a living being, and that the medium which serves as its aliment, and the water in which it lives, are remarkably well adapted for the development of a vast number of other microscopic beings, the comparative purity of yeast should surprise us even more than its deterioration does.

Now by means of microscopical observations we might often detect the existence of the evil long before we are warned of it by a defective working, which invariably entails great losses.*

In proof of this remark we may cite the following facts. In the month of September, 1871, we were permitted to go through a large London brewery, in which the microscopical study of yeast was altogether unknown. We were allowed to make certain experiments in the presence of the managers of the establishment. We first examined porter yeast, which was collected in a channel that received the yeast as it worked out of the fermenting vessels. One of the ferments of disease abounded in this yeast, as may be seen in the accompanying

* Since the publication of the author's "Studies on the Diseases of Wine, and the Dangers resulting to Wine and Beer from the Microscopic Parasites found therein," some intelligent brewers have derived considerable profit from the application of the theories laid down in that work.

sketch, which was taken on the spot (Fig. 1). It was evident that the working of the porter was extremely unsatisfactory, and had, perhaps, been so for a long time; indeed, we were told that they had obtained a change of yeast from another London brewery that same day. We made a point of examining this yeast with the microscope. It was beyond comparison purer than the preceding yeast.

It is evident that if these brewers had been in the habit of using the microscope they might have detected the unsoundness of their produce before the time when they actually made the

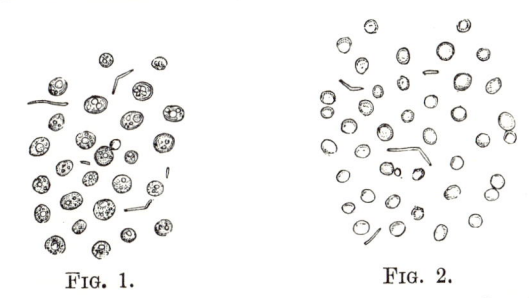

FIG. 1.   FIG. 2.

discovery, which, no doubt, was forced upon them by the complaints of their customers, or some other annoying circumstance, that led to their obtaining a change of yeast.

We next obtained permission to examine the yeast of the other beers undergoing fermentation, especially those of white beers, such as ale and pale ale.

In the sketch which we made of these yeasts one may detect the presence of the filaments peculiar to turned beer (Fig. 2).

We examined with much interest the ales which had immediately preceded those undergoing fermentation, the yeast of which we had just inspected. We were furnished with two kinds, both in casks, the one fined, the other not fined. The latter was visibly turbid, and, examining a drop of it, we discovered three or four filaments present in every field of the microscope. The ale which had been fined was nearly clear, but wanting in brilliancy; it contained about one filament to the field. We asserted in the presence of the head brewer, who had been summoned, that these ales were extremely liable to change, that it was highly necessary to dispose of them without delay, and that they were necessarily already faulty in flavour—a fact which all admitted after some hesitation—attributable, of course, to the natural reluctance which every manufacturer feels to own that his produce is not above reproach. We were shown some of the finings used in the brewery; they were swarming with the same filaments of disease-organisms.

We then propounded to the managers certain questions on the subject of the losses which a brewery may sustain from changes in its beer. We had heard from several brewers that the selling price of beer differed so greatly from the cost of its production solely in consequence of the losses which the unavoidable waste of large quantities of beer was constantly causing; several brewers have in our presence estimated these losses at 20 per cent. of the total production, on the average.

At first the English brewers returned somewhat vague answers to our questions; however, after what had taken place, they doubtless recognized the fact that a mutual understanding between a savant and a practical man may often be of considerable benefit to the latter, and in the end they confessed to us that they had stowed away in their brewery a large quantity of beer which had gone bad in cask a fortnight or so after it was brewed. Having avowed thus much they expressed their great anxiety to learn the cause of so serious a change in their beer, which was quite undrinkable. We examined it under the microscope, without being able to detect immediately any diseased ferments, but being aware that the beer had probably been clarified, by remaining undisturbed for a very long time, and that these ferments might have become inert and precipitated to the bottom of the enormous vats containing the beer, we examined the deposits which had formed at the bottom of these vats. They were composed solely of filaments of disease-organisms, without even the least trace of the globules of alcoholic yeast. The supplementary fermentation of this beer had evidently been nothing but a diseased fermentation.

The resemblance between these filaments and those which, in considerably smaller proportion, accompanied the globules of alcoholic ferment in our preceding observations, the change in the beer, which was almost as bad as beer could possibly be, along with an abundance of filaments, and the change, to a minor extent, in that beer which only presented a few filaments in a field of the microscope, impressed those managers of the brewery who were present with an entire belief in the theory which we had been endeavouring to impress on their minds concerning the causes of the badness of their beer. Some eight days afterwards we paid another visit to this same brewery, and learnt that the directors had lost no time in acquiring a microscope, and in procuring changes of yeast for all the varieties of beer, which they had put in working since our first visit.

There are some periods of the year—early spring, summer, and autumn, for instance—when the working of a brewery is a matter of great difficulty. The preservation of yeast becomes a subject requiring the most delicate treatment, in consequence of the increase in the temperature. In the early part of autumn the most important ingredients used in brewing are of inferior quality; the deteriorating influences which have been at work have covered them with a variety of parasites. All these circumstances contribute to facilitate the development of diseased ferments.

§ II.—The Absence of Change in Wort and Beer Coincides with the Absence of Foreign Organisms.

The method which we have just pursued in demonstrating the existence of a relation between the diseases of beer and certain microscopic organisms can scarcely leave a doubt, it seems to us, as to the correctness of the principles which we are advocating. In every case where the microscope reveals in a yeast, especially a yeast which is in a state of activity, products which are foreign to the composition of alcoholic ferment, properly so called, the flavour of the beer is more or less unsatisfactory, according to the abundance or nature of these minute organisms. Moreover, when a finished beer of superior quality loses in the course of time its agreeable flavour, and becomes sour, it may readily be shown that the alcoholic ferment in the deposit existing in bottles or casks, although originally pure, at least in appearance, becomes gradually intermixed with these same filiform ferments or other ones. These facts may be deduced from what precedes; nevertheless, some prejudiced minds might perhaps urge that these foreign ferments are the consequence of some diseased condition, produced by circumstances of which we know nothing.

Although this gratuitous supposition may be difficult to sustain, we shall endeavour to corroborate our preceding observations by the method of experiment which will be seen to be the more decisive.

This method consists in proving that beer never possesses any unpleasant flavour, so long as the alcoholic ferment, properly so called, is not associated with foreign ferments; that this also holds good in the case of wort, and that wort, liable to change as it is, may be preserved in a state of purity, if it is kept under conditions that protect it from the invasion of microscopic parasites, to which it presents not only favourable nutriment, but also a field for development.

By employing this second method we shall, moreover, have the advantage of proving with certainty a proposition that we just advanced, and showing that the germs of these organisms proceed from the particles of dust which the common air wafts about and deposits on every object, or which are spread over the utensils and materials used in a brewery, materials that are naturally charged with microscopic germs, which various changes in the store-houses and maltings may multiply to an indefinite extent.*

* If we put a handful of germinating barley from a maltster's cistern into a little water, and examine drops of the liquid, after it has become

Let us take a glass flask having a long neck (Fig. 3 A), and holding from 250 c.c. to 300 c.c. (*i.e.*, about 9 or 10 fl. oz.); let us put into it some wort, hopped or not, and then draw

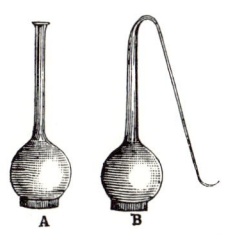

FIG. 3.

out the neck of the flask in the flame of a lamp, so as to give to it the shape B (Fig. 3); let us next heat the liquid to the boiling point, when the steam will rush with a hissing sound out of the curved end. We may then, without further precaution, permit our flask to cool, or, as an additional safeguard, we may introduce a small quantity of asbestos into the open extremity, at the very moment when the flame is taken away from the flask. Before introducing the asbestos, we may pass it through the flame, and we may repeat this after it has been placed in the end of the tube.* The air which first re-enters the flask must come in contact with the

turbid, under a microscope, we shall be amazed at the wonderful number of strange microscopic organisms that swarm on the surface of the grains and on the sides of the cistern. There is no doubt that their presence is injurious to germination, inasmuch as they absorb much oxygen; moreover, they acidify the grain and cause it to deteriorate.

* In these experiments the asbestos is only introduced by way of extra precaution. Originally, in his early experiments in connection with the subject of spontaneous generation, the results of which were published in 1860-62, the author did not use it, and he observed no ill effects resulting from the omission; now, however, he constantly makes use of it. In studies of this kind novel precautions are never thrown away; moreover, the presence of this asbestos is a sure bar to the entrance of insects. The author has preserved for a long time a flask, in the slender neck of which an insect is contained; he killed it with a flame just as it was approaching the liquid. Quite recently, M. Calmettes, a young engineer from the École Centrale, when engaged, at

heated glass and the hot liquid, and these will destroy the vitality of any germs existing in such particles of dust as this air may introduce. The re-entrance of the air will be effected very gradually—sufficiently so to enable the drop of water which the air, as it enters, forces up the curved tube, to catch all particles of dust. Ultimately, the tube will become dry, but then the passage of the air will proceed so slowly that every foreign particle will get deposited on its interior sides.

Experience tends to prove that external particles of dust cannot find their way into flasks of this pattern, having free communication with the air, at all events within ten or twelve years—the longest time that has been devoted to experiments of this kind; the liquid in the flasks, if originally clear, will not become in the least degree contaminated, either upon its surface or throughout its bulk, although the outside of the flasks may be covered with a thick coat of dust. This is an undeniable proof of the impossibility of particles of dust finding their way inside such flasks.

Wort treated thus will preserve its purity for an indefinite time, notwithstanding its extreme liability to rapid change when exposed to the air, under conditions which cause it to come in contact with the particles of dust that air contains. This also holds good in the case of wine, beef-tea, the must of grapes, and, generally speaking, of all liquids which are subject to putrefaction or fermentation, and which possess the faculty, when their temperature is raised to about 100° C. (212° F.), of destroying the vitality of those microscopic germs that are found in dust.

A flask such as we have described (Fig. 3) is all that we require when we have to demonstrate the facts that we have

Tantonville, in Tourtel's brewery, in carrying out certain practical experiments in connection with the process that will be described in one of the later chapters of this work, wrote complaining that his flasks had been suddenly invaded by a swarm of aphides, scarcely larger than phylloxeras, and that many of them had even penetrated into the inside of the curved tubes.

just reviewed, a more detailed account of which may be found in our Memoir published in the *Annales de Chimie et de Physique*, for 1862, under the title *Mémoire sur les corpuscules organisés en suspension dans l'atmosphère. Examen de la doctrine des générations spontanées.* The shape of the flask represented in Fig. 4 only differs from that of the preceding one in having a second little tube attached to the globular part of the flask; this presents great advantages for different objects of study, and it was adopted in the subsequent investigations detailed in this work.

This flask will permit us to study without difficulty every separate kind of microscopic organism in the liquid best adapted to it without fear, if we take reasonable precautions, that the subject of our study may become associated with other organisms, the accidental presence of which cannot fail to seriously affect the results of our observations.

Let us use one of those flasks in our experiment on yeast, at the same time expressly assuming that the minute germs of yeast are free from all contamination by foreign germs, an object which we shall learn how to realize by a variety of methods in a subsequent chapter.

Let us introduce some wort into our flask (Fig. 4); then,

FIG. 4.

after we have fitted an india-rubber tube to the little supplementary tube, let us boil the liquid; the steam, finding an easier exit through the india-rubber opening than through the drawn-out tube, will rush out through the india-rubber tube, and thus, as it passes, destroy any germs which may be adhering to the sides of the little supplementary tube. If we close the india-rubber tube by means of a glass stopper, the steam will immediately issue through the bent tube. On permitting the flask to cool, it will then be ready for impregnation. If there were any fear that some foreign germ of an unknown nature might have effected an entrance during cooling, or had not been destroyed by the steam (which is always a little super-heated, in consequence of the resistance which it meets in escaping), we need only place the flasks on a warm stove, and leave them there for a few days or a few weeks to ascertain whether the liquid in them has undergone any change. We should then only use those flasks which contain a sound liquid.

At the same time we must warn our readers that this cause of error does not exist once in a thousand times, especially if we use an asbestos stopper to prevent the entrance of little insects which are attracted by the odour of the liquid, and which instinctively seek to enter at the extremity of the tube, and to pass through it into the flask. In going so far, and incurring such labour in search of their food, they condemn themselves to certain death, for they are sure to be drowned, since it would require an intelligence superior to that which they possess to enable them to get out of the flask; the liquid, morever, could not fail to undergo some change, in consequence of the particles of dust that the insects would introduce into it.

After having passed the flame of a spirit-lamp quickly over the india-rubber tube, the glass stopper, the curved tube, and even over the fingers of the operator, we may withdraw the glass stopper, and introduce the pure yeast by means of a glass pipette that has been previously heated. This yeast is kept in a vessel also free from the dust floating in the air. However few globules of yeast the glass tube may take up, it is sure to introduce a hundred or a thousand times more than is necessary for the impregnation of the liquid. The glass stopper must then be replaced immediately, after having been again quickly passed through the flame. In transferring our yeast from the vessel containing it to the flask, by means of a glass pipette, it is exposed to another cause of impurity, since we cannot avoid bringing it in contact with the common air. If this risk frequently troubled us in our experiments, we might banish it or minimize it by some new arrangement; but this is unnecessary. We have suffered no inconvenience from this cause, as there does not exist in the atmosphere anything like a continuous supply of that from which the so-called *spontaneous* generation arises, as was erroneously believed to be the case before the publication of our Memoir in 1862, to which we have already alluded.

The following are the results of the experiments conducted in the manner just described.

The yeast which we sowed, in ever so small a quantity, seemed to acquire vigour, to bud, and to multiply. Soon, that is to say in the course of twenty-four or forty-eight hours or longer, according to the temperature, and, more especially, the degree of vitality in the globules, we found that the sides of our flasks were covered with a white yeasty deposit, and noticed on the surface of the liquid a fine froth, which at first appeared like little islets formed by groups of bubbles so minute that they would have been imperceptible had they not been joined together. These patches increased in size, and gradually attached themselves to each other, finally forming a thick froth. In the course of two or three days this froth fell, the fermentation proceeded less rapidly, and then ceased completely. The beer was finished. This beer might be preserved for an indefinite period in the flask without undergoing any change. The external air passes freely into and out of the flask, as the pressure of the atmosphere and the temperature vary, and the beer in the course of time becomes flat; it acquires age in much the same manner as wine does, but it never contracts any taste of disease, it never becomes sour, or sharp, or bitter, or putrid ; it does not even become covered with *mycoderma vini* as is usually the case with all beer exposed to the common air in the course of trade.

After some weeks, or perhaps months, a white ring may show itself on the surface of the liquid on the glass. This is a crown formed by a mass of young yeast globules, which grow there like a mould, by absorbing the oxygen of the air as it enters the flask. The bulk of the yeast which has been fermenting remains at the bottom of the liquid in the form of an inert deposit. This inertness, however, is apparent rather than real; the globules may be internally active, without any development of new buds, and the effects of this working may cause them to become more and more languid, and in the course of time may even destroy them.

The case is quite different when the yeast with which our wort is impregnated, instead of being pure, is mixed to any extent whatsoever with diseased ferments. Should there be any of these in the yeast with which we impregnate our wort, even though their quantity were so infinitesimal that the most skilful observer could scarcely discover them with the microscope, they would multiply in the flask after the beer had been finished, especially if the beer were left for a short time on a stove. In this manner we may secure an excellent test of the original purity of the yeast which we employ in the impregnation of our wort.

Thus it may be seen that the absence of microscopic organisms that are foreign to the nature of pure yeast may invariably be noticed in the case of a beer which is sound, and which will remain sound for any length of time, when in contact with pure air, at any temperature. We may see, too, that the presence of these organisms may invariably be detected in an unsound beer, the peculiar unsoundness of which depends upon the peculiar species of the organisms contained in it. It would be difficult to adduce clearer proofs than those which we have given as to the intimate relation existing between these organisms and the deterioration of beer. The relation between cause and effect, in the succession of physical phenomena in general, is established by proofs that are by no means more decisive.

CHAPTER III.

On the Origin of Ferments properly so called.

The new process of brewing, which it is the principal object of this work to explain, and which will follow as an immediate and inevitable deduction from the novel facts herein demonstrated, cannot be fully understood without a knowledge of all the principles upon which it is founded. One of the most essential of these has reference to the purity of our fermentation. We should gain but little from the use of a yeast uncontaminated by any foreign germs if natural organic substances had the power of organizing themselves by means of spontaneous generation, or by some transformation which took place amongst them, or even by a conversion of certain microscopic beings into certain others. Theories of this kind are still warmly advocated, but, to our thinking, rather from sentimental considerations or prejudice than from any basis of serious experimental proofs.

Be this as it may, we must free our minds from all suppositions which might qualify the exactness of the principles upon which our new process is founded, or cause any doubt in the minds of our readers as to the possibility of its application and the benefits to be derived from its adoption.

§ I.—On the Conditions which cause Variations in the Nature of the Organized Products existing in Infusions.

We have proved by experiment, in the preceding chapter,

that a few minutes' boiling renders liquids, and more especially wort, absolutely free from liability to change when in contact with pure air, that is, air which contains none of the germs of organisms that are continually floating about in the atmosphere.

What is true in the case of wort is equally so in the case of all organic liquids; there is not a single one that could not be rendered inaccessible to any subsequent change if it were brought, first of all, to a suitable temperature, which would vary with the nature of the liquids. Amongst them there are some which, like vinegar, lose their tendency to change after having been rapidly raised to a temperature of not more than 50° C. (122° F.); others, like wine, require a greater heat. Wort, to which no hops have been added, should be subjected to a temperature of not more than 90° C. (194° F.); milk to about 110° C. (230° F.).*

It is easy to show that these differences in temperature, which are required to secure organic liquids from ultimate change, depend exclusively upon the state of the liquids, their nature, and, above all, on the conditions that affect their neutrality, whether towards acidity or alkalinity; for it is not difficult to observe that the least changes in these respects lead to considerable variations in the temperatures which we must employ.† We could adduce many examples of this. The only difference between the nature of must and that of wine is caused by fermentation. We may say the same thing of wort and beer, and, better still, of new milk and sour milk. Must, to be secured from change, requires a much higher temperature than wine does; similarly, wort requires a much higher temperature than beer. Milk must be heated to about 110° C. (230° F.), as we have just stated, but sour milk would require 20° C. or 30° C.

---

* We have heard of liquids even less sensitive than these, which required a temperature of 120° C. (248° F.) or more, but we have had no opportunity of studying them.

† See Pasteur, *Mémoire sur les Générations dites Spontanées* (*Annales de Chimie et de Physique*, t. lxiv. 3ᵉ série, année 1862).

(36° F. or 54° F.) less. Wine, when fresh, ceases to be liable to change after it has been brought to a temperature below 100° C. (212° F.); it requires a temperature of more than 100° C. in the presence of carbonate of lime.

As regards the explanation of the influence which acidity or alkalinity exerts in diminishing or increasing the temperature required to protect infusions and organic matters from ultimate change, although this is a subject which claims special study, we are inclined to believe that acidity permits, and alkalinity prevents, the penetration of moisture into the interior of the cells of the germs belonging to infusions, so that in heating the outer cases of these cells in an alkaline medium we heat the germs in a dry state; and in heating the outer cases in an acid medium we heat the germs when they are moist. We all know that these conditions make a great difference in the resistance which bodies offer to the action of heat. A particle of mould which, in a moist state, cannot survive a temperature of from 60° C. to 100°. C. (140° to 212° F.), will preserve its fecundity even if heated to 120° C. (248° F.), if it has been previously well dried.[*]

The nature of the spontaneous productions which we see appear in organic liquids is affected to a remarkable extent by the smallest change in the compositions of those liquids. Generally speaking, as we have often proved in our former works, a feeble acidity is unfavourable to the development of bacteria and infusoria, and, on the other hand, favourable to the growth of mould. A liquid which is neutral or of feeble alkalinity behaves in an exactly inverse manner.

Those who support the theory of spontaneous generation seek to find in the natural differences between the organic productions of various liquids which are simultaneously exposed to the same atmosphere, an argument in favour of their doctrine. These differences, however, are only an effect of the greater or less fitness of a peculiar liquid for a certain kind of growth. When an acid organic liquid, such as the must of grapes for

[*] See my *Mémoire sur les Générations dites Spontanées*, already cited.

example, is exposed freely to the air, it is besieged simultaneously by spores of *mucedines*, as well as germs of *bacteria, leptothrix, vibrios, &c.*, but the latter germs are checked in their development, if, indeed, they are not actually destroyed, by the acidity of the liquid ; and we should never find them there in their adult state.

Most moulds, on the other hand, thrive in acid liquids, and therefore they are generally found alone. If we began by saturating must with carbonate of lime, previously dried or otherwise, we should observe opposite phenomena ; bacteria, lactic ferments and butyric vibrios would invade our fields long before the spores of mould had time to grow, since the germination of these proceeds very languidly in neutral or alkaline liquids, and an infusion once occupied by a living organism has much trouble in nourishing others ; the early developments consume the alimentary substances, especially the oxygen.

Differences as marked as these in the adaptability of certain liquids to certain growths give rise to innumerable illusions, and are one of the chief sources of error in the study of this subject. If we sow in an acid liquid, such as must, an alcoholic ferment, the development of which is not arrested by the acid character of our medium, it will multiply there, and we shall have no difficulty in growing it over and over again in the same acid medium. This being the case, let us suppose that our alcoholic ferment is impure—let us say, mixed with filaments of turned wine, which are due to a ferment checked in its development by the peculiar qualities of the must. In repeating the growth of this alcoholic ferment in the must the filaments which were, by supposition, present in our first sowing, and which cannot reproduce themselves in the must, or do so with great difficulty, will become very scarce in the fields of our microscope ; they will not, however, cease to exist, for the repetition of our attempts to grow them only serves to spread the original germs over a larger surface ; and, although the eye fails to detect them, they will only have become more difficult to discover. At this point the experimentalist is in danger of falling into error, for when he no longer perceives the foreign ferment he will be inclined to believe that it has vanished, and that he may regard the alcoholic ferment as being free from all impurity, without testing for the purity by a direct experiment.

An example of this mistake is to be found in a recent work by M. Jules Duval. This writer has published a theory according to which yeast becomes transformed into lactic ferment, and likewise into other ferments—that of urea, for example—the only condition of change, according to M. Jules Duval, being that we should cultivate it in suitable mediums. The proofs by which he supports his conclusion are altogether inadmissible, and a simple glance at his experiments enables us to detect innumerable causes of error. M. Duval believes that yeast becomes transformed into lactic ferment from the fact that he obtained a fermentation which furnished lactate of lime and lactic ferment from some sour milk to which he had added some glucose, chalk, and phosphate of ammonia before impregnating it with yeast; but he took no steps to secure himself against introducing into his medium —which was, as a matter of fact, well adapted to lactic fermentation, inasmuch as it was a little alkaline—an alcoholic ferment containing impurities. This was the crucial point in his experiments. M. Duval recognizes this, but he deceives himself when he says, without proof :—" My alcoholic ferment is pure, for I have grown it over and over again in must, preserved in flasks prepared after the manner of those which M. Pasteur uses in his experiments." Here we have merely a simple assertion ; a direct experimental test might have proved that the yeast was impure.

Yeast cannot transform itself into lactic ferment. No matter what the medium may be in which it is sown, *if it is actually pure* it will never present the least trace of lactic ferment or of any other ferments. By certain changes in the nature of the medium, the temperature, and other conditions, the cells of the ferment may become oval, elongated, spherical, and larger or smaller in size, but they will never produce the most minute quantity of lactic ferment or lactic acid. The whole theory of the transmutation of ferments, which M. Duval has published, is imaginary.*

We have asserted that the source from which we obtain our supply of the substances that we expose to contact with the air may likewise furnish a reason for the development of vegetable or animal organisms which make their appearance in our infusions. This may be easily understood. If we expose the infusions to temperatures more or less high, with the object of destroying the vitality of the germs which they may contain, we completely suppress all germs originating from two different sources—those which the infusions may have acquired directly from the atmospheric air, or from the dust upon our utensils, and those which may have been introduced by the materials used in manufacturing our infusions or decoctions, which materials must have been brought from some distance. An infusion, after having been heated to a sufficient degree, can harbour and nourish only such germs as are conveyed to it by the air after the heating. These floating germs are far from being as varied in their nature as it pleases those to believe who are tied down by their arbitrary and faulty interpretation of the knowledge that we have acquired, and the discussions in which we have taken part, during the last fifteen years. Air, unless in violent agitation, can hold only the most minute particles in suspension. The observations which have been recorded concerning organisms of spontaneous growth found in infusions, have always been made in sheltered places—in rooms or laboratories, the atmosphere of which is, relatively speaking, very still. For this reason, in liquids that have been subjected to heat, the *flora* and *fauna*—if we may use such an expression—are very poor, and all the more so because, as we have recently

---

* Jules Duval (of Versailles), *Nouveaux faits concernant la mutabilité des germes microscopiques. Rôle passif des êtres classés sous le nom de ferments.* (See the *Journal d'Anatomie et de Physiologie*, edited by C. Robin, Sept. and Oct. 1874, and *Compte-rendus de l'Académie des Sciences*, Nov. 1874). M. Béchamps had previously fallen into similar errors.

had occasion to remark, a great number of the organisms which would spring into existence of their own accord, if they were allowed sufficient time for germination, are kept back by others of a more rapid development. The truth of this is evident from the fact that we may observe greater variations in the nature and number of species of living organisms, if we divide one infusion amongst several vessels which are immediately closed up again, than if we leave our infusion in contact with an unlimited volume of surrounding air. By this means we expose each portion of the liquid to no other germs than those existing in a state of suspension in the volume of air introduced into the vessels; and it so frequently happens that we obtain a variety of germs which, coming into contact with a liquid adapted to their nutrition, without having mixed with others, finally multiply there, in consequence of no other organisms of greater activity occurring to impede their slow and laborious propagation.

The nature of the products resulting from raw infusions—that is, those obtained, without heating, from the maceration of organic substances, such as leaves, fruits, grains, or the organs of plants or animals—is much more varied. The reason of this is that such substances generally carry with them not only the particles of dust existing in air that is in motion, but also microscopic parasites, which find a congenial resting-place on their surface or its vicinity. We may cite a few accurate observations on this point, for the subject is one of great interest.

If we boil an infusion of hay, and then expose it to contact with the air in a room, all its productions will be derived from such germs as a comparatively still air can carry about; thus, we shall very rarely find any *colpoda* in our infusion, for the germs of these infusoria, consisting of rather large cells, can scarcely exist in a state of suspension in motionless air, in spite of their extraordinary diffusion in nature. On the other hand, we almost invariably find *colpoda* in macerations of raw hay. This difference is easily accounted for; the particles of dust adhering to the surface of hay, especially that which comes from marshy districts, contain the germ-cells of *colpoda* in abundance. The reason is obvious; rain falls on a meadow and forms little pools of water about the roots of the herbs that grow there; this water remains for some time, and very soon swarms with a multitude of infusoria, especially *colpoda*. Dryness follows; the *colpoda* becomes encysted, and forms a dust that is wafted by the winds on to the blades of grass, so that the mower will carry away not only his hay, but also myriads of *colpoda*, as well as spores of *mucedines* and other organisms.*

The maceration of pepper will give us some infusoria hardly ever found in other infusions, the reason of this being that such infusoria exist where the pepper grows—in other words, their germs are exotic. That the infusion of a special plant should give us special infusoria, is scarcely more surprising than the discovery of a particular parasite or insect existing on a particular plant, and not on others of a different species that grow near it. Thus it happens that the ferment-germs of must exist on the surface of grapes, whether detached or in clusters. It is only natural that we should find the organ or the plant that is destined later on to become the food of a parasite serving as a habitation for the germs of that parasite.

§ II.—Experiments on Blood and Urine taken in their Normal State, and Exposed to Contact with Air that has been Deprived of the Particles of Dust which it Generally holds in Suspension.

Recourse to the application of heat, in the first place, is an excellent means, as we have just seen, of procuring organic liquids free from all disturbing germs; but there is a still more remarkable and instructive, we may even say more unlooked for, method of securing this result, which may be described as in some measure borrowed from the nature of things. It consists in seeking purity in the natural liquids of animals and plants. It is difficult to understand how the liquids circulating in the organs of animal bodies, such as blood, urine, milk, amniotic

* On this subject see the observations of M. Coste (*Compte-rendus de 'Académie*, t. lix. pp. 149 and 358, 1864).

fluid, and so on, can possibly secrete the germs of microscopic organisms. There would be excellent opportunities for these germs to propagate themselves if they actually did exist in the liquids appertaining to the animal economy. Life in all probability would become impossible in the presence of such guests. A proof of this is to be found in the multitude of diseases which many of the greatest minds of modern times attribute to parasitic developments of this nature. Medical men of high authority agree in thinking that the questions of contagion and infection will find solutions from the obscurity in which they are now involved in a careful study of ferments, and that hygienists and physicians should labour to secure by every possible means the destruction of the germs of ferments, and should strive to check *their* development, and prevent the evils which *they* cause when developed. Great progress has already been made in this direction, and we deem it a signal honour that our researches on the subject have been considered, even by those by whom this progress has been accomplished, as the source from which they derived their first inspirations. We shall, doubtless, be excused by our readers if we recall this fact in relating certain historical details which are especially necessary in order that they may comprehend the principles that we are endeavouring to explain in these "studies."

It is a matter of regret to us, however, that the facts which we have established should have been accredited with any importance beyond that which is their due. The exaggeration of novel ideas invariably leads to a reaction, which, again, overshooting the mark, brings into disrepute even those points in which such ideas are perfectly just, or, at all events, worthy of serious consideration. There are certain symptoms of such a reaction in the case of our theories: they are evident in the tendency of unreflecting minds to give a total denial to the fact that certain diseases may be derived from certain ferments —organized and living ferments—of the nature of those which have been discovered in the course of the last twenty years. We should be guided by facts, whichever side of the question we espouse, and by facts alone we should test the truth of doubtful discoveries. We are but on the threshold of the exploration of our subject, and we should strive to discover new facts in connection with it, and should deduce from these, whatever they may be, only such conclusions as they may strictly warrant. Unfortunately, there is amongst physicians a tendency to generalize by anticipation. Many of them are men of rare natural or acquired talent, endowed with keen powers of intellect, and the art of expressing themselves fluently and persuasively; but the more eminent they are, the more they are occupied by the duties of their profession, and the less leisure they have for the work of investigation. Urged on by that thirst for knowledge which belongs to superior minds, and perhaps, in some measure, through associating with the upper classes of society, which are becoming more and more interested in science, they eagerly seize upon easy and plausible theories, readily adapted for statement which is general and vague just in proportion to the unsoundness of the facts on which they are based. When we see beer and wine undergo radical changes, in consequence of the harbour which those liquids afford to microscopic organisms that introduce themselves invisibly and unsought into it, and swarm subsequently therein, how can we help imagining that similar changes may and do take place in the case of man and animals? Should we, however, be disposed to think that such a thing must hold true, because it seems both probable and possible, we must, before asserting our belief, recall to mind the epigraph of this work: *the greatest aberration of the mind is to believe a thing to be, because we desire it.*

One of the most distinguished members of the Academy of Medicine, M. Davainne, who was the first to give his attention to rigorous experiments on the influence that organic ferments exercise on the production and propagation of infectious diseases, declares that the idea of his researches on *splenic fever* and *malignant pustule* was suggested to him by his perusal of our work on butyric fermentation, published in 1861. In 1850 this gentleman and M. Rayer discovered in the blood of animals attacked by these diseases minute filiform bodies, to which they paid little attention, and which M. Davainne recollected, when he came across our Memoir. He had the foresight to conjecture—a conjecture that was soon confirmed most decisively by his researches—that the former disease, known under the name of *sang de rate*, might be the production of a fermentation analogous to the butyric, in which the minute filiform bodies observed by Rayer and himself, in 1850, played the part which vibrios fill in butyric fermentation. Within two years of this the first works of Messrs. Coze and Feltz appeared. These clever and courageous experimentalists avowed that their beautiful researches had been suggested to them by the perusal of my work on putrefaction, published in 1863. We might also quote the striking and admirably conceived experiments of Dr. Chauveau, on castration.* We cannot, however, refrain from reproducing here a letter addressed to us in 1874 by the celebrated Edinburgh surgeon, Mr. Lister:—

"Edinburgh, Feb. 10, 1874.

"Dear Sir,—Will you permit me to beg your acceptance of a pamphlet which I forward to you by this post, and which describes certain inquiries into a subject upon which you have thrown so much light—the theory of germs and fermentation? It gives me pleasure to think that you will peruse with some interest what I have written about an organism that you

* Chauveau's experiments were directed to show that the operation *bistournage*, employed by veterinary surgeons for castrating animals by twisting and subcutaneous rupture of the spermatic cord, an operation which, though leading to the mortification and subsequent absorption of the testicles, is commonly attended with no other mischief to the animal, does, nevertheless, lead to septic effects of a serious character, provided that septic germs—decomposing serum containing *vibrios*, for example— be introduced into the blood current. From the fact that the operation is ordinarily harmless, M. Chauveau concludes that septic organisms are not produced by the action of the constituent gases of the atmosphere— always present in the blood—upon albuminous matter when outside vital influences; whilst, from the success of the direct experiment of introducing septic germs, he concludes that the phenomena always arise from the actual presence of such germs.—D. C. R.

were the first to study in your Memoir on lactic fermentation. I do not know if you ever see the records of British surgery. If you have perused them you may have observed from time to time notices of the antiseptic system which I have been endeavouring for the last nine years to bring to perfection. Permit me to take this opportunity of offering you my most hearty thanks for having demonstrated by your brilliant researches the truth of the theory of putrefactive germs, and for having afforded me in this manner the sole means of perfecting the antiseptic system.

"Should you ever come to Edinburgh I am sure that you will be truly gratified to see in our hospital the extent to which the human race has profited by your work. I need hardly add, that I should have great satisfaction in showing you how greatly surgery is indebted to you.

"Excuse the freedom which I have taken in addressing you, on the grounds of our common love for science, and believe in the profound esteem of yours, very sincerely, JOSEPH LISTER."

The wad dressing of Dr. Alphonse Guérin, surgeon at the Hôtel-Dieu, Paris, which has already rendered great assistance to surgery, and has been the subject of a very favourable report at the Academy of Sciences in Paris, was invented by its author in consequence of certain reflections suggested to him by the perusal of our researches. The commission which framed the report made, through M. Gosselin, some wise reservations in the case of certain theoretical ideas which M. Guérin had not sufficiently proved by experiment. We have no doubt, however, that when the matter is thoroughly examined, facts will confirm the truth of the wide views entertained by the surgeon of the Hôtel-Dieu.

Dr. Déclat has founded quite a new system for the treatment of infectious diseases, which is based upon the use of one of the best known antiseptics, phenic acid. His theory, which he affirms was suggested to him by our studies on fermentations, is, that the diseases which transmit themselves are, each of them, the product of a special ferment, and that both medical and surgical professors of therapeutics should make it their study to prevent exterior ferments from penetrating into the liquids of our economy, or in the event of these ferments having found their way into the system, to discover *antiferments* for their destruction, without effecting any change in the vitality of the histological elements of the liquid or tissues.

There is no doubt that extreme caution must be exercised in dealing with questions of this kind, as M. Sédillot has authoritatively remarked; but at the same time it cannot be denied that the more such questions are discussed with exactness, the more those celebrated practitioners who originated them are confirmed in the ideas which first guided them. We may give another example of this.

In 1874, in consequence of a communication addressed to the Academy of Sciences by Messrs Gosselin and A. Robin, on the subject of ammoniacal urine. we made the observation that we should endeavour to ascertain if, in all such cases, the urinary fluids were not rendered ammoniacal by the presence of the little ferment of the urea, which we have previously noticed,* and which has since then been discussed with remarkable intelligence by M. Van Tieghem, in the thesis which he maintained for his doctor's degree. The suggestion and the considerations that justified it led to a discussion before the Academy of Medicine, in which contrary opinions were maintained. We lost no time in submitting these to the test of facts. We could not find a single person suffering from ammoniacal urine, in whose case the little ferment which we mentioned was not to be detected. Our predictions were thus completely justified.

As early as 1864 the *Gazette Hebdomadaire de Médecine et de Chirurgie* published an account of urine made ammoniacal in the bladder, the author of which, Dr. Traube, makes the following observations :—" It was believed that, in consequence of the

---

* See Pasteur, *Mémoire sur les Générations dites Spontanées*. pp. 51 and 52, 1862.

retention of the liquid, and the resulting distension of the bladder, that organ became irritated and produced a larger quantity of mucus, and that this mucus was the ferment which caused the decomposition of the urea, by virtue of a chemical action peculiar to itself. This belief can no longer be held in presence of M. Pasteur's discoveries. This observer has demonstrated, in the most conclusive manner, that ammoniacal fermentation, like alcoholic and acetic, is produced by living beings, whose pre-existence in the fermentable liquid is a necessary condition of the process. The preceding fact offers a remarkable proof of M. Pasteur's theory. In spite of the long duration of the retention, alkaline fermentation was not produced by an excessive secretion of the vesical mucus or of pus: it only began from the moment when the germs of vibrios passed from the outside into the bladder."*

Finally, we may conclude with perfect truth that the liquids of our economy, blood and urine, for instance, may afford a

* DAVAINNE, *Compte-rendus de l'Académie des Sciences*, t. lvii. p. 220, 1863.

COZE and FELTZ, *Recherches cliniques et expérimentales sur les maladies infectieuses*, Paris, J. B. Baillière, 1872. Summary of all their works published before 1865.

Dr. LISTER, Medical and surgical journals, particularly the *Lancet*, 1865-67.

Dr. GUÉRIN, *Compte-rendus de l'Académie des Sciences*, March 23, 1874, and May 28, 1874, also the Report of M. Gosselin, December, 1854.

Dr. SÉDILLOT, *Compte-rendus de l'Académie des Sciences*, November, 1874, t. lxxix. p. 1108.

PASTEUR, *Mémoire sur la fermentation appelée lactique*. (*Annales de Chimie et de Physique*, t. lii. 3ᵉ série, 1875.)—*Animalcules infusoires, vivant sans gaz oxygène libre et déterminant des fermentations*. (*Compte-rendus de l'Académie des Sciences*, t. lii. 1861.)—*Recherches sur la putréfaction*. (*Compte-rendus de l'Académie des Sciences*, t, lvi. 1863.)

GOSSELIN, ROBIN, and PASTEUR, *Compte-rendus de l'Académie des Sciences*, January 5, 1874. *Urines ammoniacales.*

TRAUBE, *Gazette hebdomadaire de médecine et de chirurgie.* *Sur la fermentation alcaline de l'urine*, April 8, 1864.

CHAUVEAU, *Putréfaction dans l'animal vivant.* (*Compte-rendus de l'Académie des Sciences*, April 28th, 1873.)

STUDIES ON FERMENTATION. 47

harbour to different ferments, even in the inmost parts of the organs, when external causes enable such ferments to find their way into those liquids, and that diseases of greater or less gravity result from this cause. On the other hand, it must be admitted that the bodies of animals in a state of health afford

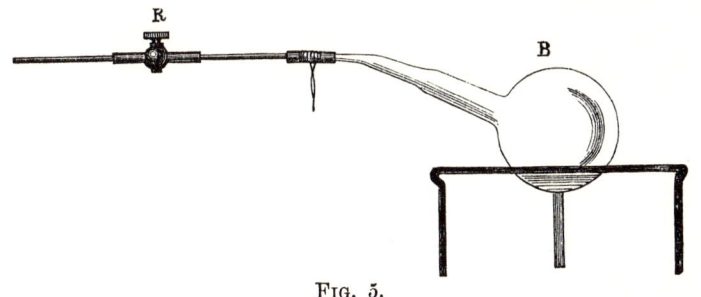

FIG. 5.

no means of entrance to these external germs. At the same time, direct experiment alone can convince the mind as to the truth of this latter assertion. Let us take some of the substances that are to be found inside living animals in perfect health, and expose them, in the same condition in which life has formed them, to contact with pure air.

For this purpose we must provide ourselves with a glass flask, joined to a copper tap by means of an india-rubber tube, as shown in Fig. 5. The two branches of the tap should be about

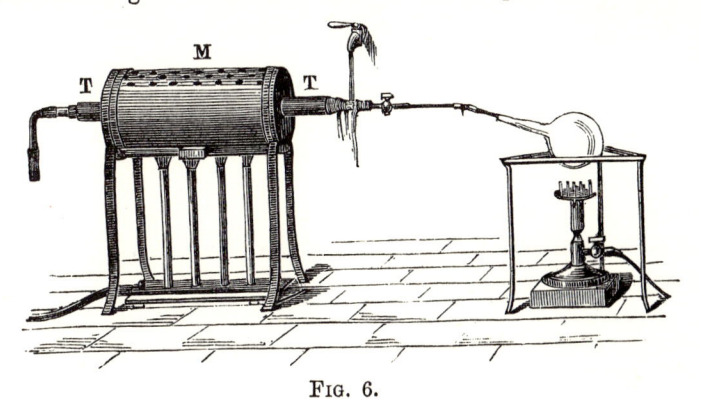

FIG. 6.

twelve centimetres long (about ½-in.), the one which is free tapering off like the end of a pipe. In order to destroy all germs which may exist in the flask, we must join the free end of the copper tube to a platinum tube kept at a very high temperature, after having carefully introduced into the flask a small quantity of water, and expelled all the air by converting the water into steam. Then as we allow the flask to cool, the air which re-enters it will necessarily pass through the hot tube (Fig. 6).

We may cause the water in the flask to boil at a temperature

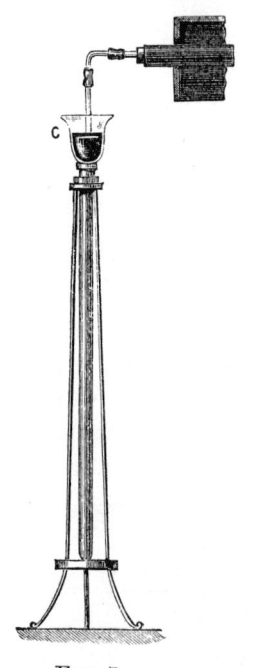

FIG. 7.

of more than 100° C. (212° F.) by fitting to the free end of the platinum tube a glass tube bent at right angles, which we plunge to any depth in a deep vessel filled with mercury (Fig. 7). Whilst the water is boiling under pressure, we must separate the tube which is plunged in the mercury; the water in the flask will continue to boil at the ordinary pressure. We must then leave the flask to cool. It will gradually become filled with air that has been heated to a high temperature, more than sufficient to burn up all the organic particles of dust which that air could have contained. When the flask is cold we must close the tap and detach it, and proceed to prepare other similar flasks. It will be advisable to close the tap when the temperature of the flask is still a few degrees above that of the surrounding atmosphere: this precaution will cause the air in the cooled flask to have a lower pressure than that of the external atmosphere.

During the interval which must elapse between the preparation and the use of a flask, it is a good thing to keep the free branch of the tap inclined towards the ground, to secure the inside of its tube from the deposit of external particles of dust. Whether this precaution be adopted or not, we must take care to heat this branch in the flame of a spirit lamp just before we bring our flask into requisition.

If we have to study blood, we must take it from a living animal—a dog, for example. We must expose a vein or an artery of the animal, and make an incision into which the end of the free tap-branch, which has previously been heated and allowed to cool, must be introduced and fixed by a ligature in the vein or artery. On opening the tap, the blood will rush into the flask; it must then be closed, and the flask placed in an oven at a certain temperature. We have successfully accomplished these manipulations, thanks to the kind help of our illustrious colleague and friend, M. Claude Bernard.

The operation is nearly the same in the case of urine. The end of the free branch of the tap is introduced into the passage of the urethra; the tap is turned at the moment when the urine is emitted, which is then allowed to pass into the flask, until it is a third or half filled.

The following were the results of our experiments:—Blood underwent no putrefactive change even at the highest temperatures of the atmosphere, but retained the odour of fresh blood, or acquired the smell of lye. Contrary to what we might have expected, the direct oxidation of the constituents of blood by slow combustion was rather sluggish. After subjecting our flasks to a temperature of 25° C. or 30° C. (77° F. to 80° F.) in an oven for several weeks, we observed an absorption of not more than 2 or 3 per cent. of oxygen, which was replaced by a volume of carbonic acid gas of about an equal bulk.*

Nearly the same results were obtained in the case of urine; it underwent no radical change; its colour merely assumed a reddish brown tint; it formed some small deposits of crystals, but without becoming at all turbid or putrefying in any way. The direct oxidation of the urinary substances was likewise very sluggish. An analysis of the air in one of the flasks, made forty days after the commencement of the experiment, gave the following results:—

Oxygen	19·2
Carbonic acid	0·8
Nitrogen	80·0
	100·0

* We must mention one curious result, which relates to what have been called the *crystals of the blood*. We could hardly have recourse to a better method of preparing these crystals, at least in the case of dog's blood, which seems to yield them with the greatest facility in any quantity we might desire to procure. Under the circumstances just recounted, in which dog's blood exposed to contact with pure air underwent no putrefactive change whatever, the crystals of that blood formed with a remarkable rapidity. From the first day that it was placed in the oven and exposed to an ordinary temperature, the serum began gradually to assume a dark brown hue. In proportion as this effect was produced, the globules of blood disappeared, and the serum and the coagulum became filled with very distinct crystals, of a brown or red colour. In the course of a few weeks, not a single globule of blood remained, either in the serum or coagulum; every drop of serum contained thousands of these crystals, and the smallest particle of coagulum, when bruised under a piece of glass, presented to view colourless and very elastic fibrine, associated with masses of crystals, without the slightest trace of blood-globules. Where our observations were protracted, it sometimes happened that all the fibrine collected into one hyaline mass, which gradually expelled every crystal from its interior.

These experiments on blood and urine which we have just mentioned date from 1863.* Ten years afterwards, in 1873, they were confirmed in an important and striking manner by the results of a very able series of experiments, which were carried out in our laboratory, by M. Gayon, who was formerly a pupil in the École Normale Supérieure. M. Gayon proved that what held good in the case of blood and urine, also held good in the case of the substances contained in eggs. He found that the whites of eggs might be exposed for any length of time to contact with air, as also might the yolks, or the white and yolks mixed, without any putrefactive change or fermentation resulting, and without the smallest microscopic germ showing itself, the sole condition being that the air must be freed from all organic particles of dust, germs of mould, *bacteria*, *vibrios*, and other organisms which it holds in suspension. This was only a part of the important facts brought to light by M. Gayon. Amongst other things, he proved that spontaneous putrefaction in eggs is invariably caused by the development of organized ferments, thereby correcting the opposite statements announced by M. Donné and M. Béchamp, who were led by their observations to believe that the change in eggs took place quite independently of the action of *vibrios* and *mucedines*.†

It is almost superfluous to remark how greatly the results of these experiments on blood, urine, and the components of the egg are opposed to the doctrine of spontaneous generation, as also to most modern theories on the generation of ferments. As long as experiments relating to the question of so-called *spontaneous* generation were made on heated substances, the advocates of *heterogenesis* had some grounds for asserting that such materials could not satisfy the conditions of spontaneous life, and that we should obtain different results by using natural organic liquids, which, if exposed to contact of pure air would

* PASTEUR, *Comptes rendus de l'Académie des Sciences*, t. lvi. p. 738, 1863.
† GAYON, *Comptes rendus de l'Académie des Sciences*, and *Annales Scientifiques de l'École Normale Supérieure*, 1874-75.

doubtless serve for the production of new beings which did not issue from parents which resembled them. This novel enunciation of the hypothesis of spontaneous generation, the only one, we think, that could be defended after the publication of our Memoir, in 1862, is condemned by the preceding facts.

The same facts completely upset the hypothesis recently maintained by Messrs. Fremy and Trécul on the subject of the causes of fermentation.

"Side by side with the immediate, definite principles which may be formed by synthesis," says M. Fremy, " such as glucose, oxalic acid, and urea, other substances of greatly inferior stability exist, the constitution of which is considerably more complicated, containing all the elements of living organs, such as carbon, hydrogen, oxygen, nitrogen, and even phosphorus and sulphur; and often salts of lime and of the alkalies besides. These bodies are albumen, fibrin, casein, the congeners of vitellin and others. Chemical synthesis cannot reproduce them. It is impossible, in my opinion, to regard them as immediate, definite principles. I designate them by the general name of *semi-organized* bodies, because they hold an intermediate place between the immediate principle and the organized tissue.

"These semi-organized bodies, which contain all the elements of organs, have the power, like a dry seed-grain, of existing in a state of organic immobility, and of becoming active under circumstances which favour organic development. By reason of the vital energy that they possess they undergo a succession of decompositions, giving origin to new derivatives, and to the advent of ferments, not by any process of *spontaneous generation*, but by a *vital energy*, which pre-exists in the semi-organized bodies, and is simply carried on, when this energy manifests itself, in these most varied organic changes."

After having expressed these hypothetical and confused opinions, M. Fremy continues :—" I do not consider, then, that these semi-organized bodies serve merely as nourishment for certain animal and vegetable organisms, which may be the sole agents of fermentations, but I give them a direct *rôle* and

admit that, under the influences which I have already cited*
they may assume a real and complete organization, and produce
ferments which are not derived, as we have seen, from a germ
or an ovum but from a semi-organized body, the vital energy of
which has become active.† It will be seen that these opinions
are quite different from those which M. Pasteur has maintained
in his works, since they attribute the origin of alcoholic and
lactic ferments to an albuminous substance. Taking the case
of alcoholic fermentation alone, I assert that, in the production
of wine, it is the juice of the grape itself which, in contact with
air, produces grains of yeast, by the transformation of the albuminous substances. M. Pasteur, on the contrary, maintains
that the grains of yeast are produced by certain germs."‡

We have combated these propositions, so extraordinary and
unsupported by any rigorous experiments, before the Academy of
Sciences, where they were first enunciated. On that occasion we
related the facts in connection with blood and urine, which we
have just discussed. Could there be any more forcible argument
against the theory of our honourable colleague than those
facts? Here we had natural albuminous substances, forming
part of matter eminently liable to putrefactive change and
fermentation, which produced no ferments of any sort whatsoever when brought into contact with air deprived of its organic
particles of dust.

Under no known circumstances is albuminous matter transformed into grains of yeast or any other organized ferment, and,
to our thinking, nothing can be more chimerical than the
gratuitous hypothesis of *hemi-organism*.

We shall proceed to new proofs of this, dealing this time
with a liquid formed by the life of a vegetable.

* Amongst these influences one of the most important, according to
M. Fremy, is " *organic impulse*,"—another gratuitous assumption.

† FREMY, *Comptes rendus de l'Académie des Sciences*, t. lviii. p. 1167,
1864.

‡ FREMY, *Comptes rendus de l'Académie des Sciences*, t. lxxiii. p. 1425,
1871. M. Trécul shares M. Fremy's opinions, and extends them to the
development of different fungoid growths.

§ III.—Experiments on the Juice contained in Grapes.

In the course of the discussion which took place, at the Academy, on the subject of the generation of ferments, properly so called, much was said about the oldest known fermentation, that of wine. We at once resolved to demolish M. Fremy's theory, by a decisive experiment on the juice of grapes.

We prepared forty flasks, capable of holding from 250 c.c. to 300 c.c. (from 9 to 11 fl. oz.) and shaped as represented in Fig. 8. These we filled with filtered must, which was perfectly

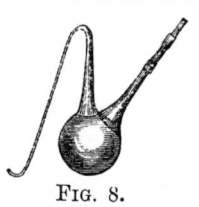

Fig. 8.

bright, and which, like all acid liquids, would remain sound, after having been boiled for a few seconds, although the ends of the long curved necks of the flasks containing the must might remain constantly open for months or years.

We washed, in a few cubic centimetres of water, part of a bunch of grapes, washing the grapes separately, or the grapes and the wood together, or even the wood of the bunch alone. This washing was easily accomplished by means of a perfectly clean badger's-hair brush, the water receiving all the particles of dust adhering to the surface of the grapes and the wood of the bunch. By means of a microscope we easily proved that this water held in suspension an infinite number of organized corpuscles, some of them bearing a very close resemblance to the spores of fungoid growths, others to alcoholic ferment, others to *mycoderma vini*, and so on.[*]

[*] This observation had already been made by Anthon and H. Hoffmann. "If we scrape the surface of a gooseberry with a blunt knife," says H. Hoffmann, "and put under the microscope the scrapings, which are of a whitish colour, we shall recognize amongst many varieties of shapeless dirt, earthy particles and other things, the same fungoid spores that we find in the expressed juice, but we shall see them there

STUDIES ON FERMENTATION. 55

We next proceeded to put on one side ten of our forty flasks, to serve for subsequent corroboration; in ten others, by means of the tube which is represented on the right hand side of the flask (Fig. 8), we put a few drops of the water in which the bunch of grapes had been washed; in a third series of ten flasks we put a few drops of the same liquid, after having previously boiled it. Lastly, we introduced into the ten remaining flasks a drop of grape-juice, taken from the inside of an uninjured grape. To do this we had to bend the right-hand tube of each of our last ten flasks, drawing it out to a fine point and closing it in the flame, as represented in Fig. 9 A. This

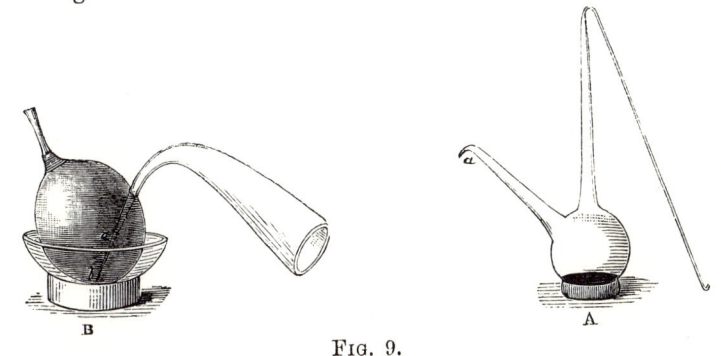

FIG. 9.

fine closed point was filed round near its extremity and then thrust, as represented in Fig. 9 B, into a grape placed on a hard substance; when the point *b* was felt to touch the substance supporting the grape it was broken off by a slight pressure sideways at the point *a*, where the file marks had been made. We had taken care to secure a slight vacuum in the flask

in infinitely larger quantities. Some of them will be of a dusky colour (*Stemphylium, Cladosporium*), and others will be colourless; the shape of these latter will be round or oval, and cylindrical. Most of them will bear resemblance to beads of the *chaplets* of *Oidium, Monilia, Torula* (that is to say, to spores of certain *Hyphomycetes*), which have been detached and carried off by the wind, and have attached themselves to the fruit. Some of these spores will be already provided with short germinating filaments. (*Annales des Sciences Naturelles, Botanique*, t. xiii. p. 21, 1860).

beforehand; this now caused a drop of the juice to be drawn into the flask. We then drew out the fine point, and closed it immediately in the flame of a spirit lamp. The vacuum was produced by heating the flasks in our hands, or over the flame of a lamp, thus causing a little air to be forced out through the end of the bent tube, which we then closed up with the lamp. When the flask was cool, the slight difference of pressure sufficed to force into it some of the juice contained in the grape, as we have just described. The drop of juice that is sucked into the flask generally remains in the curved part of the fine tube; to mix it with the must we must incline the flask so as to bring the must in contact with the drop; after that we may replace the flask in its natural position.

The following are the results presented by our four series of comparative experiments in the different cases. The first ten flasks—our standard flasks, containing must boiled in contact with pure air—showed no signs of organized products; the must might have remained in them for any number of years without change. Our second series of flasks, which contained the water in which the grapes, separately and in bunch, had been washed, had undergone alcoholic fermentation in every instance; this had manifested itself in all the flasks in the course of about forty-eight hours, the temperature being at about summer heat. At the same time that the yeast made its appearance in the form of little white lines, which gradually joining together formed a deposit on the sides of the flask, we perceived minute flakes of *mycelium* forming; sometimes as a single fungoid growth, sometimes combined with another, or with many together—these growths being quite independent otherwise of the yeast or alcoholic ferment. In several cases, too, *mycoderma vini* showed itself on the surface of the liquid in the course of a few days. *Vibrios* and lactic ferments, properly so called, could not make their appearance, on account of the nature of the liquid.

The flasks of our third series, containing the water in which the bunch of grapes had been washed, and which we boiled

STUDIES ON FERMENTATION. 57

before our experiment, remained as free from change as the flasks of our first series had done.

Lastly, our fourth series of flasks, containing the drops of juice taken from inside the grapes, remained equally free from change, although we could not be certain of having removed, in every case, without exception, all causes of error which must inevitably occur sometimes in so delicate an experiment.

These experiments cannot leave the least doubt on our minds:
That must, if boiled, will never ferment when in contact with air that has been freed from the germs which exist in it in a state of suspension.

That must may be fermented, after boiling, by introducing into it a very small quantity of water, in which a bunch of grapes has been washed.

That must will not ferment if we introduce into it some of this same water which has been boiled and afterwards cooled.

That must will not ferment if we introduce into it a small quantity of the juice contained in a grape.*

It follows, then, that the ferment which causes grapes to ferment in the vintage tub must come from the exterior, and not the interior of the grapes. Thus, the hypothesis of MM. Trécul and Fremy, according to which albuminous substances transform themselves into grains of yeast by the action of a peculiar vital force, is annihilated; *à fortiori*, there can no longer be a question concerning Liebig's theory, on the

---

* The experiments that we have described give rise to a useful remark. All the organic liquids, boiled or not, in the course of time must take up oxygen from the air. At the same time, and certainly under this influence, they assume an amber or brownish colour, but this effect is only produced when the liquids are placed under conditions of unalterability. Should fermentation or the development of fungoid growths be possible, scarcely any change of colour will take place. Doubtless this non-coloration may be attributed to the fact that these organisms consume the oxygen necessary for coloration. In these experiments on must, all the unchanged flasks assumed a pale yellowish brown colour; those which fermented or contained fungoid growths remained colourless, or nearly so.

transformation of albuminous substances into ferments, by a process of oxidation.

Our readers may be curious to know what M. Fremy has been able to oppose to such crucial experiments; they could scarcely have imagined the following:—

"In my experiments, which I have varied in every possible manner," says that gentleman, "I have found that it is almost impossible to discover alcoholic fermentation, appreciable by its results, in a single drop of grape juice, and I may add that this fermentation must be still more difficult to discover when this drop has been drowned in a large quantity of juice that has been previously boiled."*

It will be admitted that we were justified in saying, at the commencement of this paragraph, that we should demolish the theory which was opposed to ours, and which its advocates have been constrained to defend by hypotheses manifestly false.

At the meeting following the one in which M. Fremy declared *that minute quantities do not ferment*, we had the malicious satisfaction of showing a great many very small closed flasks, into each of which we had caused a single drop of the must of crushed grapes to be introduced by suction. We broke the thin points of many of them, in the presence of the Academy, and every one of them showed by a sharp hissing, which was audible at a distance, that fermentation was proceeding in the drop of liquid they contained. M. Fremy was there, but he made no remark.

We may cite some very curious facts on the subject of the period at which the germs that develop yeast are in a condition to be able to cause fermentation.

On July 25th, 1875, in the neighbourhood of Arbois (Jura), the grapes were still green and of the size of peas. We went to a vine that was far from paths and roads, and there, with a pair of small scissors, cut some grapes from off a bunch and let them fall with their short stalks into tubes half filled with

---

* *Comptes rendus de l'Académie, séance du* 28 *Octobre,* 1872.

gooseberry must, previously rendered unalterable by boiling. These tubes we closed again with all possible precautions, using corks which had been passed through the flame of a spirit-lamp and carried them to our laboratory, where we left them to themselves. Some days afterwards we saw diverse fungoid growths appear in most of the tubes, but not one of them then, or subsequently, presented the least appearance of fermentation. The germs of yeast at that period of the year did not exist either upon the woody part of the bunch, or upon the grapes. In Chapter V. we shall return to observations on this subject.

§ IV.—WORT AND MUST EXPOSED TO COMMON AIR.

If the principles which we have laid down possess all the value that we attribute to them, if the cause of change in natural or artificial organic liquids does not exist in those liquids themselves, if change considered in itself depends upon the nature and number of the particles of dust in various places, if it is, besides, radically affected by the composition of the liquids, it must necessarily follow that wort or must, whilst, under certain circumstances of exposure to air, it remains absolutely free from life and its results, will, under other circumstances, give rise to a variety of organisms and their corresponding fermentations. This is, in fact, the lesson which direct proofs will teach us. Before entering upon these new observations in detail, we must call the reader's attention to the difficulty, as experience has shown, of interpreting correctly the facts connected with the spontaneous impregnations of organic liquids.

Gay-Lussac crushed some grapes under a bell-jar filled with mercury, after having washed them in hydrogen, to expel the air adhering to the grapes and the sides of the jar. Having waited for several weeks without detecting any signs of fermentation, he introduced some bubbles of oxygen, and fermentation showed itself the following day. Gay-Lussac concluded that the fermentation of must could not commence without the help of oxygen.*

Under the conditions of his experiment nothing could be truer, and we must admire the diffidence with which this great natural philosopher interpreted the fact that he had observed. Another French natural philosopher, however, M. Cagniard-Latour, observed that the ferment of alcoholic fermentation was a little cellular plant. What was its origin in Gay-Lussac's experiment?

The advocates of the doctrine of spontaneous generation were ready with their explanation, and we have seen how MM. Trécul and Fremy, following many others, did not hesitate to maintain that the little plant with all its particles was produced by the action of oxygen on the albuminous substances contained in the juice of the grapes. The experiments, which we have given in the preceding paragraph, show us positively that germs of the ferment of must exist on the surface of the grape, and that, consequently, Gay-Lussac's experiment has a more simple and natural explanation. The germs of the ferment existing on the surface of the grape become mixed with the juice of the grape when the latter is crushed; these germs remain inactive in the presence of hydrogen; they vegetate as soon as oxygen is introduced to them.

Moreover, the results of our labours in connection with *spontaneous* generation, in 1862, teach us that in Gay-Lussac's experiment the germ of the ferment might also have had its origin either in certain particles of dust adhering to the sides of the glass bell, or upon the mercury; and, in a laboratory where alcoholic fermentation is studied, dust invariably contains dry cells of ferment. The necessity of oxygen for the success of the experiment is surprising, when we reflect that

* GAY-LUSSAC, *Annales de Chimie*, t. lxxvi. p. 245; read at the Institute, December 3rd, 1810. Long before Gay-Lussac, it had been remarked that atmospheric air had a great influence on fermentation. See M. Chevreul's articles on the history of chemistry in the *Journal des Savants*.

alcoholic fermentation often takes place in liquids that are not exposed to contact with air; but we shall prove by experiment that, notwithstanding what may happen during fermentation, oxygen has the greatest influence on the readiness with which ferment develops itself, and that this gas is indispensable to the revival of withered cells, and still more so to the germination of special cells, which we may consider to be the true germs of the little plant.

The advocates of the doctrine of *spontaneous* generation have based most of the objections which they vainly urge against their opponents upon erroneous interpretations of certain facts relating to the spontaneous impregnation of organic infusions. Taking a very wrong view of the essential conditions of the phenomena, they require that the assertors of the diffusion of the germs of microscopic organisms should be compelled to place at any one point of space, so to say, all the germs of the products of infusions; a demand which really borders on absurdity. They believe, or feign to believe, that we are bound to admit the existence of germs of must in all places and at all times, on the banks of rivers and on the loftiest mountains, and so on. " Fermentations," said one of these gentlemen one day, before the Academy, " cannot depend upon chance particles of atmospheric dust. How is it possible that germs of yeast can be present everywhere throughout the universe, ever ready to fall upon must ?" It is an established fact that grapes crushed in any part of the globe whatsoever, even on a glacier or at the highest elevations, can set up a fermentation. The explanation of this pretended impossibility is most simple, for we know, from the facts related in the preceding paragraph, that grapes carry on their skins the germs of their own ferments.

In experiments relating to the kind of organisms which we are discussing we must never fail to take into account the action of the particles of dust spread over the articles that are used. Very often an effect that should be attributed to germs adhering to the vessels and utensils used in experiments, the origin of which may be altogether special, is erroneously imputed to the dust-forming germs—that is to say, to those germs which exist in a state of suspension in the air.

In our Memoir of 1862, which we have quoted several times, we have explained that it is almost impossible to draw any serious conclusions from experiments made in a basin of mercury, because of the organic particles of dust which always exist in that metal, and which, without the knowledge of the operator, pass into the interior of the vessel, where they produce certain changes which one is tempted to impute to *heterogenesis*.

In all classical works an experiment of Appert's, reproduced by Gay-Lussac, is given. This, through a faulty interpretation, led to the hypothesis of the continuity of the causes of fermentation, if we may use such a term, in the atmospheric air.*

When we decant bottles of must, which has been preserved by Appert's method, into other bottles, all the latter soon set up a fermentation : this constitutes the experiment. If it were proved that the must, whilst being decanted, came in contact with atmospheric air alone, as Gay-Lussac believed, we should be compelled to admit, according to the theory of germs, that the must had come in contact with some particles of ferment in the air during decanting. And again, if it were shown that the experiment could succeed in any place whatsoever, we must come to the conclusion that germs of ferment exist everywhere in a state of suspension in the air.

"I have taken," writes Gay-Lussac, "a bottle of must that had been preserved for a year and was perfectly transparent, and have decanted the must into another bottle, which I then carefully corked and exposed to a temperature of 15° C. to 30° C. (59° F. to 86° F.). Eight days afterwards the must has lost its transparency ; fermentation has taken place in it, and soon my must has become transformed into a vinous liquor, sparkling like the best champagne. A second bottle of must that had been preserved for a year, like the preceding one,

* GAY-LUSSAC, *Annales de Chimie*, t. lxxvi. p. 247, *Mémoire cité*, 1810.

but which had not been brought into contact with the air, has presented no signs of fermentation, although placed under conditions most favourable to its development."

The result of this experiment, when roughly made, is correctly described by Gay-Lussac; in other words, it may be proved that if, at the time of vintage, we prepare some bottles of must, after Appert's process, and, in the course of time, open them and decant their contents into other bottles, we shall soon see the must ferment and deposit yeast. It is, nevertheless, equally certain that the inferences which have been drawn from this celebrated experiment have been founded on error, and that the germs of yeast are very rarely derived from the particles of dust floating in the air with which the must comes in contact. The germs in question are, in our opinion, generally derived, not from the air, but from the sides of the bottles, from corks, from the string employed in corking, from corkscrews, and from a variety of other things. The reason for this is that any room, vault, cellar, or laboratory where the grapes, or must, or vintage, are handled— unless special precautions, of which Appert and Gay-Lussac certainly never thought, are taken—all the utensils, as well as all articles of clothing, and all the sides of the bottles which the hands have touched, are contaminated by cells of ferment derived from must that has fermented, or by germs from the surface of grapes and clusters. Thus, at the moment of decanting the must, a thousand accidental circumstances may lead to the introduction of those germs, the origin of which, as we have seen, may be actually traced to the very grapes which served for the manufacture of the must. In other words, we believe the inference that the germs of yeast which cause the experiment to succeed, are derived from particles of dust floating in the air of the place where we decant the contents of our bottles, to be altogether an erroneous one.

Since the preceding remarks were written, we have endeavoured to repeat this experiment of Gay-Lussac's in such a manner as we believed would confirm our views, by varying the conditions in such a way as would cause it to succeed or fail, according to the circumstances of the manipulation employed.

On December 7th, 1874, we took two bottles of must which we had preserved, after Appert's process, in our laboratory from the beginning of October, 1873. Both of these were covered with dust—the dust that floated about in our laboratory. We decanted them as follows :—One bottle, which we handled without special precautions, we uncorked by means of an ordinary corkscrew, and decanted into another bottle that had been well washed, as bottles are washed when they are to be used subsequently. This bottle was taken from a number that had been standing upside down on a drainer for a fortnight. We took no precaution to remove the dust which covered the exterior of the bottle of must, or to purify the washed bottle. The second bottle of must, on the other hand, was decanted after we had removed the dust that covered it; its cork was cut off close to the string, and the flame of a spirit lamp was passed over the string and the surface of the cork; and, as a final precaution, the corkscrew was passed through the flame. As for the bottle into which we subsequently decanted the must, we first plunged it in a hot-water bath kept at 100° C. (212° F.), then took it into a garden to cool upside down in the open air. After these precautions we removed it, and immediately decanted into it the must from the second bottle.

The first bottle showed signs of growths, both on the surface and at the bottom of the must, the day after the operation, and manifested the first symptoms of alcoholic fermentation on December 16th. The contents of the second bottle remained perfectly unchanged after being exposed to the warmth of a stove for several months.

Can anything be more conclusive than these facts? They are in perfect keeping with the views that we have recently expressed, and with the principles that we have maintained for nearly twenty years, on the subject of the causes of change in organic liquids.

It is by no means our intention to assert that in the atmospheric air there exist no germs of ferment in a state of suspension, as fine dust. Beyond all doubt they do so exist in that state; but, as a rule, in comparatively small number, their abundance or scarcity being dependent upon circumstances which control their multiplication, favouring or restricting it, as we are about to prove.

On May 2nd, 1873, we uncorked two ordinary bottles filled with wort, prepared in December, 1872, after Appert's process. To avoid the causes of error which we have mentioned, we uncorked the bottles in the following manner:—The cork was cut off to the level of the neck; the cork and string were next passed through flame, regardless of burning and charring them; we then gently extracted the cork by means of a corkscrew which also had been passed through the flame.

The bottles thus prepared were placed on the table of an underground room, in which we were continually making experiments on alcoholic fermentation.

1*st bottle.*—On May 7th we observed little particles of fungoid growth on the surface of the liquid, and at the bottom were large flakes of *mycelium*.

On May 11th a veil of *mycoderma vini* had formed: there were no signs of fermentation.

On May 13th vigorous fermentation commenced; it lasted until May 23rd. The microscope revealed yeast in globules of two sizes, the larger of which were considerably less numerous than the others. There were no signs of lactic or butyric ferment.

2*nd bottle.*—May 7th, particles of fungoid growth on the surface of the liquid, and also a veil of *mycoderma vini*. On May 11th, 13th, and up to the 23rd, no signs of fermentation were visible. On May 30th fermentation was active. The microscope showed us yeast mixed with butyric *vibrios*.

In this case, alcoholic ferments had come into existence, and from the precautions taken at the moment when the liquid was brought into contact with the external air, it is certain that the advent of the germs of those ferments, as also those of the

F

other organisms which made their appearance—the fungoid growths, *mycoderma vini* and *vibrios*—could only be accounted for by the fall of particles of dust floating about in the room. It follows, then, that under certain circumstances germs of alcoholic ferment may be found floating in the air; but we can readily show that the peculiar conditions of the place had a large share in bringing about the results obtained by the foregoing experiment.

The same day, May 2nd, 1873, we uncorked, with the precautions that we have already described, four other bottles of the same must. These were placed in a room which was used less frequently than the preceding one, and in which experiments relating to fermentation were seldom conducted.

1st bottle.—On May 8th we observed on the surface of the liquid large, frothy pieces of mycelium (*mucor mucedo* or *mucor racemosus*). The liquid was perfectly bright.*

May 30th.—No signs of actual fermentation yet visible.

2nd bottle.—On May 8th we noticed a thin, greasy-looking scum on our liquid, which had become turbid and acquired a sour smell. The microscope showed that this scum was formed of *mycoderma aceti*. On May 30th the scum had assumed a whitish appearance, and seemed to be dead; there was a green spot of *penicillium glaucum* upon it. No signs of fermentation.

3rd bottle.—May 8th, patches of fungoid growth on the surface of the liquid. May 30th, thick and abundant fungoid growth, but no fermentation.

4th bottle.—May 8th, little patches of fungoid growth, and a scum of *mycoderma vini*. May 30th, still no fermentation.

Up to the month of August, 1873, not one of these bottles gave the least sign of alcoholic or other fermentation.

On December 16th, 1872, we uncorked four bottles of wort, which also had been preserved by Appert's process; these we

* It is well to notice that under the influence of fungoid growths, properly so called, the wort of beer speedily becomes bright. We may say that fungoid growths, by their rapid development, clarify the must, which serves to nourish them.

placed on an oven, where there were always vessels fermenting, at about 25° C. (77° F.), but where none of the manipulations required for the starting or final study of fermentations were practised. The next day a fungoid growth, but unaccompanied by any signs of fermentation, made its appearance, and this state of things lasted for five months, after which we ceased to keep these bottles under observation.

On May 26th, 1873, we uncorked, with all the necessary precautions, ten bottles of wort, which had been preserved from April 9th, and then left them undisturbed in a room where we were constantly engaged in the study of fermentation.

On the following day, some patches of fungoid growth appeared on the surface of the liquids.

May 30th.—Fermentation commenced in one of the bottles.

May 31st.—A second bottle likewise began to ferment.

June 9th.—Four bottles, including the two preceding ones, were now in a state of fermentation. The six bottles that had not fermented were thereupon covered with caps of paper, taken from the centre of a ream of paper and passed through a flame. After this, and up to August 1, when our observations were discontinued, these six bottles underwent no fermentation.

From these examples, which are confirmed by many others that we shall have occasion to mention in the course of this work, it will be seen that the germs of alcoholic ferment are not present in every little point of space, constantly ready to fall upon any object, not even in those places where one is perpetually dealing with that kind of growth.* If we conduct our experiments with exactness, we very soon learn that all that has been written on the facility with which saccharine

* It has already been observed in our Memoir on spontaneous generation, that alcoholic fermentation is not always to be obtained by sowing wads of cotton or asbestos, charged with the particles of dust which float through the air, in saccharine musts that are in contact with much air. The air which furnished the particles of dust, in the experiments to which we are alluding, was taken outside the laboratory, in a neighbouring street.

musts may be made to ferment, by being rapidly brought into contact with the surrounding air, is greatly exaggerated.

The germs of ferments, especially of alcoholic ferments—the yeast of beer and the yeast of wine—are not nearly as abundant in atmospheric air, or in the particles of dust spread over the surface of things, as are the spores of fungoid growths. It is easy to understand this, for spores are generally borne by aerial organs in a state of dryness, so that the least breath of wind catches them up and carries them away, whilst ferments are composed of moist cellules that do not readily become dry.

The vacuous flasks, partly filled with organic liquids, which are opened and closed again immediately, frequently give us fungoid growths, but very rarely alcoholic fermentation, although in the latter respect they may not be absolutely sterile. We may cite some proofs of this.

On June 19th, 1872, we prepared seven flasks of saccharine liquid, impregnated with yeast—our flasks were of 300 c.c. capacity (about 10 fl. oz.)—and contained 100 c.c. of the liquid; we then drew out their necks to a small opening, which was sealed during boiling, after the steam had expelled all the air.

On June 29th we opened them in the principal room of our laboratory.

On July 9th, two of the seven flasks gave no sign of organized products; the others were swarming with *mycelia*, submerged or fruiting on the surface of the liquid, and either with or without *bacteria* entangled in their flakes. In two of the flasks there were visible at the bottom of the liquid some white streaks, which is an indication sometimes of the presence of alcoholic ferment, but much more frequently of a little cellular plant resembling it in appearance, but purely aerial in its growth, that is to say, taking no part in fermentation. Some days afterward, we saw bubbles of gas rising from the bottom of one of these flasks, and then fermentation proceeded so rapidly that we were obliged to open the neck to avoid an explosion. We append a sketch of its ferment (Fig. 10).

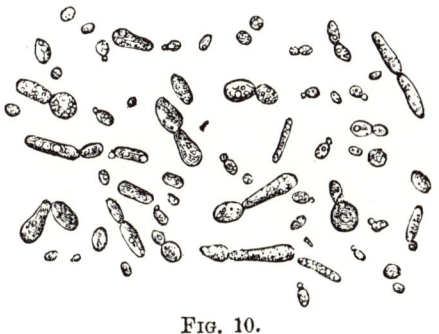

FIG. 10.

The other flask with the white streaks showed no signs of any fermentation.

In this kind of observation we rarely succeed in obtaining active ferments, the reason being that we deal with volumes of air that are too limited for the few germs of ferment that exist in a state of suspension in it.

We are more sure of success if we expose a tolerably large surface of saccharine liquid to the open air, because, under such circumstances, even if the exposure is of short duration, a considerable volume of air will pass over the surface of the liquid.

On May 29th, 1873, at five o'clock in the afternoon, we placed in the underground room previously mentioned, at a height of about two feet, ten porcelain dishes having surfaces of from thirty-five to forty square inches. We had just taken them from boiling water, and after allowing them to cool we placed in each quantities of wort to about one-third of an inch deep, which we poured from bottles uncorked with every precaution against the chance of the wort coming into contact with anything besides the floating particles of dust. On May 30th, at five o'clock, that is after twenty-four hours of exposure to the air of the room, we emptied the contents of the basins separately into glass flasks with long necks, which had been treated with boiling water and then cooled, necks downwards. The beak of the basin, by means of which the liquid was poured, and the funnels—for we used a separate funnel for each flask—had been passed through the flame. The whole ten flasks were then placed in an oven at a temperature of 25° C. (77° F.).*

On June 1st six of the flasks gave signs of fermentation, and next day all the flasks were fermenting.

The following are some of the numerous microscopic observations which we made on the liquids and their deposits.

On June 1st the liquid in one of the six flasks which had begun to ferment was covered with a continuous scum of *mycoderma vini*, below which appeared a filamentous network belonging to a *mycelium*, or other fungoid growth. But neither in the liquid itself nor in the deposit could we perceive any cells of the ferment of beer; the field, however, was swarming with active butyric *vibrios*, rather thick and short, their length being about twice their diameter. This fermentation was exclusively butyric.

On June 2nd another of the flasks showed no *vibrios*, but alcoholic ferment in small quantity, much lactic ferment, consisting of little particles contracted at the middle and non-mobile, and, finally, some slender filaments, resembling those represented in Plate I., Nos. 1 and 2.

On June 3rd we examined the liquid in the flask which showed the most marked fermentation. In addition to the flakes of fungoid growths, checked in their development through want of air, we found at least five distinct productions, which are represented in the accompanying sketch (Fig. 11).

aaa.—Thick cells of alcoholic ferment, the size of which is given in our sketch: thus, $\frac{1\cdot3}{450}$ indicates that the corresponding figure is $\frac{1\cdot3}{450}$ millimetre in length (rather more than $\frac{1}{1000}$ inch).

bbb. —Small alcoholic ferment, such as we generally see in the

* The decanting into the flasks is necessary, because of the possibility of the fermentation in the basins being masked. See further on the note on p. 75.

must of acid and sugared fruits—especially in filtered grape must. Its dimensions varied from 1 to 1½, or 2, 450ths of a millimetre.*

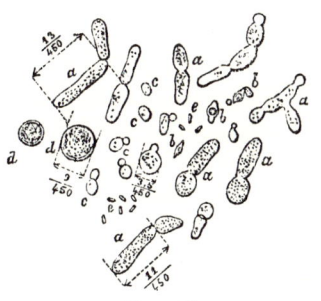

FIG. 11.

ccc.—" Low " yeast, of a type resembling that existing in other preparations fermenting in the room.

ddd.—Enlarged, distended spores of *mucor racemosus.* These are scarce, and have an old appearance. We shall come to them again in a subsequent chapter, where we shall explain their real significance.

eee.—Short *vibrios*, occurring either contracted or not near the middle. Some were motionless, others vibrating to and fro and executing other movements. These forms belong to the butyric and lactic ferments shown on Plate I.

* This small ferment is very curious, although it scarcely affects industrial fermentation. It was first described in 1862. (PASTEUR, *Bulletin de la Société chimique*, 1862, page 67, and following : *Quelques faits nouveaux au sujet des levûres alcooliques.*) It has since been described by Dr. Rees under the name *Saccharomyces apiculatus*. (Dr. Rees, Leipzig, 1870 : *Sur les champignons de fermentation alcooliques.* See also Dr. Engel, *Thèse pour le Doctorat*, Paris, 1872.) If we carefully filter some grape must at the time of vintage, we may be sure that we shall see it appear in the clear liquid at the bottom of our vessel, without intermixture with any other ferment.

Should we not filter the must this ferment will appear all the same, but it will soon become associated with another, thicker in appearance and more elongated, which also is one of the ferments peculiar to the fermentation of grape must.

The preceding series of experiments shows us that, in the case of wort exposed to the air, germs of divers organisms, amongst which various ferments—butyric, lactic, and alcoholic—are to be found, fall simultaneously from the particles of dust floating in the air. We must observe, however, that we were dealing with the air of a laboratory in which we were constantly studying analogous fermentations, and that a different atmosphere would, most likely, give us different results. We shall see a proof of this in the following paragraph, where we shall also find some new facts tending to prove that the germs of alcoholic ferment do not exist amongst the particles of dust floating in the air, in anything like the quantity usually supposed.

§ V.—New Comparative Studies on the Germs held in Suspension by the Air of Different Places which are near each other, but Subjected to Different Conditions affecting the Production and Diffusion of the Particles of Dust found in them.

We may compare the character and the greater or less abundance of similar germs existing in neighbouring localities, by studying the changes which take place in similar liquids exposed simultaneously to the action of the air in those localities. To do this, we must prepare a large number of flasks of the same size, free from air, and containing about equal quantities of a particular liquid—the same being used for all. We must open the same number of these flasks in each of the localities we have selected, and permit the air with all its particles of dust to rush into them; then we must close our flasks again, and observe, day by day, the appearances they present. The results obtained by these means will not furnish us with conclusions applicable to every kind of germ that the air contains at any given moment, but only with conclusions which apply to those germs which can develop in the particular liquid employed. Thus, for example, we could draw no inference as to the nature and relative number of *bacteria* or *vibrios*, in the

Pl. III

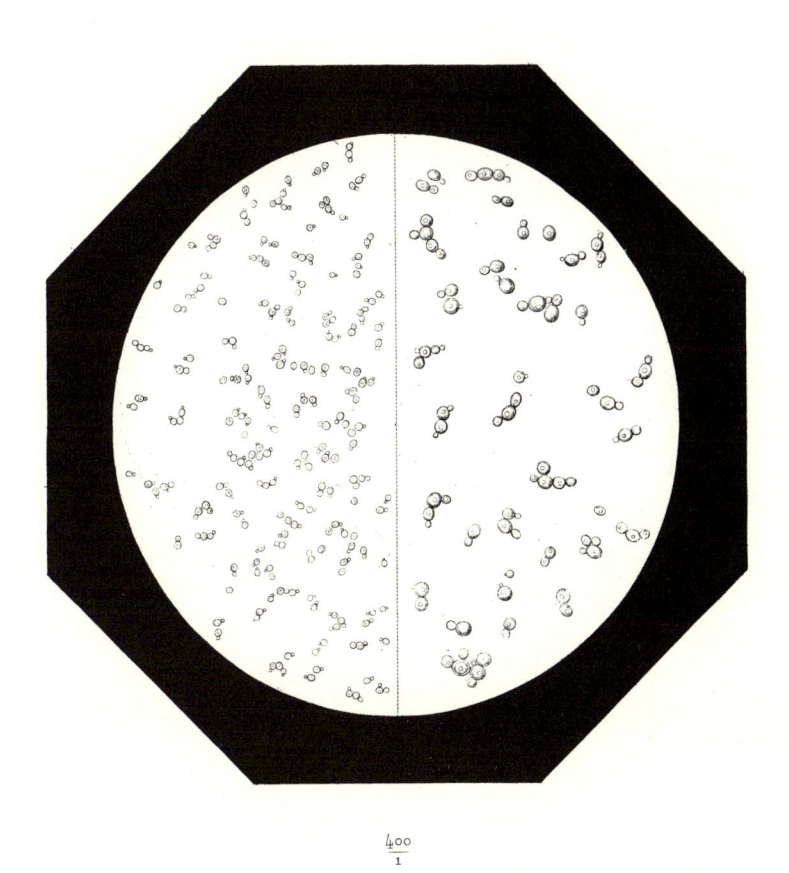

$$\frac{400}{1}$$

Deyrolle del. Picart sc

Imp Cony-Gros, Paris.

case where we employ an acid liquid; for organisms of that kind we must have recourse to neutral or slightly alkaline infusions. On the other hand, liquids having a feeble acid reaction would favour the growth of *mucedines, mycoderms,* and certain ferments, as for example, the alcoholic.

On November 26th, 1872, we opened and reclosed thirty flasks containing must kept from the last vintage.

Ten flasks were opened at the bottom of the garden of the *École Normale.*

Ten on the landing of the second floor.

Ten in the principal room of our laboratory, which had been swept out shortly before, by which operation the dust of the floor had been raised and put in motion.

Different objects made their appearance in a certain number of the thirty flasks on the following days; but from December 17th, things remained stationary. The following observations were made at that date:—

Of the ten flasks from the bottom of the garden, only one had undergone any change.

Of the ten flasks from the interior of the building, four had undergone change.

Of the ten flasks from our laboratory, all had undergone change.

The difference in the number of germs held in suspension in the three different places whence we had taken our air was, therefore, considerable.

The difference in the nature of the germs was equally marked. Those flasks of our first two series which had undergone change presented no trace of *torulæ,* or anything besides fungoid growths, whilst three of the last ten contained *torulæ* associated with fungoid growths.[*]

[*] We may remind the reader that in 1862, in our *Mémoire sur les Générations dites spontanées,* we applied the expression of *torula* to all the little cellular plants of spontaneous growth, excepting *mycelium,* propagated by budding, after the manner of the ferment of beer. At the same time, stress was laid upon the frequent occurrence of their germs, especially in our laboratory, where studies on fermentation were, even then, carried on. Plate III. represents two of these ferments.

On May 29th, 1873, eighteen flasks, free from air and with necks drawn out to a fine point, containing must, were taken into one of our rooms at the *École Normale*. A jet of gas from an ordinary burner was passed over the surface of the glass down to the surface of the liquid, with the object of burning any particles of dust that might have been deposited from the atmosphere of the laboratory.; the points of the flasks were then broken with a pair of ordinary scissors that had been passed through the flame of a spirit lamp ; and, lastly, the tops of the flasks were taken off, just above the surface of the liquid, and the eighteen flasks thus became transformed into eighteen basins, each containing about 100 c.c. (about $3\frac{1}{2}$ fluid ounces) of grape must. These eighteen basins were placed on a table in the room, and left there for five days, precautions being taken to prevent any one from entering the room.

The basins were examined on June 2nd: they all contained little flakes of floating *mycelium*, but none of them had any white streaks on their sides—a proof that they were destitute of *torulæ*—the liquid had remained very bright. With the contents of nine of the basins we filled two long-necked flasks that we had prepared for our purpose—that is to say, had heated to a certain point, just before using them, with the object of removing from their sides any foreign germs which they might have picked up in the laboratory. Up to July 10th, when we deemed it useless to carry our observations further, these flasks presented no signs of fermentation whatever. With the contents of the remaining nine basins, we filled two other long-necked flasks, but before doing so, we kept the basins for twenty-four hours (June 2nd to 3rd) in the basement of our laboratory. These two flasks soon set up an active fermentation, and deposited an abundance of yeast—an additional proof of the great difference in character of the germs floating about the room and those floating about the laboratory.

On June 3rd we exposed, simultaneously, in the aforementioned room and also in our laboratory, seven basins prepared as just described. On June 8th all the basins in the room showed signs of fungoid growths, without any trace of *mycoderma vini*, or lines indicative of the presence of *torulæ*, whilst six of the seven in our laboratory had their sides covered with a white precipitate, and on the surface of the liquids a layer of isolated patches of fungoid growth. The liquid in these latter basins was poured into a long-necked flask, which it nearly filled, and in the course of forty-eight hours it began to show signs of alcoholic fermentation.* This is another striking proof of the difference between the number of germs of ferment and *torulaceæ* in the air of our laboratory and that of an ordinary room.

We append drawings of the *torulæ* found in the six laboratory basins (see Sketches I., II., III., IV., V., VI. of Fig. 12). The abundance of the germs of these organisms in our laboratory is very striking, and is doubtless due to the nature of the work

---

* It is to be remarked that in this case, as in the case recorded § IV. p. 70, in order to detect with certainty any alcoholic ferment, the contents of the basins were transferred to a long-necked flask; since where, as in the basins, a liquid has a large surface exposed to spontaneous impregnation, the strictly alcoholic fermentation may escape observation. The reason of this is that, when a liquid of large surface but small depth is exposed to the air it affords a suitable medium for the active development of moulds, which, by absorbing the oxygen which would dissolve in the liquid, checks the growth of the ferment, or even prevents its germination altogether. As a matter of fact we shall see that for their growth and multiplication ferment *cells*, and still more ferment *germs* (the difference between the two will appear in Chap. V.), require a larger supply of oxygen just in proportion to their age, state of desiccation, and distance from the budding condition. Now, if the spores of moulds be present and effect a settlement in the liquid, the increase of the ferment, or even its actual germination, is prevented. But by collecting the liquid in a deep and narrow vessel, such as a long-necked flask, after it has been exposed to spontaneous impregnation, we deprive the moulds almost completely of oxygen, and so allow the ferment to exert its peculiar energies. The mere act of transferring enables the liquid to take up a sufficiency of oxygen, and a liberation of gas very speedily shows that fermentative action is going on. We must add further that sometimes in a liquid of large surface and shallow depth, in which but little ferment is formed, the evolution of carbonic acid gas may fail to be detected, by reason of its diffusing itself into the air slowly as it is formed.

76   STUDIES ON FERMENTATION.

carried on there, as well as to the power of endurance peculiar to the germs, or the minute vegetative cells of these microscopic plants—a tenacity of life which prevents them from losing their reproductive powers, even after being dried up into dust. But varied as are the formations represented in Fig. 12—and it will be observed that in IV. and VI. we have shown four

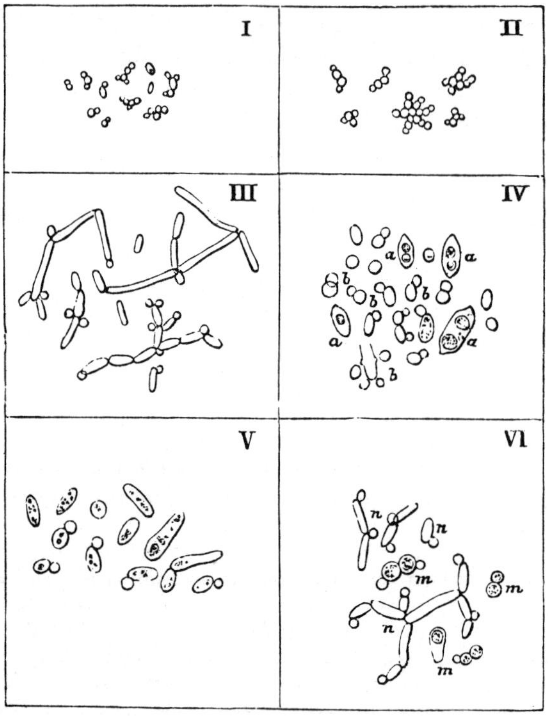

FIG. 12.

distinct forms, marked a, a; b, b; m, m; n, n respectively—it must not be supposed that they correspond necessarily to distinct species. From the ends of a compound organism like those in No. III, a little spherical cell may detach itself and then, by a process of budding, give rise to a series of other minute spherical cells reproducing the form shown in Nos. I. and II.

The forms figured in No. III. represent one of the types of *mycoderma vini*, which is often found in this branching arborescent state; but it frequently also occurs in short forms, and it is in this shape that it is generally met with on the surface of wines.

It is true that the nature of the substratum has a great influence on the changes of aspect in the organisms which we are describing, but this is not the sole cause of their morphological modifications. We are strongly inclined to believe that each of the cells, or vegetating forms so represented, differing so greatly as they do in aspect, and begotten, all of them, spontaneously in certain appropriate liquids, in a laboratory where researches on fermentation are pursued, is capable of furnishing a distinct variety. In fact, there is not a single one of the cells in the six varieties in Fig. 12, which, taken alone, has not its own peculiar characteristics, which, by hereditary transmission, it can impart, in a greater or less degree, to all the individuals of the generations that succeed it.

We may remark, on the other hand, that nothing can be more favourable to the isolation of different varieties of *torulæ* or *mycoderma vini* than the spontaneous impregnations to which we submit our liquids. For when suitable liquids contained in flasks exhausted of air are impregnated with the particles of atmospheric dust, by opening the flasks for a moment and then immediately re-sealing them, it must generally happen that we admit only one species of reproductive organism, so that we shall have a vegetation exclusively of one kind, as being derived from the same mother-cell. If we could take from a crowd composed of men and women separate couples, and forthwith transport each couple to a separate isolated and unpeopled island, they would, in the course of time, beyond doubt form so many distinct tribes.

It is very remarkable that some of the *torulæ* in Fig. 12 are not ferments; they do not cause sugar to decompose into alcohol and carbonic acid, any more than the *mycoderma vini* does; but, nevertheless, there may be an absolute similarity in aspect, development, shape, and size between the alcoholic ferment, properly so called, and these *torulaceæ*.

We must here cite a case in proof. On May 28th, 1872, in one of the rooms of our laboratory, we broke the fine points of a series of flasks, similar to those used in our previous experiments, containing must of grapes and deprived of air. We then closed up the ends immediately after the sudden entrance of the exterior air. One of these flasks developed only one kind of organism, which belonged to the *torulaceæ*. On June 7th this was sufficiently abundant to cover all the sides with a white deposit, and the surface of the liquid appeared quite free of any *mycoderma vini*. To assure ourselves that we were actually dealing with one kind of *torulæ*, unattended by fungoid growths, we waited until June 14th, but the aspect of things remained unchanged. On that day we opened the flask; there was no escape of gas to indicate that the interior pressure was greater than the exterior. We then subjected the plant to microscopic examination. It was quite homogeneous, and formed of a mass of cells, absolutely identical in aspect and size with old cells of ordinary yeast (Fig. 13).

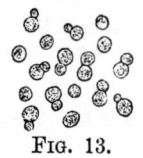

FIG. 13.

We distilled all the liquid, of which there was about 100 c.c., (3½ fl. oz.) without obtaining any trace of alcohol in our distillate; we collected 33 c.c. (about an ounce) of the distillate, which we distilled again, and we submitted the distillate a third time to distillation; but even then there were no more signs of the presence of alcohol than there had been in our first distillate.*

* Here we had to seek for a most minute quantity of alcohol, that no alcoholometer could have indicated. A certain sign of the presence of alcohol is contained in the first few drops distilled; these always assume the form of little drops or *striæ*, or, better still, oily tears, when alcohol is present in the distillate. The distillation should be effected with a

We may safely conclude that our *torula*, in the course of its development in must, with a weight that would have been very appreciable, did not produce, by its action of multiplication $\frac{1}{10,000}$ of 1 c.c. of alcohol.

Under the following conditions we obtained a slightly different result, which, nevertheless, confirmed the preceding one.

On July 5th, 1872, we opened and closed twelve flasks similar to those we had used before, the sole difference being that they contained yeast water * sweetened with ten per cent. of sugar. One of these flasks furnished us similarly with one kind of *torula*, which bore the greatest resemblance to the ferment of beer. When this *torula* was beginning to spread all over the bottom of our flask, we shook up the liquid, and turned the flask upside down, with the object of submerging the torula and depriving it of air, at least at the bottom of the neck. For some days, and even months, there were no signs of the liberation of gas. On July 22nd, 1873, after the interval of a year, we opened the flask (which gave no indication of the existence of an interior pressure) and endeavoured to discover the presence of alcohol, by means of successive distillations, as just described. In the two first distillates there seemed to be no alcohol, but in the third we detected its presence in very small quantity. We shall see, later on, that the formation of such a small quantity of alcohol may be attributed to the fact of the plant having been submerged when in full growth, and to its having continued to live for some time after its submersion quite independently of the oxygen contained in the air of the flask.

small long-necked retort and a Liebig's condenser. We must carefully watch the neck of the retort at the moment of boiling; should the liquid contain $\frac{1}{1000}$ part of its volume of alcohol, we shall observe the indications given above for a short, but appreciable time. $\frac{1}{10,000}$ of alcohol is difficult to judge, but with care and practice we may do it without failing. Collecting a third of each distillate, and supposing the limit of appreciation to stop at thousandths, in three distillations we may easily detect the presence of $\frac{1}{10,000}$ of 1 c.c. of alcohol in a total volume of 100 c.c.

* Yeast when macerated in water imparts to it certain soluble nitrogenous materials. The solution so obtained, filtered from yeast globules, is known as *yeast water*.—D. C. R.

From the previous facts it is obvious that there exist certain productions of various aspects, the germs of which are particularly abundant in the dust of a laboratory where the phenomena of fermentation are studied, productions essentially aerial, and incapable of giving rise to fermentation, although it may be impossible for the microscope to distinguish their forms from those of true alcoholic ferments.

The idea of some physiological bond between these plants and the ferments which resemble them in so remarkable a manner, is one that impresses itself forcibly and, so to say, instinctively upon the mind. This remark holds good also in the case of *mycoderma vini*, properly so called, when compared with alcoholic ferments. There appears to be no other difference between the *mycoderma vini* and the *torulæ* of which we are speaking, than that afforded by peculiarities of physical structure and a certain greasiness in the cells of the former which permits it to exist, in the form of a scum, upon the surface of liquids, that is to say unsubmerged.

We have frequently, but without success, endeavoured to bring about the conversion of these unsubmerged *torulæ* and *mycoderma vini* into alcoholic ferments; in other words, we have never succeeded in imparting to these *torulæ* or to *mycoderma vini*, which bear so striking a resemblance to alcoholic ferments, the permanent fermentative character peculiar to the latter. At one period of our researches, in 1862, and more recently, in 1872, we thought that we had discovered the conditions under which such conversion might be possible, but, as we shall explain in a subsequent chapter, our experiments were affected by certain errors that had escaped our notice.

---

* It is possible that this greasiness in the cells of the common *mycoderma vini* arises simply from the composition of the liquid in which it vegetates. It is in saccharine liquids that the submerged *torulæ* are found; fermented liquids more readily give birth to the forms of *torulæ* and *mycoderma vini* which exist as a scum. In all probability, however, there is no radical difference between these two kinds of little cellular plants of aerial growth, the floating *torulæ* and *mycoderma vini*.

§ VI.—Yeast may become Dry and be Reduced to Dust without losing its Faculty of Reproduction.

In the preceding paragraphs we have given examples of liquids becoming impregnated with self-sown alcoholic ferments. We shall proceed to show that this little cellular plant may actually exist in the form of dust, floating in the air, after the manner of spores of fungoid growth and the encysted forms of certain infusoria, without losing its powers of reproduction.

On December 16th, 1872, we collected and pressed all the yeast resulting from a brewing of about one hectolitre (about 22 gallons). From the centre of the cake we took a few grammes (50 or 60 grains) of yeast, which we mixed in a porcelain mortar with five times its weight of plaster—both mortar and plaster having been heated, just before, in an oil bath, to a temperature of about 200° C. (392° F.), and then cooled rapidly. The powder thus prepared was immediately done up in a twist of paper, which had been passed through the flame of a spirit lamp, and the twist and its contents were then placed in an oven at a temperature of from 20° C. to 25° C. (about 75° F.). The object of these several precautions was to free the powder composed of the yeast and plaster, if not from the germs contained in floating particles of dust, at all events from those contained in the dust existing on the surface of the articles we used—the mortar, plaster, and paper.

On December 18th, we took up with a platinum spatula,

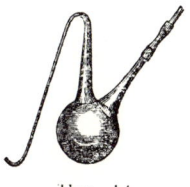

Fig. 14.

previously passed through the flame, a pinch of the yeast-and-plaster powder, and sowed it in a two-necked flask (Fig. 14) containing some pure wort. We then placed the flask in an oven, at 20° C.

On December 21st, three days after we had sown the powder, fermentation began to manifest itself by the appearance of patches of froth on the surface of the wort. On December 19th and 20th the yeast was sensibly developing, although there was no liberation of gas to denote the presence of actual fermentation. The yeast, examined under the microscope, appeared very pure.

On March 5th, 1873, we took another pinch of the yeast-and-plaster powder from the twist of paper, and placed it in a flask of pure wort, as in the foregoing experiment.

On March 9th, that is, after having been subjected to a heat of 20° C. (68° F.) in the oven for four days, fermentation began to manifest itself by the appearance of patches of froth on the surface of the wort. From this it was evident that the yeast had not been destroyed, but only retarded in its revival.

On July 25th, 1873—that is, after a lapse of seven months and a half—we resumed our experiments, and sowed some more of the yeast-and-plaster powder in another flask of wort. On August 2nd, eight days from the time of our sowing, the little islets of froth appeared on the surface of the liquid. Observed under the microscope, the yeast still seemed pure, and resembled the original yeast; we append a sketch, which will give an idea of its shape (Fig. 15).

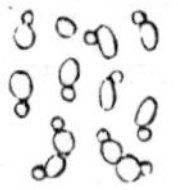

FIG. 15.

On November 7th, 1873, we once more sowed some of the powder. This time the yeast was dead; we observed the flask which contained it, day by day, until February 1st, 1874, without detecting the slightest sign of fermentation or development of the yeast that we had sown. On February 1st, we made a microscopical examination of the yeast, and found it mixed with the plaster and absolutely inert at the bottom of the saccharine liquid; its cells were isolated, very old-looking and granulated, without any appearance that might denote the possibility of their ever budding again.

Thus we determined that alcoholic ferment may be dried at the ordinary temperature of the atmosphere, and preserved, in the form of dust, for a period of seven months or longer, without losing its faculty of reproduction. This faculty evidently diminishes in the course of time, for our dried yeast, after having been kept for seven months and a half—all the other conditions of the two experiments having been precisely the same—required about eight days to develop sufficiently to reveal fermentation, whilst, immediately after the drying, it cnly required three or four days to accomplish the same thing.

Side by side with these experiments on alcoholic ferment, we carried on exactly similar ones with yeast obtained from "high fermentation" breweries. On December 16th, 1872, we prepared a powder of this yeast and plaster as before. Our last sowing took place on July 25th, 1873, in a flask of pure wort, which showed signs of fermentation on July 27th. We append a sketch (Fig. 16) which gives the general aspect of

FIG. 16.

this "high ferment," when revived after such a lapse of time; it had preserved the distinctive features of the cells of "high ferment."

These facts can leave no doubt whatever as to the possibility of cells of yeast existing, in a state of suspension in the air, in the form of fine dust, particularly in a laboratory where researches on alcoholic fermentation are pursued.

CHAPTER IV.

THE GROWTH OF DIFFERENT ORGANISMS IN A STATE OF
PURITY: THEIR *AUTONOMY*.[*]

OUR observations in the preceding chapter will have shown that organic liquids, natural or artificial—the wort of beer amongst others—if exposed to contact with the air, rapidly develop various forms of life. This is a natural consequence of the mode of impregnation. The fertility of the liquid depends on the various microscopic germs which are deposited

[*] In the course of this work we shall combat, by means of experimental proofs which appear to us irrefragable, the opinions which many writers entertain on the subject of certain transformations of organisms —that of *penicillium glaucum* into ferment, or *mycoderma;* of *bacteria* into lactic ferment; of ferment into *vibrios;* of *mycoderma aceti* into ferment, and so on. Nevertheless, we shall pronounce no *a priori* opinion on the question whether the inferior organisms, which will be the subject of this chapter, and which include yeast and the ferments properly so called, are perfect beings in their habitual form, or whether they are susceptible of polymorphism. It is with this reservation that we employ the word *autonomy*. If we claim polymorphism for any species, we shall not do so without furnishing proofs. Some organs detached from higher organisms, and some beings in a certain phase of their existence, may reproduce themselves under a special form, with special properties, when brought into media and under conditions that are unfit for the production of the plant or animal under its other shape or ordinary mode of reproduction. Modern Science affords many examples of this, and certain alcoholic ferments present us with analogous facts; but to wish to stretch these facts beyond their due significance, and to admit a polymorphism that cannot be proved, in consequence of a belief that it is possible, or on the faith of confused observations, is to indulge in gratuitous assertion from a mere spirit of system.

in it by the common air, and these, again, as regards their nature and number, are dependent upon the situation of the vessel containing them, its height above the ground, the time of year, the disturbance of the atmosphere, and other causes.

The fortuitous association of other forms, in growths which we believe to be uniform and independent, constitutes one of the principal difficulties that occur in the study of the lower organisms, particularly that of fungoid growths. The fact that the germs of many of these little beings exist in the atmosphere in the form of dust, invisible to the naked eye, or, as such, spread over the surface of the different materials and objects used in experiments, exposes the student to constant risk of wrongly interpreting the results which come under his notice. He has sown a plant, and is observing the course of its development. Without his knowledge, spores of another plant have got mixed with his growth, and germinated. In his ignorance, he will attribute all that he sees, all the changes which he describes and which he sketches, and all the conclusions which he draws, to the one plant which engages his attention. If he is dealing with *bacteria, vibrios*, and, generally speaking, the infinite variety of mobile microscopic organisms, his embarrasment will be greater still. Again, inasmuch as the medium which serves as substratum for growths has a considerable influence on the fertility of the germs in contact with it, as well as on their ulterior development, it often happens that germs deposited fortuitously by the particles of dust which fall from the atmosphere or collect on objects are fertile and multiply with rapidity, whilst those which have been directly sown, no matter in what number, remain sterile, or multiply very slowly. If we place in a young wine some *mycoderma aceti*, we shall obtain *mycoderma vini;* by placing some *mycoderma vini* in an old wine, especially if it is a little acid, we shall obtain *mycoderma aceti*.* It is from facts of

* See, on this subject, the author's *Études sur le Vinaigre*, Paris, 1868, p. 76, note; and especially *Études sur le Vin*, 2nd Edition, 1873, p. 19.

this kind, wrongly interpreted, that many errors have crept into our knowledge of the lower organisms, and that we are constantly seeing old discussions crop up, both on the subject of so-called *spontaneous* generation and on that of the theory of fermentation. At every step in the course of this work we shall see the trace of these complications, as well as the influence they have had on the progress of our knowledge.

In opposition to these results, we will study the case of wort sown directly with germs distinctly of one kind, unmixed with any other.

§ I.—Growth of Penicillium Glaucum and Aspergillus Glaucus in a State of Purity—Proofs that these Fungoid Growths do not become Transformed into the Alcoholic Ferments of Beer or Wine.—Preliminary Enquiry into the Cause of Fermentation.

Let us again take one of the flasks furnished with two necks such as we have already described, and let it be supposed that this flask contains a quantity of saccharine wort, brewed some considerable time ago, which has undergone no change whatever, except in colour, the slow process of oxidation having gradually darkened the original colour of the liquid. What we have to do is to drop into this unchanged and fertile liquid some grains or spores of *penicillium* which are free from the slightest trace of the spores or germs of other microscopic organisms.

One means of effecting this consists in taking up with a pair of metallic forceps, previously heated, a piece of platinum wire, one or two centimetres (about ¾ in.) in length, which we also pass through the flame of a spirit lamp, and with which, as soon as it is cold, we touch a mass of sporanges of a growth of *penicillium*. No matter how few spores may be taken up on the end of the platinum wire, we shall have far more than we require for the impregnation of the liquid. At the moment of charging the point of the wire we withdraw the glass stopper which closes the india-rubber tube on the right-hand neck of the flask (Fig. 14) and drop the wire through that tube ; we then replace the glass stopper, after having, by way of additional precaution, passed it rapidly through the flame of the lamp. There is no doubt that we expose ourselves to error in consequence of having to convey the wire through the surrounding air, and also, in consequence of having previously to open the flask ; but, as we have already remarked, this double cause of error has never, we may say, interfered with the exactness of our experiments, the volume of air with which we are concerned being exceedingly limited. Moreover, our flask being in free communication with the exterior air, by means of the opening in the curved, slender tube, there is no inrush of air when we withdraw the stopper. The chance of encountering a spore or fecund germ and introducing it into the flask on the wire that is charged with the others, is so remote that we have considered it unnecessary to adopt a more perfect apparatus, which might easily have been devised had we felt that it was necessary.

A more serious cause of error may occur in the preceding method ; resulting from the possible impurity of the spores taken from a field of *penicillium* which has developed in contact with common air. This field receives, every instant, and has received throughout its growth, particles of dust which have fallen from the atmosphere ; thus, it may not be, and, as a matter of fact, is not, free from the germs of other fungoid growths.*

* Some observations in the preceding chapter enable us to account for the vast number of germs which are constantly falling on the surface of everything. We may here allude to the use we have made of flasks, shaped as in Fig. 17, and holding from 250 c.c. to 300 c.c., which are a third part filled with an organic liquid, and are closed up when boiling. They contain no air when cool, and are opened in series of 10, 20, &c., out of doors, and closed up again immediately. The air rushes violently into the vacuum, and thus we introduce about 200 c.c. of air, with all the particles of dust contained in that air, into each flask. It has been proved that a certain number of these flasks undergo change in the

88   STUDIES ON FERMENTATION.

The operator, without knowing it, may frequently sow, besides the *penicillium*, which is all he can see, spores of *mucor mucedo* and *mycoderma vini*, in short, of all the most common fungoid growths.

This process of impregnation, therefore, does not afford us sufficient safeguards, but by means of the following device we shall

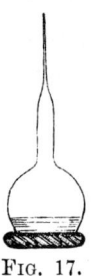

FIG. 17.

render it more satisfactory. Let us take a series of flasks shaped as in Fig. 17, containing an organic liquid suitable to the development of fungoid growths, that is to say, slightly acid—yeast-water, plain or sugared, the wort of beer, or Raulin's fluid *

course of time, the number of those changing and the nature of their changes being in close proportion to the probable number and nature of the floating germs able to develop in the particular nutritive liquid used. If we work at great elevations, far from houses and the dirt of towns and inhabited plains, as we did at Montanvert, near the *Mer de Glace*, change will seldom occur. The opposite will be the case if we work in a place like the living-room of the little, dirty, ill-kept inn at Montanvert. In a laboratory where fermentation is studied we obtain certain kinds of germs which often differ from those found in the air of the open country. If we desire to have organisms in all our flasks, we have only to stir up the dust on the ground or on surrounding objects at the moment when we open the flasks. This simple and easy experiment clearly shows us that it is impossible for a field of sporanges of fungoid growth, existing in an uncovered vessel or on the surface of a fruit, to escape becoming mixed with germs that are foreign to the little plant; in other words, the student who sows spores of *penicillium*, which he has collected from one place or another on a brush, exposes himself to serious causes of error.

* M. Jules Raulin has published a well-known and remarkable work on the discovery of the mineral medium best adapted by its composition

will answer our purpose; let us boil the liquid, and having previously drawn out the necks, let us close the ends in the flame of a lamp whilst the steam is escaping, as soon as we judge that the air has been nearly all expelled. Having prepared ten or twenty of these flasks in this manner, when they are cold we may break their points in any place we may be in. The air will rush into the flasks, and we must then seal them up again in the flame of the lamp, and put them aside for future observations. In a certain number of these flasks, as we have already explained in our experiments carried on after this fashion, we shall see some fungoid growths appear, first in the shape of flakes of *mycelium* floating in the liquid, and afterwards coming to the surface to fructify. Now, it often happens that *penicillium glaucum* appears alone, so numerous are the spores of this fungus floating in the air. Under such conditions, we shall evidently obtain a field of sporanges quite free from the presence of other organisms. If we now take off the neck of one of the flasks containing the pure *penicillium*, and take out some of the germs with our platinum wire, * we

to the life of certain ordinary fungoid growths; he has given a formula for the composition of such a medium. It is this that we call here "Raulin's fluid" for abbreviation.

Water 1,500	Carbonate of Magnesia ..	0·4
Sugar Candy 70	Sulphate of Ammonia....	0·25
Tartaric Acid 4	Sulphate of Zinc	0·07
Nitrate of Ammonia 4	Sulphate of Iron	0·07
Phosphate of Ammonia .. 0·6	Silicate of Potassium	0·07
Carbonate of Potassium .. 0·6		

J. RAULIN. Paris, Victor Masson, 1870. *Thèse pour le doctorat.*

* If we do not wish to take the chance of procuring the pure *penicillium* by means of these spontaneous sowings, effected by opening and then closing in the flame a certain number of flasks with drawn-out points, we may utilize one of the flasks, which, having been opened and closed again, has notwithstanding developed no organized forms, as follows:—
We impregnate the contained liquid directly, by dropping into it from a metallic wire spores taken from any growth of *penicillium* exposed to the common air; and then from the new field of sporanges formed by this sowing in the flask that has been re-closed, we must, later on, take the pure spores that we require. This method is quicker and almost as safe.

shall thus obtain with most certainty spores of *penicillium* free from impurities.

Our readers will excuse the length of these details and the minutiæ of our precautions, but we shall again and again see that to neglect them, or any part of them, is to expose ourselves to hazard in drawing sure conclusions from facts which come under our observation.

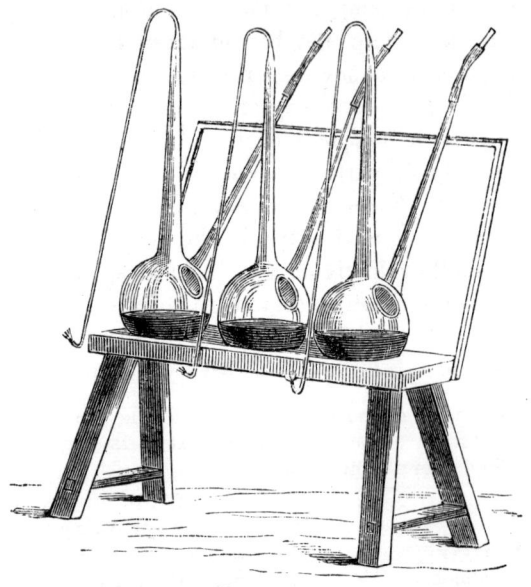

FIG. 18.

On June 17th, 1872, we placed some pure spores of *penicillium* in a series of three flasks containing wort (Fig. 18), observing all the precautions that we have indicated. We shall designate

We should add that, if we wish to use for our purpose spores of *penicillium* from a closed flask, in which the plant has fructified, we must be careful not to leave the plant too long closed up. A few days after the sowing the growth of the fungus is arrested, in consequence of all the oxygen being absorbed, and its place being supplied by a mixture of carbonic acid and nitrogen; and the spores, if kept too long in this atmosphere, will all perish.

these flasks by the letters A, B, C. On the following day the spores germinated, and the liquid became full of flakes of mycelium, some of which came to the surface to fructify. The temperature varied between 25° C. and 30° C. (77° to 86° F.).

On June 22nd, small patches, with whitish borders and green centres, developed on the liquids. We then shook up the flask A, in order to submerge the plant and the spores.* We also shook the flask B, after observing the precaution of sealing up the slender bent tube.† The flask C was attached on one side to an aspirator, on the other to a tube filled with cotton, and every day we renewed the air in it.

During the weeks and months over which our observations extended, there was not the least formation of yeast in these flasks; moreover, we have frequently repeated this and other experiments of a similar kind, without ever detecting the appearance of either ordinary yeast or any other true alcoholic ferment. The experiments may be made with saccharine juices that are highly favourable to the development of *bacteria* and lactic ferment. These latter appear equally incapable of transformation into yeast, which has never been seen to develop in experiments where they were used, if proper precautions have been taken to secure a pure growth. Should we neglect any of the precautions that are necessary to secure the purity of our spores, we may of course obtain different results. If, for instance, we sow spores of *penicillium* grown in free contact with

---

* To shake the liquid without danger of introducing exterior particles of dust, we apply the flame of the spirit lamp to the drawn-out neck of the flask, and close up the open end; we may then shake our flask without risk. We must afterwards reopen the end of the drawn-out neck for the purpose of re-establishing communication with the exterior air.

† The flask B was closed with the lamp in consequence of one of the objects of these experiments being to test M. Trécul's experiments on the transformation of *penicillium* into ferment. Strangely enough, according to M. Trécul, as we shall see later on, the spores of *penicillium* refuse to change into ferment, if the vessels in which they are sown are not "perfectly air-tight."

the atmosphere, and consequently exposed to the particles of dust floating therein, we shall frequently observe, mixed with the fruiting hyphæ of the fungoid growth, yeast and *mycoderma vini* and *torulæ*, or even *bacteria* and lactic ferment. Thus we shall be led to believe, in all good faith, that we have under our eyes examples of the changes of spores of fungoid growth into cells of ferment, or proofs of the conversion of *bacteria* or lactic ferment into the same cells.

Causes of error of this nature have induced some German naturalists to believe that they have succeeded in proving, beyond the possibility of doubt, that a number of fungoid growths may produce alcoholic ferment, and that they have clearly demonstrated that spores of these fungi may become transformed into yeast. In 1856 M. Bail, and, about the same time, Berkeley, and, later on, H. Hoffmann and Hallier, have successively entertained these views, which were introduced into science by M. Turpin. We have combated them since the year 1861.* Since that period they have lost rather than gained ground abroad, in spite of the growing favour bestowed on the Darwinian system. One of the mycologists who enjoy the most legitimate authority beyond the Rhine, M. de Bary, has arrived, as we have, at absolutely negative results.

A simple perusal of what has been written in favour of the transformations which we are discussing causes us to entertain the gravest doubts as to the correctness of results which are quoted as decisive. We need only give one example, which we extract from a paper by M. H. Hoffmann.

"In some cases," this author writes, " and under favourable circumstances, I have been able to see the ferment produce filaments, both small specimens that could be examined immediately under the microscope, and also large specimens, and I have recognized, amongst other varieties, *penicillium glaucum, ascophora mucedo, ascophora elegans,* and *periconia hyalina,* sometimes isolated, sometimes intermixed. This result is most easily to be

* *Bulletin de la Société Philomathique.*

obtained by the following method:—Pour a small quantity of water into a test-tube, which should then be placed slantingly: introduce some fresh yeast into the middle part of the tube, and close the tube with a wad of cotton, to prevent the entrance of exterior particles of dust. In this vapour-filled receptacle we shall sometimes see flakes develop. It seems that Messrs. Berkeley and G. H. Hoffmann have also obtained *penicillium* from ferment, by a similar process."*

Why, however, should it not be admitted that *penicillium* found under such conditions may be derived from spores of that growth, adhering to the sides of the tube before it is closed with the wad, or mixed with the yeast that is put into the tube?

The facts alleged during the last few years by M. Bail, who persists in his views, in spite of their apparently greater exactness, are also far from being satisfactory.†

M. Trécul, who is almost the only one in France, besides Messrs. Ch. Robin and Fremy, to participate in these errors, does not confine himself to affirming the change of the spores of *penicillium* into yeast, and *vice versâ*; his system is a far more extensive one. "According to my observations," he says, "there would be the following series of changes: albuminous matter changed into *bacteria*, or directly into alcoholic ferment, or into *mycoderma*; *bacteria* into lactic ferment, there becoming immoveable; lactic ferment into alcoholic ferment; alcoholic ferment into *mycoderma cerevisiæ*; finally, *mycoderma cerevisiæ* into *penicillium*. ‡

M. Trécul does not stop here. He goes on to explain the

* HERMANN HOFFMANN, *Études Mycologiques sur la Fermentation.* Botanische Zeitung and *Annales des Sciences Naturelles*, 4ᵉ série, t. xiii. p. 24, 1860.

† *Communication sur l'Origine et le Développement de quelques Champignons.* Dantzig, 1867.

‡ TRÉCUL, *Comptes rendus de l'Académie*, t. lxxiii. p. 1454; December 28, 1871.

principal of these changes, as though his testimony were quite beyond refutation:

"If we use a perfectly filtered wort, containing no granulations, and prepared at a temperature between 60° C. and 70° C. (140° F. and 160° F.), there will first of all appear a multitude of fine granules that will develop into active bacteria, which, losing the faculty of motion, will constitute lactic ferment, as I have repeatedly pointed out. A few days after the appearance of the first granules, we shall perceive others rather larger in size and isolated. These will increase in size, and, in the course of time, assume the form of little globuloid, or elliptic cells; they will not commence to bud before they have attained a comparatively large size, approaching that of ordinary yeast, consequently, there will be a considerable interval of time, during which the young cells will present no buds, especially if we work at a low temperature, as from 20° C. to 35° C. (68° F. to 95° F.)

"As for the transformation of the spores of *penicillium* into alcoholic ferment, the possibility of which M. Pasteur also denies, I have very often obtained it by using liquids, such as boiled wort and sugared barley water, which had stood for a month or six weeks without setting up an alcoholic fermentation. These liquids, sown with spores of different forms of *penicillium*, chosen when young and in full growth, fermented after a varying number of days, even at a temperature of 12° C. (54° F.), the condition of fermentation being that the flasks were closed with very elastic corks, which had been boiled for a quarter or half an hour; these corks, as I have already pointed out, it is best to keep for a month after the boiling, to make sure, by drying them thoroughly again, of destroying any *mycelia* adhering to them. It is necessary to keep the flasks stoppered that the corks may be always moist, and it is also advisable to shake the flasks once or twice a day, to secure the submersion of the spores. If these conditions are carried out, we shall soon see the spores increase in size, gradually lose their green colour and then bud, and often a very active fermentation will manifest itself. All

STUDIES ON FERMENTATION. 95

the spores will be transformed, if the flasks are perfectly air-tight."*

Such is the manner in which M. Trécul regards these changes. His is entirely a system of spontaneous generation, worked out into minutest detail, from the transformation of the albuminous substances to the formation of cells of the higher organisms, passing from the disintegration of the original substances to the formation of very fine granules, from these to the creation of active *bacteria*, which last, in their turn, become lactic ferment through the simple cessation of their faculty of moving and so on. We regard all this as purely imaginary. As a matter of fact, M. Trécul's argument is based on the successive phenomena which manifest themselves in filtered wort " containing no granulations." As M. Trécul reasons, this condition is a necessity, for he starts with the assertion that the albuminous substances in the wort become changed into granulations " that will develop into active bacteria." This is another of M. Trécul's illusions. No doubt we may filter hopped wort to almost perfect clearness, but we can only do this when it is cold. If we filter it warm, it will be bright as long as it remains warm, but as soon as cold it will appear turbid, in consequence of the great number of minute granules floating in it. Again, cold wort, however little it may be or has been in contact with air, undergoes a process of oxidation, and this oxidation, which acts principally on the colouring or resinous matter, causes a deposit of fine granules, the number of which is constantly increasing as oxidation goes on. These granules form an absolutely inert precipitate which, under no possible circumstances, can become

* TRÉCUL, *Comptes rendus de l'Académie*, t. lxxv. p. 1169, November 11, 1872. A proof of M. Trécul's carelessness in experiments of this kind is the fact that in studying the fertility of an impregnated wort, he often obtains different productions. Our experiments give opposite results. If we sow nothing, we obtain nothing. If we sow a plant, we obtain a similar plant; or, should there be any difference, the change may be traced, beyond question, to its origin in the plant sown, and is the consequence of some alteration in the conditions of our experiment.

transformed into active bacteria. Nothing can be easier than to prove this fact, by taking some of our two-necked flasks (Fig. 4) and preparing pure wort in them, by boiling, and then leaving it to cool and undergo the process of oxidation. In wort thus exposed to the air—the air being pure and free from germs—there will be formed a granular deposit, which will never become active or transform itself into any kind of organism whatever.

We may also remark that whilst M. Trécul used wort in his experiments, he does not tell us if it was hopped or not. Had M. Trécul informed us that the facts which he described applied to unhopped wort, we should reply that a temperature of 60° C. or 70° C. (140° F. or 160° F.) is quite insufficient to kill the germs of bacteria existing in such a wort. Hopped wort should be heated to 70° C. or 75° C. (160° F. to 170° F.), that it may remain inert after having cooled down in contact with pure air; unhopped wort must be heated to about 90° C. (194° F.).

In short, whatever may be the case, it must be evident to our readers that the active bacteria observed by M. Trécul existed in the form of germs in the wort that he used, and that what he observed was nothing more than the development of these germs when brought into contact with the air held in solution in the liquid.

As for the success of M. Trécul's experiments on the *penicillium*, we have no doubt that that gentleman has sown germs of yeast or *torulæ*, which bear so striking a resemblance to yeast, at the same time that he sowed spores, since he took his spores from sporangia of *penicillium* that had been exposed to contact with ordinary air. The conditions under which M. Trécul conducted his experiment rendered it difficult for the spores—although, relatively, much more numerous than the contaminating germs of ferment with which they happened to be associated—to make way against these latter, since the spores were unable to continue their development in a medium that was deprived of oxygen. On the other hand, the cells of ferment might easily have multiplied to such an extent as to make the discovery of the spores that had been sown a matter of some difficulty, since those spores would have been lost amongst the great number of cells of ferment. This was, probably, one of the causes which led to the mistaken notion that such spores underwent conversion into cells of ferment. Now although botanists describe several varieties of *penicillium glaucum*, we do not suppose that the cause of the difference between our results and those obtained by M. Trécul can be attributed to our having operated upon a different variety of *penicillium* from that which he used. Supposing that there had been a great difference between our two varieties, still M. Trécul declares that he has realized the phenomenon with numerous varieties of this fungus.

M. Trécul expresses himself as follows : " I have used spores of *penicillium* of several varieties in these experiments : Firstly, thick, green, elliptic spores of a variety of *penicillium* that grows on lemons ; secondly, elliptic spores of a bluish colour and smaller than the preceding, of another variety of *penicillium* found on lemons ; thirdly, spherical spores of the variety termed *penicillium crustaceum* ; fourthly, spores of the *penicillium* that develops on the yeast of beer.[*]

This criticism of M. Trécul's opinions was written on the occasion of a discussion at the Academy, after we had been induced to read over again the remarks which he had published on the subject. We were so impressed by the positive manner in which his conclusions were stated, that we asked ourselves, once more, which of us could be mistaken, and once more, also, we applied ourselves to fresh experiments, which we conducted with every possible precaution, following, as far as we could without falling into the errors of which we accuse the learned botanist, the mode of procedure that he adopted. As his descriptions struck us as being at times insufficient, we resolved to ask him for certain explanations *vivâ voce* (November 3rd, 1873), which he gave us with the greatest willingness.

[*] *Comptes rendus des Séances de l'Académie des Sciences*, t. lxxv. p. 1220; Nov. 18, 1872.

"Every variety of *penicillium*," said M. Trécul, "especially when young and vigorous, is amenable to transformation into ferment. This is the way in which I operated: I had some little flasks of 30 c.c. to 40 c.c. (about 1½ fluid ounces) in capacity, filled quite full with wort, or, at least, containing very little air, closed perfectly air-tight with corks which I had kept for a quarter of an hour in boiling water. These flasks when corked were heated to 60° C. or 70° C. (140° to 158° F.). After they had cooled I uncorked them, and introduced into them the spores which had been prepared as follows: I placed on a piece of glass some spores of the variety of *penicillium* that I wished to study, taken with a pair of forceps from a mouldy lemon, and I mixed these spores with a drop of wort and observed them under the microscope to assure myself that they contained nothing of a foreign nature; then I poured my drop of wort from the piece of glass into one of the flasks, which I recorked and laid down. The transformation into ferment took place next day."

Provided with these new data we set to work again and prepared a series of little flasks which were filled quite full with hopped wort, or contained but very little air, as M. Trécul had recommended. These we heated in a hot water bath to 70° C. (158° F.) at least; we then impregnated them, observing the necessary precautions, which we described at the commencement of this paragraph—not working in the evidently defective manner in which M. Trécul had done. Taking his spore-seeds from a field of sporanges exposed to the air, and afterwards manipulating them, in contact with the air, in water on a piece of glass, before he made his microscopical examination, his experiments were conducted under circumstances in every way conducive to the introduction of causes of error. One of the most serious of those causes is that which results from the substratum of the spores as taken from a mouldy lemon. If M. Trécul will examine under the microscope the water in which any lemon has been washed—even a sound lemon, unattacked by any fungoid growth—he will immediately see the cause of error to which his method of working exposes him. Germs of microscopic organisms exist abundantly on the surface of all fruits.

Having impregnated the liquids in our flasks with spores from a quantity of pure sporangia grown in a closed vessel, gathered on the point of a platinum wire, which had first been heated and then allowed to cool, we found that in each case, without exception, germination took place, then a *mycelium* was developed, which soon, however, ceased to grow from want of a proper supply of air; but not in any single case was there the faintest trace of fermentation, formation of yeast, or appearance of *bacteria* or lactic ferment.

We repeated these experiments, using unhopped wort instead and obtained similar negative results. We had previously determined that it was necessary to heat flasks of hopped wort to 70° C (158° F.), at least, and those of unhopped wort to 90° C. (194° F.) to secure them from further change.

In short, contrary to the assertions of M. Trécul, M. H. Hoffmann, and other naturalists, it is not true that the spores of *penicillium* can change into alcoholic ferment.

Regarded from another point of view, growths of pure *penicillium* will give us some remarkable results, the interpretation of which seems to us to be intimately connected with the physiological theory of fermentation that we shall discuss in a subsequent chapter. It is a question as to the production of alcohol whilst the life of the plant is carried on under certain conditions of growth.

If we distil saccharine liquids on the surface or in the body of which we have grown *penicillium*, and repeat the distillation in the manner that we have already described for the detection of the minutest quantities of alcohol, we shall readily find that those liquids frequently do contain a little ordinary alcohol. Moreover, if we regard the quantities of alcohol produced, which are always very minute, seldom exceeding 1 or 1·5 thousandth of the total volume of the liquids, we shall find that there is no fixed proportion between this alcohol and the weights of the plants formed. It is possible, for instance, that we may obtain more alcohol from one plant than from another weighing a hundred times as much. Often, however, when the vegetation is abundant we cannot make out the occurrence of alcohol in spite of the sensitiveness of the process described (p. 78).

What can be the cause of these varying results relating to the production or non-production of alcohol in the vegetation of the little plant? The numerous experiments that we have made seem to demonstrate positively that they are dependent upon variations in the amount of air or oxygen that is supplied to the fungoid growths, whether, that is, the vegetating mycelium alone be submerged, or the whole plant with its organs of fructification. When the plant has at its disposal an excess of oxygen, as much as its vitality can dispose of, there is no alcohol, or very little, formed. If, on the other hand, the plant vegetates with difficulty, in presence of an insufficiency of oxygen, the proportion of alcohol increases; in other words, the plant shows a certain tendency to behave after the manner of ferments.

Some time ago, wishing to assure ourselves that the spores of *penicillium* could not become transformed into ferment, we sowed some pure spores in small flasks, holding from 50 c.c. to 100 c.c. (from 2 to 4 fl. oz.), which contained very little air, and which were sealed hermetically after the sowing. Under these conditions, the germination and growth of the spores proceeded with great difficulty, and soon ceased through want of air. The total weight of the little plant was too small to be determined. In cases of this kind, if we distil the whole of the liquid we shall often see the alcohol appear in the second distillation, even though the weight of the plant may have been scarcely appreciable. If, on the other hand, side by side with experiments of this kind, we grow pure *penicillium* in flasks containing air and having quantities of saccharine liquids equal to the quantities in the small flasks of which we have been speaking, the plant, in consequence of the large volume of air at its disposal, will develop vigorously, and in the course of even a few days will have become perceptibly heavier. In distilling the subjacent liquid, however, we shall generally find that it contains no alcohol at all, even though the weight of the plant be half a gramme, or more (6 or 7 grains).

These results apply to all the fungoid growths that we have studied, but they vary considerably with the nature of the organisms. *Aspergillus glaucus* is, in this respect, one of the most curious.

On June 15th, 1873, we impregnated three flasks of wort, A, B, C, with pure spores of *aspergillus glaucus*. The development was rapid and the fructification abundant. On June 20th, we shook up the liquid and the supernatant fungoid growths in the three flasks; the flasks A and B were then treated as follows:—

We distilled the liquid in A to discover the presence of alcohol, but could find none.

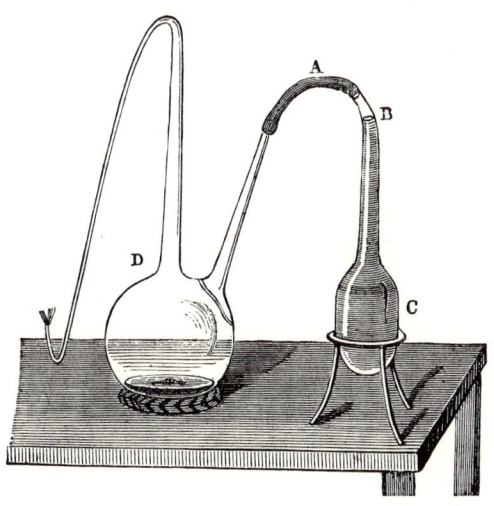

FIG. 19.

The flask B was connected with a test flask (Fig. 19), into which the liquid, together with its fungoid growth, was transferred from B. The next day, June 21st, the mycelium which was on the surface of the liquid, in the neck of the flask, was studded with bubbles of gas; these we dispersed by shaking. On June 22nd, many others had formed again, and a large flake of mycelium that had risen from the bottom of the test flask had been stopped at the bottom of the neck, quite distended by gas bubbles. We liberated the gas by shaking, but the bubbles formed again by the next day, and this effect continued for several days; nevertheless the liberation of gas was not continuous, as is the case in an ordinary fermentation.

On July 20th we drew off the liquid and distilled it; it was still very sweet, but though it contained a sensible quantity of alcohol, the microscope failed to detect a single cell of ordinary alcoholic ferment.

These results show that the *aspergillus* when in full growth, with plenty of air at its disposal, does not yield alcohol, and that if we submerge it, so as to prevent the oxygen of the air from readily coming into contact with its various parts, it decomposes sugar, after the manner of yeast, forming carbonic acid gas and alcohol.

These effects were still more marked in the case of the flask C, the liquid in which, after having been shaken up, was not decanted to any great depth in our test flask, as had been the case with B. From June 21st, there was *mycelium* on the surface of the liquid, studded with large bubbles of gas, which formed again after having been liberated by shaking. This last flask was examined on November 1st, 1873. Its aspect was unchanged; the liquid was covered with *mycelium* loaded with sporanges and borne up by large old bubbles that had not disappeared. The following was the analysis of the liquid :—

Alcohol	1·2
Glucose	84·0
Dextrine (?)	32·0

The liquid was very bright, and contained an amorphous granular deposit, formed by the wort after it had been boiled, at the time when we prepared our flasks. We crushed a small

STUDIES ON FERMENTATION. 103

quantity of mycelium that had risen to the surface of the liquid, and obtained a field such as is represented in Fig. 20. Amongst

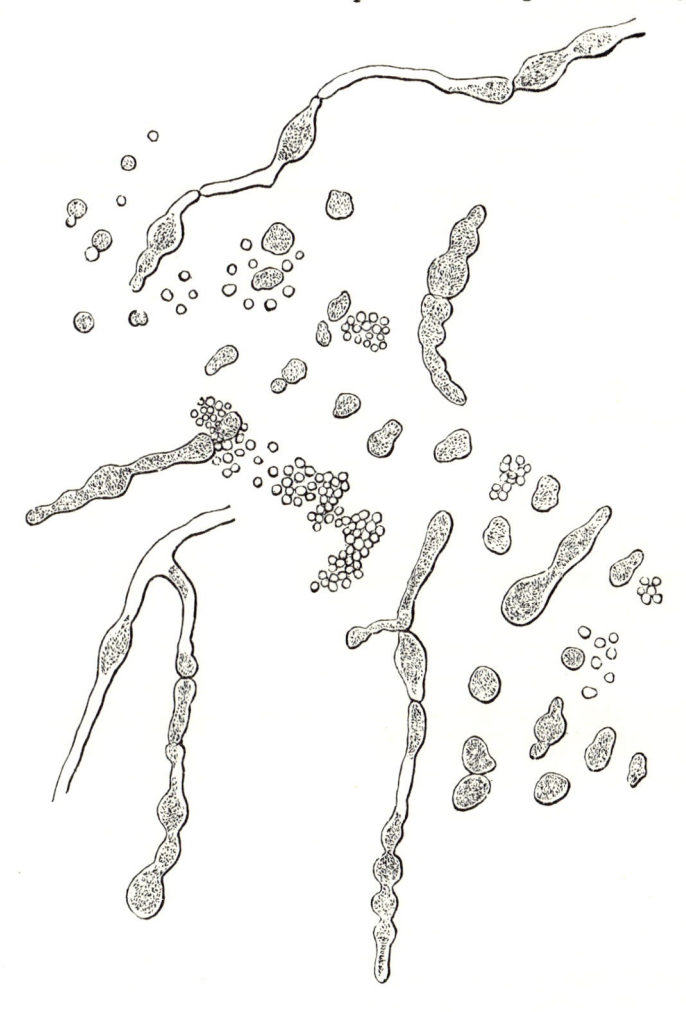

FIG. 20.

the ordinary filaments of mycelium belonging to the plant, which are not represented in our engraving, and which were not more than $\frac{1}{300}$ of a millimetre (nearly $\frac{1}{7500}$ in.) in diameter, we perceived much larger ones, swollen and contorted in the most singular manner, and measuring as much as $\frac{1}{30}$ of a millimetre across their broadest parts. There was also a multitude of the ordinary spores of *aspergillus* mixed with others of larger size, and big, inflated cells, with irregular or spherical protuberances, full of granular matter. As there are all the stages between the normal spores of the plant and the big cells, and between these latter and the filaments, it must be admitted that the whole of this strange vegetation results from spores which change their structure under the influence of special conditions to which they are exposed.* Beyond all doubt these cells and irregularly shaped segments, in vegetating with difficulty, gave rise to the fermentation, which, although insignificant, was sufficiently marked to produce more than a gramme (15 grains) of alcohol. The oxygen of the air failing, or existing in insufficient quantity for the regular development of the filaments of mycelium belonging to the plant, and for the germination of its submerged spores, filaments and spores vegetated as the yeast of beer might have done if deprived of oxygen.

If we study the vegetation of *aspergillus glaucus* with this preconceived idea, we shall soon recognize the fact that these spherical forms of mycelium are the result of a greater or less deprivation of air. The filaments of this mycelium which develop freely in the aerated liquid are young and transparent, small in diameter, and exhibit the ordinary ramifications. Those which are situated about the centre, in the denser or

---

* Since writing the above we have experienced some doubt as to whether the forms of development represented in Fig. 20 are actually those of the *aspergillus glaucus*, which we supposed our fungoid growth to be. In some of the later sketches of our observations we find similar forms, which belong to a bluish kind of *penicillium*, with rather large spores. Fortunately, this doubt affects our argument in no essential particular. It matters very little what variety of fungoid growth it is that gives rise to alcoholic fermentation attended by peculiarities of shape that only occur in the development of its spores when air fails it.

STUDIES ON FERMENTATION.

Aspergillus glaucus.

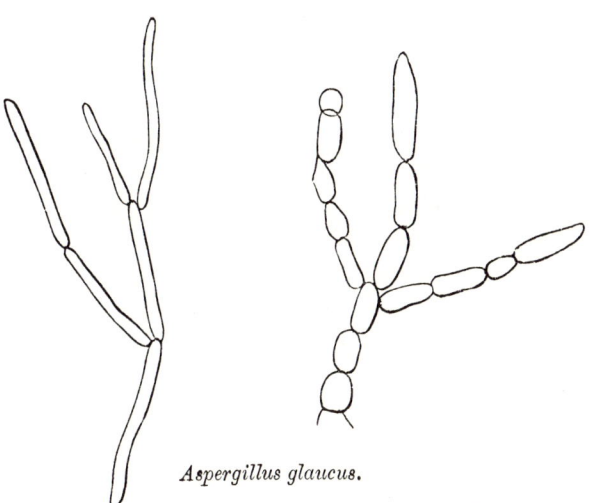

Growth with abundant air-supply at the edge of the mycelium crust.

Growth with reduced air-supply in the central and deeper parts of the mycelium.

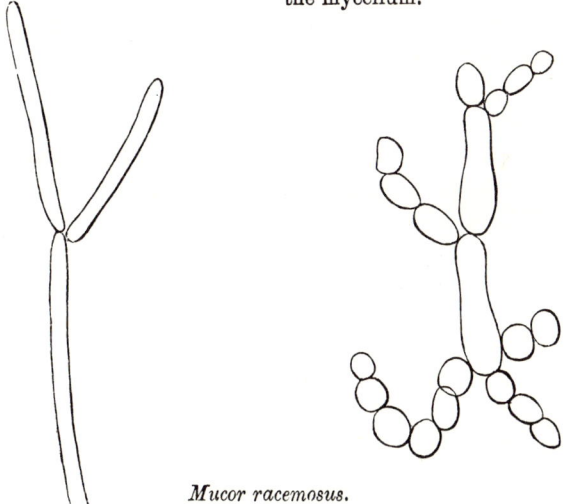

Mucor racemosus.

Growth with abundant air-supply at the edge of the mycelium tuft.

Growth with reduced air-supply in the central and deeper parts.

Fig. 21.

more complicated parts, to which the oxygen cannot penetrate in consequence of its absorption by the surrounding parts, are more granular in appearance as well as larger, and inclined to develop swellings. We can observe no *conidia** on these filaments, but we may say that they are on the point of appearing, for the spherical segments often tend to assume an appearance of close jointing, as when they take the form of those rows of swelling, or cells, which has given rise to the idea of the *chaplets of the conidia-cellules*. This is represented in the accompanying sketches (Fig. 21), which we have purposely contrasted with two similar ones which relate to the *mucor*, of which we shall soon speak. The *conidia* of these latter are very remarkable, and their fermentative character becomes apparent as soon as their growths are deprived of air.

It is scarcely necessary to add that in these vegetations of aspergillus, which were accompanied by a corresponding alcoholic fermentation, it was impossible to find cells of yeast; and that, notwithstanding this, the liquid was so adapted to ordinary alcoholic fermentation, that, when we added a small quantity of yeast to it, in the course of a few hours, a most active alcoholic fermentation declared itself.

We may give some other facts relating to a crop of *aspergillus glaucus* which was also grown in ordinary hopped wort, and which was left to itself for a year.

A two-necked flask, holding 300 c.c. (rather more than 10 fl. oz.) was prepared and impregnated on December 21st, 1873, and was then placed in an oven at a temperature of 25° C. (77° F.). The fungoid growth developed in isolated tufts, which subsequently united, but without entirely covering the surface of the wort. A few tufts also vegetated at the bottom of the liquid; those on the surface soon became surrounded by large bubbles of gas.

On December 12th, 1874, we examined the liquid and the plant, which for a long time had appeared dead. Its mycelium was

* By the term *conidia* is meant certain chains of cells, which are in reality mycelial spores.

STUDIES ON FERMENTATION. 107

formed of aged, granulated filaments, with few swellings. The weight of the dry fungoid growth was 0·50 gramme (about 8 grains) for a total volume of liquid of 122 c.c. (4¼ fluid ounces). We obtained 4·4 c.c. of alcohol of 15°, which was about seven times the weight of the plant. Finally, we determined the acidity of the liquid, and found 2·8 grammes, in equivalents of sulphuric acid, a quantity greatly in excess of the total acidity of an equal volume of wort, a fact which shows us that fermentation caused by *aspergillus glaucus* is accompanied by the formation of an organic acid, the nature of which it would be interesting to determine. M. Gayon has commenced the study of this subject in our laboratory.

In concluding our observations on the *aspergillus glaucus*, we may give the comparative results of two growths that were obtained under precisely similar conditions, in flasks of exactly the same size, but differing in this respect—that one of them was constantly subjected to a current of pure air that played on the liquid. In the course of a few days, when the fungoid growth in the flask that had been aerated had attained a considerable size, in comparison with the other, we broke the flasks in order that we might take out the two growths and compare their weights. After drying them at 100° C. (212° F.) we found :—

Growth in the aerated flask .. 0·92
Growth in the closed flask .. 0·16
Ratio of weights, $\frac{92}{16} = 5·75$.

Again, although we had taken the precaution of condensing in a U tube, over which cold water played, the vapours carried away by the current of air, the liquid in the aerated flask gave no evidence of alcohol. That in the other flask contained a very appreciable quantity, although the weight of fungoid growth in that flask was scarcely a sixth part of what it was in the other.

The preceding facts taken altogether, seem to us to demonstrate once more, in the most conclusive manner :—

Firstly, That neither *penicillium* nor *aspergillus glaucus* can change into yeast, even under conditions that are most favourable to the life of that ferment.

Secondly, That a fungoid growth which vegetates by using the oxygen of the air, and which derives from the oxidating action of that gas, the heat that it requires to enable it to perform the acts necessary to its nutrition, may continue to live, although with difficulty, in the absence of oxygen; that, in such a case, the forms of its mycelian or sporic vegetation undergo a change, the plant, at the same time, evincing a great tendency to act as alcoholic ferment, that is to say, decomposing sugar and forming carbonic acid gas, alcohol, and other substances which we have not determined, and which probably vary with different growths.

Such, at least, is one interpretation of the facts that we have reviewed. The observations in the following paragraphs and chapters may the more incline our readers to accept it as the true one.

§ II.—Growth of Mycoderma Vini in a state of Purity—Confirmation of our original Conjectures as to the cause of Fermentation—Mycoderma Vini does not Change into Yeast, although it may give rise to Fermentation.

The efflorescence of wine, cider, and beer is pretty generally known.* Fermented liquors cannot be exposed to the air without soon becoming covered with a white film, which grows thick and becomes wrinkled in a marked manner in proportion as it is deprived of room wherein to spread horizontally, in accord with the extraordinary multiplication of the cellules that compose it. The rapidity of this multiplication is sometimes astounding. During the heat of summer, when the medium is well adapted to the life of the plant, we may count the number of cells which grow in the course of a few hours by millions. The absorption

* See Pasteur, *Études sur le Vin*, 1st Edition, pp. 20 and following.

of the oxygen necessary to the activity of this growth, and the heat developed in the film, as well as the liberation of carbonic acid gas, that result from it are considerable. A piece of glass covering the mycoderma, at some distance above it, becomes wet with moisture, that soon accumulates to form large drops of water. The quantity of oxygen absorbed is so great that we never see any other fungoid growth on the surface of this film, although the air is constantly depositing on it, as dust, spores of an entirely different character; for, notwithstanding that the warm and moist surface is in contact with an atmosphere that is being continually renewed, yet the *mycoderma* appropriates to itself all the oxygen contained in the air. When, however, the vegetation begins to languish, we often find, on the other hand, that the plant becomes associated with other species of mycoderma, notably *mycoderma aceti*, as well as other fungi, amongst which *penicillium glaucum* generally appears. This is one of the facts which, wrongly interpreted, have led to the belief that *mycoderma vini* or *cerevisiæ* may possibly, or even readily, become transformed into *penicillium*, and *vice versâ*.* As the study of the growth of

* Since writing this paragraph, we have found in M. Ch. Robin's *Journal d'Anatomie et de Physiologie*, an article signed by that gentleman, and entitled *Sur la Nature des Fermentations*, &c. (July-August, 1875), in which the learned microscopist says:—"The *torula cerevisiæ* is derived from the *mycoderma cerevisiæ*. My observations leave no doubt on my mind that *penicillium glaucum* is one of the forms evolved from spores or ferments that have preceded it, as M. Trécul showed a long time ago, and that, moreover, the spores of *penicillium*, germinating in suitable media, give us the sporical form termed *mycoderma*."

We take the liberty to observe that these assertions of M. Robin's are purely gratuitous. Up to the present time it has been impossible to discover a suitable medium for the proof of these different transformations or polymorphisms. From the time of Turpin, who firmly believed that he had observed these changes, to our own, none of the microscopists who have affirmed these transformations have succeeded in adducing any convincing proof of them, and M. Trécul's latest observations, especially as regards *penicillium* and its transformation into ferment or into the *mycoderma* of beer, have been positively disproved by ours, supported, as they are, by proofs that we consider irrefutable.

110 STUDIES ON FERMENTATION.

mycoderma vini on the surface of saccharine liquids and in their depths, unaccompanied by any other species, has the most important bearing on the theory of alcoholic fermentation, we may pursue it through a few examples with all the detail that it allows of.

On June 21st, 1872, we sowed some *mycoderma vini* in three flasks, with double necks, A, B, C (Fig. 22), containing some

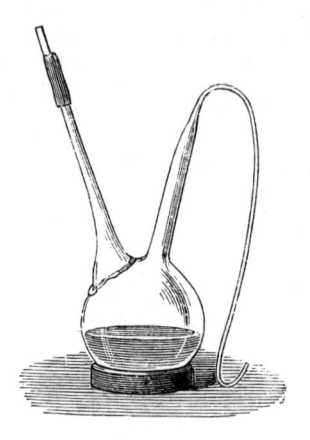

FIG. 22.

wort. The spores employed for the purpose were obtained from plants growing on sweetened yeast-water in an ordinary closed flask. This had been impregnated with spores from plants grown on wort, which in turn had sprung from spores taken directly from *mycoderma vini* growing on wine.

The several impregnations were effected by means of a platinum wire, held by forceps, both having been first cleaned by passing through flame, and then smeared with the fungoid films.

By this series of growings in closed vessels, which were but momentarily open at the time when we dropped the spores into them, we secured the separation of the mycoderma from all foreign organisms; and more particularly from germs of *myco-*

derma aceti, which is generally found along with it, but which propagates with difficulty in neutral saccharine liquids.

On the following days films of *mycoderma vini* had spread over the surface of the liquid in the three flasks. To all appearance they were very pure; and the microscope showed the complete absence of any mixture of *mycoderma aceti*, lactic ferment, or other foreign growths.*

On June 26th we decanted and distilled the liquid in A without finding any trace of alcohol. We shook up the liquids in B and C, with all due precautions, so as to submerge their films as much as possible, and then we raised the temperature of the flasks to 26° C. or 28° C. (82° F.). For some days afterwards we saw a constant succession of minute bubbles of carbonic acid gas rising through the liquid, which remained bright under the part of the film that had not fallen in. It had all the appearance of a slow but continuous fermentation.

On June 29th we decanted and distilled the liquid in B, and found in it an appreciable quantity of alcohol, which showed itself in the first distillation. The flask C, which was shaken afresh, continued to give signs of fermentation, but, some days later, the evolution of the bubbles ceased.

On July 15th, 1873, we examined the flask with its film and its deposit of *mycoderma vini*, without finding a trace of any foreign growths, either in the shape of *penicillium glaucum*, or *mucor mucedo*, or *rhyzopus nigrans*, or *mycoderma aceti*, or, in short, any of the organisms which could not have failed to appear on the surface of a substratum so peculiarly adapted to their development, had it been in the nature of *mycoderma vini*

---

* It is a very easy matter to study the liquids and growths in our flasks during the course of a single experiment. We take out the glass stopper that closes the india-rubber tube on the straight-neck, and, by means of a long rod or a glass tube previously passed through the flame, take up a quantity, which we draw out immediately for microscopical examination. We then replace the glass stopper, taking care to pass it through the flame before doing so, to burn up any organic particles of dust that it may have picked up from the table on which we laid it.

to transform itself into one or other of those common fungoid growths. The liquid, moreover, still remained sweet, and did not contain any cells of actual yeast. We may conclude then that when one or more of these fungi occur, after an interval of some days, in a growth of *mycoderma vini* conducted in contact with common air, it does so in consequence of that air having, without the knowledge of the observer, impregnated the liquid spontaneously with germs of these foreign organisms.

There might perhaps be room for some fear that the conditions of growth in our flasks were not favourable to the simultaneous appearance of these common fungoid growths along with the *mycoderma vini*. On June 24th, 1872, we sowed, in three flasks of sugared yeast-water, prepared as before—in the first, *mycoderma vini*, together with *penicillium glaucum*; in the second, *mycoderma vini*, together with *mucor mucedo*; in the third, *mycoderma vini* alone.

We effected this by plunging the platinum wire, which we used for impregnating the liquids, into the pure film of *mycoderma vini*, and then touching with the wire the sporanges of the other fungus. On June 29th, we saw on the surface of our first flask some green patches of *penicillium*, along with some spots of *mycoderma vini*; in the second flask a voluminous mycelium of *mucor mucedo*, distended by large bubbles, had risen to the surface of the liquid, and was entirely covered by a film of *mycoderma vini*. As for the liquid in the third flask, there were only a few spots of very pure *mycoderma vini*. This last flask, after being kept in an oven at 25° C. (77° F.) for several months, still contained nothing but *mycoderma vini*, unmixed with any other fungoid growth whatever.

We may therefore be sure that *mycoderma vini*, vegetating on the surface of liquids adapted to its nutrition, in contact with air deprived of its germinating dust, will not present the least sign of a transformation into any of these other common fungi, or into yeast, however long may be the duration of its exposure to contact with that pure air.

We may now return to that feeble and limited production of

carbonic acid gas and alcohol, the formation of which we have shown experimentally to take place at a high temperature, after submerging the film of *mycoderma vini*.* There can be no doubt that we have here a phenomenon similar in every point to that presented by *penicillium* and *aspergillus*, which we studied in the preceding paragraph. When the germs or jointed filaments of *mycoderma vini*, growing on a saccharine substratum in contact with the air, are in the full activity of life, this activity is carried on at the expense of the sugar and other materials in the liquid, in the same way that animals consume the oxygen of the air and evolve carbonic acid.

The consumption of the different materials is attended with a proportionate formation of new materials, development of structure, and reproduction of organisms.

Under these conditions, not only does the *mycoderma vini* not form a sufficiency of alcohol for analytical determination, but, if any alcohol exists in the subjacent liquid, the *mycoderma* consumes it, converting it into water and carbonic acid gas, by

* We may prove the occurrence of alcoholic fermentation by the cells of submerged *mycoderma vini* in a different manner. To do this, after having made all our preparations as before and shaken up the film of *mycoderma vini* in its liquid, we must attach our flask to a test flask (Fig. 19), and pass the turbid liquid into the latter. On succeeding days we shall detect a very protracted fermentation in the test flask; there will be a succession of minute bubbles rising from the bottom, but in small number at a time. The fermentation is very evident whilst it lasts, but is rather sluggish, and, although of very long duration, ceases long before the sugar is exhausted.

This experiment proves better than any other the non-transformation of *mycoderma vini* into other ordinary fungoid growths. For after decanting the liquid into the test flasks, the sides of the experimental flask remain covered with streaks of *mycoderma vini* along with some of the liquid. Moreover, the flask is refilled with air, and this air is being constantly renewed, in part, by variations of the temperature of the oven, so that the *mycoderma* remaining on the sides is thus placed under the most favourable conditions for transformation into other fungoid growths, if that were possible. It is still more easy to detach the experimental from the test flask, and to pass pure air into it, once or twice a day, or constantly. In any case, we shall never see anything besides the *mycoderma vini* spring up within it.

I

fixation of the oxygen of the air.* If, however, we suddenly submerge the *mycoderma*, we shall obtain a different result. If, on the one hand, the conditions of life of this fungus are incompatible with the altered circumstances in which it is placed, the plant must perish, just as an animal does when deprived of oxygen. But if, in spite of these changed conditions of nutrition, it can still continue in life, we should expect to see marked changes in its organic structure, or chemical metamorphoses. The result of our observations points to the continuance of life, in a distinct though sluggish and fugacious activity, accompanied by the phenomena of alcoholic fermentation, that is, the evolution of carbonic acid gas, and the production of alcohol.

If we take a drop of liquid charged with disjointed cells of *mycoderma*, a day or two immediately after the submersion of the film, we shall observe changes, small but appreciable, in the aspect of a great number of these cells; they will show increase in size, their protoplasm will be in process of modification, and many of them will have put forth little buds. It will be quite evident, however, that these acts of interior nutrition and the changes of tissue resulting from them, proceed with difficulty; the buds when they form will soon wither, and there will be no multiplication of new cells. These changes will, nevertheless, be accompanied by the decomposition of sugar into alcohol and carbonic acid.

In comparing these facts with those which we have pointed out in connection with the cultivation of *penicillium* and *aspergillus*, we are compelled to admit that the production of alcohol and carbonic acid gas from sugar—in one word, alcoholic fermentation—is a chemical action, connected with the vegetable life of cells which may differ greatly in their nature, and that it takes place at the moment when these cells, ceasing to have the power of freely consuming the materials of their nutrition by respiratory processes—that is, by the absorption of free oxygen

* See PASTEUR, *Comptes rendus des Séances de l'Académie des Sciences*, t. liv., 1862, and t. lv., 1862. *Études sur les Mycodermes*, &c.

STUDIES ON FERMENTATION. 115

—continue to live by utilizing oxygenated matters which, like sugar or such unstable substances, produce heat by their decomposition. The character of ferment thus presents itself to us, not as being peculiar to any particular being or to any particular organ, but as a general property of the living cell. This character is always ready to manifest itself, and, in reality, does manifest itself as soon as life ceases to perform its functions under the influence of free oxygen, or without a quantity of that gas sufficient for all the acts of nutrition. Thus we should see it appear and disappear concomitantly with that mode of life; feeble and fugacious in its action when the conditions of this vitality are of a similarly restricted character; intense, on the other hand, and of long duration and productive of large quantities of carbonic acid gas and alcohol, when the conditions are such that the plant or cell can multiply with facility in this novel manner. To this we may attribute all possible degrees of activity in fermentation, as well as the existence of ferments of every variety of form and of very different species. It may readily be imagined that sugar may undergo decomposition in a quite different manner from that of which we have spoken, that instead of alcohol, carbonic acid gas, glycerine, and similar substances, it may yield lactic, butyric, acetic, and other acids. It would be only one definite class of cellular organisms, the members of which resembled each other more or less, that decomposed sugar into alcohol and carbonic acid; others, specifically different, would act in a different manner. In short, we may say that the number of these living organisms is a measure of the number of different ferments.

Plate IV. represents in its two halves the condition of the *mycoderma vini* at two different and unequal periods after its submersion. In the left-hand semi-circle, it is evident that many of the figures are swollen, that modification of their protoplasm has taken place, and incipient budding is going on in several of them. A budding of this kind would not wither; the buds would grow and, detaching themselves, would form new cells capable of budding in their turn. We should have

I 2

under our eyes all the characteristics of a yeast, which, beyond doubt, would give rise to a very active fermentation, inasmuch as it would belong to the order of phenomena of nutrition and vital energy of which we are speaking. Instead, however, of insisting upon the acceptance of our interpretations, based on a few facts merely, let us go on to accumulate facts, varying the conditions as much as possible. Our examples, taken singly, may seem insufficient to establish the theory that it will be our endeavour to substantiate, but taken together we trust that they will secure our readers' confidence.

We may now, perhaps with advantage, introduce two new expressions to embody the preceding facts, by the help of which we may often shorten our subsequent explanations. Since life can continue, under certain conditions, away from contact with the oxygen of the air, and since the altered nutrition is accompanied by a phenomenon which is of great scientific as well as industrial importance, we may divide living beings into two classes, *aërobian*, that is those which cannot live without air, and *anaërobian*, which, strictly speaking, and for a time, can do without it; these latter would be ferments, properly so called. Again, since we can conceive, in an entire organism, some organ or even a cell capable of existing, at least momentarily, apart from the influence of the air, and endowed at a given moment with the character of a ferment, we may, in like manner, make use of the expression *anaërobian* cell, in opposition to a cell that is *aërobian*.

As long ago as 1863, in our work on putrefaction, we proposed to adopt the preceding expressions, and since then we have had the satisfaction of seeing them used by different authors in France and other countries.

One of the principal assertions in this paragraph relates to the non-transformation of *mycoderma vini* into other moulds or into yeast.*

For a long time, like Turpin and many other observers, although we had no belief in the transformation of *mycoderma vini* into any

---

* In a subsequent chapter we shall prove that yeast is likewise incapable of transformation into *mycoderma vini*.

Pl. IV

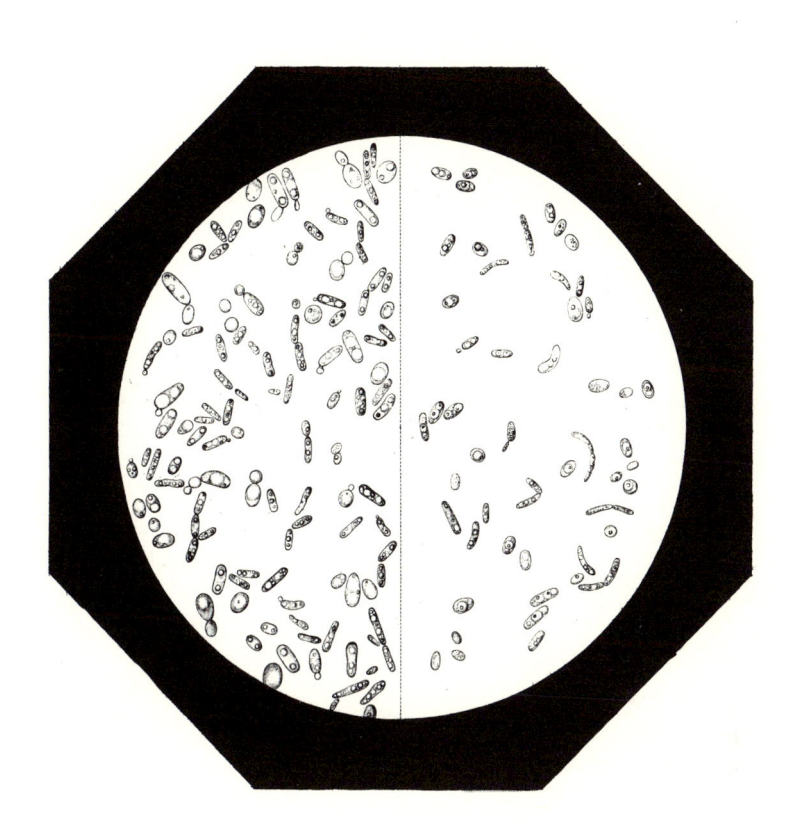

$$\frac{400}{1}$$

Deyrolle del. Picart sc.

Imp Geny-Gros. Paris

one of the common moulds, yet we did believe in its transformation into alcoholic ferment. In the course of more elaborate researches, however, we at last discovered that our previous experiments had been vitiated from the same source of error which we have so often had occasion to point out as affecting the observations of our opponents, namely, the fortuitous and spontaneous introduction, unknown to the experimentalist, of germs of the very plant for whose appearance by way of transformation he is seeking.

When we consider that every fermented vinous liquor, when put on draught, is liable to efflorescence, it is difficult to avoid the supposition that this efflorescence is primarily due to cells of the yeast that has caused the liquid to ferment, from which cells the liquid could not be completely freed, no matter how bright it might have been, and which come to the surface of the liquid to live after the manner of fungoid growths. We wished to test this supposition by means of experiments. So great, however, was the resemblance between the forms possible to yeast and mycoderma, of which latter efflorescence is really composed, that we quite despaired of being able to solve the question by microscopical examination, that is, by observing the actual conversion of a cell of yeast into a cell of mycoderma. In order, then, to overcome that difficulty, we endeavoured to produce an inverse transformation—that of mycoderma into yeast. We imagined that we should doubtless obtain this result by submerging some of the efflorescence of wine or beer in a saccharine liquid well adapted to alcoholic fermentation. By submerging the mycoderma we would do away with the ordinary conditions of life in this kind of fungoid growth; for we would thus prevent the supply of oxygen from the air, since that oxygen would always be excluded, in the most effectual manner possible, by the portion of mycoderma that would remain on the surface of the liquid, even after the submersion process; and on the other hand, we would be subjecting our growth to the ordinary conditions of ferment life, which acts at the bottom or in the bulk of liquids fermenting.

Our experiments were conducted in the following manner :—
In some flat porcelain basins, we grew some pure *mycoderma vini** on fermented liquids, such as wine or beer, or on artificially vinous liquids, such as alcoholized yeast-water, taking care to boil these liquids previously to kill any germs of yeast or other organism that they might contain. The basins themselves, as well as the plates of glass with which they were to be covered, were plunged into boiling water just before they were wanted for use. As soon as the film of mycoderma had become well developed and thick, and even wrinkled—a process requiring not more than two or three days during summer heat—we decanted the subjacent liquid, by means of a siphon, so as to leave the film on the bottom of the basin. We then diffused the whole mass of efflorescence in a saccharine liquid that had been boiled and afterwards cooled down in a closed vessel; generally, we used wort or must preserved by Appert's process. After that, we emptied the mixture of saccharine liquid and efflorescence into long-necked flasks that had likewise been previously heated, as also had the funnels used in the process of transference.

It seemed to us that experiments conducted with all these precautions must be free from causes of error. It was true that we were working more or less in contact with atmospheric air, but all that we had to fear for the soundness of the conclusions which we might draw was the presence of germs of alcoholic ferment, and we considered how few of these there are amongst floating particles of dust. Consequently, if we succeeded in observing the advent of yeast in each of the long-necked flasks, accompanied by an active alcoholic fermentation, we thought that we might, without danger of error, admit as a fact the transformation of cells of mycoderma into cells of yeast. Again, we thought that we should probably find in the forms of the cells of yeast which were directly derived from the cells of

---

* We secured the purity of our mycoderma by the same means that we have already described for the procuring of spores of *penicillium* or other fungoid growths in a state of purity.

mycoderma, a more or less elongated structure, which would be a convincing proof of the transformation that we were seeking, if, indeed, such transformation were possible.

Strange to say, everything happened in a manner that seemed to realize our expectations. The saccharine worts in the flasks in which we had mixed and submerged the mycoderma, fermented in the course of a few days; the yeast first appeared in elongated shapes; lastly, we could see under the microscope that many of the cells or jointed filaments of mycoderma were inflated and presented the appearance of undoubted gradations between their natural state and that of the cells of yeast which soon formed part of the deposit in the vessels. In spite of all this, however, we were the victims of an illusion.

In experiments conducted as we have just described, the yeast which appears, and which soon sets up an active alcoholic fermentation, is introduced in the first place by atmospheric air, from which germs are constantly falling either upon the film of mycoderma or upon the objects that are employed in the successive manipulations. Two peculiarities in these experiments first opened our eyes to the existence of this cause of error. We sometimes found at the bottom of the flasks in which we had submerged the efflorescence, along with the cells of mycoderma, large, spherical cells of *mucor mucedo* or *racemosus*, ferment-cells that we shall soon learn to recognize in studying this curious fungoid growth. The existence of *mucor mucedo* or *racemosus*, where we had only sown *mycoderma vini*, was to us a proof that one or more spores of that mucor had been introduced by the surrounding air. If then, we reasoned, the air can introduce spores of mucor into our field of operations, why should it not introduce cells of yeast, especially in our laboratory? Again, it sometimes happened that a negative result was obtained. Harassed by doubts about the reality of this transformation, which accorded so well with the physiological theory of fermentation we had been led to adopt, we repeated the experiments many times, and in some cases we failed to detect any appearance whatever of a transformation of mycoderma into yeast cells, although the conditions under which each of the experiments was conducted had been as similar as could be.

We were at a loss to account for this inactivity in the cells of the mycoderma. Even in the most favourable cases of the supposed fermentation, it was evident that a host of cells of *mycoderma vini* did not become cells of yeast; but how could it possibly be admitted that amongst the millions of submerged cells, none were adapted for transformation, if that transformation were at all possible?

Thereupon, to find a way out of the difficulty, we resolved to modify completely the conditions of our experiments, and to apply to the research that we had in view a mode of cultivation that might completely, or nearly so, obviate the sole cause of error that we suspected, namely, the possible fall of cells or germs of yeast during the manipulations. We secured this by the use of flasks with two tubes, the right hand one of which was closed by means of a piece of india-rubber tubing with a glass stopper, the other one being drawn out in the shape of a swan's neck. The use of these flasks, which was then new to us, permitted us to grow mycoderma and to study it under the microscope without fear of disturbance from exterior particles of dust. This time we obtained the results given in the first part of this paragraph. We no longer observed yeast or alcoholic fermentation following the submersion of the efflorescence, either in the flasks themselves, or in the test-flasks attached to them, as represented in Fig. 19. We observed, however, that kind of alcoholic fermentation of which we have already spoken and which is due to the mycoderma itself, a fermentative action that is still more instructive than the one which we thought we had determined, and certainly not less calculated to support the theory of fermentation which we have already briefly sketched.

In an age when ideas involving transformation of species are so readily accepted, perhaps in consequence of their requiring no rigorous experimental work, it is not without interest to consider that, in the course of our researches upon the growths of microscopic plants in a state of purity, we once were inclined to believe in the transformation of one organism into another—the transformation of *mycoderma vini* or *cerevisiæ* into yeast, and that, on that occasion, we were altogether wrong, through having ourselves fallen a victim to the identical source of error which confidence in our theory of germs had led us so frequently to detect as affecting the observations of others.

§ III.—GROWTH OF MYCODERMA ACETI IN A STATE OF PURITY.

The study of *mycoderma aceti* has not escaped the numerous causes of error which are apt to attend all observations made on microscopic organisms. This little fungus is still believed by many authors to be one of those polymorphous species capable of great modifications, according to the conditions of their cultivation—it could be, in turns, bacterium, vibrio, yeast, &c. Respecting it, we have seen resuscitated under a modern name, in the course of the last few years, the old hypothesis of Buffon concerning *organic molecules*, that of Turpin concerning the *punctiform globulines* of barley, milk, and albumen, and the theory maintained by Dr. Pineau, of Nancy, and by Pouchet concerning *proliferous pellicles*.[*]

M. Béchamp, Professor in the Faculty of Medicine at Montpellier, disdaining to adopt the expressions which we have just used, has substituted for them that of *microzyma*, whilst adhering to the opinions and errors represented by the other expressions. This savant designates under the name of *microzyma* all those punctiform globulines that are met with in most organic liquids when submitted to the microscope; and attributes to them, with Turpin, the faculty of playing the part of ferments, as well as of transforming themselves into yeast

[*] BUFFON, *Histoire de l'Homme*, t. viii., edition 12mo, 1778; TURPIN, *Mémoires de l'Académie des Sciences*, t. xvii.; Dr. PINEAU, *Annales des Sciences Naturelles*, t. iii., 1845; POUCHET, *Traité de la Génération dite Spontanée*, p. 335, 1859. See also our *Mémoire sur les Générations dites Spontanées*, 1862, pp. 100 and following, in which we give a *resumé* of some of these theories.

and various other organisms. They are contained in milk, blood, eggs, the infusion of barley, and such like ; nay, we may even find them in chalk, and so we have the fine discovery of *Microzyma cretae* as a distinct species !

Those who, like ourselves, cannot see in these granulations of organic liquids ought besides things whose nature is still undetermined, term them *molecular granules*, or, in reference to their Brownian movements, *mobile granules*. Indefinite expression is the best exponent of imperfect knowledge; when a precise terminology is invented, without any basis of precise ideas derived from a rigid observation of facts, sooner or later the hypothetical facts disappear, but the terminology prematurely created to explain them, hangs about the Science, and, bearing an erroneous interpretation, retards rather than promotes real progress.

We may here introduce a summary of Turpin's system, as given by himself. It forms a complete biogenesis, which leaves far behind it M. Béchamp's theory of *microzymata*, M. Fremy's descriptions of *hemi-organism*, and M. Trécul's account of the genesis of bacteria and lactic ferment :—

" When a mucous substance presents nothing visible through the microscope, as, for example, gelatinous matter, dissolved gum, the white of eggs, or plant-sap, simply thickened on its way to *cambium*, we call it *organic matter* or *organizable matter*. We attribute to it the fecundating power of organic life in the simplest degree ; we consider it as material still isolated from organization. We suppose that the invisible molecules, of which this organizable matter is composed, come together, combine and serve through this association in the construction of the different elementary forms of future tissues.

" May we not with greater truth believe that organizable matter is of varied origin, formed of innumerable globulines, too minute and transparent as yet to be observed by our present microscopical means, and that these globulines which are always endowed with motion and a special vital centre, are all capable, although many of them *do* abort, of separate development either into a formative element of tissue or into a mucedinous plant?

"Organizable matter may, according to its successive states of development or age, and according to the different forms it takes in the tissues, be distinguished by special names:—

"1.—We may term matter *organizable* as long as the globulines composing it are not yet visible to microscopes of existing power.

"2.—We may speak of *amorphous* or *globuline tissue* when even the globulines, previously invisible, have increased so as to be seen under the microscope, the term amorphous, or shapeless, being here applied to the association of globulines, and not to the globulines themselves.

"3.—Then we have *vesicular tissue*, when the globulines, continuing to increase, have developed in such a manner as to present a mass of continuous vesicles, still empty or already containing a new generation of globulines.

"4.—Lastly we have *filamentous* or *tubular tissue*, when the globulines, instead of vesiculating, form threads or tubes."*

* The following is Turpin's application of his theory to the formation of the ferments of fruits (*Mémoires de l'Académie*, t. xvii., 1840, p. 155), where also, on p. 171 the above quotation will be found:—*Ferments Produced by the Filtered Juice of the Pulp of Different Fruits*—"By the word pulp we mean the soft and juicy cellular tissue of the fleshy part, mesocarp or middle layer of the pericarp of certain ripe fruits. This cellular tissue, which is very abundant in the peach and all stone-fruit, in the apple and pear, in the orange and grape, and similar fruits, is the same as that which forms the body of a leaf. Being in every case composed of a simple agglomeration of contiguous mother-vesicles, which are always filled with globulines that are more or less developed, more or less coloured, and individually endowed with a special vital centre, it is not surprising that its globulines when free and detached from the compound organisms to which they belong, and from association with its vegetable life, should, when placed in a suitable medium, themselves vegetate and become transformed, under these new influences, into a mucedine, with filaments and articulations. Such are the very fine, and, consequently, very transparent globulines, which, when left to themselves in sweetened water, grow and become vesicular, producing other globulines in their interior, then bud, vegetate into mucedinous filaments, decompose sugar, and produce all the effects that constitute what we term *alcoholic fermentation*."

Such are the purely hypothetical and exploded ideas which MM. Fremy, Trécul, Béchamp, H. Hoffmann, Hallier, and others would revive in our own day, in opposition to a theory so clear and so well supported by facts as that of germs floating in the air, or spread over the surface of objects, as fruits, dry or green wood, and so on.

M. Béchamp believes that he has discovered that *mother of vinegar*, introduced into various saccharine liquids, in the presence of carbonate of lime, generates bacteria, which, with the sugar or dregs, produce butyric, lactic, and acetic acids, and that this same mother of vinegar, without the addition of the carbonate of lime, "generates, on the other hand, the fine cells, which produce the normal alcoholic fermentation of cane sugar." Further, M. Béchamp advances the hypothesis that mother of vinegar is a conglomeration of *microzymata*, and, as he fails to see in the experiments on which he bases the conclusions which we have just given, that bacteria and ferment cells are the result of spontaneous impregnation, having no connection with the presence of mother of vinegar, on which he experimented, he arrives at this conclusion: "In the experiments which I have just described, things happened as though the microzyma, under some peculiarly favourable conditions, had been the parent both of the bacteria and the cells."* . . . .

The object of the following experiments was the study of these assumed transformations of the *mycoderma aceti* in saccharine liquids, in the presence and in the absence of carbonate of lime.

We prepared some two-necked flasks, containing as a growing medium a liquid composed of one-third of Orleans vinegar, and two-thirds of a white wine used by vinegar-makers in Orleans. This liquid is peculiarly adapted to the development of *mycoderma aceti*.

On December 13th, 1872, we sowed the little plant in a state

* BÉCHAMP, *Recherches sur la Nature et l'Origine des Ferments* (*Annales de Chimie et de Physique*, 4ᵉ série, t. xxiii., and *Comptes rendus de l'Académie des Sciences*, Oct. 23, 1871).

of purity, by means of a piece of platinum wire, in the manner already explained in connection with propagation of other fungoid growths. On December 19th a young and thin film of *mycoderma aceti* covered the surface of the liquid. We then poured out the liquid through the right-hand tube, at the same time heating the end of the bent tube, to purify the air that passed into the flask. The whole film of *mycoderma aceti* remained adhering to the interior sides of the flask during this decanting. The question then was how to convey this film of the little plant into a saccharine liquid of a particular kind. We effected this easily by the following means: After having emptied the flask, as just described, instead of re-closing the india-rubber nozzle on the end of the right-hand tube, we attached it to a test-flask containing the saccharine liquid on which we wished to operate. This had been previously boiled in the test-flask, and when we attached the neck of the test-flask, previously slightly drawn out and curved, to the india-rubber tube, the liquid was still very warm. We permitted the liquid in the test-flask to cool down, and, then, taking up the test-flask, we decanted its contents into the other flask, in which, as we have already said, the film of *mycoderma aceti* had been left. In this way the film became partly submerged, partly spread over the surface of the new liquid. Experiments were made with two saccharine liquids, must and wort. In the case of the latter, from December 22nd the whole surface of the liquid was covered by a film of *mycoderma aceti*, which even spread up the moist sides of the flask above the level of the liquid. In the case of the must, on the other hand, the plant for some time did not seem to be developing; on December 24th, however, it was visibly spreading over the surface of the must. The following days we frequently shook up the films to separate them, and spread them over the subjacent liquid. There were no signs of alcoholic fermentation.

On December 30th we introduced several grammes (50 or 60 grains) of carbonate of lime into each of the flasks, an operation of little difficulty, which we effected in a manner similar to that just described. We substituted for the test-flask another flask—or, better still, a simple glass tube—containing carbonate of lime that had been subjected to great heat in the flask or tube, and there left to cool down. When cold, we poured the powdered carbonate of lime into the liquid in the flask, in this way avoiding the possibility of any error from the introduction with the carbonate of lime of any foreign germ.

In neither case did we obtain alcoholic fermentation, nor was there any appearance of lactic fermentation, or bacteria, or *vibrios*, properly so called. The flasks remained in the oven, at a temperature of about 25° C. (77° F.), until the end of January, 1873, when we made a microscopical examination of their deposits, exercising greater care and precaution than we had adopted in the case of those examinations which we had made from time to time in the course of the experiment to assure ourselves of the nature of the organisms present.* The result was that we never found anything besides the *mycoderma aceti*, which had developed, although with great difficulty, on the surface of the liquids neutralized with carbonate of lime. The beaded filaments had, under these circumstances, only become a little larger than they had been in the unsweetened acid liquids.

Mycoderma aceti, then, grown on sweetened acid or neutral liquids, grown in the absence or in the presence of carbonate of lime, undergoes no transformation into bacteria or vibrios or yeast, if only we operate with pure germs, free from the dust floating in the air, and from that which, unknown to the operator, may be introduced by means of the vessels and materials employed. It may be asked, do we, therefore, absolutely, reject the theory of the polymorphism of *mycoderma aceti* ?

* We need scarcely here observe, having done so on previous occasions, that whenever we opened our flasks to obtain specimens, we made use of a fine tube, previously passed through the flame of a spirit lamp, and that we also passed this flame over the surface of the india-rubber, glass stopper, &c., to consume the organic particles of dust which floating about might introduce themselves at the moment when we opened the right-hand tube of the flask.

On the contrary, we have endeavoured to prove the existence of this polymorphism again and again in a variety of ways. We have been mostly concerned with physiological polymorphism; that is, our efforts have been directed to ascertain if *mycoderma aceti* might be, for example, the *aërobian* form of a ferment from which it differed physiologically, as, for instance, lactic ferment, which, in shape, sometimes bears a striking resemblance to *mycoderma aceti*. We have not succeeded in discovering anything of the kind up to the present time.

What, in view of the positive proofs to the contrary, we do absolutely reject in the matter of this mycoderma, is the theory of polymorphisms, advocated by M. Béchamp and other authors, which, in our judgment, can only be founded on incomplete and erroneous observations.

§ IV.—GROWTH OF MUCOR RACEMOSUS IN A STATE OF PURITY
—EXAMPLE OF LIFE MORE ACTIVE AND LASTING WHEN REMOVED FROM THE INFLUENCE OF AIR.

Side by side with the facts explained in the last paragraph, the study of varieties of the genus *mucor*, grown in natural or artificial saccharine liquids, is of great importance to the establishment of the physiological theory of fermentation, which we shall explain later on. There is a very remarkable work on the subject of this mucedinous fungus by a German botanist, M. Bail, who, in 1857, declared that *mucor mucedo* caused alcoholic fermentation, and could change into ordinary yeast. The first assertion, relating to the alcoholic fermentation that this fungoid growth which is everywhere so abundant may cause, is quite correct; the second which relates to its faculty of changing into yeast is erroneous.*

* Ever since the year 1861 (see p. 92), this question of the possible transformation of the ordinary fungi, especially *penicillium* and *mucor mucedo*, into yeast has engaged our attention. The results attained have been entirely negative; but hitherto only the conclusions of our work have been published, some account of which was given at the meeting of the *Société Philomathique* of March 30th, 1861. The following extract is

On June 13th, 1872, we sowed by the help of a platinum wire in some wort, contained in two-necked flasks, A, B, and C, several of the minute sporange-bearing filaments of *mucor* along with the heads containing the spores.

On June 14th, there was no mycelium visible to the naked eye in the liquids.

from the *Bulletin* of the society:—" Meeting of March 30th, 1861. At this meeting a paper was read by M. Pasteur 'On the supposed changes in the form and vegetation of yeast-cells, depending on the external condition of their development.' It is well-known that Leuwenhoeck was the first to describe the globules of yeast, and that M. Cagnard-Latour discovered their faculty of multiplying by budding. This interesting vegetable organism has been the subject of a host of researches by chemists and botanists. The latter, from the days of Turpin and Kutzing, have almost unanimously regarded yeast as a form of development of various inferior vegetable types, especially *penicillium*. The studies of this subject which seem to have won most favour during the last few years are those of MM. Wagner, Bail, Berkeley, and H. Hoffmann. The researches of these botanists seem to strengthen and confirm the original observations of Turpin and Kutzing. M. Pouchet has, quite recently, expressed the same ideas, and has determined certain points in connection with them with much precision of detail. M. Pasteur has long studied this important question, which is so intimately connected with the essential nature of yeast and with those phenomena of the polymorphism of the inferior types of vegetable life, to which most of the remarkable works of M. Tulasne relate; he has, however, arrived at results that are altogether negative, and he declares that he was unable to detect the transformation of yeast into any of the *mucedines* whatsoever, and, inversely, that he could never succeed in producing the smallest quantity of yeast from ordinary *mucedines.*" These same results we communicated to the *Société Chimique* of Paris, at a meeting held April 12th, 1861. Throughout the investigation of which we have just indicated the conclusions, we insisted on the necessity of cultivating the separate organisms in a state of purity in all researches relating to these inferior forms of life, if we desire to attain to sure inferences about them; and the method of working, which we recommended, did not differ essentially from that adopted in the present work. Since then the study of these growths has been conducted with the utmost precautions; and other apparatus, perhaps as safe as those which we employ and better adapted than ours for the study of polymorphism of species, have been invented by botanists of great skill—M. de Bary, in Germany, and M. Van Tieghem, in France.

On June 15th mycelium was very abundant, and was borne up by bubbles of gas. In addition to this there were a few scattered patches of bubbles on the surface of the liquid, showing that fermentation had commenced.

On June 16th fermentation continued to show itself by the frothy state of the crusts of mycelium buoyed up by the bubbles of gas.

On June 17th we attached B and C separately, as indicated in Fig. 19 (p. 101) to test-flasks, into which we transferred nearly all their contents. Some clusters of entangled filaments of mycelium remained on the surface of the liquids in the test-flasks.

On June 18th a very slow fermentation commenced in the test-flasks; it continued for some days without becoming more active. A little bubble would slowly rise from the bottom of the vessel, succeeded after a short interval by another, and so on. The temperature of the oven was 24° C. (75° F.). On June 22nd we raised it to 28° C. (82° F.). The fermentation became more rapid, a constant succession of bubbles rose quickly from the bottom of the test-flasks; still there was none of the vivacity of an alcoholic fermentation produced by yeast.

On June 25th the fermentation was in much the same condition, if anything rather less active.

On June 28th temperature 25° C. (77° F.); fermentation had stopped.

On June 29th we raised the temperature to 27° C. (81° F.) again, and some slight revival of fermentation manifested itself.

The increase in temperature, therefore, as might have been expected, exercises a considerable influence on this kind of fermentation.

The vessels were then left to themselves, and during the course of three months they did not show the least sign of fermentation; moreover, we did not observe, either on the interior walls of the empty flasks, or on the surface or throughout the body of the liquid in the test-glasses, any fungoid production or organism whatever different from *mucor* itself.

The same observations apply to the vessel A; in this case the

K

liquid that remained in the flask was covered with a gelatinous and frothy mycelium.

On October 20th, 1872, after a lapse of three months and a half, we poured the liquid from the test-flask attached to flask C back again to that flask. The test-flask connected with flask B we left untouched alongside the other flasks to serve as a means of comparison.

On October 21st, 22nd, 23rd, we observed nothing; on succeeding days, however, some patches of bubbles appeared on the surface of the liquid in flask C, and clusters of mycelium buoyed up by the bubbles of gas which they imprisoned. Life had resumed its course, and with life fermentation had recommenced. What had been the cause of this change in the condition of the liquid, after an absolute quiescence of three months? There can be but one answer to this question: for in the other vessels there was no corresponding movement, or sign of life to be detected. In this vessel, however, an aeration of the plant had evidently taken place, consequent on the decantation and contact with the atmosphere of the flask, which communicated with the exterior air through the curved tube. This aeration had been absent or ineffective before decantation, in consequence of the great depth of liquid in the test-flask, the surface of which, too, was covered by a mass of mycelium filaments, itself effectually opposing any aeration of the liquid. Moreover, the surface of the liquid in the narrow neck of the test-flask had necessarily been covered by a layer of carbonic acid gas. We may investigate more thoroughly the influence of aeration, and its relation to the resumption of life in the mycelium of *mucor*, by restoring the liquid to its previous condition of depth and so cutting off again contact with the air.

For this purpose, on October 31st we decanted once more the liquid and its deposit from the flask into the test-glass. The same evening a slight but continuous fermentation, with formation of froth, appeared on the surface of the liquid in the neck of the test-glass. Fermentation although never vigorous, continued the following days, and until December 20th.

Between December 20th and 23rd, it ceased altogether to manifest itself by liberation of gas. As for the flask B, during all this time it had remained quite inactive and in the same state in which it had existed since June 29th, although the oven had on several days been heated to 28° C. (82° F.).

On December 23rd, 1872, wishing to assure ourselves of the state of the plant in flask B, we subjected it to the same operation to which the flask C had been subjected on October 20th : that is to say, we poured the contents of the test-glass back into the connected flask, with the object of supplying the plant with oxygen.

On December 24th, 25th, 26th, 27th, there was no apparent change.

On December 28th bubbles of gas began to be evolved carrying up clusters of mycelium to the surface of the liquid. It was evident, therefore, that the quiescence in the test-glass attached to flask B, was solely due to deprivation of air, as had happened in the case of the test-glass attached to flask C, up to the date of October 31st.

On this day, December 28th, we re-decanted the contents of the flask into the test-glass, and the following day a continuous but feeble fermentation proceeded. This lasted until January 22nd, although very sluggish in character ; it is evident that these effects were exactly the same as those which took place in flask C.*

We should observe before we proceed further, that we took

* We found, after the lapse of another year, in December, 1873, that the ferment of the *mucor* in the test glass might still be easily revived ; that it was able to propagate, both in the mycelium and in the cellular form, in wort, and that it might produce a fermentation, more or less active, according to the condition of aeration ; in short, that it was capable of producing all the characteristic phenomena described. By means of the method of cultivation that we employ, our study, which was continued for years, was pursued without the least fear of any foreign fungoid growths being introduced into the vessels, although they remained constantly open, and the air in them was being perpetually renewed by the action of diffusion and variations of temperature. In 1875 nothing remained alive in our flask, and further revival became impossible.

specimens from the flasks A, B, C, at different times between June and January, and that the microscope never revealed the least trace of yeast in them. We may note besides that, during this interval, we impregnated fresh flasks of wort with specimens taken from the deposits in the flasks A, B, C, and that we always obtained reproduction of the *mucor* and its peculiar fermentation without the least appearance of ordinary ferment.

The inferences from the results that we have just detailed follow readily, and are besides of great interest. In the first place, it is evident that even if the *mucor mucedo* may be able to produce alcoholic fermentation, it is totally incapable of changing into yeast. The two plants are necessarily and radically distinct, and, if different authors have succeeded in obtaining them mixed one with another in growths of *mucor*, this intermixture was doubtless the result of a spontaneous sowing of the yeast, the germs of which abound, particularly in the particles of dust existing in the atmosphere of any laboratory in which studies relating to fermentation are pursued.

This, however, is not the most striking inference from the facts which the cultivation of these organisms revealed. The *mucor* is evidently a plant, at the same time *aërobian* and *anaërobian*. If we had sown the spore-bearing filaments of *mucor* on slices of pear, lemon, or similar fruit, we should have seen the spores germinate, tubes of mycelium ramifying on the surface of the substratum, and reproducing sporiferous aerial *hyphae*. In this case the plant would have effected all its phenomena of nutrition by absorbing oxygen and emitting carbonic acid, after the manner of animals, as, in our essay on the organic corpuscles which exist in a state of suspension in the atmosphere, we have shown to be the case generally with fungoid growths. Under these circumstances, the only sugar decomposed would have been a quantity equivalent to that assimilated in forming the cellulose of the young tissues of the fungus, or in entering into combination, either with the elements of ammonia or with the sulphur of the sulphates, or the phosphorus of the phosphates, to form the albuminous substances of the interior of the cells.* In this case the sugar used up would furnish no alcohol, or at least, if alcohol were formed, it would be decomposed immediately. All *aerial* growths take place in the same manner; and such is the nature of nutrition and life in all the larger forms.

In our flasks, on the other hand, the life of the little plant functions quite differently. Deprived of oxygen, or having at its disposal but an insufficient quantity of that gas, after a life of activity in contact with air, it can, nevertheless, live apart from the direct action of that element, and the combinations to which it gives rise. On the other hand, we see all the signs of alcoholic fermentation appear; that is, a notable proportion of sugar, in comparison with the weight of solid matter assimilated and fixed by the plant, is decomposed into alcohol and carbonic acid gas; and this decomposition continues as long as life itself continues in the cells, and they remain submerged, this last condition being effected by the decantation of the liquid and its deposit into the test-glass. Along with the disappearance of the phenomena of vital activity in the cells, the fermentation ceases absolutely, or at least is no longer visible externally, by reason of its extreme feebleness. The cells then assume an old, shrivelled, worn-out appearance, with irregular outlines and granular markings. Their life is merely suspended, however, not extinct; for if they be supplied once more with oxygen, and suffered to exist under the influence of that gas, they will vegetate again, and become capable of producing fermentation afresh, even after having been excluded from the air for a considerable time.

Oxygen then presents itself to us as being endowed with a certain determining stimulus in the matter of nutritive action enabling this action to be prolonged beyond the point where

* We do not here take into account certain phenomena of oxidation of which the fungoid growths are the seat, and which remind us of those that are presented in so remarkable a degree by *mycoderma vini* and *mycoderma aceti*.

the direct influence of oxygen ceases. In time the energy that has been imparted to the cells will die away, and then also fermentation will cease, to be resumed, however, when the plant is once more submitted to the revivifying action of the gas. It seems as though the vital energy derived from the influence of gaseous oxygen were capable of effecting an assimilation of oxygen, not in the gaseous state, but existing in some state of combination, and hence its power of causing the decomposition of sugar. Looking at the matter in this light, it seems to us that we may discover in it a fact of general occurrence, that this peculiar action of the oxygen and the cells is to be seen in all living beings. For indeed is there any cell which, if suddenly and completely deprived of air, would perish forthwith, and absolutely ? Probably there is not a single one that would do so. With certain modifications of greater or less amount the assimilative and excretive acts which have taken place during life must be carried on after the suppression of oxygen, resulting in fermentations ordinarily obscure and feeble, but in the case of the cells of ferments, properly so called, manifesting an activity both greater in amount and more enduring.

Let us now proceed to compare the weight of alcohol formed by the *mucor* during fermentation with the weight of the plant itself.

First experiment.—One of the double-necked flasks contained at starting 120 c.c. (about 4 fl. oz.) of wort.

On January 2nd, 1873, we attached this flask to a test-glass, containing a deposit of *mucor* ferment (Fig. 19, p. 101), a few drops of which we poured into the wort in the flask, to impregnate it. On January 3rd we decanted the wort from the flask into the test-glass; under these conditions we have seen that the wort must ferment.

On January 18th the fermentation in the test-glass ceased. On July 31st, 1873, we transferred the liquid from the test-glass back to the flask. On August 4th, 1873, we again decanted this same liquid from the flask into the test-glass. On December

25th, 1873, we once more removed the liquid from the test-glass to the flask, and allowed it to remain so until December 23rd, 1874, on which day we submitted it to examination. It was found to contain per 100 c.c. (3½ fl. oz.)

	Grains.	Grammes.*
Total weight of the fungus	5·7	0·37
Absolute alcohol	50·9	3·3
Acidity, estimated in its equivalent of sulphuric acid	1·7	0·11
Sugar, determined by cupric solution	82·2	5·2
Dextrine (?)	24·6	1·6

The total weight of fungoid growth being 0·37 gramme, and the total weight of absolute alcohol for the 120 c.c. of fermented liquid being 4 grammes, we had, consequently, from ten to eleven times by weight more alcohol than fungus.

Second experiment.—On June 13th, 1872, we sowed two or three sporiferous heads of *mucor* in some wort contained in one of the double-necked flasks. The temperature of our oven varied between 23° C. and 25° C. (73° F. to 77° F.) The total volume of liquid was 120 c.c., as before.

June 15th, mycelium had developed, buoyed up on bubbles of gas.

June 16th, patches of bubbles, due to fermentation, covered the surface of the liquid.

June 17th, we transferred the liquid to the test-glass.

June 28th, fermentation in the test-flask had ceased.

June 28th, fermentation recommenced, the temperature of the oven being raised to 27° C. (80° F.).

October 20th, the liquid was transferred back from the test-glass to the flask.

October 24th, mycelium had developed, supported by big bubbles on the surface of the liquid in the flask.

October 31st, we retransferred the liquid to the test-glass.

[* There are 15·43 grains in the gramme.]

November 1st, a feeble, but continuous fermentation commenced. This was kept up until January 2nd, 1873, on which day we transferred the liquid, with its deposit from the test-glass to the flask, when it now seemed to be quite inert. We left it in this flask until December 24th, 1874, without its manifesting during this long interval any sign of fermentation; nor did the fungus appear to grow at all.

We then submitted the liquid to analysis, and found in it, per 100 c.c.—

	Grammes.*
Total weight of fungoid growth	0·25
Absolute alcohol	3·4
Acidity, estimated in its equivalent of sulphuric acid	0·12
Sugar, determined by copper solution	6·2
Sugar, determined after treatment by boiling with sulphuric acid, and deduction of amount of sugar already obtained (dextrine)?	1·0

The total weight of absolute alcohol for the 120 c.c. of fermented liquid was 4·1 grammes—that is, the weight of the alcohol was sixteen or seventeen times that of the plant.

The structure of the plant differs considerably when it lives surrounded by air, and when it is more or less completely deprived of that fluid. If it has an abundance of air at its disposal, if it vegetates on the surface of a moist substance or in a liquid in which the air held in solution may be renewed without being incessantly displaced by carbonic acid gas, we shall see it develop as an ordinary fungoid growth, with a mycelium consisting of filaments more or less slender, branching, and entangled, sending up from the surface of the liquid aerial organs of fructification. This is the well-known form of vegetation of the common *mucor*. On the other hand, if we compel the *mucor* to live in a saccharine liquid with insufficiency of air, at least for some of its parts, the mode of vegetation will change completely, as we have seen in the case of *penicillium, aspergillus,*

[* For English equivalent see Experiment 1, p. 135.]

Pl. V.

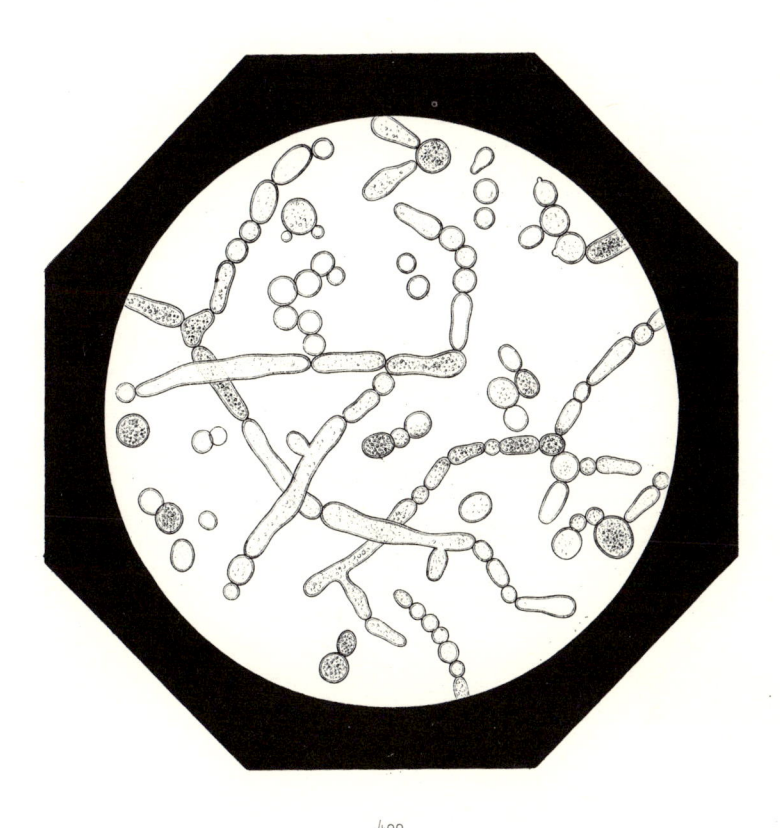

$\frac{400}{1}$

Lackerbauer del. Picart sc.

and *mycoderma vini* when submerged, but with this difference, that in the case of the *mucor* the changes in question, and the activity of nutrition under these new conditions, are much more marked than in the case of those other organisms. The spores grow larger and the filaments of mycelium which do develop are much stronger than those in the normal plant. These filaments put forth, here and there, other filaments which detach themselves and vegetate at the side of the others, being terminated or interrupted by chains of large cells, species of spores which can live by budding and reproducing cells similar to themselves or by elongating into filaments.

Plate V. represents the living plant submerged at a little depth, and having, consequently, still at its disposal a certain quantity of air, insufficient, however, to supply the oxygen needed for all the acts of nutrition. In this case the *mucor* appears very different, morphologically, from what it is when in free contact with air. Here it forms short filaments, having a diameter double or triple that of the filaments of the ordinary mycelium with branches and buds all over, and what is especially characteristic, forming a network of chains of cells, sometimes spherical, sometimes oval or pear-shaped, which are the actual spores. These, as soon as they are detached, bud in their turn, and reproduce either cells or branching tubes; these cells or the chaplets which they form being known under the name *mycelian spores* or *conidia*. Our plate gives these different aspects very correctly, and affords us a good idea of the luxuriant state of this remarkable vegetation.

Plate VI. represents the plant living at a greater depth with less air, expending, by means of sugar as source of heat, the energy which it acquired in vegetating under the influence of the oxygen of the air. The filaments are fewer and older in aspect, and the number of cellular forms is proportionately larger than in the former case, the budding giving rise by preference to spherical or oval cells. On a single cell we often see two, three, four, five, six, and even more buds.

When the buds of the oval or spherical cells detach themselves whilst young, they often resemble in form and size cells of ordinary yeast, nor can even considerable experience in this kind of observation always enable us to distinguish them. Hence we may easily understand how many have come to believe, with so skilful a botanist as Dr. Bail, in the transformation of *mucor* into yeast.

With the forms represented in Plates V. and VI., the plant is more of a ferment than of a fungoid growth. In such cases the weight of sugar decomposed in comparison with the weight of new cell-globules formed is very considerable, an effect which is more marked the less air the plant has at its disposal. Under the latter conditions, however, vegetation is slow and laborious, and the ferment very soon assumes an aspect of age, and we must constantly rejuvenate the cells by bringing them into contact with oxygen, and subjecting them to the action of limited quantities of that gas, and so promote their vegetation and prolong their fermentative activity. This effect we brought about when we retransferred the liquid and its deposit of *mucor* from the test-glass to the flask, thus bringing them into contact with fresh air. We saw cells that appeared old, dark, and highly granulated, become inflated, grow more transparent, and fill with a gelatinous protoplasm, the few granulations which they still exhibited assuming a brilliant appearance when we succeeded in distinguishing them; and finally, a very active budding was set up. Under this reviving influence life could continue once more away from the air, although with difficulty, so that fermentation would be most intense if the large filaments and their conidia were constantly being removed from and to the action of air.

The preceding plates show several instances of this rejuvenescence of the old cells of *mucor* ferment.

We have omitted to represent amongst the old cells some cells which have their granulations collected about the centre, with an empty space between the granulations and the exterior

Pl VI

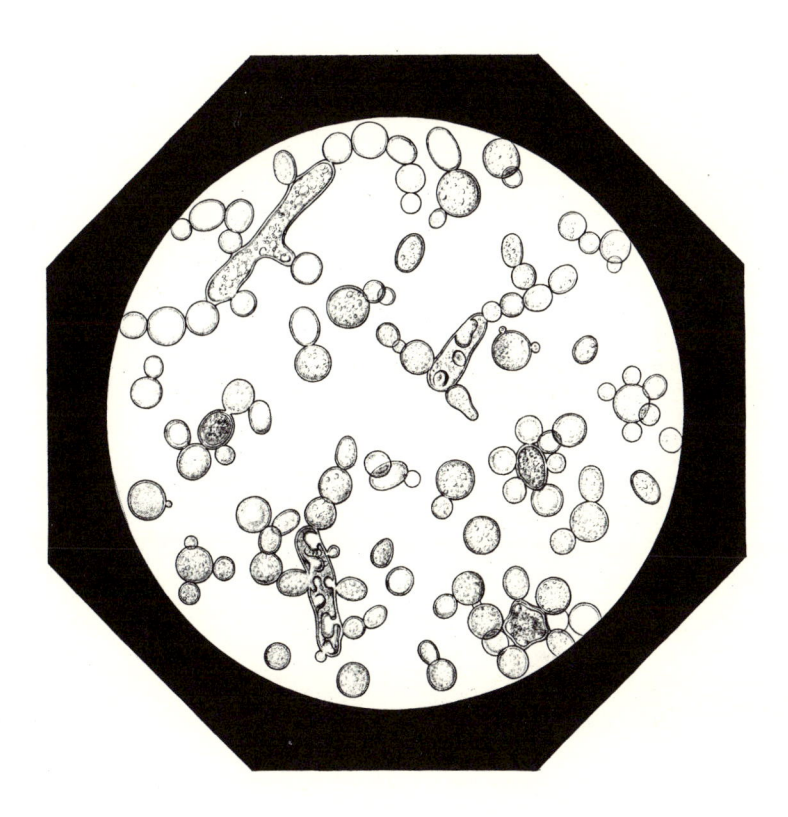

$\frac{400}{1}$

Lackerbauer del. Picart sc

borders.* In this state, cells are generally dead and incapable of any revival. It is impossible to avoid being impressed by the striking analogies which exist between all these facts and those presented by cells of yeast.

In concluding our study of the vegetation of *mucor* as a mould and *mucor* as a ferment, we may again remark that the most striking analogies also exist between the preceding observations and those we have seen in the case of *penicillium aspergillus*, and *mycoderma vini*. These latter plants do not furnish alcohol or carbonic acid gas by direct fermentation of the sugar, as long as we let them vegetate with plenty of air at their disposal. Once submerged, however, their vital aspect changes; on the one hand the cells or filaments of the mycelia evince a tendency to become larger; on the other hand there is a tendency to greater closeness in these latter, and, consequently, a transition to the state of *conidia*. Lastly, there is a correlative budding of cells, accompanied by a

* The figure given below supplies this omission. The cells that are isolated or are in chains, *b.b.b.*, show this state of the old cells. The cells *a.a.a.* are younger, and may be more easily revived. We may see by the dimensions of some of these how greatly, in certain cases, the cells of *mucor* resemble cells of yeast; nevertheless, in the state of the contents and the aspect of the outlines, there are always some differences sufficiently appreciable to strike the practised observer.

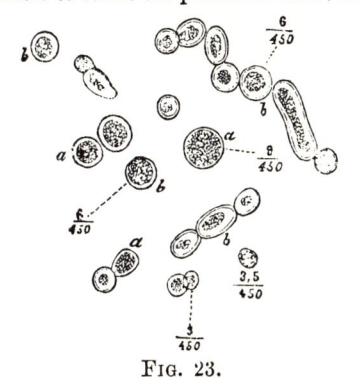

FIG. 23.

The figures adjoining the cells indicate fractions of a millimetre. (A millimetre may be taken as $\frac{1}{25}$-in.)

formation of alcohol and liberation of carbonic acid gas; in short, all the ordinary signs of alcoholic fermentation.

The principal difference in the case of *mucor* consists in this, that the vegetation of this latter, under the conditions of insufficient aeration or none at all, is more decided, both as to extent and duration.

It may be thought that all the varieties of *mucor* are capable of yielding the kind of ferment that we have just mentioned. But this is not the case; and here we have another striking proof of the great physiological differences presented by forms of vegetation so intimately connected with each other that, in botanical classifications, they must be put as closely as possible together. Of this fact we have the most striking example in *mycoderma vini* and the alcoholic ferments, properly so called, which so closely resemble each other in form and development that they might be supposed to be identical, at least, according to our present knowledge, but which differ so widely in their physiological aspects.

On November 17th, 1873, we found a very beautiful specimen of *mucor mucedo* on a pear, under a glass bell jar. It was a mass of perfectly straight filaments, simple and isolated, very large in comparison with those ordinarily met with, each terminating in a sporange, identical to that of *mucor mucedo*, and proportionately well developed. We are able to distinguish *mucor racemosus* from *mucor mucedo* only by the circumstance of its having on its sporange-bearing hyphæ lateral branches which also terminate in sporanges.

We sowed only one of the terminal heads of the large erect hyphae in some wort, in which it soon produced an abundant mycelium, but without the least appearance of gas. For a very long time, up to January 7th, 1875, we studied the developments of this organism, which remained all the time perfectly pure, in consequence of our having cultivated it in one of our two-necked flasks on pure wort.

The total volume of liquid, which was 130 c.c., (4·57 fl. oz.) contained 2·3 grammes (35·3 grains) of alcohol. In spite of

STUDIES ON FERMENTATION.   141

this rather large proportion of alcohol, a clear sign of undoubted fermentation, the plant had yielded no *conidia* at all, nor any cell-globules of ferment. Some of the filaments, however, were larger than the rest, and exhibited irregularly-shaped swellings, which in some cases were of enormous size. Whilst the natural mycelial filaments, by which we mean the vegetating part of *mucor*, which were supplied with abundance of air, only measured $\frac{3}{450}$ of a millimetre* in diameter, the filaments that had grown probably with an insufficiency of oxygen, and performed the functions of ferment, measured $\frac{8}{450}$, and the swellings as much as $\frac{30}{450}$ of a millimetre in diameter, as represented in Fig. 24.

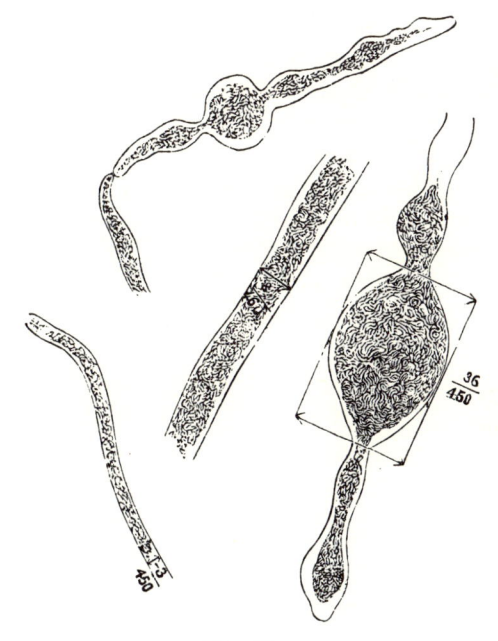

FIG. 24.

In concluding this paragraph, we may mention a very able research on fermentation which we have lately studied, the

* [0·000089 in., 0·00026 in. and 0·00089 in. respectively.]

author of which, Dr. Fitz, communicated it to the Chemical Society of Berlin in 1873. In section II., page 48, this author explains his observations in a manner conformable to our own views, as may be seen from the following passage of the memoir:—

" In the presence of oxygen, the ferment of *mucor* develops into a mycelium and consumes the sugar; in the absence of oxygen, on the other hand, the spores develop into ferment of *mucor*, that buds and decomposes the sugar into the products of fermentation.

" The properties of *mucor mucedo* in a fermentable liquid, in the presence or in the absence of oxygen, accord perfectly with the theory of fermentation established by Pasteur in 1861 (*Comptes rendus de l'Académie des Sciences*, t. lii., p. 1260). According to this theory a fermentative fungus needs oxygen for its development; if it finds any free oxygen it utilizes the whole of it, assimilating one part of the sugar and burning the other; whilst in the absence of free oxygen, the fungus appropriates what it requires from the sugar."

CHAPTER V.

THE ALCOHOLIC FERMENTS.

§ I.—ON THE ORIGIN OF FERMENT.

AMONGST the productions that appear spontaneously, or, we should rather say, without direct impregnation, in organic liquids exposed to contact with the air, there is one that more particularly claims our study. It is that one which, by reason of its active energy as an agent of decomposition, has been distinguished and utilized from the earliest times, and is considered as the type of ferments in general; we mean the ferment of wine, beer, and more generally, of all fermented beverages.

Yeast is that viscous sort of deposit which takes place in the vats or barrels of must or wort that is undergoing fermentation. This kind of ferment presents for consideration a physical fact of the most extraordinary character. Take a morsel of the substance and put it in sweetened water, in must, or in dough, which always contains a little sugar; after a time, the length of which varies, a few minutes often sufficing, we see these liquids or the dough rise, so to speak. This inflation of the mass, which is due to a liberation of carbonic acid gas, may cause it to overflow the vessels containing it, if their capacity is not considerably greater than the volume of the matters fermenting. It is equally remarkable that these phenomena are natural and spontaneous; that is to say that the must, the wort, and the dough are able to rise, as we have termed it, when left to themselves, without the least addition of foreign substances. The only difference that may occur in these phenomena is a certain amount of retardation, in cases where the yeast does not reach the saccharine matters in a perfectly natural form, inasmuch as it then requires a certain time to get itself together before it can begin to act.

It is necessary, indeed, that sugar should be present; for if we abstracted by some means or other from the must or dough all the sugar contained in it, without touching the other constituents, the addition of yeast would produce no gas. Everything would remain quiet until the moment when signs of a more or less advanced putrefaction showed themselves. Yeast is one of the most putrescible of substances, and it is worthy of notice that its alteration is also the consequence of the formation of one or more ferments, very different, however, from that of which we are speaking. As for the nature of yeast, the microscope has taught us what it is. That marvellous instrument, although still in its infancy, enabled Leuwenhoeck, towards the close of the 17th century, to discover that yeast is composed of a mass of cells. In 1835 Cagnard-Latour and Schwann took up Leuwenhoeck's observations, and by employing a more perfect microscope, discovered that these same cells vegetate and multiply by a process of gemmation. Since then the physical and chemical phenomena already mentioned, such as the raising of the mass, the liberation of carbonic acid gas, and the formation of alcohol, have been announced as acts probably connected with the living processes of a little cellular plant, and subsequent researches have confirmed these views.

In introducing a quantity of yeast into a saccharine wort, it must be borne in mind that we are sowing a multitude of minute living cells, representing so many centres of life, capable of vegetating with extraordinary rapidity in a medium adapted to their nutrition. This phenomenon can occur at any temperature betweeen zero and 55° C. (131° F.), although a temperature between 15° C. and 30° C. (59° F. and 86° F.) is the most favourable to its occurrence.

As regards the rapidity of the budding, the following observations will give some idea of what it is in the case of one of the ferments of natural must. The temperature was between 12° C. and 13° C. (55° F.).

"On October 12, 1861, at ten o'clock in the morning, we crushed some grapes, without filtering the juice that ran from them; afterwards, at different times during the day, we examined the juice under the microscope, until at last, although not before seven o'clock in the evening, we detected a couple of cells, as represented in Fig. 25, *a*.

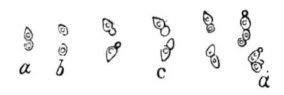

FIG. 25.

From that time we kept these contiguous cells constantly in view. At 7.10 we saw them separate and remove to some little distance from each other (Fig. 25, *b*). Between 7 and 7.30 we saw, on each of these cells, a very minute bud originate and grow little by little. These buds developed very near the point of contact, where the disjunction had just taken place. By 7.45 the buds had increased greatly in size (Fig. 25, *c*). By 8 they had attained the size of the mother-cells. By 9 each cell of each couple had put forth a new bud (Fig. 25, *d*). We did not follow the multiplication of the cells any farther, having seen that in the course of two hours two cellules had furnished eight, including the two mother-cells." *

An increase like this, which would have been more rapid at a temperature between 15° and 25° (59° and 77° F.), and still more so between 25° and 30° (77° and 86° F.), may indeed seem surprising. It is really, however, nothing to what sometimes occurs. In choosing proper conditions of temperature and medium, of state and nature of yeast, it has sometimes happened that the bottom of a vessel has become covered with a white deposit of yeast cells, in the course of not more than five or six hours

* Extract from a Note which I inserted in 1862 in the *Bulletin de la Société chimique* of Paris.

146 STUDIES ON FERMENTATION.

after we had sown a quantity of yeast so small as to effect no change at all in the transparency of the liquid contained in the vessel after it had been shaken up. Such a rapidity of vegetation reminded us of those exotic plants which are said to grow several feet in height in the course of twenty-four hours.

Budding commences in the form of a simple protuberance on the cell—a kind of little boss, as represented in Fig. 26, No. 1.

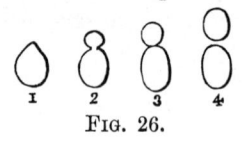

FIG. 26.

This protuberance goes on increasing, and assumes a spherical or oval form. At the same time, there is a tendency in the points of attachment in the young cell to meet—a kind of strangulation occurs (Fig. 26, No. 2). The junction takes place a little sooner or later, according to the species (Fig. 26, No. 3); the two individuals then separate (Fig. 26, No. 4). In certain cases a single cell may give rise to several protuberances, and, consequently, to several daughter-cells. Where there is only one protuberance or bud we generally see it originate at the thick end and a little on one side of the apex of the oval outline, which, in a greater or less degree, characterizes the cells of the majority of ferments.

Certain authors have maintained that the method of budding which we have just described, and which we think was first promulgated by Mitscherlich, is merely an illusion, and that the cells of yeast break up and scatter their granular contents, and that these scattered granules eventually attach themselves to the cells, growing there, and so giving the appearance of buds or daughter-cells. This error has been revived quite recently.[*] Nothing can be less admissible. We could count the number

[*] Schützenberger, in his work on "Fermentation," following Dr. de Vauréal. Paris, 1875, p. 278. [See pp. 61, 62 English version in International Scientific Series (H. S. King & Co., London, 1876). This appears to be the only reference to this subject in the English copy.—D. C. R.]

of yeast cells which we have seen undergo this process of rupture in the course of some ten years of observation, every day of which, we may say, thousands of these cells have passed under our eyes. This breaking up of the cells is really of the most rare occurrence, and may always be explained by some abnormal circumstance affecting the yeast; being indeed a mechanical accident, not a physiological fact. We may easily convince ourselves of this by growing some yeast in a saccharine wort, filtered perfectly clear, and, consequently, deprived of all granular amorphous deposit that might deceive the observer. The cells will be observed to bud and multiply without exhibiting the most minute appearance of granulation, or disruption; moreover, there will always be cells of all sizes, ranging from the smallest visible up to the largest. This very simple piece of observation may be made in all the alcoholic ferments, and with any wort capable of fermenting, and in its presence the hypothesis, which we have been repudiating, cannot hold its own.

In Plate VII. (left side) there is represented a field of yeast, magnified 400 times. We see a mass of disjointed cells, such as appear after fermentations without sufficient aliment; of the kind represented some are nearly spherical, others oval or cylindrical, more or less elongated. If we mix a little of this yeast, of about the size of a pin's head, with wort, and put the wort into a small, shallow, flat-bottomed basin, having a surface of about 1 square decimetre (10 sq. ins.) exposing it to the surrounding temperature, we shall find next day the bottom of the basin covered with a fine white deposit, of the forms of which we give a sketch in the right half of the plate. In this it will at once be observed that the cells sown have lost their interior granulations, having become more transparent and filled with a gelatinous protoplasm. The principal difference between the two halves of the plate consists in this, that whereas the cells in the left half are isolated and granular, those in the right half are more inflated, more transparent, and provided with buds, which may be seen in every stage of development, from their first appearance till they become as large as the parent cells. They continue to grow until they detach themselves; then they bud in their turn, so that the same figure may furnish examples of cells of the first, second, and third generations. In the right half, the protoplasm contained in the cells exhibits circular spots or vacuoles, which may be made to appear lighter or darker than the rest of the cell by slight movements of the object-glass of the microscope. These spots are due to a migration of the protoplasm towards the sides; they commonly occur in yeast cells the vitality of which, from deficient nourishment, has become suppressed—the shrivelled appearance which they then assume being due to their being forced to live upon themselves, so to speak. However, by introducing such cells into a nutritive and aerated liquid the vacuoles quickly disappear.

In the ordinary yeast, as met with in breweries, the majority of cells show one or more of these vacuoles; if, however, we place a little of this yeast in an aerated wort, and watch under the microscope the changes that occur in the cells, we shall witness, often in the course of a few seconds, a kind of turgescence, a greater tension of the cell-walls, which seem to grow thinner, and a complete disappearance of the vacuoles. At the same time the interior gelatinous matter will become filled with fine granulations that are scarcely visible, but which at a certain distance appear brilliant. At the same time protuberances begin to show themselves, and next day the budding will have already become very active. The newly-formed cells will have such a delicacy of aspect and contour as to be scarcely discernible in the field of the microscope. There will also be a tendency to ramification in the budding, which appearance will be more or less marked according to the kind of alcoholic ferments present, as we shall see presently, attaining its maximum in each case when the cells have been revived after exhaustion by rest and want of food. In the latter case, the process of rejuvenescence may be protracted; but this is not the case with cells of commercial yeast, which is always used within a few days of its formation.

Pl. VII

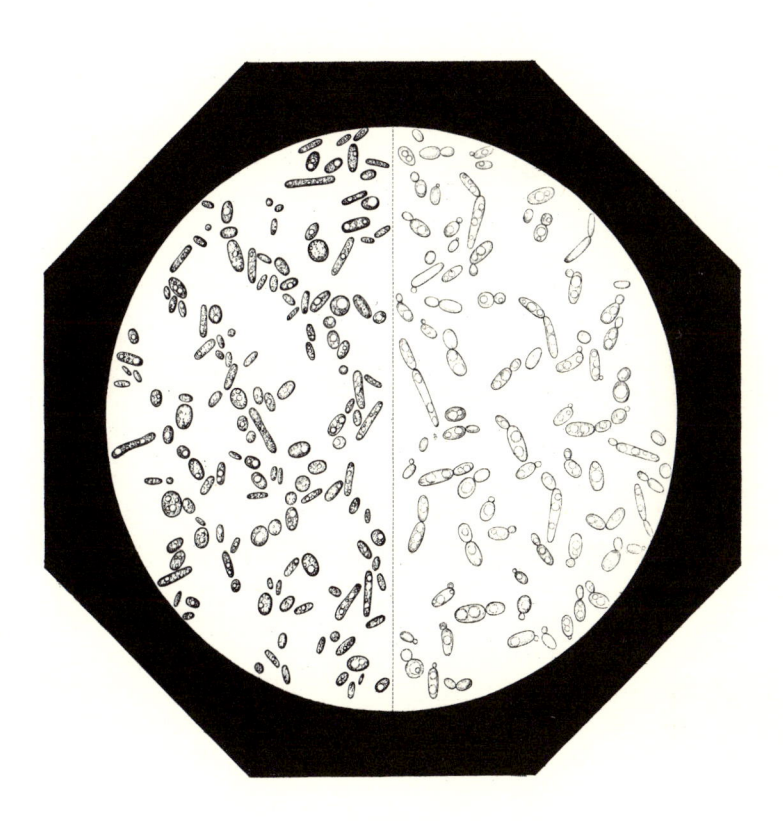

$\frac{400}{1}$

Deyrolle del. Picart sc.

Imp. Cuny Gros. Paris.

And thus, as I said a little ago, speaking of these cells, they often manifest the first signs of their budding in a few seconds.

In our preceding remarks we have expressly assumed that there are many kinds of alcoholic ferment. This is, beyond doubt, the case, as we have given incontestable proofs, first in 1862, in the *Bulletin de la Société chimique* of Paris, and later on, in 1864 and 1866, in a Note in the *Comptes rendus*, on the diseases of wines, as well as in our "Studies on Wine." Moreover, we know that brewers have long recognized two distinct methods of fermentation—"high" fermentation and "low" fermentation—and two corresponding yeasts. It is true that the differences presented by these fermentations were believed to be caused by the different conditions under which they took place, and that it was supposed that we might change "high" yeast into "low" yeast, or inversely, by subjecting the first to a low temperature, or the second to a high one. In our observations of 1862, which we have just mentioned, we discovered that must gives rise to several yeasts; that the ferment of "high" beer cannot develop except with great difficulty in must, whilst one of the ferments of the grape grows rapidly and luxuriantly in wort; that it is easy to isolate the smallest of the ferments of the grape from its congeners, by subjecting filtered must to fermentation; and finally, that the secondary fermentations of wines which remain sweet furnish a remarkable ferment, very different in aspect to the ferment of beer.

We have not given specific names to these different ferments, any more than we have to the other microscopic organisms which we have had occasion to study. This was not from any disregard for names, but from a constant fear that, since the physiological functions of these minute forms was the exclusive object of our study, we might be led to attach too much importance to exterior characters. We have often found that forms, having nothing apparently in common, belong to one and the same species, whilst similarity of form may associate species far apart. We shall give some fresh examples of this fact in the present paragraph. A German naturalist, Dr. Rees, who has discovered new proofs of the diversity of alcoholic ferments, putting aside, perhaps rightly, such scruples, has attached specific names to the different kinds of ferments, in his *brochure* published in 1870, which we have already cited (p. 71). Indeed, we have often ourselves, for brevity's sake, made use of the names proposed by Dr. Rees.*

In a Note inserted in the *Bulletin de la Société chimique de Paris*, in 1862, we figured a ferment of small dimensions, which develops spontaneously in must, filtered or unfiltered, and which is very different from the ordinary ferment of wine. It is the first to make its appearance in the fermentation of the grape, and may even appear alone if the must has been previously well filtered, doubtless because its germs, being smaller than those of other ferments, pass through the filter more easily and in greater number. Fig. 27, extracted from our

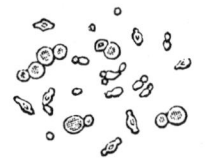

FIG. 27.

Note of 1862, represents this ferment, together with some spherical cells of *high* yeast, with the object of giving a more exact idea of the relative dimensions of these two ferments and their dissimilarities. Dr. Rees has named it *saccharomyces apiculatus*.

* The principal result of Dr. Rees' labours consists in the discovery of a sporulation peculiar to yeast cells, that is to say, to a formation in the interior of these cells, and under particular conditions—such as when the growth occurs on slices of cooked potatoes, carrots, &c.—of two, three, or four smaller cells, which, when placed in fermentable liquids, act like the germinating spores of ferments. The mother-cell may be regarded as an *ascus*, and the daughter-cells as *ascospores*, and so the genus *saccharomyces* may be classified among the group of fungi termed *ascomycetes*. These facts have been frequently confirmed, notably by

STUDIES ON FERMENTATION. 151

The same savant has given the name of *saccharomyces pastorianus* to the yeast of the secondary fermentations of sweet liquids, such as wine that has remained sweet after its principal fermentation. We have described this yeast in a Note published in 1864, on the diseases of wine, from which we give the following extract:—*

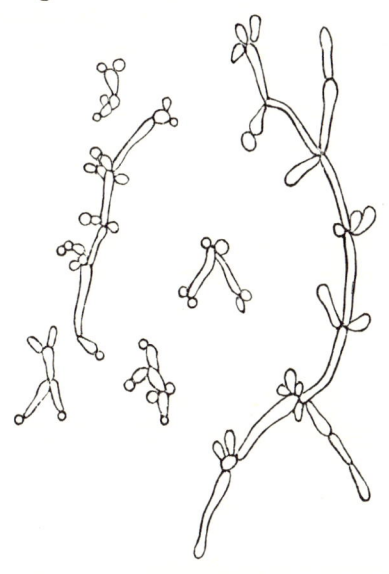

FIG. 28.

" Fig. 6 (Fig. 28 in this work) represents a very interesting Dr. Engel, professor of the Faculty of Medicine, at Nancy. Previously to Dr. Rees' discovery, M. de Seynes (*Comptes rendus*, t. lxvii., 1868) had described an endogenous formation of spores in *mycoderma vini*, particularly in the elongated cells, followed by the rupture of the mother-cell, and subsequent absorption of cell-walls and other contents after the issue of the endospores, which we have just termed *ascospores*. We ourselves had also previously called attention to those refractive corpuscles which appear amongst vibrios as probably being reproductive corpuscles, and we had likewise witnessed the reabsorption of the parts surrounding them. The plate on page 228 of our "Studies on the Silkworm Disease" represents the phenomena in question.

* See *Comptes rendus de l'Académie des Sciences*, vol. lviii. p. 144.

variety of alcoholic ferment. It happens pretty often, especially in the Jura, where the vintage takes place about October 15th, when the season is already cold and little favourable to fermentation, that the wine is still sweet at the moment when it is put into casks. This is especially the case in good years, when the sugar is abundant and the proportion of alcohol high, a circumstance which prevents the completion of fermentation when effected at a low temperature. The wine remains sweet in cask sometimes for several years, undergoing a continuous but feeble alcoholic fermentation. In such wines we have always observed the presence of this peculiar ferment. In form it consists of a principal stem, forming nodes at various points, from which short branches arise, ending in spherical or ovoid cells. These cells readily detach themselves, and act as spores of the plant. It is rarely, however, that we see so perfect a vegetation as we have represented, because the different parts fall to pieces, as we have shown in the left half of the figure."

What is the origin of cellular plants of this remarkable type? Where and how are the ferments of the grape generated?

In Chapter III. § 3 we were on our way to a solution of this question. It has been shown that fermentation cannot take place in the juice of crushed grapes if the must has not come into contact and been mixed with particles of dust on the surface of the grapes, or of the woody part of the bunch. It would, however, be sufficient that a vintage vat, of any capacity whatsoever, should receive the particles of dust existing on a single bunch in some cases, on even a single grape, for the whole mass to enter into fermentation.

What, then, we must ask ourselves, is the nature of these particles of dust? On September 27th, 1872, we picked from a vine, in the neighbourhood of Arbois, a bunch of grapes, of the variety called *le noirin*. The bunch selected, without any injury to a single grape, was brought to our laboratory in a sheet of paper that had been previously scorched in the flame of

Pl VII

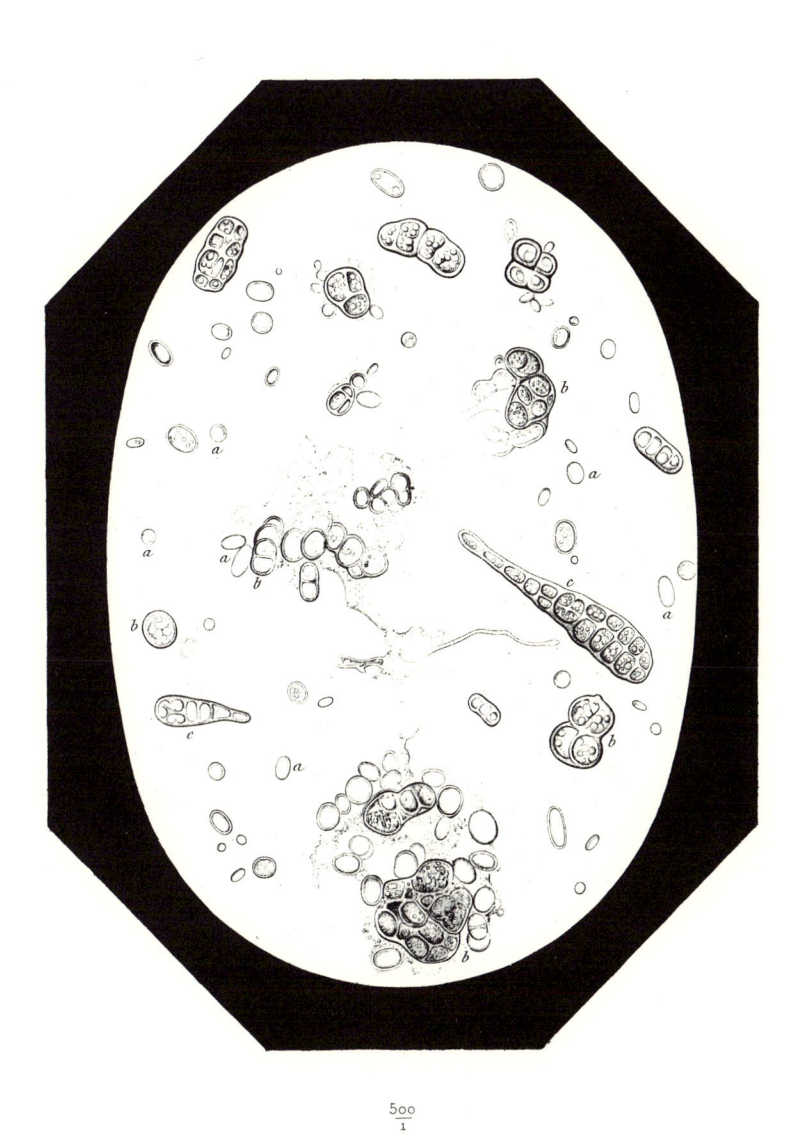

$\frac{500}{1}$

Deyrolle del.   Picart sc.

Imp. Gony frès. Paris.

a spirit lamp, and the grapes were cut off with a pair of fine scissors, which had also been passed through the flame. By means of a badger-hair brush, thoroughly purified in water, each grape to which a portion of its peduncle remained attached, was washed in a little pure water. The successive washing of a dozen grapes in 3 c.c. of water was sufficient to make the water turbid; we then examined it under the microscope. Each field contained many little organized bodies, accidentally associated, now and again, with some very scarce crystalline spicules. As a rule, the organisms consisted of simple, transparent, colourless cells; some, indeed, of larger size had a yellowish brown colour, and were detached or united in irregular masses; and, lastly, there were club-shaped or bottle-shaped vessels, full of spores ready to germinate. We repeated this experiment with bunches of other varieties of grape, and also submitted to examination water in which the outer surfaces of gooseberries, plums, and pears had been washed; the result was in each case the same, that is, we found a great number of the same colourless cells, and the same irregular masses of darker cells, which latter, however, we must not confound with the masses of dead cells sometimes found covering parts of the epidermis of certain fruits.

As we had purposely left each fruit attached to part of its peduncle, we wished to ascertain if these corpuscles proceeded from the grapes or from the wood of the peduncle. For this purpose we washed separately the surface of the grapes and the woody part of the bunch. The water in which the latter was washed was visibly more charged with the minute organisms than that in which the grapes was washed, although the latter was by no means free from them.

Plate VIII. represents these corpuscles as they exist on the surface of fruits, magnified 500 times. The groups, $b, b, b,$ ... , $c, c,$ ... are of a brown colour, more or less dark, or of a reddish yellow; the cells $a, a,$ ... are transparent. Amongst them are some spores of ordinary fungoid growths, and several cells which are probably the issue of a germination that had commenced in certain groups which have a hard, yellowish appearance, and which are provided with what seems to be a double case—*b, b, b,* ..., *c, c,* ..., a result of the moisture of the woody part of the bunch, or of rain that fell just before the commencement of our observations.

It is an easy matter to trace the germination of these different varieties of cells with the microscope. We put a drop of the water in which the woody part of a bunch of grapes has been washed into a small quantity of wort, previously boiled and filtered bright. Plate IX. presents a series of developments observed in the case of simple or grouped cells, A, D, G, and J. The process is as follows: The yellowish-brown cells soften and grow larger in the nutritive medium, and gradually become almost transparent and colourless. At the same time we see some very young buds appear on their margins; these rapidly increase in size, and detaching themselves to make room for others, move off as young cells that after a time bud in their turn. The rapidity with which these cells bud and multiply is often extraordinary. The group A and the cell D produced the groups C and F within twenty-four hours, passing through the intermediate stages represented in groups B, E. The cells A and D did not give rise to any filamentous growths, at least whilst under our observation. Some groups of cells, however, put forth, from the first, long filaments, having cross-partitions and resembling the mycelium in ordinary fungoid growths. Together with these, and along their whole length, was an abundance of cells, often in clusters, as represented by Fig. G, the whole of which growth took place in less than twenty-four hours.* But apart from contact with the air, there was a complete absence of life.

The figures H, I, J, K, represent other aspects of developing cells and filaments. The cells H are spherical; the cells I have numerous buds, as also have those marked K. These

* The plates referred to in this paragraph were exhibited at a meeting of the Academy of Sciences, November 18, 1872, and commented upon by the perpetual secretary, M. Dumas.

$$\frac{500}{1}$$

Deyrolle del. Picart sc

Imp. Gony-Gros. Paris

different forms were all produced in the course of twenty-four hours by the cell which may be observed in the centre of the group J. In connection with this same group, J, we may remark that on September 30, 1872, at 10 A.M., we witnessed the detachment of three oval cells at the points a, b, c; by 10.45 other buds of the size represented in our engraving had formed in their place; by about five o'clock that same afternoon these buds, a, b, c, having become transformed into cells, fell off in their turn.*

* For these observations, we employed small glass cells, which we made out of some St. Gobain glass by punching holes through it, and then cementing on one side one of the little glasses used for covering objects in microscopical examinations. In this manner we made small troughs, in which we placed some wort that had been boiled, and a drop of the water in which grapes had been washed. To prevent evaporation we covered the cells with a sheet of glass. We examined the liquid in these cells by inclining our microscope to the angle required. (*a*)

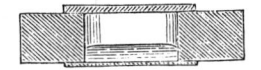

FIG. 29.

We also made use of cells similar to those employed by MM. Van Tieghem and Lemonnier (*b*) in their researches on *mucorines* (Fig. 30).

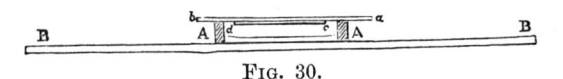

FIG. 30.

An apparatus similar to that employed by M. Duclaux in 1853 (*c*) would do equally well. We should be able to work with even greater facility if we employed bulbs like some which we ordered in Germany, some twelve years ago, of the well-known glass-blower, Geissler. We have heard that these bulbs now sold by that maker are much used by German microscopists. They consist of a tube blown out into a flat

(*a*) In our essay on acetic fermentation, published in 1864, we have already described this apparatus, which we employed to follow the multiplication of the jointed filaments of *mycoderma aceti*. See PASTEUR, *Etudes sur le vinaigre*, p. 64, Paris, 1868.

(*b*) VAN TIEGHEM and LEMONNIER, *Annales des Sciences naturelles*, 5th series, *Botanique*, t. xvii. 1873.

(*c*) DUCLAUX, *Comptes rendus des séances de l'Académie des Sciences*, t. lvi. p. 1225.

156   STUDIES ON FERMENTATION.

It may be asked, what proof have we that amongst the filamentous and cellular growths which spring from the small, dark bodies existing in the particles of dust adhering to the surface of fruits, and which we here see bud and multiply with such marvellous rapidity, the ferment or ferments of vintage do actually exist? A very simple experiment will prove conclusively that this is the case. When in the course of twenty-four or forty-eight hours, by contact with saccharine must, and in presence of excess of air, the revival and development of the cells has taken place on the bottom of the little troughs employed in our observations; if then we fill up the trough with the same must, so that there remains no free air under the cover-glass, within a very short time—an hour, half-an-hour, or often less—we shall see bubbles of gas rise from the bottom, accompanied by an increase in the deposit of cells. This will be

bulb, the sides of which, in the centre, come sufficiently close together to enclose but a very thin layer of liquid, and to admit of microscopical

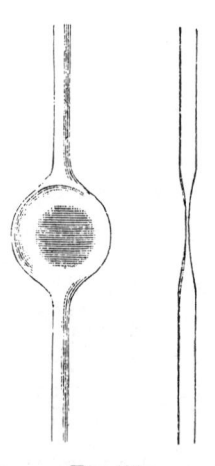

FIG. 31.

examination. We may fill these tube-bulbs completely with liquid, to the exclusion of air or we may surround the central drop with air.

the must fermenting after the submersion of the cellular plants. It follows that the cells, or groups of cells, of a dark colour which cover the grapes, or the woody part of the clusters, are actual germs of the cells of yeast; more correctly speaking, that germs of yeast-cells exist amongst these groups, for it would not be consistent with truth to say that the various germinating forms present in the dust on the surface of grapes must all of them give rise to actual corresponding ferments. Thus the flask-shaped spores *c, c,* ... in Plate VIII., are reproductive organs of *alternaria tenuis,* which have probably nothing in common with alcoholic ferment or ferments, properly so called, except their outward form. We may repeat, however, and it is a point of great importance to bear in mind, that the cells of yeast originate from some or other of the little, brownish, organized bodies, which the microscope reveals in such numbers amongst the particles of dust existing on the surface of fruits.

The impossibility, which we have already demonstrated (Chapter III., § 3), of making grape juice ferment apart from the action of external particles of dust, and the knowledge which we have just acquired, that the particles of dust on the surface of the grapes and woody peduncles, at the moment when the grapes have attained maturity, contain certain reproductive cells which give rise to certain ferments, naturally lead us to the investigation of another point, which concerns the period at which these germs make their appearance on the different parts of the vine plant. The two following experiments tend to prove that the ferment can only appear about the time when the grapes attain maturity, and that it disappears during the winter, not to reappear before the end of the following summer.

I. In the month of October, 1873, we procured from a vineyard in the canton of Arbois some of the woody parts of very ripe clusters of grapes, taking the precaution to cut off all the grapes, one by one, with a very clean pair of scissors, whilst still on the vine; we then wrapped up the woody parts of the clusters, thus deprived of their grapes, in thin paper, to convey them to Paris. Our only object at that time was to secure for use in our subsequent studies the ferment-bearing dust found in October on the woody part of the vine, and, more particularly, on the clusters themselves, as already stated. After our return to Paris, and during the course of our experiments in October and November, it sufficed to wash a few scraps of the bunches in a little pure water, in order to obtain the grape-ferment in abundance; but later on in the winter we were astonished to find that the same procedure yielded no ferment, only some moulds. The bunches which, when put into boiled and filtered must, in October, very readily caused that must to ferment, at the end of winter could no longer produce the same effect, however favourable might be the temperature to which we raised the must. The particles of dust on the bunches had, therefore, become sterile, as sources of alcoholic ferments.

II. On February 17th, 1875, we purchased of Chevet, a dealer in provisions, two bunches of white grapes, which were perfectly sound, presenting not the slightest trace of injury or bruise. We took an iron pot full of mercury, which had been heated to 200° C. (392° F.), and then covered over its surface with a sheet of paper that had also been subjected to flame. When the mercury had cooled down we placed several of Chevet's grapes, singly and in small bunches, on the surface of the metal, and, after having enclosed them in a glass cylinder that had been previously heated with and by means of the mercury, we crushed them in this vessel, in contact with air, by means of a strong, crooked iron wire that had been passed through the flame of a spirit lamp. The object of all these precautions was to prevent any cause of error, such as might have resulted from the accession of particles of dust associated with the mercury, or floating about our laboratory. We then placed our cylindrical jar in an oven, at a temperature of 25° C. (77° F.); but though the experiment was continued for several days following, no fermentation manifested itself. At last, to assure ourselves that the pulp and liquid were, notwithstanding this, well adapted to fermentation, we introduced into the test-flask an almost imperceptible quantity

STUDIES ON FERMENTATION. 159

of yeast. This readily developed, and promptly produced fermentation.*

It seems possible, therefore, that the germs of ferment may not exist on bunches of sound grapes during winter, and that the well-known experiment of Gay-Lussac on the influence of air on the fermentation of the must of crushed grapes cannot succeed at all times.

The following observations will afford more than sufficient proof of this statement, being, after all, but an easy method of carrying out Gay-Lussac's experiment, without having recourse to the use of mercury.

It may already be inferred from the preceding facts that there must be, in the course of the year, between the end of winter and autumn, a period when the vegetation of the cellules from which yeast proceeds undergoes a revival. When does this period occur? In other words, how long after winter does sterility of the plant continue, until it is again capable of yielding ferment? To ascertain this, we conducted numerous experiments during the summer and autumn of 1875 and the winter of 1876. Having to conduct them in a vine-growing country —in the vineyards of Arbois, Franche-Comté—at a distance from our laboratory, we were compelled to adopt a simple form

* In experiments of this kind there is always a slight increase in the volume of air in the jar. This increase may be very perceptible even when the experiment made with fresh grapes, in August, for instance, causes no fermentation due to the action of yeast. After the oxygen of the air has been absorbed and replaced by carbonic acid gas, either by direct oxidation or by the action of moulds, the grapes, although crushed, act like fruits plunged into carbonic acid gas (a), and this effect is even more marked in the case of imperfectly crushed grapes. The reason is, that the crushing is never so perfect as to injure all the cells of the parenchyma. We may easily convince ourselves that the experiment on the liberation of carbonic acid gas and the formation of alcohol by grapes and fruits in general when plunged into carbonic acid succeeds very well in the case of fragments of fruits or grapes, and succeeds better the less the parts are crushed.

(a) See paragraph: Fermentation in saccharine fruits immersed in carbonic acid gas, Chap. vi , § 2, p. 266.

of apparatus for our experiments, which, besides being very convenient, was at the same time sufficiently exact for the object we had in view.

Into common test-tubes we poured some preserved must; we then boiled it, with the object of destroying all the germs that it might contain, and then, having passed the flame of a spirit lamp over the upper sides of the tubes, we closed them with corks which had been held in the flame until they began to carbonize (Fig. 32). Having provided ourselves with a

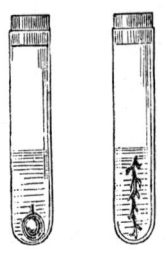

Fig. 32.

series of tubes prepared in this manner, we carried them to a vine, and there dropped into some of them grapes, into others bunches, from which we had taken all the grapes, by cutting their peduncles; into others, fragments of leaves or the wood of the branches. The corks were again passed through the flame and replaced successively in each tube. Some of the grapes we dropped in whole, some we crushed at the bottom of the tubes with an iron rod that had previously been passed through the flame; others, again, at the same moment that we introduced them into the tubes, were cut open with scissors, likewise passed previously through the flame, so that a portion of their interior juice might mix with the must in the tube.

Our experiments gave the following results:—As long as the grapes were green, about the end of July and during the first fortnight of August, we obtained no fermentation in our must. Between the 20th and 25th of August a few tubes underwent fermentation, by the action of the little apiculated ferment; and in the course of September the number of tubes that fermented increased progressively. In each series of tubes, however, we always found a few in which there was a complete absence of fermentation.

Here are a few actual examples. In the beginning of September we placed grapes in thirteen tubes, into some whole, into others crushed ones, taken from bunches of the variety known as the *ploussard*, the fruit being already sufficiently ripe to be very pleasant to the taste. All the tubes of this series failing to give us any trace of fermentation, or anything besides ordinary moulds—which indeed appeared in all our experiments, whether there was or was not fermentation—we began a new series of experiments, under similar conditions, on September 28th, as follows:—

Nos. 1, 2, 3 and 4 tubes containing one uncrushed grape.

No. 5 tube containing two uncrushed grapes.

No. 6 tube containing two crushed grapes.

No. 7 tube containing two crushed grapes, in 2 c.c. of water previously boiled.

No. 8 tube with a fragment of a bunch from which grapes had been cut, and occupying the entire depth of liquid.

No. 9 tube with a fragment of wood from a branch.

Nos. 10, 11, and 12 tubes with a fragment of leaf.

On September 29th and 30th there was no appearance of fermentation in any of the flasks, but all contained flakes of fungoid mycelium. On the 1st of October fermentation more or less marked and active occurred in 2, 3, 4, and 5, in which uncrushed grapes were, accompanied by a general turbidity of the liquid, and a suspension of the development of the fungoid growths. It was still absent in 1, 6, and 7, of which the first contained an entire, the latter crushed grapes. No. 8, containing the woody part of the bunch, was in active fermentation. Nos. 9, 10, 11, and 12, with fragments of branch or leaves, showed no signs of fermentation. The following day No. 1 was fermenting; but from October 5th onwards there was no alteration in the number of fermenting tubes.

In this series we determined the presence of the small apiculated form of yeast (*S. apiculatus*) in the tubes that fermented, only once finding it associated with *saccharomyces pastorianus*.

We need hardly say that the grapes which we employed were perfectly ripe, the vintage having already commenced in some of the Jura cantons.

This experiment shows that, even when the grapes are perfectly matured, it by no means follows that each individual grape must carry germs of ferment, and that some grapes may be crushed, in some instances several together may be crushed, without being able to set up a fermentation. In the presence of these novel facts, those who support the hypothesis of the transformation of the albuminous matter contained in the juice of grapes into yeast will no doubt admit the untenability of their opinions, since their hypothesis requires that every grape or number of grapes, when crushed, should ferment, in contact with air.

On the same day we prepared another series of tubes, using grapes of a variety called the *trousseau*.

Nos. 1, 2, 3, and 4 tubes containing one whole grape.

Nos. 5 and 6 tubes containing some of the wood of a branch.

No. 7 tube containing some of the wood of a branch from which the grapes had been detached.

In the course of the following days fermentation took place in 4, 5, and 7.

In this case three out of four of the uncrushed grapes did not cause the must in which they were placed to ferment; whilst the same must fermented in one of the two tubes containing wood of the branch, and in the other remained unchanged; and, lastly, the tube containing the woody peduncles of the bunch fermented.

We have already remarked that it was more particularly the wood of the bunch that was charged with germs of ferment. The truth of this assertion was proved by the following series of experiments.

On October 2nd, 1875, we charged at the vineyard twenty-four tubes, all of which were about a third filled with pure must that had been previously boiled.

Nos. 1, 2, 3, 4, 5, and 6 tubes containing one crushed grape.

No. 7 tube containing two crushed grapes.

No. 8 tube containing one crushed grape.

Nos 9, 10, 11, and 12 tubes containing some wood of a branch of the vine.

Nos. 13, 14, 15, 16, 17, 18, 19, 20, 21, 22, 23, and 24 tubes containing a fragment of the wood of a bunch from which the grapes had all been detached and removed.

In the course of the following days some of these tubes began to ferment; but in others only fungoid mycelia were visible.

On October 7th the following tubes were fermenting: the second of the first eight containing whole or crushed grapes; not one of the four that contained wood of the branches; whilst, on the other hand, of the tubes containing wood of the bunches, 15, 17, 20, 21, 22, 23, and 24 were all in full fermentation. In short, fermentation, and therefore germs of yeast, were present in one single tube out of eight containing grapes; in none of the four tubes containing wood of the vine branch; but in seven out of the dozen containing wood of the bunches. There was no subsequent change in the number of tubes that fermented.

The same day that we arranged this series of tubes we prepared twenty-four other similar ones, using *the wood of bunches preserved from the vintage of the preceding year*. Not one of these twenty-four tubes showed the least sign of fermentation, although they contained grape juice in presence of the wood of the bunches; this was a further confirmation of the sterility of the germs of ferment in the case of bunches of grapes preserved for a sufficient time.

The next question to be considered was, what length of time after the vintage do the germs on the surface of the woody part of bunches of grapes preserve the faculty of producing yeast? The following experiments were undertaken to determine this point.

We have just seen that on October 2 fragments of the woody peduncles introduced with must, on the spot, caused that must to ferment in seven cases out of twelve. In order that we might test the wood of these same bunches during winter we took care to wrap some fragments up in paper previously passed through the flame. We afterwards took occasion to test portions of these fragments as follows:—

On December 21st, 1875, we conducted an experiment with twelve. On the following days all began to show flakes of mycelium, or numerous multiplying cells of *mycoderms, torulæ,* and *dematium;* and only four subsequently produced yeast and alcoholic fermentation. From this we may conclude that, three months after the vintage, a large number of the germs of yeast spread over the woody part of the bunches lose their vitality, through desiccation by the surrounding air, since two-thirds of the examples taken had become sterile by that time.

On January 21st we conducted a similar experiment with twelve other tubes. At a temperature between 20° and 25° C. (68° to 77° F.) fermentation occurred in only two of them. On March 2nd we undertook another experiment, again using twelve tubes, and again fermentation occurred in two tubes.

By the beginning of April the sterility was absolute. At that period of the year (April and May) we made numerous experiments of this kind, using the woody parts of fresh bunches of grapes and white grapes preserved from the last vintage, plenty of which were still to be had in a state of freshness at the provision store. We also operated on some wood obtained from a vineyard at Meudon. In a great number of cases no fermentation occurred; it even happened that a whole bunch of fresh black grapes, very ripe, which were bought at Chevet's on April 16th, and which had been grown in a hothouse, after having been crushed, did not ferment at all.

Up to March not one of the tubes containing the wood of dry bunches brought from the Jura, which had fermented, showed any signs of *apiculatus* or of *pastorianus,* or anything besides the ordinary low yeast of wine, *saccharomyces ellipsoideus.**

It would be a study of much interest to determine if yeast exists on other species of plants besides the vine. During the winter we could discover it on no others. Once during the winter, experimenting on box, we obtained fermentation in one of our tubes which contained must. In a great number of other experiments we obtained nothing besides moulds and growths of *dematium, alternaria,* and *torulaceæ.*

Our observations in Chap. III. § 6, taken in connection with those which we have just made, prove that the yeasts of fermentation, after being dried, preserve the faculty of germination longer than the germ-cells which are scattered over the dead wood of the vine.

As might be expected, a microscopical examination of the particles of dust scattered over the surface of the fruit and woody peduncles of grapes, reveals great differences in the number of these fertile particles at different periods of the vegetation of the grapes. As long as the grapes are green and the vine in full activity we find scarcely any, or, at all events, very few spores which seem to belong to ordinary fungoid growths. Towards autumn, however, when the grape is ripening and the leaves becoming yellow, fungoid growths and numerous productions of great fertility accumulate on the vine, on the leaves, the branches, and the bunches. At this period we find the water in which the grapes and the woody parts of the bunches are washed swarming with different kinds of organized corpuscles; it is at this period, too, that the ferment-

* Dr. Rees has given the name *saccharomyces ellipsoideus* to the ferment of wine represented in Plates VIII. to XI. of our "Studies on Wine," which we have termed the *ordinary* ferment of wine, from its being the most abundant of the ferments found at the end of the fermentation that produces the wine.

yielding moulds attain that phase of their vegetation in which, when mixed with the juice of grapes, they produce fermentation.

In the Jura district a peculiar kind of wine, called straw wine (*vin de paille*), is manufactured, which seems to contradict what we have said as to the advent of sterility towards the end of winter in the yeast-germs formed on the surface of preserved bunches of grapes. This straw wine is made of grapes preserved for long after the vintage on straw. From what we have said it might be supposed that fermentation could not occur under these circumstances. We have, in fact, no doubt that it is often really produced by quite different yeast-germs from those which cause fermentation in the vintage gathered in autumn. Fermentation as effected in the manufacture of straw wine is probably due to yeast-dust spread over the utensils of the vine-grower, and derived from the preceding vintage. We have seen (Chap. III. § 6) that yeast may be dried and reduced to powder, and yet preserve its faculty of germination for several months. It would be useful, however, to submit this surmise to the test of experiment, and it would be easy to do so provided we took care to crush the grapes so preserved in very clean vessels, previously heated to a temperature of 100° C. (212° F.), having first rejected every bunch containing injured grapes, which might have fermented or given occasion to the development of yeast. Fermentation, we believe, would not then take place.

Another consequence results from the various facts that we have brought out in relation to the origin of the wine-ferments, which is, that it would be easy to cultivate one or more vine-stocks so that the grapes gathered from them, and crushed to extract their juice, would be unable to ferment spontaneously *even in autumn.* For this purpose it would be sufficient to keep the bunches out of contact with particles of dust during the vegetation of the bunches and the ripening of the grapes, and then to effect the crushing in vessels thoroughly freed from germs of alcoholic ferments. Moreover, every fruit and

Pl X.

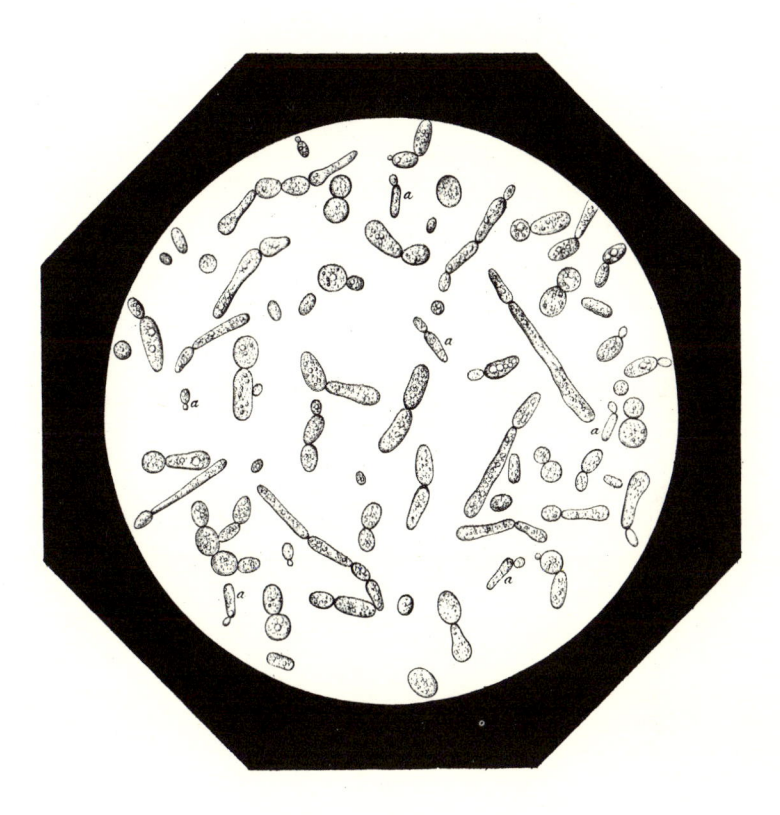

$$\frac{400}{1}$$

Deyrolle del.   Picart sc

every vegetable might be submitted to important investigations of this kind, the results of which, in our opinion, could hardly be doubtful.

The following observations, which relate to the polymorphism of *saccharomyces pastorianus*, seem to me to have an important bearing on the history of alcoholic ferments, as presenting a close analogy between the species of ferment and fungoid growths of a higher order, for example, such fungi as *dematium*, which are generally found on dead wood; and we would say that between the vine and other shrubs there is only this difference, that amongst the *dematium* forms of the vine there occur one or more which are anaërobian, at a certain period of the year, whilst, on the other hand, the *dematia, alternaria*, &c., of other shrubs are more generally aërobian. There would be nothing surprising in this result, considering that amongst the mucors, for instance, we find both aërobian and anaërobian forms, and that there are likewise torulæ-ferments or anaërobian forms, as well as torulæ-forms exclusively aërobian.

When *saccharomyces pastorianus* begins to develop from its natural germs, such as are scattered over the surface of acid fruits, it takes the form of elongated jointed filaments, branching, often pear-shaped, and more or less voluminous. In proportion as the oxygen held in solution in the liquid disappears and the buddings are repeated, the length and diameter of the filaments and cells diminish, and such is the transformation that we might, at last, suppose that we were dealing with a different ferment of smaller dimensions.

Plate X. represents this ferment, at the commencement of fermentation in cherry juice. In the course of a short time there is nothing to be seen but cells of comparatively small size, disjointed and round or oval, and filaments comparatively short and slender. This appearance is indicated in our drawing by the cells *a, a, a*. As these latter forms multiply with great rapidity, we soon have to search widely over the microscopic field before we find any of the long forms from which they spring. Instead of the forms given in Plate X., we have only those represented in Plate XI. In other words, the aspect of these ferments changes daily, from the very commencement of fermentation. Thus the yeast would appear to grow smaller, coincidently with the progress of fermentation passing from a condition in which it consists of large cells and long ramified filaments, to a condition in which the cells are small and the filaments short. These changes are principally due to an alteration in the method of budding and in the life-processes of the yeast, which speedily exhibits itself when the air supply is reduced, and not through any intermixture of foreign ferments. So, at least, all our observations up to the present time lead us to believe. As soon as the oxygen has been absorbed the cells which form are oval or globular, and the filaments do not lengthen or become so plump.

This is, however, not the only cause of these changes in form and aspect, although the presence of air, in greater or less quantity, has a marked influence on the earlier developments of yeast; there is another circumstance to be taken into account, difficult indeed to state shortly, but which is demonstrated clearly by the microscope, and is connected with the actual state of the germ cells. As a general rule the budding of a cell is not an identical process when the cell is quite young, and when it has become exhausted from want of nourishment. Between these two conditions there is a difference which may be compared with that which exists, for example, between a newly-formed grain which would not germinate, and the same grain matured by rest, if we may use the expression, that is, which has been kept long enough for its germination to be possible. In other words, and as far as our subject is concerned, we are not to expect that, by reviving our old yeast cells and putting them to grow with abundance of air, in a saccharine, nutritive medium, we shall obtain the appearance of the earlier developments of the germ-cells on the surface of sweet and acid fruits. We see this clearly in Plate VII., the right-hand half of which represents the recruited budding of cells, such as those

Pl. XI

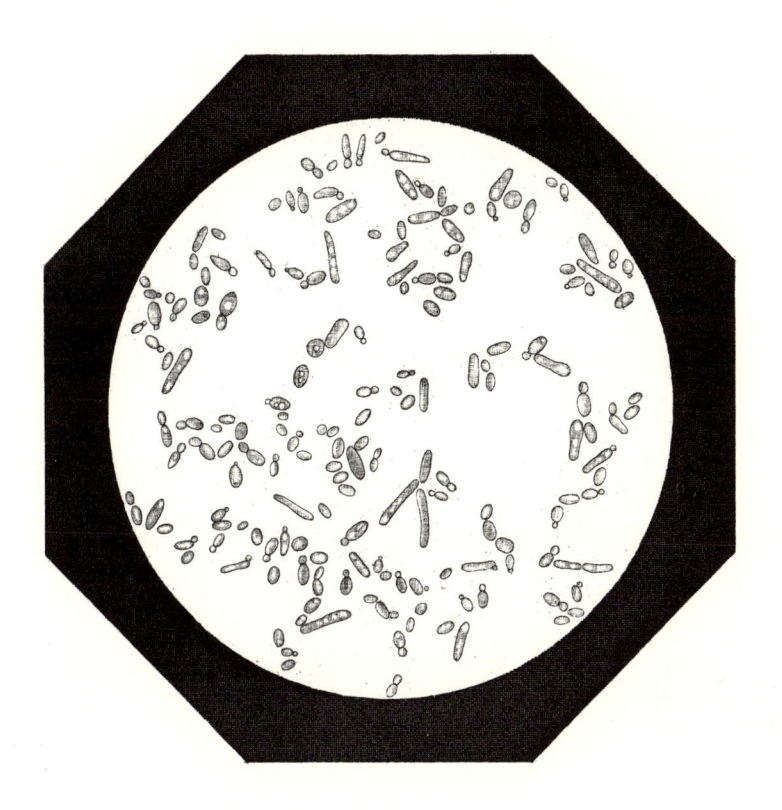

$\frac{400}{1}$

Lackerbauer del. E. Hellé sc.

Imp. Geny-Gros, Paris

represented in the left-hand half, in a medium peculiarly adapted to their vitality, *and in the presence of much air*. As regards the length and size of filaments and cells, there is little appreciable difference between the two sides. The principal difference consists in the relative freshness and the budding going on in individuals in the right-hand half.

There is a simple means of transforming the small, disjointed forms of the yeast as it occurs in a deposit, at the end of a fermentation, back into the long, tubular, pear-shaped forms peculiar to the germination of the germ-cells, which exist amongst the particles of dust spread over the surface of fruits. Plate X. illustrates the result of the process. For this purpose we must effect as complete an exhaustion as possible of the ferment *saccharomyces pastorianus*, by leaving it to itself for a very long time, without aliment, in contact with pure air, in a damp state; or, better still, in presence of sweetened water. We cultivate some yeast in wort, in one of our two-necked flasks, and then carefully decanting the fermented liquid through the right-hand neck, leave the deposit of yeast on the sides of the flask. The glass stopper which closes the india-rubber tube must be replaced, and the moist yeast be left thus, in contact with pure air. The cells will steadily continue their activity, and so gradually age, without meanwhile losing their vitality. We use the word *age*, as we have already observed, because the period of rejuvenescence in the case of such a yeast is so much the slower the longer the plant has remained in that state.

Under these conditions the yeast rarely dies. It becomes attenuated and shrivelled but still preserves its vitality, that is, the power of reproducing itself after a lapse of several months or even several years. In the end, however, it dies, a fact which is proved by the cells, when sown in a nutritive medium, remaining inert.

To exhaust yeast, without destroying it, sweetened water is preferable. Having decanted the beer, we substitute in its place water sweetened with 10 per cent. of pure sugar. By effecting the substitution in the following manner, we escape the risk of introducing germs from floating particles of dust, which would nullify all experiments of this kind. We prepare, then, a flask containing sweetened water, free from all foreign germs, which we attach to the other flask [*i.e.*, two of M. Pasteur's flasks with two necks, one straight and wide, the other bent and narrow (Fig. 8)]. This is done by taking the india-rubber tube off the flask containing yeast, and removing the glass stopper from the other india-rubber tube attached to the flask containing the sweetened water; then, introducing the right-hand neck of the yeast flask into the india-rubber tube connected with the other, we raise the latter flask so as to pour the sweetened water on to the yeast. At the same time an assistant passes the flame of a spirit-lamp over the bent part of the curved tube attached to the water flask, with the object of destroying the vitality of the germs in the floating particles of dust, which enter the flask in proportion as it is emptied into the other.

The sweetened water, which is thus brought into contact with yeast of greater or less freshness, soon begins to ferment. Fermentation accomplished, the vinous liquid is decanted and replaced by fresh sweetened water, which ferments in its turn, although even at this stage with greater difficulty than the first; this second dose is again decanted, and again replaced by fresh sweetened water, and this process is repeated three or four times. The yeast becomes weaker and weaker, and eventually is unable to cause any fermentation in sweetened water poured on it.

This exhaustion of yeast in sweetened water may be produced more quickly by the following means:—It is sufficient to sow a mere trace of pure yeast in a large quantity of sweetened water, say 100 c.c. (nearly four fluid ounces), that is, instead of pouring the contents of a bottle of sweetened water upon the whole deposit of yeast in the flask which contained the fermented wort, we simply take a little yeast, by means of a fine tube, from the deposit at the bottom of the flask, and introduce it into the flask of sweetened water. This large proportion of liquid is itself sufficient to exhaust the small quantity of yeast, quickly checking the feeble fermentation which it had induced, so feeble indeed as frequently not to be detected by the eye, from the fact that the amount of liquid present is more than sufficient to dissolve any bubbles of carbonic acid gas that might otherwise have been liberated.

It is a remarkable fact that the yeast, which during its protracted stay in the sweetened water becomes enfeebled to such a degree that it can no longer excite the least fermentation in that water, but will remain in its presence for an indefinite time in a state of inert dust, does not die. In some of my experiments the yeast has remained alive in the sweetened water for more than two years.* It is almost unnecessary to point out that these results are altogether out of keeping with the various properties that are usually attributed to yeast.†

In these experiments we may use yeast-water ‡ instead of water sweetened with sugar. Into some flasks of pure yeast-water we put a little yeast, taking all precautions to prevent the introduction of foreign germs. No fermentation results, there being no sugar present; the yeast, however, begins to bud, and this budding is more or less marked according to the quantity

* The alcoholic ferments in general, subjected to these weakening influences, have not all the same power of resistance. That one which seems to possess this power in the highest degree is the *saccharomyces pastorianus*, which ferment we had in view in writing the above.

† The term *exhaustion* (*épuisement*), which we have just used, was, perhaps, not altogether felicitously chosen. No doubt we exhaust the cells of yeast when we sow an imponderable weight of them in a large quantity of sweetened water; it might, however, be better to say that in such a case we adopt a particular method of preserving the vitality of the cells, without suffering them to die of exhaustion, or to multiply by budding. We may remark that the yeast, in this case, exists in a state of latent life, which resembles that of cells on the surface of fruit. The cells on the surface of fruits, bunches, or barks, can no more find around them sufficient aliment for their propagation than can our yeast-cells in a great excess of sweetened water. We would not, however, say of the spores on the surface of fruits, or their woods, that they are in a state of exhaustion; the term would be misapplied.

‡ See foot note p. 79.—D. C. R.

of carbohydrate food which we introduce along with the specimen. An interior chemical action also goes on, causing a gradual change in the aspect of the yeast. The plasma of the cells collects about the centres, assuming a yellowish-brown colour, becoming granular, and forming within the cells masses more or less irregular in shape, very rarely spherical.

We may observe here that these conditions seem to be peculiarly adapted to show the character of the interior sporulation of the cells discovered by Dr. Rees. Notwithstanding this we have never succeeded in finding it distinctly, under these circumstances.

The fact which should claim all our attention, we repeat, is, that this exhausted, shrivelled-up, aged-looking yeast preserves its faculty of germination for several years; that, moreover, this faculty may be aroused by placing it in aërated nutritive media, in which case it will exhibit all the peculiarities which, under similar conditions, characterize some of the germ-cells found on the surface of our sweet domestic fruits. In other words, this yeast, instead of multiplying, as it always does in the course of several growths in saccharine musts, in the form of cells which detach themselves readily as soon as they have nearly attained the form and size of the mother-cells, begins to shoot out into such beautiful forms as those of *dematium pullulans*, producing like that ferment long, well-grown, branching filaments, as well as plump and frequently pyriform cells, as represented in Plate X.

The following figures (33 to 37) and descriptions of the observations to which they relate will furnish fresh proofs of our assertions. In these figures we see *saccharomyces pastorianus*, which has been exhausted in sweetened water or in yeast-water, undergo revival in saccharine musts, give rise to elongated, branching, pear-shaped forms, such as belong to the original ferments of fruits, and afterwards assume the most minute forms that we find in fermentations progressing or completed.

Let us examine Fig. 33. The history of this growth is as follows:—

STUDIES ON FERMENTATION. 173

Some spontaneous yeast which, after repeated cultivation, had acquired the aspect represented in Plate XI.—which aspect the *saccharomyces pastorianus* generally assumes under these circumstances—was exhausted in sweetened water, and subsequently revived in must at 10° C. to 11° C. (51° F.). At this temperature germination was not very marked before the end of eight days ; at a temperature of 20° C. (68° F.), it only took three days, under similar conditions. The sketch includes but one

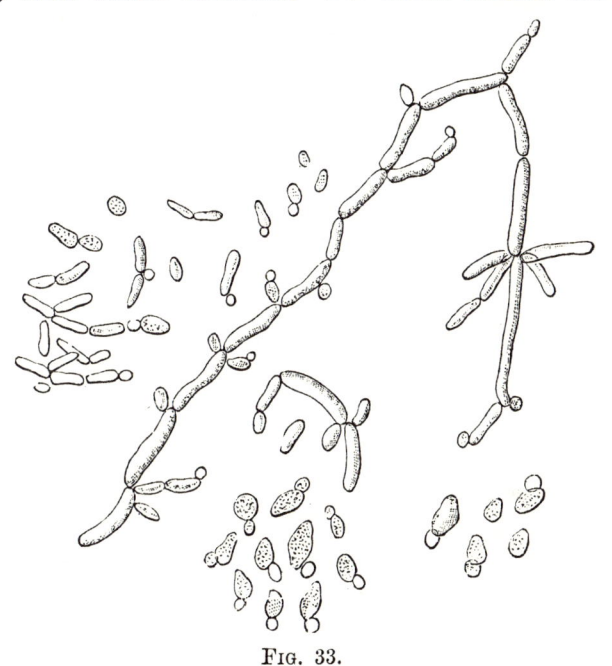

FIG. 33.

of the long branches from which the ferment cells and the budding joints took rise, but there were a great number more. Some of the forms represented in the figure bear a striking resemblance, it appears to us, to some of those of *dematium*, in Plate IX. ; and even we may trace out the several peculiarities of form which distinguish the figures in the latter plate.

The next figure (34) represents the earliest forms of germination of another specimen of *saccharomyces pastorianus* in

174   STUDIES ON FERMENTATION.

wort, after it had been exhausted by four successive growths in sweetened water. We here see the large ferment-form which appears at the commencement of fermentation, in acid fruits, such as cherries and gooseberries (Plate IX.), associated with smaller forms, which follow it and emanate from it, in proportion as the process of budding is repeated. The field was covered with this minute form, and we had to search about considerably before we could find any of the large cells and the long, branching, jointed filaments which we have sketched. The reason of this was, that these large, extended

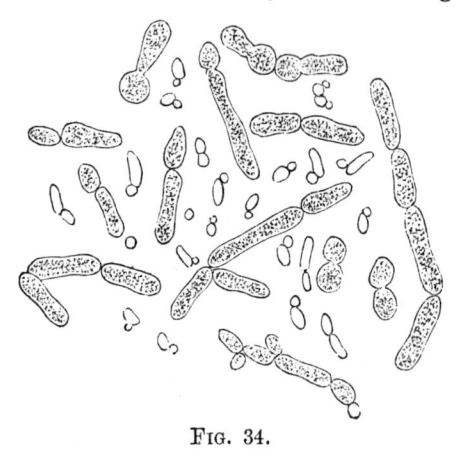

FIG. 34.

filaments only appear at the beginning, when there is still an abundance of air, giving place, after repeated budding, to minute cells or short filaments, the ever-increasing number of which soon hides the others from sight.

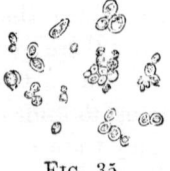

FIG. 35.

Fig. 35 represents *saccharomyces pastorianus* again, as it appears after having been exhausted by two years preservation in yeast-water, in contact with pure air. Strange to say, it has lost its elongated appearance, and would appear to have originated from a round ferment. The cells are much exhausted, and most of them seem to have a double border; their interior is very granular and of a yellowish colour. One might readily take the specimen to be a dead old ferment, which, however, it by no means is.

Fig. 36 represents the germination of this ferment, which had previously been revived in a flask of wort, at the temperature of the air, in May, 1875. The following are the details of our observation:—

We sowed a trace of the exhausted yeast (Fig. 35) in a flask of wort on May 16th. The sketch (Fig. 36) was made on May 19th, but on the 18th there was a sensible revival. It will be seen how much the little ferment had developed in the course of three days from the time when the process commenced. If we had waited a few days longer before taking our sample, we should probably have had difficulty in finding any cells or filaments of the large ferment form, as there would have been so few of them in comparison with the others.

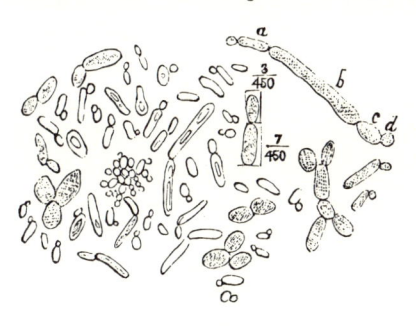

Fig. 36.

In the above figure we should remark the chain of large cells and long-jointed processes, *a, b, c, d :* *d* is one of the cells that we sowed; it has become transparent, and its contents, which are slightly granular, have lost their brownish tint; *c* is a large cell which sprang from the preceding one; its outline is clear, and it is full of fine, yellowish granules, which present a perfect resemblance to the large ferment-cells of fruits, proceeding from the germ-cells on the surface of those fruits, when it begins to appear in sweet juices; *b* is a long filament, sprung from the preceding cell; and, last of all, *a* is a joint and its bud, in which the border is not yet very clearly defined; it has scarcely any granules, and is finer than the others, belonging, in short, to the small ferment form represented in Plate XI. Here, then, we see the transition of the large ferment to the small, on the same branch, after two generations from the germination of the germ-cell *d*. This observation corroborates the opinion maintained by us, that in Figs. 33, 34, 36, as in Plate X., we have not a mixture of two ferments, the one consisting of large, elongated filaments, the other of small cells, but one and the same ferment, the differences in the form and size of which depend on particular conditions. The smallest ferment-form very soon becomes the only one visible, and it preserves its peculiar appearance in successive growths from inability to return to the full, elongated, filamentous forms before undergoing a prolonged exhaustion. The ferment of *mucor* would probably afford similar indications: it would be very interesting to find out.

The following is one of the most curious of the forms presented by *saccharomyces pastorianus*, occurring after exhaustion in a sweet mineral liquid. The ferment, taken from a closed vat, in which it had been used for beer, was sown in the mineral liquid on July 4th, 1873. The following days the ferment developed feebly, but perceptibly, and gradually increased in bulk. The flask was left to itself in an oven at 25° C. (77° F.) until December 3rd, when we ascertained that all the sugar had fermented. We then sowed a trace of the deposit, which had become abundant, in a flask of pure wort. On December 4th there was no perceptible change. On December 5th, however, fermentation was in active progress; a large quantity of froth covered the surface of the liquid, and a considerable deposit of ferment had already taken

STUDIES ON FERMENTATION. 177

place at the bottom. We made a microscopical examination of this deposit, a sketch of which we append (Fig. 37). The dark, double-bordered cells are those which were sown but did not rejuvenesce. We may notice in different places several

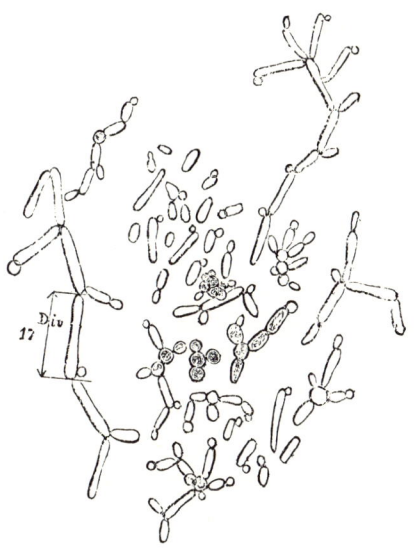

1 Div. = $\frac{1}{450}$th of millimetre ($\frac{1}{11250}$th of in.).
FIG. 37.

of these same cells, recognizable by their granular contents, which they are beginning to lose, to make room for germinating cells and joints, often numerous. For instance, in the group at the bottom of our figure one of the cells is in course of rejuvenescence and germination, and has given rise to no fewer than six cells, filaments, or groups of filaments. In different fields of our microscope we met with a crowd of branches, more or less ramified, and chains of cells, of greater or less length, of which we have sketched a few. In proportion as the budding of these branches is repeated, the cells and joints become more readily disunited, grow small, and assume the appearance of *saccharomyces pastorianus* in ordinary

N

growths, almost as represented in Plate XI. At first, when the old, exhausted cells begin to germinate, their appearance rather resembles that of *dematium pullulans,* as seen in the germination of many of the corpuscles on the surface of clusters of grapes or fruits, or their woody parts, some specimens of which are to be found in Plate IX.

We may briefly summarize the leading facts demonstrated in the above paragraph. We have seen that there are different alcoholic ferments. In the fermentation of natural saccharine juices, which, especially when acid, so readily undergo a decided alcoholic fermentation, the ferments originate in certain germ-cells, which are spread in the form of minute spherical bodies of a yellow or brown colour, isolated or in groups, over the exterior surface of the epidermis of the plant, and which are gifted with an extraordinary power of budding with ease and rapidity in fermentable liquids. The presence of atmospheric oxygen is indispensable to the germination of these germ-cells, a fact which explains Gay-Lussac's observation that atmospheric oxygen is necessary for the commencement of spontaneous fermentation in must.* Of these

---

* M. Béchamp (*Comptes rendus*, November 18th, 1872) asserts that *the air has no direct influence on the production of ferment or on the process of alcoholic fermentation.* That experienced chemist deduces this erroneous assertion from experiments on sweetened water, to which bunches of grapes, petals of corn-poppies and petals of *robinia pseudo-acacia* had been added. As may be seen in our "Studies on Wine" (p. 7, 1st edition, 1866), these experiments conducted by M. Béchamp in 1872 were merely a reproduction of those made long before with vine leaves, petals of elder-flowers, leaves of sorrel, &c., by the Marquis de Bullion, Fabroni, and other experimentalists. M. Béchamp has modified his later experiments by not adding the bunches of grapes, leaves, &c., to the sweetened water before having introduced carbonic acid gas into the liquid. Fermentation having still taken place in spite of this change, M. Béchamp wrongly concluded that *air has no direct influence on the production of yeast on an alcoholic fermentation.* The introduction of the carbonic acid gas could not remove all the air imparted to the sweetened water by the objects placed in it, and it was this air which remained adhering to these objects that permitted the production of fermentation. We may avail ourselves of the opportunity here presented to add that, in this same

various ferments one deserves special mention—namely, the variety termed *saccharomyces pastorianus*. As is the case with all ferments, when we gather it from the deposits produced in must that has been fermented by its action, it is composed entirely of oval or spherical cells or of short joints. When again placed in a similar must it buds, like all the ordinary ferments, and the buds detach themselves from the joints or mother-cells as soon as they have attained the size of these latter, from which time in the new deposit is reproduced the original ferment-form from which it sprung, and so on. Under certain conditions of exhaustion, however, which may be easily obtained, and which we have already accurately described, the cells undergo an absolute change as regards their capabilities of budding and germinating. Each cell, modified in its structure by the conditions we have mentioned, shows a tendency to shoot out all around its surface, with astonishing rapidity, into a multitude of buds, from many of which spring branching chains, covered in parts, and more especially at the internodes, with cells and jointed filaments, which fall off and bud in their turn, soon to present the forms of the yeast deposit. In this way *saccharomyces pastorianus* seems to afford a kind of bond of union between the race of ferments on the one hand, and certain kinds of ordinary fungoid growths on the other. Of these latter the plant which De Bary has named *dematium*, and which is generally found on the surface of leaves or dead wood, more especially, however, on the wood of the vine at the end of autumn, the time of the vintage, presents a striking example.

There seems every reason to believe that at this period of the year one or more of the varieties of *dematium* furnish cells of yeast, or even that the ordinary aërobian varieties of

Note of November, 1872, M. Béchamp commences by making various assertions concerning the forms assumed by cells of the alcoholic ferment of the grape when in process of fermentation. This question was discussed by us ten years before, and our conclusions supported by sketches, in a Note which appeared in the *Bulletin de la Société chimique de Paris*, for 1862.

dematium produce at a certain stage of their vegetation, in addition to aërobian cells and torulæ, other cells and torulæ which are anaërobian, that is, alcoholic ferments.

In this manner we arrive at the confirmation of an idea entertained by most authors who have studied yeast closely—namely, that it must be an organ detached from some more complex vegetable form. We may also add that in the case of *saccharomyces* the chains of filaments, both tubular and fusiform, and septate cells more or less pyriform originating in them, when attentively observed, remind us forcibly of the filamentous chains and spore-balls, or conidia of *mucor racemosus* when submerged, so that one might suppose that the spore-ferment of our *dematium* is itself an organ detached from some still more complex vegetable form, in the same way that conidia-ferment of *mucor racemosus* belongs to that more complex fungoid growth.

In the following passage De Bary uses, for the first time, the words *dematium pullulans* (Hofmeister, vol. ii. p. 182, 1866). The German naturalist begins by citing the opinions of Bail, Berkeley, and H. Hoffmann, the first of whom maintains that *mucor mucedo* becomes transformed into the yeast of beer, the second that yeast is a peculiar state of *penicillium*, and the third that it may be generated by fungi of very different nature, and especially by *penicillium glaucum* and *mucor mucedo*. He goes on to say: "I have taken great pains to repeat the experiments of Bail, Berkeley, and H. Hoffmann, but I have never been able to confirm the results which they have stated, either in the case of growths in microscopic cells or in experiments performed in test-tubes with the purest possible substances—specially prepared solutions or must of wine and spores of penicillium, *mucor mucedo, botrytis cinerea*, &c." On this point M. De Bary arrives at exactly the same results which we communicated to the *Société Philomathique* and the *Société Chimique* of Paris, as already given in Chap. IV. § 4, p. 128, note.

M. De Bary goes on to say: "In researches of this kind

it is difficult to eliminate two sources of error. On the one hand, it is beyond doubt that cells of ferment are actually scattered over everything, and that, consequently, they may easily get into the experimental liquid along with the spores that we sow, and so occasion mistakes.* On the other hand, there are a great many fungi which develop budding processes similar to yeast, but incapable of producing fermentation, which yet in some cases spring directly from spores as well as from mycelium, especially we may instance *exoascus*. This last observation is especially applicable to the extraordinarily numerous variety of fungi which rank under the Dematiei and Sphaeriacei, and which I shall term, for convenience of naming, *dematium pullulans*.

We shall conclude this paragraph with a remark that has doubtless presented itself to the minds of our readers, which is, that it would be impossible to carry out the experiments we have described if we could not make sure of dealing with pure ferments, or, at least, with mixtures the components of which are sufficiently well known for us to assign to each the effect produced by it in the total phenomena observed. It would be extremely difficult to continue growths of yeast-deposit in sweetened water or in a moist atmosphere if the little plant were mixed with spores of other fungoid growths, a variety of ferment-forms, and germs of bacteria, vibrios, or

* The germs of ferments are less widely diffused than M. de Bary supposes, as may be seen from our observations in Chap. III. See, too, our Memoir of 1862, *Sur les Générations dites Spontanées*, p. 49. It is only in a laboratory devoted to researches on fermentation, or places such as vaults, cellars, and breweries, that the air holds appreciably in suspension cells of ferments, ready to germinate in saccharine media. If we except these particular circumstances, ferment is not very largely diffused, save on the surface of fruits and the wood of the trees which bear them, and perhaps, also, on some other plants. The particles of dust held in suspension in any atmosphere whatever rarely produce fermentation in pure must even when we take all possible precautions, so that the action be not overlooked; for true fermentation may be hidden by fungoid growths, when there is much air and but a small quantity of saccharine liquid present.

infusoria in general. All these foreign organisms would tend to develop just in proportion as the conditions of the media were more or less favourable to their growth, and, in a very few days, our flasks would be filled with swarms of beings which, in most cases, would entirely conceal the facts relating to those forms, the separate study of which it was our object to follow out. We shall have occasion, therefore, to examine, in a subsequent paragraph, the preparation of ferments in a state of purity. At present we may state that yeast, which in its ordinary condition is a mass of cells so liable to change that its preservation in a moist state is impossible, manifesting in the course of a few days during the winter, and in twenty-four hours during the heat of summer, all the signs of incipient putrefaction, thereby losing its distinctive characteristics, is nevertheless capable, when pure, of enduring the highest atmospheric temperatures for whole years without showing the least signs of putrid change or contamination with any other microscopic organisms, and without the cells losing their power of reproduction. In the presence of facts like these, the theory of spontaneous generation must seem chimerical. The hypothesis of the possible transformation of yeast into *penicillium glaucum*, bacteria, and vibrios, or conversely, which the theories of Turpin, H. Hoffmann, Berkeley, Trécul, Hallier, and Béchamp involve, is equally refuted by these facts.

§ II.—On "Spontaneous" Ferment.

The expression *spontaneous ferment* may be applied to any ferment that appears in a fermentable liquid without having been purposely sown in it. In this respect the ferments mentioned in the preceding paragraph, those of all saccharine juices of fruit which ferment when left to themselves—the ferments of wine, for example—are spontaneous. The term, however, is not altogether appropriate, because, after all, the process is the same as if an actual sowing had been made, since, as we have shown, it is absolutely necessary for the juice to come into contact with the surfaces of the fruit, so that the ferment may be mixed with it, and so produce subsequent fermentation. Therefore, although we may apply the term *spontaneous ferment* to the ferments of fruits, we intend that expression to apply in this paragraph solely to those ferments that are generated in a saccharine liquid, in which, by previous boiling, we have destroyed all ferment germs, and which, nevertheless, enters into fermentation after being exposed in free contact with air. In such a case it is entirely from the particles of dust floating in the air that the ferment germs that appear in the liquid are derived. Such are typical *spontaneous* fermentations, and it is of the ferment so obtained that we are about to speak.

In the course of the researches which we undertook in order to ascertain whether *mycoderma vini*, or vinous efflorescence, became transformed, in the case of beer, into actual alcoholic ferment—researches which were the more protracted and varied in consequence of their leading to the condemnation as erroneous, on the faith of new and more precise experiments, such as those given in Chap. IV. § 2, of that transformation, in which we had for long believed—we had occasion to observe several spontaneous fermentations of this kind in various saccharine liquids. We then proceeded to describe our method of conducting the experiments. Having brought about the development of a film of *mycoderma vini* or *cerevisiæ* on the surface of a liquid, fermented or not, we submerged that film in wort, which we afterwards put into long-necked flasks, in which alcoholic fermentation generally took place in the course of a few days. This fermentation in no way resulted from the transformation of the cells constituting the efflorescence into ferment. The mycodermic film merely acted as a receptacle of true ferment germs, wafted thither with the particles of dust floating in the air of the laboratory, which germs developed in the liquid into actual alcoholic ferments amongst the cells of the submerged mycoderma. By conducting experiments in this manner we brought about several spontaneous fermentations, the germs of which could have been introduced by nothing but the particles of dust in the air. These fermentations, which we were obliged to follow very carefully with the microscope from the time when they first manifested themselves, on account of the transformation that we were seeking, which transformation we thought might possibly be that of the cells of *mycoderma vini* into cells of ferment, generally gave us during the first days of fermentation the large, elongated, branchy ferment represented in Plate X., which was succeeded by the small ferment represented in Plate XI.*

Here let me describe one of these experiments. In the beginning of March, 1872, we grew some *mycoderma vini*, obtained from wine, on some wort contained in a shallow basin. On March 6th we submerged the efflorescence and put it all together, liquid and film, into a long-necked flask. On March 9th we detected incipient fermentation, and on March 12th we took a sketch of the yeast of the deposit, as given in Plate XII. This is the large and long branching, more or less pear-shaped form, which occurs at the beginning of fermentation in the sweet and acid musts of our domestic fruits. On March 16th we made another sketch of the deposit, in which the proportion of cells, in the form of elongated segments and filaments, reminded us, in some measure, of the filamentous mycelium of typical fungoid growths much diminished. In this case, however, the majority of cells were oval, round, and in short segments. On this day, March 16th, we added some fresh wort to that which had fermented, with the object of prolonging the duration of

* In these experiments the apiculated ferment appeared sometimes, but much less frequently than *saccharomyces pastorianus*. We also met with the ellipsoidal ferment. We should probably have a greater variety of ferments if our experiments could be conducted in the open air, but insects and particles of dust of all kinds brought by the wind render experiments under such conditions difficult and untrustworthy. In a laboratory we have not these difficulties to contend against, but, unfortunately, the operations ordinarily carried on there cause the results of our experiments to be of a less general character than they would be if obtained in free contact with country air.

Pl. XI

Deyrolle del

$\frac{400}{1}$

E. Helle sc

Imp. Geny-Gros, Paris

fermentation and increasing the proportion of yeast. On March 19th we made a fresh sketch, which it is not necessary either to reproduce; suffice it to say, that the yeast was now considerably more regular and uniform in appearance.

Spontaneous ferment, therefore, very often occurs in this large ferment-form, which, by repeated developments in the act of fermentation, becomes reduced by degrees after successive generations to the ferment which, following Dr. Rees, we have named

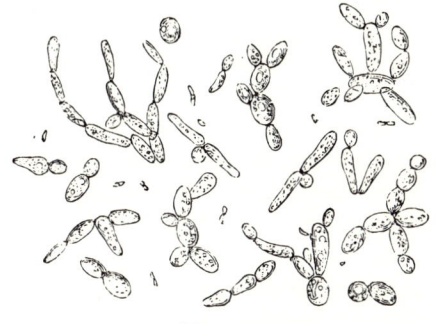

FIG. 38.

saccharomyces pastorianus, a polymorphous ferment which must be studied closely that it may not be confounded with others, inasmuch as it is so universally diffused that we very seldom fail to find it in any ferment which has been exposed in contact with ordinary air, at least, we may repeat, in a laboratory devoted to researches on fermentation. We have found the same thing occur in a brewery, being there mixed with the ferments used in brewing.

There are, no doubt, several varieties of this *saccharomyces*. We sometimes find amongst the spontaneous ferments which repeated growths have brought to a more or less uniform state, the forms represented in Plate XI., but the cells and segments much smaller. Amongst others, Dr. Rees has distinguished a *saccharomyces exiguus*.

Fig. 38 represents another spontaneous ferment, which appeared in a boiled saccharine wort, which entered into fermentation after being exposed to the air of the laboratory.

The sketch was made directly after the fermentation had commenced. Probably this is simply one of the earlier forms assumed by the *saccharomyces*, or by one of its varieties. It will be seen that the alcoholic ferment is associated with another little filiform ferment, probably the lactic. The spontaneous ferments are almost always impure, a circumstance that may be readily understood if we bear in mind the results described in Chapters III. and IV.

§ III.—On "High" and "Low" Ferments.

The ferments mentioned in the preceding paragraphs do not belong, properly speaking, to industrial products; that is to say, in actual practice there are no operations in which the ferments of fruits and spontaneous ferments are employed for the purpose. It is quite true that these ferments are the cause of the fermentations from which wine, cider, gin, rum, gentiana, mead, &c., are derived, but these fermentations are spontaneous, they take place without the intervention of man, and without man's directing their production, or taking any notice of the agent which starts them.

In the manufacture of beer, on the other hand, the practice is quite different. We may say that the wort is never left to ferment spontaneously, the fermentation being invariably produced by the addition of yeast formed on the spot in a preceding operation, or procured from some other working brewery, which, again, had at some time been supplied from a third brewery, which itself had derived it from another, and so on, as far back as the oldest brewery that can be imagined. A brewer never prepares his own yeast. We have already had occasion to remark that the interchange of yeasts amongst breweries is a time-honoured custom, which has been observed in all countries at all periods, as far back as we can trace the history of brewing. The yeasts which in the present day produce beer in the brewery of Tourtel, near Nancy, in that of Grüber, at Strasburg, that of Dreher, at Vienna, and others, came originally from breweries, where and when it would be hard to say. In the case of the first working brewery, the yeast was, no doubt, derived from some spontaneous fermentation, which took place in an infusion of barley that had been left to itself, or, from some natural spontaneous ferment, and nothing could be easier than to realize this fact again. In the brewing industry there are two distinct modes of fermentation :—" high " fermentation and " low " fermentation, some of the distinctive characteristics of which we have pointed out in Chapter I. It may be questioned whether the spontaneous yeast employed in the first brewery, or that which a wort left to itself in the present day would yield, would be of the " high " or " low " type. It may be concluded from what we have said on the subject of spontaneous fermentations in wort, that wort, left to itself, would furnish ferments more or less resembling those of wine. We have never obtained in spontaneous fermentations of wort either a distinctly " high " ferment, or a distinctly " low " one, properly so called ; nor, further, have we ever obtained either one of these distinct kinds, with its industrial characteristics, in experiments on the ferments of fruits. What, then, was the origin of the " high " and " low " ferments now used by brewers ? What was the nature of their original germs ? These are questions which we are unable to answer, but we are very much inclined to think that we have here another example of the modifications which plants as well as races of animals undergo, and which become hereditary in the course of prolonged domestication. We know nothing of corn in its wild state, we cannot tell what its first grain was like. We know nothing of the silk-worm in its original state, and we are ignorant of the characters of the race that furnished the first egg.

These reflections may seem to favour the supposition that there is a real difference between " high " yeast and " low " yeast, and that both of these differ from spontaneous ferments and the ferments of domestic fruits. These are propositions demanding most careful consideration, for it is generally admitted

188   STUDIES ON FERMENTATION.

that these ferments become intermixed, that their morphological differences are merely a question of medium, and that the transition of one to the other is a simple matter. The following facts seem to contradict such statements.

"High" Ferment.—Fig. 39 represents some "high" yeast

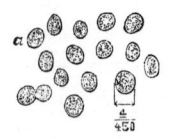

FIG. 39.

taken from a deposit after fermentation, and Fig. 40 the same yeast in course of propagation in some aerated wort. In comparing "high" yeast with other alcoholic ferments at the same stage of development, there are three points which are especially striking: the diameter of its cells is relatively large, their general aspect is rounder, and when they are undergoing propagation their mode of budding produces a markedly ramified appearance, so that the cells always occur in clusters and branches. Fig. 40 gives a very exact idea of these characters. To investigate satisfactorily the branching habit of growth peculiar to this ferment we should examine it during the first few hours of its propagation, when, under the influence of the oxygen dissolved in the fermentable liquid, its vital activity is greatest. Later on, often on the day following the sowing, the groups become disconnected, and at the end of the fermentation the cells have quite separated from each other, not more than 2 or 3 per cent. remaining united, and even these in groups of not more than two cells together. This is represented in Fig. 39.

To give an idea of the rapidity with which this ferment multiplies, we may state that our sketch (Fig. 40) was made under the following conditions:—On April 28th, 1874, we caused a flask of wort to ferment by means of a trace of "high" yeast. On the morning of the next day, that is

STUDIES ON FERMENTATION. 189

fourteen hours afterwards, an appreciable deposit of yeast had formed, and some frothy patches appeared on the surface of the liquid, showing that fermentation had set in. On May

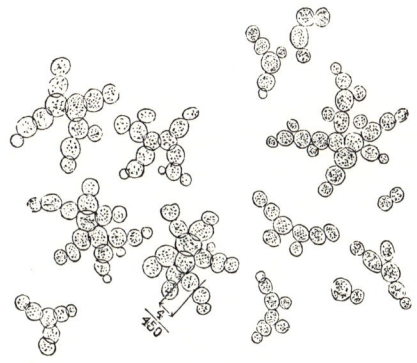

FIG. 40.

1st we decanted the beer, substituting for it water sweetened with 10 per cent. of sugar. On May 2nd we decanted the sweetened water, and substituted a fresh quantity containing the same percentage of sugar. On May 3rd, at mid-day, we took some of the fermenting liquid from this flask and put it into a flask of wort; five hours after the introduction of the ferment we made the sketch in question. The field is covered with branching clusters, the groups being sketched exactly as they occurred in the field. Their activity was due to the condition of the ferment, and to the perfect fitness of the nutritive medium for its vegetation. In sweetened water the budding of the cells was considerably less active; no branching groups of cells are to be found. Budding, nevertheless, occurs to a considerable extent, but it is limited to one bud, or two at the most, to each cell. Fermentation in pure sweetened water is mostly correlative with the duration of vital activity in the globules already formed.

Let us next suffer our yeast to exhaust itself by keeping it in a great excess of sweetened water for a very long time; we shall then be able to observe its process of revival, and see if we can find any facts analogous to those presented by *saccharomyces pastorianus* (Chapter V. § 1).

With this object in view, on May 6th, 1874, we impregnated two fresh flasks of sweetened water with some of the contents of the before-mentioned flask, which we had refilled with sweetened water on May 2nd. On May 13th we decanted the liquid, which was still very sweet, from one of these two fresh flasks, which could hardly be said to have fermented at all—the quantity of yeast in them being so small—and replaced it with some wort. Strange to say, on the morning of the 14th we found an appreciable growth of yeast, and a froth of carbonic acid gas on the surface of the liquid. The yeast therefore was not dead, although its fermentative powers had been exhausted. There was, however, no remarkable feature in connection with its revival, nor did we find the slightest trace of any of the elongated ferment-form. What we got was simply the ramified groups of "high" yeast again, in round cells, but nothing more.

Fearing that our yeast might not have remained for a sufficient time in the sweetened water for exhaustion, we set aside, for a whole year, the other flask which we had prepared on May 6th. On May 16th, 1875, we decanted the sweetened liquid and replaced it with wort. This time, however, there was no revival of the yeast; it had perished. Fortunately, we had also saved the flask of yeast and sweetened water which was prepared on May 2nd, 1874, as already mentioned, and in this case, as will be seen, the vitality of the yeast had not been extinguished, doubtless, in consequence of the formation of what we shall presently designate by the name of *aërobian ferment*. On May 16th, 1875, we decanted the liquid from this last flask, and replaced it with wort. On the next day the surface of the wort was covered with a thin froth, indicating the commencement of fermentation. The microscope revealed nothing extraordinary, or indicative of the fermentation of any special ferment. To assure ourselves that our ferment had remained "high," we sowed some of it in a fresh flask of wort on May 19th, and then, seven hours after impregnation, submitting it to examination, we could find nothing but ramified groups in fine condition, without a single elongated cell, indeed, it would have been impossible to find a more beautiful specimen of " high " yeast, or one of a more decided character.

It would seem, therefore, that "high" yeast cannot, under any circumstances, assume the form and character of the ferment *saccharomyces pastorianus*, or of other known ferments. We are justified, therefore, in regarding it as a distinct species of ferment, an opinion which is supported by other circumstances.

1. In equal quantities of saccharine wort a considerably greater growth of "high" yeast is obtained than of other yeasts. We need no very rigorous proofs to convince ourselves of this fact: for by simply causing equal volumes of the same wort to ferment, the one being pitched with *saccharomyces pastorianus*, for example, the other with "high" yeast, we shall obtain a perceptibly greater volume of "high" yeast than of the other, in certain cases even five or six times as much.

2. " High " yeast is of a tougher texture than the others, separating, when the fermented liquor and its deposit is shaken up, into lumps which refuse to disappear; whereas *saccharomyces pastorianus* diffuses through the whole liquid with the greatest ease.

3. " High " yeast produces a special beer, with a peculiar flavour, well known to consumers, but little esteemed at the present day. Hence the gradual displacement of breweries worked on the old "high" fermentation system by others in which " low " yeast (of which more anon) alone is employed.

4. Lastly, one characteristic of "high" yeast, which it shares in common with some other ferments, although not with all, and which, from a practical point of view, deserves special mention, is that as fermentation proceeds the yeast rises to the surface of the liquid. Whilst the process of the manufacture of beer by this ferment is going on, the yeast is seen to work out of the bung-holes, flowing over in considerable quantity. The ferment named after the author, as well as " low " yeast, does not possess this property: it remains

at the bottom of the vessels. When "high" fermentation takes place in vessels that are not filled, the ferment forms a thick layer, a kind of cap on the surface of the beer. This characteristic may be witnessed even in the fermentation of very small quantities of liquid. In our flasks, in which the volume of fermenting wort does not exceed 100 c.c. or 150 c.c. (about 4 or 5 fluid ounces), we may perceive, as the violence of fermentation subsides, and the head falls, the sides of the vessel covered to a height of from 1 cm. to 2 cm. (about ¾-in.) above the surface of the liquid, with particles of yeasty matter, in little masses, or in a thin film, raised to that height by the head, and left behind when that fell.

"Low" Ferment.—Whilst high yeast performs its functions in the breweries in which it is used at somewhat high temperatures—namely, between 16° C. and 20° C. (60° F. to 68° F.)—"low" yeast is never employed at a higher temperature than 10° C. (50° F.), and it is even thought preferable that it should not be subjected to more than 6° C., 7° C., or 8° C. (43° F. to 46° F.). At these comparatively low temperatures "high" yeast would have no perceptible action, whereas it is at such temperatures that "low" yeast best performs its functions.

In our Memoir on alcoholic fermentation, published in 1860, in the *Annales de Chimie et de Physique*, the idea of the identity of the two yeasts was accepted; but we had at that time made no special observations of our own on the subject.

Upon closer investigation we are inclined to believe that the two yeasts are quite distinct. We might keep our "high" yeast at the lowest temperatures that it can bear, and repeat our growths under these conditions; or, on the other hand, we might subject the "low" yeast to temperatures higher than those at which it ordinarily grows, without ever succeeding in changing the first into the second or the second into the first, supposing, of course, that each of our yeasts was pure to begin with. If they were intermixed the change in the conditions of development would cause one or the other to preponderate, and incline us to believe that a transformation had really occurred.

It is true that brewers generally are of a different opinion. Most of them assert that "low" yeast cultivated at a high temperature becomes "high" yeast; and conversely, that "high" yeast becomes "low" by repeated growths at a low temperature. Many have told us that they have proved this. Nevertheless it is our belief that the success of such transformation has been but apparent, attributable in each case to the fact, as we have just stated, of their having operated on a mixture of the two yeasts.

Mitscherlich, and various authors after him, have asserted that "high" yeast propagates by budding, and "low" yeast, on the contrary, by spores, formed by the endogenous division of the protoplasm of the cells, and set free by the rupture of the cell-wall, which then, increasing in size, assume the character of ordinary cells. But we have never been able to confirm this.

Fig. 41 represents a field of low yeast, taken from the deposit in a vat after the fermentation of the beer was finished. The granular matter mixed with the cells is altogether amor-

FIG. 41.

phous, although in many cases perfectly spherical. It is a product in no way related to this yeast (see Plate I., No. 7).*
"High" yeast and all the ferments of beer have this kind

* [A rather serious clerical error appears to have here crept into the original, for on referring to Plate I. and the letterpress descriptive of No. 7 (p. 5), we find it applies to a very formidable species of diseased ferment, whereas the author is here speaking of an amorphous deposit, harmless in character, and more or less associated with all yeasts. Doubtless No. 7 should stand No. 6, see p. 6.—D. C. R.]

of deposit associated with them. There is no doubt that confused observations as regards these minute bodies have been the cause of the error which we had to deal with in connection with a particular mode of reproduction of low yeast, as to which we have already fully expressed our views (Chap. V. § 1, p. 146).

Comparing Fig. 41 with Fig. 40 (p. 189), it may be seen that the general aspect of low yeast is distinguished, in its early stages, although in no very decided manner, from that of "high" yeast, by being slightly smaller and less round or spherical in its cells than the latter.* These differences, however, would escape an unpractised eye.

As to the case of "high" yeast, the deposits of "low" yeast after fermentation appear as scattered, isolated cells; we do not find more than two or three per cent. of united cells. Nevertheless the two yeasts present, as we shall see, quite marked differences in the character of their budding and multiplication.

On May 28th, 1875, we put a trace of pure, unicellular, "low" yeast, taken at the end of a fermentation, into a flask of wort. On May 29th, sixteen hours after impregnation, the temperature during the night having been 15° C. (59° F.), we made a sketch of the yeast before its development had become apparent to the naked eye. No perceptible development, that is to say, no visible deposit at the bottom of the liquid and formation of patches of froth on the surface, took place before May 30th. A mere glance at Fig. 42 will be sufficient to enable us to detect a considerable difference between it and Fig. 40, which represents the multiplication of the cells of "high"

* [We would here call the reader's attention to the following extract from Dr. Graham's appreciative review of this work in "Nature," January 11th, 1877. He says: "M. Pasteur seems to be in error in stating (p. 190, Fr. ed.) that the bottom yeast may be distinguished by being less spherical than top yeast. It is true that in London and Edinburgh yeast, the cells will be found usually round; hard water, however, such as that at Burton, or artificially made so, yields yeast in which the cells are distinctly ovoid in appearance, resembling very closely Bavarian bottom yeast."—D. C. R.]

yeast. The cells of the "low" yeast are slightly smaller and rather more oval, as we have already had occasion to notice, and the budding processes are considerably less ramified, in consequence of which there is a comparative absence of

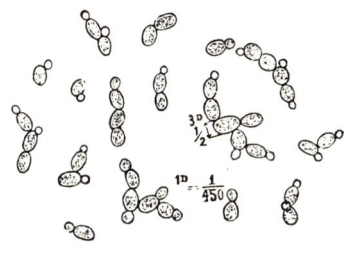

FIG. 42.

globular clusters which are so striking a feature in the development of "high" yeast, when examined early enough. Moreover, if we cause our "low" yeast to age, by leaving it for a longer or shorter time in the beer which it has formed, or if we exhaust it in sweetened water by leaving it for whole months in a volume of sweetened water considerably larger than what it is capable of fermenting, and then proceed to revive it and cause it to propagate in an aerated saccharine wort capable of nourishing it, this yeast will resume its original aspect, as sketched and described. At most we shall observe certain minute differences in the size of the cells in successive growths. A very remarkable industrial characteristic of this yeast is the fact that it never rises to the surface, no matter at what temperature it may be working, whether between 6° C. and 8° C. or 15° C. and 20° C.;* in other words, it is not buoyed up by the carbonic acid gas when the fermentation is at its height. At the end of the fermentation, the surface of the liquid and the sides of the vessel above the level of the liquid are clean and not covered with the yeast, which remains altogether at the bottom of the fermented liquid. Moreover,

* [43° F. to 46° F. or 59° F. to 68° F.]

the weight of new yeast which it yields is always less than that yielded by "high" yeast, for the same quantity of fermentable liquid, although greater than that which *saccharomyces pastorianus* would give. Lastly, the beer possesses a flavour and delicacy which cause it to be held in higher esteem by consumers than beers produced by means of other ferments.*

§ IV.—ON THE EXISTENCE AND PRODUCTION OF OTHER SPECIES OF FERMENT.

Our present knowledge of the alcoholic ferments embraces the following, without taking into account the ferment-form of *mucor* :—

The ferment named after the author, which is found associated with the ferments of the grape and other domestic fruits, and with spontaneous ferments in general.

The ferment of "high" beer.

The ferment of "low" beer.

To these must be added the ordinary ferment of wine, and that called *apiculatus*, although, indeed, these last are of little practical importance, since, in general, they soon become lost amongst others of greater vitality, in the spontaneous fermentation of fruits. These are not the only alcoholic ferments; a study of the germ-cells diffused over the surface of fruits, grains, and stalks of all vegetables in different countries, would doubtless lead to the discovery of many new ones. We are even inclined to believe that one ferment might give rise to a multitude of others. The investigations which we have undertaken in this direction are as yet not far advanced; we may, however, be allowed merely to state the principle which governs them. A ferment is a combination of cells, the individuals of which must differ more or less from each other. Each of these cells

* [On this point again Dr. Graham expresses some dissent ("Nature," loc. cit.) : " Here surely M. Pasteur must be thinking rather of the inferior products of the surface fermentation in France and Germany, than of those of England and Scotland."—D. C. R.]

has certain generic and specific peculiarities which it shares with the neighbouring cells; but over and above this, certain peculiar characteristics which distinguish it, and which it is capable of transmitting to succeeding generations. If, therefore, we could manage with some species of ferment to isolate the different cells that compose it, and could cultivate each of these separately, we should obtain as many specimens of ferments, which would, probably, be distinct from one another, inasmuch as each of them would inherit the individual peculiarities of the cell from which it originated. Our endeavours are directed to realizing this result practically, by first thoroughly drying a ferment and reducing it to fine powder. We have seen (Chap. III. § 6) that this mode of experiment is practicable, that in a powder composed of yeast and plaster the ferment preserves its faculty of reproduction for a very long time. If we now drop a small quantity of this powder from a sufficient height, and then, at a certain distance below the cloud of dust so formed, open several flasks previously deprived of air and containing a fermentable liquid that has been boiled, immediately closing them all up again, under such circumstances it is conceivable that some of the cells of yeast diffused in the cloud of dust, and separated widely in the act of falling, will enter some of our flasks singly, and there develop an appreciable weight of ferment, all the cells of which will have sprung from the same mother-cell. We have proved that flasks may be easily impregnated under these conditions, and our preliminary observations, although incomplete, seem to favour the idea that numerous varieties of ferment are to be obtained by these means.

Spontaneous ferments, properly so called, of which we have already spoken, are, after all, the result of sowings of this kind. Originating in liquids which have been boiled, and then left to themselves in contact with the air in a place where cells or germs must have existed, these ferments must necessarily often spring from single germs or from a limited few, and this also would probably be a means of developing distinct varieties of ferments.

Without dwelling longer on the practical consequences likely to result from the ideas which we have just expressed, we shall proceed to describe two new alcoholic ferments, which differ widely from those already mentioned.

New " High " Ferment.—We met with this ferment accidentally, under the following circumstances:—On February 12th, 1873, we had brewed in the laboratory about $2\frac{1}{2}$ hectolitres (rather over 50 gallons) of wort, 10 litres (about two gallons) of which were set aside to cool in a white-iron trough, and left during the night exposed to free contact with air in the underground part of the laboratory, where we have a small experimental brewery. Next day we put some of this latter into a bottle; the wort soon began to show evidence of change, various productions made their appearance on the surface of the liquid, and a deposit of yeast settled at the bottom. On May 23rd, perceiving bubbles of gas and a steady fermentation set up in the wort, which remained all the time corked up, and fearing that the bottle might burst by the increasing internal pressure, we drew the cork. A considerable liberation of gas at once took place, accompanied by a voluminous foam which half emptied the bottle. A microscopical examination of the deposit from the disturbed liquid led to the discovery of a very homogeneous yeast, associated with various other organisms; it was clearly a yeast which we had not hitherto met with amongst the spontaneous ferments which we had had occasion to study. Thinking that this might be a new species of ferment which would probably produce a beer that was also unknown, we set to work to purify it by cultivation in flasks of pure wort, during the months of May, June, and July. Our last growths, of August 4th, 1873, were preserved, in order that we might assure ourselves of the purity of the beer, and, consequently, of the ferment. On November 15th its purity was established. On that date we made some beer with this ferment, which had now been left to itself for several months in contact with pure air. The beer which we obtained resembled no known variety; consequently the ferment must

STUDIES ON FERMENTATION. 199

itself have been a distinct one, differing from others, especially those which we have been considering in this chapter.

Fig. 43 represents the rejuvenescence of this ferment.

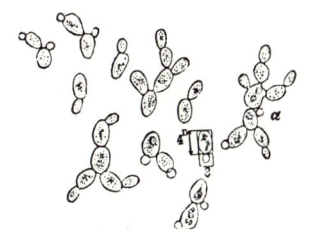

FIG. 43.

Comparing this figure with Fig. 42, we see that this ferment presents a considerable resemblance to "low" yeast in dimensions, method of budding, and oval shape; but the feature which distinguishes it essentially from "low" yeast is that it rises to the surface, like "high" yeast. Buoyed up by the gas during fermentation, it forms a layer of yeast on the surface of the fermenting liquid, where it remains after the head has fallen. Some of this head of yeast likewise adheres to the sides of the vessel above the level of the liquid.

In short, by the greater regularity of its forms and the uniform dimensions of its cells, this ferment is to be easily distinguished from *saccharomyces pastorianus;* its aspect, which is oval instead of spherical, and the ramified form of its chains of cells, which is less marked than in the case of "high" yeast, also prevent our confounding it with the latter ferment; in its *rising* character it differs absolutely from "low" yeast; lastly, it may be distinguished from all other ferments by the flavour of the beer that it produces.

The ferment which we discovered in this accidental way may be utilized. Indeed, we may ask, is it not to be found already in our beer? We are inclined to believe that it is. After the war of 1870, some Viennese traders established at Maisons-Alfort, near Paris, a manufactory of yeast for bakers. They saccharified by means of malt a mixture of the meals of rye,

maize, and barley, which they then caused to ferment. One
day we had occasion to study the yeast produced in this establishment, and although we did not submit it to a sufficient
number of consecutive experiments to enable us to speak
positively, we are under the impression that the yeast produced
at Maisons-Alfort is a "high" one, differing from what may
be properly termed the "high" yeast of breweries in which
"high" fermentation is practised, but presenting a great
resemblance to the "high" yeast of which we have been
speaking. It would be interesting to confirm the opinion of
their possible identity by fresh studies, and the best way of
doing this would be to compare the qualities of beer which the
two yeasts could produce.

Caseous Ferment.—We give the title *caseous* for a reason that
will presently appear, to a ferment which we came across also
accidentally. We were trying different methods of purifying
yeasts, and for this purpose had composed a liquid formed of:

Ordinary wort .. .. 150 c.c.*
Water saturated with bi-tartrate of potash .. 50 c.c.
Alcohol of 90° .. .. 25 c.c.

Quantities of this liquid were placed in several of our double-
necked flasks, submitted to boiling, then, after cooling, impregnated with different ferments, and kept in a water-bath at
50° C. (122° F.) for one hour.

In operating under these conditions with brewers' "high"
yeast, say, for instance, with what is called Dutch yeast, a kind
well known in distilleries, fermentation shows itself in the
course of a few days, in spite of the increased temperature to
which our liquid, which is hopped and slightly acid and
alcoholic, has been subjected. The time required for the
resumption of fermentation depends both upon the degree of
temperature to which the yeast has been exposed and upon the
duration of its exposure. These, however, are not the points

* [28·4 c.c. = 1 fl. oz. approximately.]

upon which we now wish to dwell. It is of greater importance to notice that the new yeast has none of the characteristics of "high" ferment, of which Dutch yeast seems to be exclusively composed, if we do not take into account impurities which cannot be avoided in a commercial product of this nature. Other specimens of Dutch yeasts would give the same results.

Figs. 44 and 45 represent this new ferment magnified to the same extent as the other ferments have generally been, that

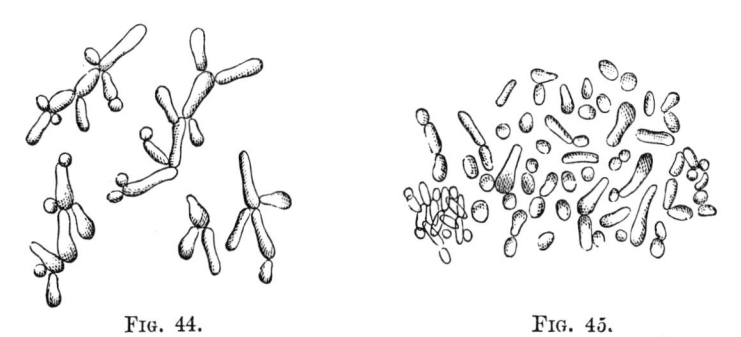

FIG. 44.   FIG. 45.

is $\frac{400}{1}$; it will readily be seen how different its form is from that of "high" yeast, how far it is from having the spherical aspect and mode of budding characteristic of that ferment. In Fig. 45 the ferment is represented in a mass; in Fig. 44 we see the ramified groups, the cells and segments of which form, after separation, the yeast of the deposit. It thus appears to be composed of jointed branches of greater or less length, which, at the junctions of the segments, put forth similar cells or segments of a round, oval, pyriform, cylindrical, or other shape; in all its characters recalling the description of *dematium*. Moreover, the cells and segments exhibit a greater sharpness of outline, as well as a more marked transparency and refractive power than are found in the majority of ferments; but the most curious physical characteristic of this ferment is its plasticity and elasticity, if we may use those terms. It can only be made to diffuse through water with great difficulty; when shaken up in it, it sinks to the bottom quickly as a clotted sediment, and the supernatant liquid appears scarcely at all charged with globules in suspension. Again, when placed on a microscope slide and compressed by the cover-glass, it returns to its original form on removal of the pressure. It is from these considerations that we have given to it the name of *caseous ferment*.* Lastly, this ferment produces a beer of a peculiar kind, which cannot be confounded with other kinds of beer known in the present day. We should add that it preserves its characteristics in repeated growths, and that we have never found it reproduce ordinary " high " yeast.

When caseous ferment is sown in a saccharine medium charged with mineral salts, its aspect, form, and mode of budding differ completely from what they are when the ferment exists in a natural medium, such as wort or other liquid adapted to the nutrition and life of ferments.

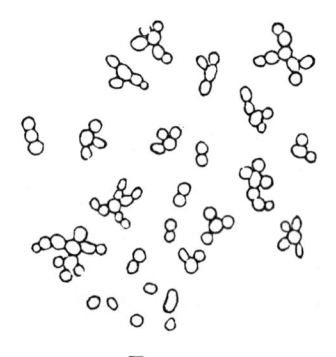

FIG. 46.

Fig. 46 represents this ferment in course of development, forty-eight hours after it had been sown in a saline medium (we employed Raulin's fluid, substituting bi-tartrate for the

* [M. Pasteur has evidently employed the word " caseous " to express the curdy nature of the ferment he is describing, its plasticity and other peculiarities of physical character; but we are, nevertheless, tempted to suggest that he may have had in mind also the peculiar " cheesy " odour given off by these very yeasts, which he refers to in the text as containing a considerable intermixture of " caseous ferment."—F. F.]

nitrate of ammonia). It will be seen how different its aspect is from that of the preceding figures; it is still capable, however, of resuming the forms of the latter if cultivated afresh in natural saccharine worts.

"High" yeast from a "high" fermentation brewery in the Ardennes, after having been exposed to heat under the conditions given above, likewise produced caseous ferment, without a trace of "high" ferment, just as happened in the case of the Dutch yeast. All the "high" yeasts used in brewing seem to behave in the same manner.

What conclusion are we to draw from these facts? Apparently that "high" yeast is modified by heat in an acid and alcoholic medium, giving rise to caseous ferment. On the other hand, it might be conceived that the "high" yeasts on which we experimented were not pure, but contained, in a state of intermixture, some caseous ferment, and that by the application of a temperature of 50° C. (122° F.) to our alcoholic medium, the high ferment was all killed and the caseous ferment alone survived. It is a remarkable fact that this latter hypothesis, improbable as it seems, inasmuch as the microscope revealed no intermixture of ferments, seems, nevertheless, to be a true one. As a matter of fact, if we subject to a temperature of 50° C. for one hour in the medium in which it acts, not the "high" yeast of commerce but "high" yeast that is *absolutely pure*, this will perish utterly, and the wort after cooling may remain for years in an oven without either undergoing fermentation or developing any growth whatever of "high" ferment or "caseous" ferment.

On the other hand, if we impregnate this same alcoholic liquid with some of the caseous ferment and then heat the vessel to 50° C. for one hour, the caseous ferment will go on reproducing itself after the liquid has cooled down.*

---

* The caseous ferment, however, must not be exposed to heat, under the afore-mentioned conditions, when it is too young. At the commencement of its development, for instance, within a few days of having been sown. In such case, it would be in danger of perishing, probably in con-

It seems, therefore, impossible to admit that caseous ferment results from a modification of "high" ferment, and we are led to believe that in the preceding experiments it must have been the progeny of cells of caseous ferment present in the "high" yeasts of commerce, which cells, probably in consequence of their scarcity, the microscope was unable to reveal, but which, nevertheless, did exist, and went on reproducing themselves alone after the heating.

This conclusion is supported by the following fact, which also tends to prove that in the case of the "high" English *pale ales*, caseous ferment plays a most important part. In the medium already described, we sowed the deposit from a bottle of good English pale ale. After having been heated the yeast went on growing, and we obtained the very beautiful specimen of caseous ferment represented in Fig. 47. The two dark globules

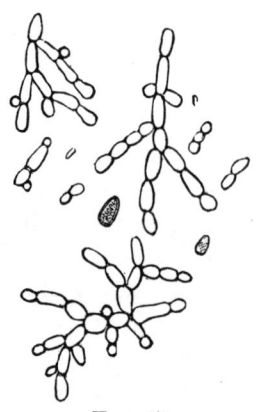

FIG. 47.

are dead cells which had been killed. Two minute segments of lactic ferment are also visible in the sketch—the yeast which we sowed was, of course, impure—and their presence

sequence of the tenderness of its tissues. At the end of a fermentation, and even several months afterwards, it might be safely heated to 50 C. (122° Fahr.) without any harm to it. "Low" yeast also can withstand a temperature of 50° C. in the medium in question.

proves, we may observe, by the way, that lactic ferment also can withstand a temperature of 50° C. (122° F.) in the medium which we here employed. The yeast as sowed is represented in Fig. 48; it reminds us forcibly of certain forms of the caseous ferment. Amongst the globules, which for the most part were transparent and very young, there were some which appeared aged and of a yellowish colour and granular. These

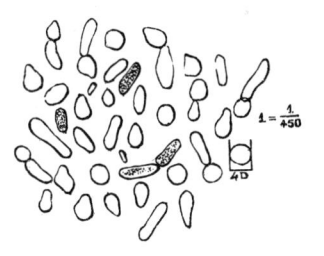

FIG. 48.

latter probably belonged to the yeast of manufacture. Their shape distinguishes them from "high" yeast, properly so called, as on the other hand it causes them to appear more like cells of a recent growth to which, there is no doubt, beer, after it is put in bottle, owes its effervescence and head. These various circumstances incline us to believe that the caseous ferment forms part of certain commercial yeasts, especially those used in the celebrated breweries of Bass and Allsopp, at Burton-on-Trent, in the manufacture of pale ale. Caseous yeast is, moreover, a "high" ferment, that is to say, it rises to the surface.

§ V.—ON A NEW RACE OF ALCOHOLIC FERMENTS: AËROBIAN FERMENTS.

Mention has already been made of certain researches which we undertook with the object of ascertaining whether *mycoderma vini*, or efflorescence of wine, and *mycoderma cerevisiæ*, or efflorescence of beer, which grow equally well in all fermented liquids, have the power of becoming transformed into actual alcoholic ferment. The result of those researches was stated to be that these mycodermata do not become transformed into ferment, properly so called, and that whenever any such transformation has been supposed to have taken place, the ferment produced was derived from germs introduced by the air or by the utensils employed. What we did ascertain of the ferment-producing power of *mycoderma vini*, was merely that this plant, when submerged, is capable of causing sugar to ferment, in consequence of a certain continuous life possible to its cells, apart from the oxidations resulting from the presence of free oxygen, but without any generation of new cells taking place.

Whilst engaged in these researches, we were pursuing others in relation to the converse of the proposition just discussed, that is to say, respecting the possibility of ferment becoming transformed into *mycoderma vini* or *mycoderma cerevisiæ*. Our experiments in connection with this subject chiefly consisted in various endeavours by way of exhausting the yeast and subsequent revival of its growth. This exhaustion was effected by growing the yeast in excess of sweetened water, and at other times in unsweetened yeast-water, our efforts being directed to deprive it of all power of fermenting. We afterwards caused it to develop afresh in highly aerated, nutritious liquids, in order that we might see how it reproduced itself, and if its new form were that of a mycoderma. The yeast after having lost its power as a ferment, and being no longer able to act in pure sweetened water, nevertheless reproduced itself when placed in fermentable media, holding in solution materials adapted to its nutrition; yet we never succeeded in obtaining any organism besides the ferment, and, indeed, the identical variety of ferment on which we had operated. In no case was *mycoderma vini* or *cerevisiæ* produced, and we concluded that we were justified in stating that whenever the *mycoderma vini* appeared on the surface of a fermented or fermentable liquid, its germ must have been introduced by the surrounding air, or have previously existed in the liquid, and that the reason why this germ multiplied so abundantly was because the liquid in question had been peculiarly adapted to the vitality of the plant.

In a laboratory where alcoholic fermentations are studied, these germs of *mycoderma vini* exist in great abundance on the surfaces of different objects. This fact admits of easy proof; we have merely to open in such a laboratory some flasks containing yeast-water deprived of air, or yeast-water sweetened, or any natural saccharine medium, or any fermented liquid, which till the moment when our flasks were closed had been kept boiling (Chap. IV.); it would be a very rare thing, indeed, if *mycoderma vini* did not develop in most of these flasks after the air was readmitted, especially if, shortly before this operation, the dust lying on the surface of the tables or floor of the laboratory had been stirred up by dusting or sweeping.

This series of experiments, the salient points of which we have just given, conducted with a view to ascertain whether yeast could be transformed into mycoderma, has led the way to certain results of special interest, results which concern all alcoholic ferments, and which in all probability will be found in the long run to apply to all aërobian ferments.

It being necessary for the conduct of our experiments to preserve our yeast in a state of purity for an indefinite period, often for a great length of time, in contact with pure air, we discovered that yeast was possessed of extraordinary vitality, and that it rarely perished completely throughout, inasmuch as we could almost invariably cause it to revive by bringing it into contact with fresh, fermentable liquid. This revival of the yeast—and it is to this point that we are most anxious to direct the attention of our readers—is effected from two distinct sources:—

1. By those cells of yeast which have not perished.
2. By cells of new formation.

We may give an example to explain this more clearly. In one of our two-necked flasks we cause some pure wort to ferment by employing yeast also in a state of purity. Fermentation completed, we leave the liquid to itself, not touching the flask again. The fermented liquor covers a deposit of yeast, apparently inert, and no trace of *mycoderma vini* makes its appearance on the surface of the liquid. Let us suppose that we go on daily for a considerable time introducing a little of the yeast from this flask to a different flask of wort: the fresh flasks will begin to ferment. The only appreciable difference which these successive flasks will present, their impregnation having been effected at intervals of twenty-four hours, will be that, *ceteris paribus*, fermentation in them will be more and more slow in making its appearance. This difference, as we have already explained, will be due to the fact that the yeast in the first flask will, in the course of time, undergo, in each of its cells, a process which we cannot better describe than as a progressive *senescence*. The cells gradually become filled with amorphous granulations, their interior becomes yellow, and the protoplasm collects, either at the centre or near the borders; in short, the vitality of the yeast becomes feeble. When, however, it is taken out of the liquid in which it has fermented and introduced into a fresh saccharine wort, it gradually resumes its transparency, and then begins to germinate. These effects are the less rapidly brought about the longer the cells remain exhausting themselves in the first fermented liquid. They might be left in that liquid for such a length of time that they would eventually perish, a fact which would manifest itself in their absolute sterility and quiescence when sown in a fresh medium. In general, however, matters are not carried far enough for this to take place, and the yeast, preserved in a state of purity in its fermented liquid, retains the capacity of revival, which may then go on indefinitely. As a matter of observation, the cells of yeast, after causing the liquid to ferment, instead of remaining inactive, and so by living at their own expense gradually passing into a state of exhaustion, begin to bud again; at least this is true of many of them. Multiplying afresh in the fermented medium, under the influence of the air, they form a kind of mycodermic film on the liquid surface, or a ring round the sides of the flask, on a level with the liquid. This development might often be mistaken for *mycoderma vini* or *cerevisiæ*; in reality there is not a single cell of *mycoderma* formed. If we sow a trace of the new growth in a saccharine medium it will behave exactly as yeast would, budding and multiplying, and setting up fermentation in the liquid. And thus, in spite of its mycodermic aspect, this growth is nothing but yeast, since it gives rise to true alcoholic fermentation; but it is a kind of yeast which, under the foregoing conditions, lives after the manner of fungoid growths, absorbing the oxygen of the air and emitting carbonic acid gas. It appears on the surface of all fermented liquids, especially those which, like beer, contain carbohydrates, and its quantity is the greater, and its action the more rapid, in proportion as it has more perfect access to the air. We have termed this yeast *aërobian ferment* or *fungoid ferment*.

It may easily be understood how this kind of production has escaped notice up to the present time. The conditions of our experiment were, in many respects, novel; a saccharine liquid had never before been caused to ferment by means of pure yeast, absolutely free from foreign germs; a fermented liquid had not previously been exposed to contact with pure air for an indefinite time. On the other hand, all ordinary fermented liquids, when left to themselves in contact with air, are a ready prey to *mycoderma vini* or *aceti* at their surface, and then give rise to true fungoid growths. The appearance of these organisms, which always takes place soon, has thus constantly concealed or prevented the development of the true aërobian ferments. In repeating the experiment described any alcoholic ferment may be used, and each one will be found to produce its own peculiar fungoid form of ferment. Another point worthy of notice is that these aërobian ferments, when they put forth buds in the act of fermentation, reproduce the forms of the original ferment, at least apparently so. In this respect they cannot be distinguished, notwithstanding the fact, sur-

P

prising as it seems, that the two kinds of ferments are not identical. If we operate on a "low" yeast its aërobian ferment will differ physiologically from the ferment from which it sprung, presenting various special peculiarities which are not to be found in the original "low" yeast. In most of our experiments we have found the new aërobian ferment to be similar in its action to "high" yeast, rising to the surface, and producing a beer which possesses a greater fragrance than beer brewed with the identical "low" yeast from which it was derived. Lastly, the properties of an aërobious ferment are not peculiar to first growth, but are hereditary; by repeating the growth of the first aërobian ferment we do not cause them to disappear, we find them again in succeeding generations.

Notwithstanding these facts, it would be difficult to discover any very appreciable differences between the forms of the cells of any particular yeast and those of its aërobian ferment in course of development. So true is this, that the aërobian ferment of *saccharomyces pastorianus* might even be caused to put on the forms of *dematium pullulans*, which we have had occasion to observe specially characterize this ferment after the cells have been subjected to a prolonged process of senescence.* This is evident from the following example, which will once

* Although we believe that the aërobian ferment of a particular yeast may be produced by a kind of transformation of the cells of the latter, yet we admit that this question is open to some doubt. The facts which we unexpectedly discovered in connection with the *caseous* ferment should make us extremely careful, and disposed to inquire whether aërobian ferments do not originally, in a state of intermixture, form part of the ferments from which they spring. One reason which might incline us to believe this, is the fact that a ferment sometimes perishes without the appearance of aërobian ferment on the surface. There is nothing very natural indeed in the hypothesis that we advance, which sets aside the supposed intermixture; but, on the other hand, if the aërobian ferment is a particular ferment, simply intermixed with some other variety and developed by change of conditions, how are we to account for its great resemblance in appearance and mode of budding to the ferment on the surface of which it appears? This resemblance, however, might be accounted for very naturally if the two ferments were originally related.

again show the remarkable extent to which the forms of a particular organism may be varied by changes in composition of the nutritive medium :—

On August 6th, 1873, we took some of the ferment *saccharomyces pastorianus* from a flask of wort that had undergone fermentation, and sowed a scarcely perceptible quantity of it in another flask containing a saline medium, composed as follows :—

Water containing about 10 per cent. of sugar-candy	150 c.c.	(5¼ fl. oz.)
Ash of yeast	0·5 gramme	(8 grs.)
Ammonic bitartrate	0·2 ,,	(3 grs.)
Ammonic sulphate	0·2 ,,	(3 grs.)

In the course of the following days the ferment began to develop, although with difficulty, the fermentation revealing itself by collections of bubbles appearing here and there on the surface of the liquid. We left the flask undisturbed till the 25th of November following. On that day we found a very white deposit of ferment covering the yeast-ash that had not been taken into solution, and a ring of aërobian ferment on a level with the surface of liquid; all the sugar had disappeared; the liquid contained 5·2 per cent. of alcohol, by volume, at a temperature of 15° C. (59° F.); and, lastly, in consequence of the purity of the materials employed, there was no trace of the formation of fungoid growths, whether of *mycoderma vini* or of *mycoderma cerevisiæ*, on the surface of the liquid, or of vibrios or lactic-ferment below the surface.

Thus then we see—and several other examples throughout this work confirm the fact—that saccharine liquids holding mineral salts in solution are as capable of complete fermentation as any media of natural composition. It is true that ferment develops slowly and with difficulty in them, and at times takes on rather curious forms, but, nevertheless, it does develop in the media and carry on a fermentation in which not the minutest particle of sugar is left undecomposed. This is true, at least, in the case of *saccharomyces pastorianus*, but there are other ferments which in such media are checked in their multiplication and in their continued action on sugar. One condition indispensable to the accomplishment of fermentation in such a sweetened mineral medium, by means of *saccharomyces pastorianus*, is the absolute purity of the materials and of the ferment. It is necessary that the life and physiological action of the latter should be in no way interfered with by the presence of other microscopic organisms. We shall have occasion to revert to this important detail in connection with our growths.

Fig. 49 represents the ferment as it appeared when examined on August 11th, 1873. We can no longer recognize in it any

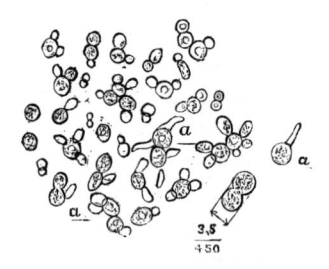

FIG. 49.

saccharomyces pastorianus. The general appearance is spherical, and there are a number of clusters of budding cells which remind one at first sight of the mode of germination of brewers' "high" yeast. At *a, a, a*, we see globules from which irregular abortive filaments have sprung, a proof of difficult germination. No such monstrosities could ever have occurred if we had used beer-wort or must as our nutritive medium.

On November 25th we made another examination and sketch of the ferment, the appearance of which did not differ materially from that given above. The general appearance was the same, consisting mostly of globules joined together in clusters of two or three or more. No separation, such as occurs in the case of

STUDIES ON FERMENTATION. 213

ferment formed in natural worts, had taken place. The ferment, moreover, was very irregular, and comprised cells of all sizes. We sowed some of it in a flask of pure wort. On November 26th there was no apparent development : on November 27th, however, not more than forty-eight hours after impregnation, there was a considerable deposit of white ferment at the bottom of the liquid, and fermentation was so active that the surface of the liquid was covered with an abundant froth. This shows us the wonderful vitality and recuperative power possessed by germs which, left to themselves for about four months, revived so readily. It proves too that the reviving influences took effect on some aërobian ferment. From the mode of life of this latter being similar to that of a surface fungoid growth, it does not become exhausted as the cells of ordinary ferment do. Now the cells which, sown on August 6th, had become exhausted by prolonged stay in the mineral liquid, and were almost inert, would have required several days for their revival; but in the experiment described the revival was rapid, and this rapidity proves, as we have said, that the revival must have taken place in cells of aërobian ferment.

Taking some fresh yeast from the bottom of the liquid we examined and made a sketch of it (Fig. 50). The field was filled with round and oval cells, jointed and ramified filaments,

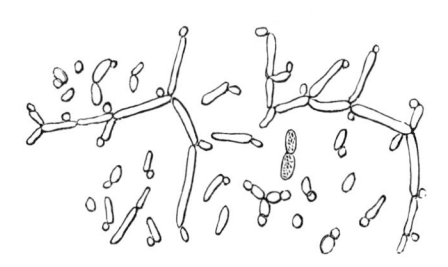

FIG. 50.

budding and multiplying in the most remarkable manner, reminding us of the germination of the cells of yeast exhausted in sweetened water, and also of the germination in the form of *dematium pullulans* of certain germ-cells which are spread over the surface of sweet, domestic fruits. We could never grow tired, as we wrote it in our original notes, of sketching this beautiful plant, which establishes very clearly a transition between one of the best defined cellular ferments, viz., *saccharomyces pastorianus*, and certain forms of very common fungoid growths, those of *dematium*, and even of the most common mould, *mucor mucedo* or *racemosus*, when it vegetates beneath the surface of a liquid and acts as a ferment.* We have here, as in these cases, filamentous chains branching into other similar chains, composed of more or less elongated cells, which at length fall off and germinate exactly as the conidia-bearing *hyphae* of *mucor* do.

The aërobian ferment of "high" yeast, in whatever medium we cultivated it, presented no peculiarity, as far as its forms were concerned. It was composed of cells of spherical shape, like ordinary "high" yeast, and germinated in the same way as the latter.

Fig. 51 represents the revival of this aërobian ferment.

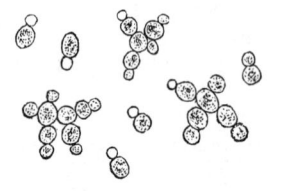

FIG. 51.

We recognize here the branched mode of budding and spherical contour characteristic of "high" yeast proper. Nor does the aërobian ferment of "low" yeast present any special

* We insist on this fact, that Fig. 50 represents the forms on revival of the aërobian ferment of *saccharomyces pastorianus*, *when this has grown in a mineral medium*. When produced on the surface of fermented wort, the aërobian ferment of which we are speaking presents no peculiarity, nor is there any irregularity in its forms or in its development, and

STUDIES ON FERMENTATION.   215

peculiarities, in forms, dimensions, and mode of growth closely resembling the "low" yeast from which it is derived. At the commencement of its restoration, however, if this is performed in sweetened water, the cells in the groups are larger than those which are subsequently developed.

Fig. 52 represents the aërobian ferment of yeast used in "low"-fermentation breweries, examined forty-eight hours

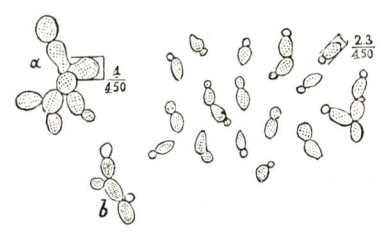

FIG. 52.

after pitching. We find that groups resembling that at a are of very rare occurrence. They are to be seen only at the very beginning, generally only for the first few hours of the renewed activity. Very soon, however, they develop cells which are of the size of the oval cells budding at b.

Fig. 53 represents the aërobian caseous yeast which forms

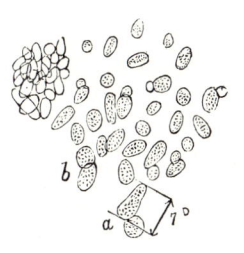

FIG. 53.

when we proceed to cultivate it in a natural saccharine medium, or in wort, it does not produce any forms of *dematium*, as in the preceding case; but the reason of this is that, in consequence of the nature of the first medium, which is better adapted to its nutrition, it assumes at once, in the second medium, the forms of deposit-yeast in the course of ordinary germination.

rather rapidly, in thick, greasy-looking pellicles, on the surface of liquids which have been fermented by means of caseous ferment. The larger form of cells, *a* and *b*, is not often met with.

On May 27th, 1875, we sowed, in a flask of wort, a trace of a pellicle of this kind, which had formed on the surface of a flask in which fermentation had been set up by means of caseous yeast in May of the preceding year. On May 30th fermentation began to reveal its presence by a voluminous froth, and the newly-formed yeast had reached the bottom of the flask. A small quantity was taken out by a capillary glass tube, and a sketch of the ferment made; this is given in Fig. 54. Amongst the cells which occupy the field there are groups of some of larger size. These are not distinct forms mixed with the others, but simply another illustration of the fact that old cells in course of revival, especially when they

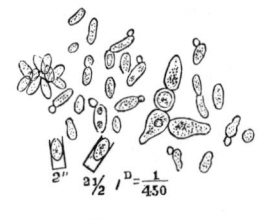

Fig. 54.

have been exhausted in sweetened water, as we have just observed of the aërobian ferment of "low" yeast, commence with forms of larger diameter or more elongated than the ordinary forms peculiar to the ferment which at a later stage are developed from them. We have seen how marked and exaggerated this feature was in the case of *saccharomyces pastorianus*.

Let us again call attention to the forms of aërobian ferment furnished by the yeast which we have already described under the name of *new* "*high*" *yeast*. Fig. 55 represents this aërobian ferment, as taken on November 27th, 1873, from a pellicle of rather greasy and moist appearance, on the surface of a flask of fermented beer-wort which had been impregnated on July 21st, 1872. It might readily be mistaken for ordinary "high" yeast, yet no two ferments can be more distinct.

On November 27th, 1873, we sowed a trace of this ferment in a flask of wort. From the 29th, with a continuous temperature of 25° C. (77° F.), a considerable deposit of yeast began to form, and the froth of fermentation covered the whole

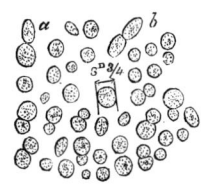

FIG. 55.

surface of the liquid. We took a little of this deposit for examination; it is represented in Fig. 56. The field is

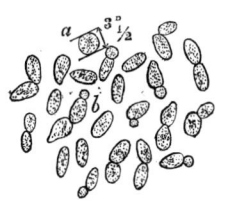

FIG. 56.

occupied with oval cells of great uniformity. We recognize the aspect of the original yeast (Fig. 43). Here and there, indeed, we come across some cells of larger size, such as those at *a* and *b*, which is another illustration of the remark that we have just made respecting the forms which revived exhausted cells take on at the commencement of a new germination.

The physical aspect of the several aërobian ferments is in general so characteristic that we are often able by simple inspection to distinguish between them as they occur on the surface of liquids. *Saccharomyces pastorianus* in its aërobian state forms a crown of cells round the sides of the vessel at the surface of the liquid, which crown is broken up by the least agitation of the liquid; its vitality continues for years.

The aërobian ferment of "high" yeast appears in the form of small isolated teats on the surface of the fermented liquid. It develops rather sluggishly, and has no great vitality.

The aërobian form of "low" yeast develops as a somewhat fragile layer, the least agitation precipitating it to the bottom of the vessel in a cloud of very small irregular flocks, that do not diffuse through the liquid as they fall. With free access to air it retains life for a long time.

The aërobian ferment of caseous yeast forms a continuous greasy-looking pellicle, gradually thickening, which breaks up into fragments when shaken. With a supply of air it lives very long, and the pellicle gradually increases in thickness.

In reviewing these ferments we may naturally ask ourselves the question whether the "high" ferments of which we have spoken—the industrial one concerned in the "high" fermentation of breweries, and the other which we have termed *new "high" ferment*—are not aërobian ferments of "low" yeasts. We are inclined to think that the ferment which in the preceding paragraph we termed *new "high" ferment*, may, perhaps, be the aërobian form of the "low" yeast employed by Alsatian and German brewers. We have studied this new "high" ferment side by side with the aërobian ferment of "low" yeast, and the result we have arrived at is, that in appearance and mode of germination, as well as in the flavour and quality of the beers which they produce, they greatly resemble one another. In the last respect, however, we cannot say that the identity is quite absolute, and hence it is with some doubt that we suggest the possible identity of the two ferments. As regards the ordinary "high" yeast of breweries, it may well be supposed, both from its power of rising to the surface during fermentation and from the peculiar smell and flavour of its beer, that we have in it the aërobian ferment of some "low" yeast, as to the identity of which, however, we can say nothing, having no knowledge as to where it is to be found; or, indeed, any certainty that such a yeast actually exists.

In writing these lines an idea suggests itself which might be profitably made the subject of serious experimental study. What would be the peculiar properties of the aërobious ferment-form of an aërobian yeast? Certain facts incline us to believe that these forms differ from each other just as a "low" yeast differs from its aërobian ferment. If this were actually the case it would be very interesting to compare the peculiar properties of an indefinite series of aërobian ferments, all derived from a common origin. We find recorded in our laboratory notes that a certain aërobian ferment of the second generation produced a beer different from that produced by the same ferment of the first generation, being possessed of a fragrance so marked that, on entering our laboratory, in which only a few litres of this beer were fermenting, we were at once struck by the powerful odour which it emitted.

§ VI.—The Purification of Commercial Yeasts.

We have already stated that the researches detailed in the preceding chapter require for their successful prosecution that the ferments on which we experiment should be absolutely free from germs of other organisms, and we have shown how impossible it would be, if this condition were not complied with, to follow for weeks or months, sometimes even years, the changes which occur in a yeast maintained in contact with air, either in sweetened water or in a liquid which has fermented under its influence. Equally necessary is it that the saccharine worts employed should also be exempt from these impurities, as well as the air, which is being constantly renewed at the surface of the liquids. These last conditions may be realized by the adoption of our double-necked flasks, with which a laboratory for research of this kind should be furnished, always ready for use, filled with the different kinds of liquids that may be required.

In general, the inconveniences resulting from the impurity of a yeast employed do not immediately manifest themselves, in consequence of the enormous preponderance of the true yeast, which, in comparison with the foreign germs that contaminate it, may be so great that microscopical examination fails to reveal even the presence of these latter. Again, it is a well-known fact that the abundance of one growth in a limited medium operates to the prejudice of a less abundant one, inasmuch as the first consumes the nutritive materials at the expense of the second, and more particularly the needful amount of oxygen. It follows, that when a saccharine liquid is impregnated with commercial yeast, nothing but yeast may be detected for a time, and one is led to believe in the purity of the subsequent growth. This, however, supposes that the external conditions, as well as those of the medium of growth, are equally adapted to the life of the yeast and that of those organisms present as impurities; for if these conditions rather favoured the nutrition of the latter, we should be sure to find their proper developments appearing at an early stage. For example, when the growth of yeast becomes sluggish, we have invariably the development of such after-growths. The principal germs, having exhausted the saccharine liquid which has fermented under their influence and is no longer adapted for their growth, cease to develop, and have their place taken by ferments of disease, spores of moulds, mycodermata, &c., the growth of which proceeds more or less rapidly, in proportion as the character of the liquid and the surrounding temperature are more or less suited to their growth.

Here, too, we have an explanation of the rapid change that

occurs in brewers' yeast when left to itself after fermentation. In such a mass of cells, kept apart from any food-supply, and only with difficulty able to keep themselves in life by consuming their own soluble contents, we have an excellent field for the development of foreign germs. In this way we may have a rapid putrefaction in yeast, to which there will be a correspondingly rapid growth of organisms in the liquid, where they find, as well as in the yeast-cells, appropriate nourishment. Nothing could better confirm this view of the matter than the array of facts, by way of antithesis, already described, in which we have seen a pure yeast remain for an indefinite time in contact with pure air, without undergoing any putrefaction, or manifesting other changes than those which result from the combustions peculiar to living cells when left to support themselves, in a moist state, in contact with oxygen.

In the process of brewing, as soon as fermentation is finished, or rather, as soon as certain physical effects are produced, for instance, when the beer falls bright, or, as the French say technically, when the yeast breaks up,* the beer is racked; subsequently the yeast, which is left in a plastic layer at the bottom of the vessels, is collected, washed, and kept under water in a cool place, to be used again in the course of twenty-four or forty-eight hours. Brewers never care to keep their yeast for a longer time before using it, especially in summer. We can understand how this practice prevents the foreign germs which are mixed with the yeast from living and reproducing; but although the conditions of brewing, as far as the treatment of the yeast is concerned, may, in a certain measure, prevent the development of these germs of disease, nevertheless they are there, and from their extreme minuteness, pass into the beer in greater or less number, however bright it may have been rendered by racking. There they only await conditions favourable to their existence to enable them to develop, and to affect more or less injuriously the qualities of that delicate beverage.

* "La cassure de la levûre."

On December 15th, 1872, we bought nine samples of beer in different large cafés in Paris, which had all come from the best breweries of Strasburg, Nancy, Vienna, and Burton. After leaving them for twenty-four hours, we decanted all our samples, and then sowed a drop of the deposit of each in flasks of pure wort. On January 2nd, 1873, we examined the ferments formed in these worts, which had been kept in an oven at a temperature of 20° C. (68° F.), and also tasted the beers produced; they all had an abominable taste, and each contained diseased ferments.

At the same time, by way of comparison, we impregnated other flasks of wort with pure ferments. None of the beers of this series acquired a bad taste or produced foreign ferments; they only became flat.

When we review the operations of the brewer's art, we are surprised by the comparative perfection to which that art has been brought by the laborious experience of years, and the more so when we consider that, as regards the question of the diseases of beer, the brewer has never been guided by any such rigorous principles as those which we have explained in this work. We have already given proofs of this in our first chapter.

The beer is racked and separated from its yeast before fermentation has entirely ceased. The principal reason for this is that it is necessary that the beer, after being run into cask, should work again and undergo a secondary fermentation, in order that it may not be invaded by the parasites, of which we have already spoken, as would not fail to be the case if the beer were suffered to remain in a state of perfect quiescence. Not only is the beer racked before it has attained its limit of attenuation, but in addition to this, and also with the view of checking the development of parasites, it is placed in cellars sensibly cooler than the temperature of fermentation, low as that is in the case of "low" beers: the temperature of the cellars being not higher than 2° or 3° C. (36° F.).

Unfortunately, the requirements of trade prevent our complying with these exigencies to the end. When the beer is sold it is conveyed away, no matter what the season may be, and deposited in the retailer's cellar, for a longer or shorter time, according to the variations of consumption. On a warm day beer will be in great demand; the next day, if rain or cold have come on, the demand will be very limited, since beer is, in our climate at least, a drink for hot weather. From causes of this nature, the beer may have to remain a long time in the cellars of the retailers or consumers. By way of precaution, indeed, it is put into very small casks, which permit of a frequent renewal of the supply, and is conveyed to distances by express trains, and during the night; it is even sent away in wagons provided with a kind of double case, the outer jacket being filled with ice, which keeps the air surrounding the casks constantly cold. Such are some of the troublesome measures taken to obviate the danger that we have pointed out. They operate very injuriously in restricting the trade and raising the price of beer. It is a matter of extreme importance, then, that our produce should be better removed from the action of those microscopic enemies which beer contains; in other words, that this beverage should have less cause to fear circumstances favourable to the development of the germs of impurity with which it is always contaminated, as a natural consequence of the methods of manufacture at present adopted. The question of alteration in the flavour of beer should be regarded from another point of view which merits equal attention. We have seen that there are different kinds of beer, each of which corresponds to a special ferment from which it derives its flavour and aroma, and, in a word, everything which gives it a value in the eyes of the consumer. It very often happens, especially in badly-managed breweries, and more particularly in those in which several beers are manufactured, that the yeast is a mixture of different ferments. The evil effects of such a mixture are experienced in the course of manufacture, and still more so in the beer after manufacture. Brewers in good "low" fermentation breweries, who brew what is called *stock* beer, during the winter months, for consumption in summer, up to August and September, are very anxious to prevent the development of a *vinous* flavour in beers of this kind. According to our observations, this vinous flavour seems to be principally due to an intermixture with the pitching yeast of *saccharomyces pastorianus* or its varieties, one of the peculiarities of which ferment is that in the course of time it imparts a decided vinous flavour to beer. If this ferment were not present amongst the yeast-cells—and here we are speaking of an absolute, so to say, mathematically absolute absence—the beer produced would gradually grow old in the store cellars, without ever acquiring any vinous flavour, properly so called.

This vinous flavour develops more especially in English beers when these are kept. It is an easy matter to show that in English beers, after their manufacture, *saccharomyces pastorianus* and the ferment which we have termed *caseous*, which also imparts a peculiar flavour, form almost exclusively, notwithstanding the fact that the yeast used in the manufacture of English beer is a ferment essentially distinct from *saccharomyces pastorianus*.

The secondary fermentation which takes place in "high" and "low" beers stored in cask after manufacture, is very often due to this same ferment, which may be recognized by elongated jointed cells, at times more or less ramified, as well as by the influence which it exercises upon the flavour of the beer.

We may add that the general result of our researches has convinced us that "high" yeast cannot transform itself, any more than "low" yeast can, into the ferment of which we are speaking, and that whenever a beer produced by means of "high" or "low" yeast develops a foreign ferment, this ferment must have existed in the original yeast in the form of germs, which, from their extreme scarcity, often fail to be detected by means of the microscope. The best proof that we can give of this is the fact that a beer produced by means of "high" or "low" yeast, if left to itself for months or years, will never contain in its deposit anything besides the yeast that was used in its manufacture, provided that that was pure to begin with. Now this can never be the case in dealing with actual commercial beers, no matter what they may be or in what brewery they may be produced. In all beers, in the course of time, in addition to diseased ferments, ferments essentially different from those used in their manufacture will appear, and notably *saccharomyces pastorianus;* this result must be attributed to the general impurity of commercial yeasts.

In certain cases the intermixture of ferments is to be feared almost as much as the presence of diseased ferments, when these latter have not developed to any great extent. We have often seen our fermentations invaded by ferments differing absolutely from those which we originally employed. The repetition of growths, and more particularly changes in the composition of our fermentable media, purposely made with the view of attaining certain results, often produce complications of this kind. For a long time we were unable to realize the true significance of the results of some of our experiments, in consequence of the facts which we have just explained, as well as those detailed in the preceding paragraph, having escaped our notice; indeed, our ignorance of those facts added greatly to the difficulty and length of our researches. Our labours from the commencement of this work to the date of its publication have extended over not less than five years, and no one can know better than ourselves with what advantage we might devote a still longer time to it; but, as Lavoisier says, one would never give anything to the world if he delayed doing so until he fully attained unto his ideal aims, which always seem more distant the more one increases one's efforts in the attempt.

Our preceding observations show how extremely important it is to employ pure yeasts to obtain, on the one hand, well flavoured beers, whilst adhering to the processes at present existing in breweries, and on the other, beers of good keeping qualities, less liable to injury, less dependent on actual commercial requirements, capable, that is, of withstanding conditions favourable to the development of ferments prejudicial to the soundness of the produce, what we have named ferments of disease.

In the case of intermixture of alcoholic ferments, we may sometimes manage to effect their separation by taking advantage of their unequal vitalities in different media of cultivation. On December 17th, 1872, we made a powder of commercial Dutch yeast and plaster, as described in Chapter III. § 6. The Dutch yeast was a "high" ferment.

On July 25th, 1873, we sowed a portion of this dried mixture in a flask of pure wort. From July 27th patches of bubbles from fermentation were visible on the surface.

On August 2nd the fermentation was completed. The yeast, examined under the microscope, was *apparently* pure, formed of spherical cells of a fine "high" ferment. We poured away the fermented liquid, observing every necessary precaution, and left in the flask almost all the deposit of yeast, and not more than one or two cubic centimetres (about half a tea-spoonful) of beer.

On November 15th following the yeast, examined afresh, still seemed pure and still exhibited the form of round cells of "high" yeast, only that they had taken on a very aged aspect, showing a double contour, and filled with granulations collected irregularly about the centre. Such are the precise characteristics of dead cells; nevertheless it was still possible that some living cells yet remained. To assure ourselves of this we took some of the yeast and placed it in a flask of pure wort. On the 19th a little froth from fermentative action appeared on the surface. We then examined the yeast and discovered that it was no longer "high" yeast, but a small ferment of rather irregular appearance, in which the jointed cells of *saccharomyces pastorianus*, as it usually appears after a succession of growths, predominated. It must not be imagined here that what we saw was a transformation of one yeast into another. The phenomena are to be explained much more simply. The Dutch yeast employed being very impure must have contained traces of foreign ferments, especially of *saccharomyces pastorianus*. Reduced to a dry powder on December 17th, 1872, the two or more varieties of cells comprising it had preserved their vitality in consequence of the plaster, and this vitality had continued at all events until July 25th, 1873. Subsequently, when cultivated in wort, they had multiplied in that medium. The *saccharomyces* had revived like the rest, but its quantity, compared with the high Dutch yeast, was so small that the microscopical observations made on August 2nd, when the flask was decanted, failed to discover its presence. Between August 2nd and November 15th the high yeast must have perished entirely: the cells of *saccharomyces*, on the contrary, still maintained their vitality, and these alone multiplied in the flask of wort impregnated on November 15th. Here we have an example of the separation of alcoholic ferments, through the unequal resistance they sometimes offer to adverse conditions to which they may be subjected. We may also conclude that if we had prepared a quantity of beer with the "high" yeast, which in our experiment of August 2nd, 1873, seemed to have developed in a state of entire purity, this beer when made and stored in cask or bottle could not have failed to undergo a secondary fermentation, in consequence of a development of *saccharomyces pastorianus*.

Let us take, as another example of purification of the same kind, the case of the different ferments of the vintage. When must begins to ferment the apiculated ferment invariably appears, and becomes afterwards associated, more or less, with the *saccharomyces pastorianus*, in the presence of which the multiplication of the apiculated ferment soon ceases. *Saccharomyces pastorianus*, in its turn, is gradually displaced by the ferment which we have termed the ordinary ferment of wine, and which Dr. Rees has named *saccharomyces ellipsoïdeus*. On the subject of these changes in the proportion of the ferments of wine, the Note which we published in 1862 in the *Bulletin de la Société chimique* may be consulted. Now, these various ferments mutually interfere with each other : whereas if *saccharomyces apiculatus* were there alone it would multiply to a greater extent, and with greater advantage to the fermentation of the must. This result is obtained by filtering the must, as we have already observed.

It is evident from what we have just said that the principal part of the deposits of yeast in the sediment of fermented grapes, at the time when the wine is first racked, which in the Jura, is called *l'entonnaison*, is composed of the ordinary ferment of wine, the *saccharomyces ellipsoïdeus*, and that the cells of apiculated ferment are scarcely discoverable with the microscope, being scattered amongst an infinite multitude of other ferments.*

We procured from Arbois, on January 20th, 1875, some wine yeast taken from a large barrel of the preceding vintage, racked on January 18th. The ferment was very irregular. Some of its cells were very old, of a yellowish colour, and full of granulations—amongst these a certain number formed jointed segments, rather elongated, and probably belonging to *saccharomyces pastorianus*. The other cells were transparent, and apparently still young. This mixture of the two ferments is represented in Fig. 57. No doubt if we had searched carefully we should also have found some cells of *saccharomyces apiculatus*. On January 21st we sowed a small quantity of this

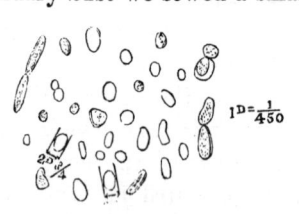

FIG. 57.

* We have reason to believe that the ratio of the proportions of these ferments depends greatly on the climatic conditions preceding the period of vintage, on the state of dryness or humidity, as well as the temperature at the time of gathering the grapes, and also on the nature of the vines.

raw yeast in a flask of sweetened water. On the 24th we poured off the liquid, and supplied the deposit with fresh sweetened water. The exterior temperature was 12° C. (54° F.). On the 27th we took some of the deposit and put it into a flask of wort. The following days there was a development of yeast, accompanied by fermentation. We obtained, however, neither the large forms of the ferments of fruits, nor those of the more minute ferments represented in Plate XI. The *saccharomyces pastorianus*, represented in the yeast which we sowed by aged, granular, elongated cells, had, therefore, not revived. Fearing that this result might have been attributable to insufficiency of the exhaustion, which had only lasted for a few days, we raised the temperature of the flask of sweetened water to 25° C. (77° F.), at which we kept it until February 20th. On that day we sowed some of this yeast in wort. There was a very perceptible revival the next day, but it was still impossible to detect with the microscope the forms we have just mentioned, nor did *saccharomyces pastorianus* appear in fresh, succeeding growths.

Fig. 58 represents the yeast formed, which evidently had

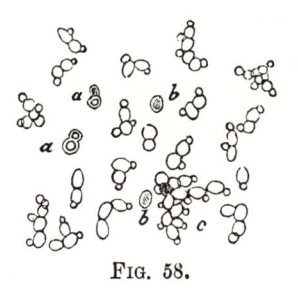

FIG. 58.

sprung from the transparent cells seen in Fig. 57, and doubtless belonging to the ordinary ferment of wine, *saccharomyces ellipsoïdeus*. Here we have another example of the natural separation of ferments brought about by the death of one or two of them, or by extreme differences in the time of their revival.

We cultivated this yeast (Fig. 58), to some considerable extent, in beer-wort. It produced a peculiar beer, of vinous character, in fact a true *barley wine*. This proves, we may here remark, that ordinary wine, in its flavour and quality, depends to a great extent on the specific nature of the ferments which develop during the fermentation of the vintage; and we may fairly assume that if we were to subject the same must to the action of different ferments we should obtain wines of different characters. With a view to the practical application of this idea, it would be well to undertake new studies in this direction; and the methods of cultivating and managing ferments, explained in this work, would be of great value in such researches.

The purification of ferments may be accomplished by various methods, according as we have to deal with an intermixture of ferments, or to regard as our principal object the expulsion of ferments of disease, such as vibrio germs, lactic ferment, the filamentous ferment of turned beer, *mycoderma aceti* or *mycoderma vini*.

One method of easy application consists in sowing the yeast in water sweetened with 10 per cent. of sugar. This liquid should be first boiled, and preserved in the two-necked flasks which we have so often described. Sweetened water is a very exhaustive medium for ferments, and the organisms mixed with them. A great many cells perish in it, and the chances are that the foreign germs, which are always scarce in comparison with the great number of cells of ferment, may be amongst those which die, or those which become so exhausted that when the yeast, after this treatment, is sown in wort, they disappear, and allow those cells which have remained vigorous enough to develop alone. The addition of a little tartaric acid to the saccharine solution—say, from $\frac{1}{1000}$ to $\frac{2}{1000}$ part by weight—often facilitates the destruction of certain germs of impurity. *Mycoderma aceti* and *mycoderma vini* do not find suitable life-conditions in the sweetened water; they soon disappear if cultivated alternately in sweetened water and wort.

In the place of flasks we may make use simply of shallow basins, covered with sheets of glass, such as we have already had occasion to describe, for cultivating yeast in wort after it has been for a longer or shorter time in the sweetened water. The success of these methods of purification is mainly due to the fact that wort is highly aerated, and experience shows that the principal disease-ferments of beer are as much checked in their development by the presence of air as they are favoured by its absence, the inverse of which holds good in the case of alcoholic ferments. So true is this that, working with commercial yeast, which is invariably impure, it would be impossible in our opinion to make beer in closed vessels; and, indeed, as a matter of fact, one has never succeeded in doing this, although the attempt has often been made. To do so requires, much more than in methods actually in use, the employment of pure yeast.

There is, therefore, this advantage in cultivating yeasts in shallow basins, that the multiplication of the alcoholic ferments is promoted, and that of most of the disease-ferments is checked. There is an exception, indeed, in the case of mycodermata; but of all disease-ferments these are the most easily got rid of, by repeating our growths before they make their appearance. Notwithstanding this, our two-necked flasks, which also contain much air at first, are to be preferred to the shallow basins, inasmuch as they are a perfect safeguard against the germs floating in the surrounding air, as well as those of the ferment *saccharomyces pastorianus*.

Another method is suggested to us by the curious results of which we have already spoken, obtained by sowing yeasts in a wort rendered acid and alcoholic by the addition of bi-tartrate of potash and alcohol. Experience proves that many disease-ferments find great difficulty in withstanding a succession of growths in wort to which 1½ per cent. of tartaric acid and from 2 to 3 per cent. of alcohol have been added. Such a mixture, however, is equally well adapted to the requirements of *saccharomyces pastorianus*, and we must always assure ourselves that this organism has not taken the place of the yeast we are endeavouring to purify. Growths at a very low temperature are of great help in enabling us to get rid of all ferments that are foreign to "low" yeast, and should be resorted to in all cases where this yeast is to be purified.

Another method of purification, which is perhaps quicker, although inferior in other respects, consists in the employment of carbolic acid—that is to say, in purifying our yeast by successive growths, we may add to every 100 c.c. (3½ fluid ounces) of wort that we employ from ten to twelve drops of phenol water, containing 10 per cent. of the acid. The action of the phenol, which at first is invariably combined with that of the oxygen of the air, tends to destroy the vitality of many of the cells sown, involving to some extent also the yeast which we are interested in preserving. But amongst the number of cells that are affected those which are less abundant, that is to say, those which are present as impurities, are paralyzed relatively in much greater proportion. If the acid does not destroy them it greatly checks their development, and the cells of yeast, which multiply continuously in vast numbers (for the fermentation goes on in spite of the phenol, if this is added in small quantity), gradually choke the foreign germs in a succession of growths.

By these different means, which are employed separately or combined with one another, we generally manage to obtain the yeast which we wish to purify in a very pure state. We need scarcely add that it is always well, in the case of our purifications, to begin with specimens which are already as pure as it is possible to obtain them. In making our choice the microscope is our best guide, but it is not a sufficient one. We should be strangely deceived if we believed in the purity of a yeast for the sole reason that when examined under the microscope it appeared to contain nothing of a foreign nature. The best means of assuring ourselves of the purity of a yeast consists in making some beer in one of our two-necked flasks, and leaving this flask, after fermentation, in an oven at a temperature of 20° or 25° C. (68° to 77° F.). If the beer, in the course of a few weeks, does not thicken, or become covered with efflorescence, if its deposit is microscopically pure, if, in short, it only tastes flat, we may have every confidence in the purity of the yeast which produced it. After we have purified a yeast we are, unfortunately, never sure that it has not undergone some change in the course of the manipulations to which it has been subjected in purification. It is indispensable, therefore, that we should test it, and see if the flavour of the beer produced by it is really the one that we want—viz., that of the beer from which we took the yeast that we submitted to purification.

In the course of a series of practical experiments that we were carrying out in the large brewery of Tourtel, at Tantonville, in 1875, in connection with the new process of brewing, which will be explained in Chap. VII., the following circumstance occurred. We had purified some of the yeast of the brewery, by means of a succession of growths and adding a few drops of phenol, and had obtained a yeast of irreproachable purity. It happened that this yeast, which was repeatedly cultivated in the brewery during the summer of 1875, from six to ten hectolitres (130 to 220 gallons) of wort being used on each occasion, always produced a beer that had a yeast-bitten flavour and defective clarifying powers, notwithstanding that it possessed remarkable keeping properties, which it owed to the pureness of the ferment employed. As a matter of fact, the beer suffered no injury from journeys of more than 300 miles, by slow trains, in ordinary casks, containing from 50 to 100 litres (10 to 20 gallons), during the great heats of June and July, or from being subsequently stored for two months in a cellar, the temperature of which rose during that time from 12° to 18° C. (54° to 65° F.) The temperature of fermentation had been 13° C. (55° F.). Beer from the same brewery, made with the same wort by the ordinary process, did not remain sound for three weeks in this same cellar.

To what may we attribute the peculiarity of the beer as just described? It is probable that during our processes of purification some ferment had taken the place of the principal yeast. Commercial yeasts, even those with which the brewer is thoroughly satisfied, generally contain various ferments, which are maintained in their relative proportions, or very nearly so, by the uniform conditions under which work is carried on in a brewery; but these proportions, it is obvious, might be very seriously affected by any radical change in the conditions of growth.

CHAPTER VI.

THE PHYSIOLOGICAL THEORY OF FERMENTATION.

§ I.—ON THE RELATIONS EXISTING BETWEEN OXYGEN AND YEAST.

THE object of all science is a continuous reduction of the number of unexplained phenomena. It is observed, for instance, that fleshy fruits are not liable to fermentation so long as their epidermis remains uninjured. On the other hand, they ferment very readily when they are piled up in heaps, more or less open, and immersed in their saccharine juice. The mass becomes heated and swells; carbonic acid gas is disengaged, and the sugar disappears and is replaced by alcohol. Now, as to the question of the origin of these spontaneous phenomena, so remarkable in character as well as usefulness for man's service, modern knowledge has taught us that fermentation is the consequence of a development of vegetable cells, the germs of which do not exist in the saccharine juices within fruits; that many varieties of these cellular plants exist, each giving rise to its own particular fermentation. The principal products of these various fermentations, although resembling each other in their nature, differ in their relative proportions and in the accessory substances that accompany them, a fact which alone is sufficient to account for wide differences in the quality and commercial value of alcoholic beverages.

Now that the discovery of ferments and their living nature, and our knowledge of their origin, may have solved the mystery of the spontaneous appearance of fermentations in natural saccharine juices, we may ask whether we must still regard the reactions that occur in these fermentations as phenomena inexplicable by the ordinary laws of chemistry. We can readily see that fermentations occupy a special place in the series of chemical and biological phenomena. What gives to fermentations certain exceptional characters, of which we are only now beginning to suspect the causes, is the mode of life in the minute plants designated under the generic name of *ferments*, a mode of life which is essentially different from that in other vegetables, and from which result phenomena equally exceptional throughout the whole range of the chemistry of living beings.

The least reflection will suffice to convince us that the alcoholic ferments must possess the faculty of vegetating and performing their functions out of contact with air. Let us consider, for instance, the method of vintage practised in the Jura. The bunches are laid at the foot of the vine in a large tub, and the grapes there stripped from them. When the grapes, some of which are uninjured, others bruised, and all moistened by the juice issuing from the latter, fill the tub— where they form what is commonly called the *vintage*—they are conveyed in barrels to large vessels fixed in cellars of a considerable depth. These vessels are not filled to more than three-quarters of their capacity. Fermentation soon takes place in them, and the carbonic acid gas finds escape through the bunghole, the diameter of which, in the case of the largest vessels, is not more than ten or twelve centimetres (about four inches). The wine is not drawn off before the end of two or three months. In this way it seems highly probable that the yeast which produces the wine under such conditions must have developed, to a great extent at least, out of contact with oxygen. No doubt oxygen is not entirely absent from the first; nay, its limited presence is even a necessity to the manifestation of the phenomena which follow. The grapes are stripped from the bunch in contact with air, and the must which drops from the wounded fruit takes a little of this gas into solution. This small quantity of air so introduced into the must, at the commencement of operations, plays a most indispensable part, it being from the presence of this that the spores of ferments which are spread over the surface of the grapes and the woody part of the bunches derive the power of starting their vital phenomena.* This air, however, especially when the grapes have been stripped from the bunches, is in such small proportion, and that which is in contact with the liquid mass is so promptly expelled by the carbonic acid gas, which is evolved as soon as a little yeast has formed, that it will readily be admitted that most of the yeast is produced apart from the influence of oxygen, whether free or in solution. We shall revert to this fact, which is of great importance. At present we are only concerned in pointing out that, from the mere knowledge of the practices of certain localities, we are induced to believe that the cells of yeast, after they have developed from their spores, continue to live and multiply without the intervention of oxygen, and that the alcoholic ferments have a mode of life which is probably quite exceptional, since it is not generally met with in other species, vegetable or animal.

Another equally exceptional characteristic of yeast and fermentation in general consists in the small proportion which the yeast that forms bears to the sugar that decomposes. In all other known beings the weight of nutritive matter assimilated corresponds with the weight of food used up, any difference that may exist being comparatively small. The life of yeast is entirely different. For a certain weight of yeast formed, we may have ten times, twenty times, a hundred times as much sugar, or even more decomposed, as we shall experimentally prove by-and-bye; that is to say, that whilst the

* It has been remarked in practice that fermentation is facilitated by leaving the grapes on the bunches. The reason of this has not yet been discovered. Still we have no doubt that it may be attributed, principally, to the fact that the interstices between the grapes, and the spaces which the bunch leaves throughout, considerably increase the volume of air placed at the service of the germs of ferment.

proportion varies in a precise manner, according to conditions which we shall have occasion to specify, it is also greatly out of proportion to the weight of the yeast. We repeat, the life of no other being, under its normal physiological conditions, can show anything similar. The alcoholic ferments, therefore, present themselves to us as plants which possess at least two singular properties: they can live without air, that is, without oxygen, and they can cause decomposition to an amount which, though variable, yet, as estimated by weight of product formed, is out of all proportion to the weight of their own substance. These are facts of so great importance, and so intimately connected with the theory of fermentation, that it is indispensable to endeavour to establish them experimentally, with all the exactness of which they will admit.

The question before us is whether yeast is in reality an anaërobian plant, and what quantities of sugar it may cause to ferment, under the various conditions under which we cause it to act.

The following experiments were undertaken to solve this double problem:—We took a double-necked flask, of three litres (five pints) capacity, one of the tubes being curved and forming an escape for the gas; the other one, on the right hand side (Fig. 59), being furnished with a glass tap. We filled this flask with pure yeast-water, sweetened with 5 per cent. of sugar candy, the flask being so full that there was not the least trace of air remaining above the tap or in the escape tube; this artificial wort had, however, been itself aerated. The curved tube was plunged in a porcelain vessel full of mercury, resting on a firm support. In the small cylindrical funnel above the tap, the capacity of which was from 10 c.c. to 15 c.c. (about half a fluid ounce) we caused to ferment, at a temperature of 20° or 25° C. (about 75° F.), five or six cubic centimetres of the saccharine liquid, by means of a trace of yeast, which multiplied rapidly, causing fermentation, and forming a slight deposit of yeast at the bottom of the funnel above the tap. We then opened the tap, and some of the liquid in the funnel entered the flask, carrying with it the small deposit of yeast,

STUDIES ON FERMENTATION. 239

which was sufficient to impregnate the saccharine liquid contained in the flask. In this manner it is possible to introduce as small a quantity of yeast as we wish, a quantity the weight of which, we may say, is hardly appreciable. The yeast sown multiplies rapidly and produces fermentation, the carbonic acid gas from which is expelled into the mercury. In less than twelve days all the sugar had disappeared, and the fermentation had finished. There was a sensible deposit of yeast adhering to the sides of the flask; collected and dried it weighed 2·25 grammes (34 grains). It is evident that in this experiment the total amount of yeast formed, if it required oxygen to enable it to live, could not have absorbed, at most, more than the volume which was originally held in solution in the saccharine liquid, when that was exposed to the air before being introduced into the flask.

FIG. 59.

Some exact experiments conducted by M. Raulin in our laboratory have established the fact that saccharine worts, like water, soon become saturated when shaken briskly with an excess of air, and also that they always take into solution a little less air than saturated pure water contains under the same conditions of temperature and pressure. At a temperature of 25° C. (77° F.) therefore, if we adopt the coefficient of the solubility of oxygen in water given in Bunsen's tables, we find that 1 litre (1¾ pints) of water saturated with air contains 5·5 c.c. (0·3 cubic inch) of oxygen. The three litres of yeast-water in the flask, supposing it to have been saturated, contained less than 16.5 c.c. (1 cubic inch) of oxygen, or, in weight, less than 23 milligrammes (0·35 grains). This was the maximum amount of oxygen, supposing the greatest possible quantity to have been absorbed, that was required by the yeast formed in the fermentation of 150 grammes (4·8 Troy ounces) of sugar. We shall better understand the significance of this result later on. Let us repeat the foregoing experiment, but under altered conditions. Let us fill, as before, our flask with sweetened yeast-water, but let this be first boiled, so as to expel all the air it contains. To effect this we arrange our apparatus as represented in the accompanying sketch (Fig. 60). We place our flask, A, on a

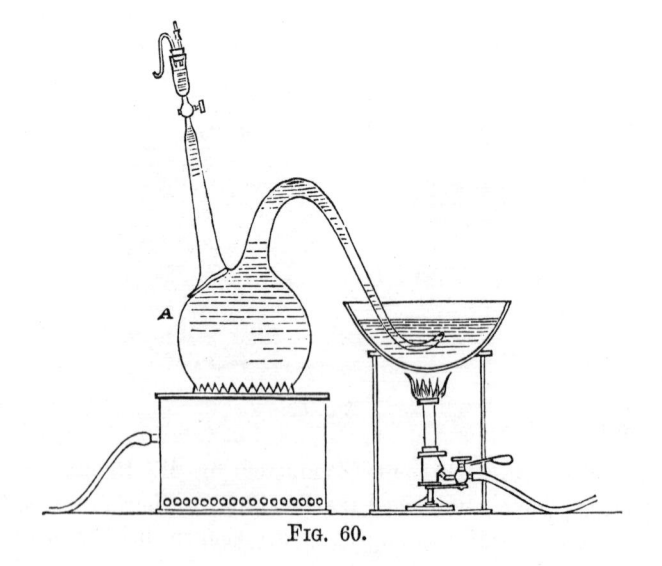

Fig. 60.

tripod above a gas flame, and in place of the vessel of mercury substitute a porcelain dish, under which we can put a gas flame, and which contains some fermentable, saccharine liquid, similar to that with which the flask is filled. We boil the liquid in the flask and that in the basin simultaneously, and then let them cool down together, so that as the liquid in the flask cools some of the liquid is sucked from the basin into the flask. From a trial experiment which we conducted, determining the quantity of oxygen that remained in solution in the liquid after cooling, according to M. Schützenberger's valuable method, by means of hydrosulphite of soda,* we found that the three litres in the flask, treated as we have described, contained less than one milligramme (0·015 grain) of oxygen. At the same time we conducted another experiment, by way of comparison (Fig. 61). We took a flask, B, of larger capacity than

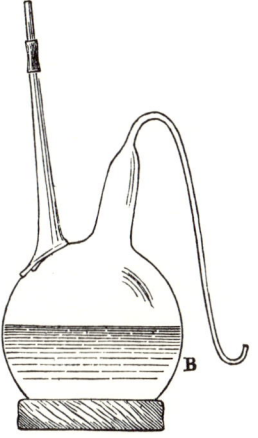

FIG. 61.

the former one, which we filled about half with the same volume as before of a saccharine liquid of identically the same composition. This liquid had been previously freed from alterative germs by boiling. In the funnel surmounting A, we put a few cubic centimetres of saccharine liquid in a state of

* [NaH SO$_2$, now called *Sodium hyposulphite.* See p. 355, footnote.—D.C.R.]

fermentation, and when this small quantity of liquid was in full fermentation, and the yeast in it was young and vigorous, we opened the tap, closing it again immediately, so that a little of the liquid and yeast still remained in the funnel. By this means we caused the liquid in A to ferment. We also impregnated the liquid in B with some yeast taken from the funnel of A. We then replaced the porcelain dish in which the curved escape tube of A had been plunged, by a vessel filled with mercury.

The following is a description of two of these comparative fermentations and the results they gave.

The fermentable liquid was composed of yeast-water sweetened with 5 per cent. of sugar-candy; the ferment employed was *saccharomyces pastorianus*.

The impregnation took place on January 20th. The flasks were placed in an oven at 25° C. (77° F.).

Flask A, *without air*.

January 21st.—Fermentation commenced; a little frothy liquid issued from the escape-tube and covered the mercury.

The following days, fermentation was active. Examining the yeast mixed with the froth that was expelled into the mercury by the evolution of carbonic acid gas, we found that it was very fine, young, and actively budding.

February 3rd.—Fermentation still continued, showing itself by a number of little bubbles rising from the bottom of the liquid, which had settled bright. The yeast was at the bottom in the form of a deposit.

February 7th.—Fermentation still continued, but very languidly.

February 9th.—A very languid fermentation still went on, discernible in little bubbles rising from the bottom of the flask.

Flask B, *with air*.

January 21st.—A sensible development of yeast.

The following days, fermentation was active, and there was an abundant froth on the surface of the liquid.

February 1st.—All symptoms of fermentation had ceased.

As the fermentation in A would have continued for a long time, being so very languid, and as that in B had been finished for several days, we brought to a close our two experiments on

February 9th. To do this we poured off the liquids in A and B, collecting the yeasts on tared filters. Filtration was an easy matter, more especially in the case of A. Examining the yeasts under the microscope, immediately after decantation, we found that both of them remained very pure. The yeast in A was in little clusters, the globules of which were collected together, and appeared by their well defined borders to be ready for an easy revival in contact with air.

As might have been expected, the liquid in the flask B did not contain the least trace of sugar; that in the flask A still contained some, as was evident from the non-completion of fermentation, but not more than 4·6 grammes (71 grains). Now, as each flask originally contained 3 litres of liquid, holding in solution 5 per cent. of sugar, it follows that 150 grammes (2,310 grains) of sugar had fermented in the flask B, and 145·4 grammes (2,239·2 grains) in the flask A. The weights of yeast after drying at 100° C. (212° F.) were—

For the flask B, with air .. 1·970 grammes (30·4 grains).
For the flask A, without air .. 1·368 grammes.*

The proportions were 1 of yeast to 76 of fermented sugar in the first case, and 1 of yeast to 89 of fermented sugar in the second.

From these facts the following consequences may be deduced:

1. The fermentable liquid (flask B), which since it had been in contact with air, necessarily held air in solution, although not to the point of saturation, inasmuch as it had been once boiled to free it from all foreign germs, furnished a weight of yeast sensibly greater than that yielded by the liquid which contained no air at all (flask A), or, at least, which could only have contained an exceedingly minute quantity.

2. This same slightly aerated fermentable liquid fermented much more rapidly than the other. In eight or ten days it contained no more sugar; while the other, after twenty days, still contained an appreciable quantity.

Is this last fact to be explained by the greater quantity of

* [This appears to be a misprint for 1·638 grammes=25·3 grains.—D. C. R.]

yeast formed in B ? By no means. At first, when the air has access to the liquid, much yeast is formed and little sugar disappears, as we shall prove immediately; nevertheless the yeast formed in contact with the air is more active than the other. Fermentation is correlative, first to the development of the globules, and then to the continued life of those globules once formed. The more oxygen these last globules have at their disposal during their formation, the more vigorous, transparent, and turgescent, and, as a consequence of this last quality, the more active they are in decomposing sugar. We shall revert hereafter to these facts.

3. In the airless flask the proportion of yeast to sugar was $\frac{1}{89}$; it was only $\frac{1}{76}$ in the flask which had air at first.

The proportion that the weight of yeast formed bears to the weight of the sugar is, therefore, variable, and this variation depends, to a certain extent, upon the presence of air and the possibility of oxygen being absorbed by the yeast. We shall presently show that yeast possesses the power of absorbing that gas and emitting carbonic acid, like ordinary fungi, that even oxygen may be reckoned amongst the number of food-stuffs that may be assimilated by this plant, and that this fixation of oxygen in yeast, as well as the oxidations resulting from it, have the most marked effect on the life of yeast, on the multiplication of its cells, and on their activity as ferments acting upon sugar, whether immediately or afterwards, apart from supplies of oxygen or air.

In the preceding experiment, conducted without the presence of air, there is one circumstance particularly worthy of notice. This experiment succeeds, that is to say, the yeast sown in the medium deprived of oxygen develops, only when this yeast is in a state of great vigour. We have already explained the meaning of this last expression. But we wish now to call attention to a very evident fact in connection with this point. We impregnate a fermentable liquid; yeast develops and fermentation appears. This lasts for several days and then ceases. Let us suppose that, from the day when fermentation first appears in the production of a minute froth, which gradually increases till it whitens the surface of the liquid, we take, every twenty-four hours, or at longer intervals, a trace of the yeast deposited on the bottom of the vessel and use it for starting fresh fermentations. Conducting these fermentations all under precisely the same conditions of temperature, character, and volume of liquid, let us continue this for a prolonged time, even after the original fermentation is finished. We shall have no difficulty in seeing that the first signs of action in each of our series of second fermentations appear always later and later in proportion to the length of time that has elapsed from the commencement of the original fermentation. In other words, the time necessary for the development of the germs and the production of that amount of yeast sufficient to cause the first appearance of fermentation varies with the state of the impregnating cells, and is longer in proportion as the cells are further removed from the period of their formation. It is essential, in experiments of this kind, that the quantities of yeast successively taken should be as nearly as possible equal in weight or volume, since, *ceteris paribus*, fermentations manifest themselves more quickly the larger the quantity of yeast employed in impregnation.

If we compare under the microscope the appearance and character of the successive quantities of yeast taken, we shall see plainly that the structure of the cells undergoes a progressive change. The first sample which we take, quite at the beginning of the original fermentation, generally gives us cells rather larger than those later on, and possessing a remarkable tenderness. Their walls are extremely thin, the consistency and softness of their protoplasm is akin to fluidity, and their granular contents appear in the form of scarcely visible spots. The borders of the cells soon become more marked, a proof that their walls undergo a thickening; their protoplasm also becomes denser, and the granulations more distinct. Cells of the same organ, in the states of infancy and old age, should not differ more than the cells of which we are speaking, taken in their extreme states. The progressive changes in the cells, after they have acquired their normal form and volume, clearly demonstrate the existence of a chemical work of a remarkable intensity, during which their weight increases, although in volume they undergo no sensible change, a fact that we have often characterized as "the continued life of cells already formed." We may call this work a process of maturation on the part of the cells, almost the same that we see going on in the case of adult beings in general, which continue to live for a long time, even after they have become incapable of reproduction, and long after their volume has become permanently fixed.

This being so it is evident, we repeat, that, to multiply in a fermentable medium, quite out of contact with oxygen, the cells of yeast must be extremely young, full of life and health, and still under the influence of the vital activity which they owe to the free oxygen which has served to form them, and which they have perhaps stored up for a time. When older, they reproduce themselves with much difficulty when deprived of air, and gradually become more languid; and if they do multiply, it is in strange and monstrous forms. A little older still, they remain absolutely inert in a medium deprived of free oxygen. This is not because they are dead; for in general they may be revived in a marvellous manner in the same liquid if it has been first aerated before they are sown. It would not surprise us to learn that at this point certain preconceived ideas suggest themselves to the mind of an attentive reader on the subject of the causes that may serve to account for such strange phenomena in the life of these beings which our ignorance hides under the expressions of *youth* and *age;* this, however, is a subject that we cannot pause to consider here.

At this point we must observe—for it is a matter of great importance—that, in the operations of the brewer there is always a time when the yeasts are in this state of vigorous youth of which we have been speaking, acquired under the influence of free oxygen, since all the worts and all the yeasts of commerce are necessarily manipulated in contact with air, and so impregnated more or less with oxygen. The yeast immediately seizes upon this gas and acquires a state of freshness and activity, which permits it to live afterwards out of contact with air, and to act as a ferment. Thus, in ordinary brewery practice, we find the yeast already formed in abundance even before the earliest external signs of fermentation have made their appearance. In this first phase of its existence, yeast lives chiefly like an ordinary fungus.

From the same circumstances it is clear that the brewer's fermentations may, speaking quite strictly, last for an indefinite time, in consequence of the unceasing supply of fresh wort, and from the fact, moreover, that the exterior air is constantly being introduced during the work, and that the air contained in the fresh worts keeps up the vital activity of the yeast, as the act of breathing keeps up the vigour and life of cells in all living beings. If the air could not renew itself in any way, the vital activity which the cells originally received, under its influence, would become more and more exhausted, and the fermentation eventually come to an end.

We may recount one of the results obtained in other experiments similar to the last, in which, however, we employed yeast which was still older than that used for our experiment with flask A (Fig. 60), and moreover took still greater precautions to prevent the presence of air. Instead of leaving the flask, as well as the dish, to cool slowly, after having expelled all air by boiling, we permitted the liquid in the dish to continue boiling whilst the flask was being cooled by artificial means; the end of the escape tube was then taken out of the still boiling dish and plunged into the mercury trough. In impregnating the liquid, instead of employing the contents of the small cylindrical funnel whilst still in a state of fermentation, we waited until this was finished. Under these conditions, fermentation was still going on in our flask, after a lapse of three months. We stopped it and found that 0·255 gramme (3·9 grains) of yeast had been formed, and that 45 grammes (693 grains) of sugar had fermented, the ratio between the weights of yeast and sugar being thus $\frac{0·255}{45} = \frac{1}{176}$. In this experiment the yeast developed with much difficulty, by reason of the conditions to which it had been subjected. In appearance the cells varied much, some were to be found large, elongated, and of tubular aspect, some seemed very old and were extremely granular, whilst others were more transparent. All of them might be considered abnormal cells.

In such experiments we encounter another difficulty. If the yeast sown in the non-aerated fermentable liquid is in the least degree impure, especially if we use sweetened yeast-water, we may be sure that alcoholic fermentation will soon cease, if, indeed, it ever commences, and that accessory fermentations will go on. The vibrios of butyric fermentation, for instance, will propagate with remarkable facility under these circumstances. Clearly then, the purity of the yeast at the moment of impregnation, and the purity of the liquid in the funnel, are conditions indispensable to success.

To secure the latter of these conditions, we close the funnel, as shown in Fig. 60, by means of a cork pierced with two holes, through one of which a short tube passes, to which a short length of india-rubber tubing provided with a glass stopper is attached; through the other hole a thin curved tube is passed. Thus fitted, the funnel can answer the same purposes as our double-necked flasks. A few cubic centimetres of sweetened yeast-water are then put in it and boiled, so that the steam may destroy any germs adhering to the sides. When cold the liquid is impregnated by means of a trace of pure yeast, introduced through the glass-stoppered tube. If these precautions are neglected it is scarcely possible to secure a successful fermentation in our flasks, because the yeast sown is immediately held in check by a development of anaërobian vibrios. For greater security, we may add to the fermentable liquid, at the moment when it is prepared, a very small quantity of tartaric acid, which will prevent the development of butyric vibrios.

The variation of the ratio between the weight of the yeast and that of the sugar decomposed by it now claims special attention. Side by side with the experiments which we have just described, we conducted a third lot by means of the flask C

(Fig. 62), holding 4·7 litres (8¼ pints), and fitted up like the usual two-necked flasks, with the object of freeing the fermentable liquid from foreign germs, by boiling it to begin with, so

Fig. 62.

that we might carry on our work under conditions of purity. The volume of yeast-water (containing 5 per cent. of sugar) was only 200 c.c. (7 fl. oz.), and consequently, taking into account the capacity of the flask, it formed but a very thin layer at the bottom. On the day after impregnation the deposit of yeast was already considerable, and forty-eight hours afterwards the fermentation was completed. On the third day we collected the yeast, after having analyzed the gas contained in the flask. This analysis was easily accomplished by placing the flask in a hot-water bath, whilst the end of the curved tube was plunged under a cylinder of mercury. The gas contained 41·4 per cent. of carbonic acid, and, after the absorption, the remaining air contained—

Oxygen .. .. 19·7
Nitrogen .. .. 80·3
          100·0

Taking into consideration the volume of the flask, this shows a minimum of 50 c.c. (3·05 cub. in.) of oxygen to have been absorbed by the yeast. The liquid contained no more sugar, and the weight of the yeast, dried at a temperature of 100° C. (212° F.), was 0·44 gramme (6·8 grains). The ratio between the weight of the yeast and that of the sugar was, therefore, $\frac{0\cdot 44}{*10} = \frac{1}{22\cdot 7}$. On this occasion, where we had increased the quantity of oxygen held in solution, so as to yield itself for assimilation at the beginning and during the earlier developments of the yeast, we found instead of the previous ratio of $\frac{1}{76}$ that of $\frac{1}{23}$.

The next experiment was to increase the proportion of oxygen to a still greater extent, by rendering the diffusion of gas a more easy matter than it is in a flask, the air in which is in a state of perfect quiescence. Such a state of matters hinders the supply of oxygen, inasmuch as the carbonic acid, as soon as it is liberated, at once forms an immovable layer on the surface of the liquid, and so separates off the oxygen. To effect the purpose of our present experiment, we used flat basins having glass bottoms and low sides, also of glass, in which the depth of the liquid is not more than a few millimetres (less than ¼-inch) (Fig. 63). The following is one of our experiments so con-

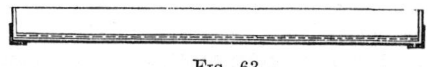

FIG. 63.

ducted:—On April 16th, 1860, we sowed a trace of beer yeast ("high" yeast) in 200 c.c. (7 fl. oz.) of a saccharine liquid containing 1·720 grammes (26·2 grains) of sugar-candy. From April 18th our yeast was in good condition and well developed. We collected it, after having added to the liquid a few drops of concentrated sulphuric acid, with the object of checking the fermentation to a great extent, and facilitating filtration. The sugar remaining in the filtered liquid, determined by Fehling's

* [200 c.c. of liquid were used, which, as containing 5 per cent., had in solution 10 grammes of sugar.—D. C. R.]

solution, showed that 1·04 grammes (16 grains) of sugar had disappeared. The weight of the yeast, dried at 100° C. (212° F.), was 0·127 gramme (2 grains), which gives us the ratio between the weight of the yeast and that of the fermented sugar $\frac{0\cdot127}{1\cdot04} = \frac{1}{8\cdot1}$, which is considerably higher than the preceding ones.

We may still further increase this ratio by making our estimation as soon as possible after the impregnation, or the addition of the ferment. It will be readily understood why yeast, which is composed of cells that bud and subsequently detach themselves from one another, soon forms a deposit at the bottom of the vessels.

In consequence of this habit of growth, the cells constantly covering each other prevents the lower layers from having access to the oxygen held in solution in the liquid, which is absorbed by the upper ones. Hence, those which are covered and deprived of this gas act on the sugar without deriving any vital benefit from the oxygen—a circumstance which must tend to diminish the ratio of which we are speaking. Once more repeating the preceding experiment, but stopping it as soon as we think that the weight of yeast formed may be determined by the balance (we find that this may be done twenty-four hours after impregnation with an inappreciable quantity of yeast) in this case the ratio between the weights of yeast and sugar is $\frac{0^{gr}\cdot024 \text{ yeast}}{0^{gr}\cdot098 \text{ sugar}} = \frac{1}{4}$. This is the highest ratio that we have been able to obtain.

Under these conditions the fermentation of sugar is extremely languid: the ratio obtained is very nearly the same that ordinary fungoid growths would give. The carbonic acid evolved is principally formed by the decompositions which result from the assimilation of atmospheric oxygen. The yeast, therefore, lives and performs its functions after the manner of ordinary fungi : so far it is no longer a ferment, so to say ; moreover, we might expect to find it cease to be a ferment at all if we could only surround each cell separately with all the air that it required. This is what the preceding phenomena teach us; we shall have occasion to compare them later on with others which relate to the vital action exercised on yeast by the sugar of milk.

We may here be permitted to make a digression.

In his work on fermentations, which M. Schützenberger has recently published, the author criticises the deductions that we have drawn from the preceding experiments, and combats the explanation which we have given of the phenomena of fermentation.* It is an easy matter to show the weak point of M. Schützenberger's reasoning. We determined the power of the ferment by the relation of the weight of sugar decomposed to the weight of yeast produced. M. Schützenberger asserts that in doing this we lay down a doubtful hypothesis, and he thinks that this power, which he terms *fermentative energy*, may be estimated more correctly by the quantity of sugar decomposed by the unit-weight of yeast in unit-time; moreover, since our experiments show that yeast is very vigorous when it has a sufficient supply of oxygen, and that, in such a case, it can decompose much sugar in a little time, M. Schützenberger concludes that it must then have great power as a ferment, even greater than it has when it performs its functions without the aid of air, since under this condition it decomposes sugar very slowly. In short, he is disposed to draw from our observations the very opposite conclusion to that which we arrived at.

M. Schützenberger has failed to notice that the power of a ferment is independent of the time during which it performs its functions. We placed a trace of yeast in one litre of saccharine wort; it propagated, and all the sugar was decomposed. Now, whether the chemical action involved in this decomposition of sugar had required for its completion one day, or one month, or one year, such a factor was of no more importance in this matter than the mechanical labour required to raise a ton of materials from the ground to the top of a house would be affected by the

* [International Science Series, vol. xx., pp. 179-182. London, 1876.—D. C. R.]

STUDIES ON FERMENTATION. 253

fact that it had taken twelve hours instead of one. The notion of time has nothing to do with the definition of work. M. Schützenberger has not perceived that in introducing the consideration of time into the definition of the power of a ferment, he must introduce, at the same time, that of the vital activity of the cells, which is independent of their character as a ferment. Apart from the consideration of the relation existing between the weight of fermentable substance decomposed and that of ferment produced, there is no occasion to speak of fermentations or of ferments. The phenomena of fermentation and of ferments have been placed apart from others, precisely because, in certain chemical actions, that ratio has been out of proportion; but the time that these phenomena require for their accomplishment has nothing to do either with their existence proper, or with their power. The cells of a ferment may, under some circumstances, require eight days for revival and propagation, whilst, under other conditions, only a few hours are necessary; so that, if we introduce the notion of time into our estimate of their power of decomposition, we may be led to conclude that in the first case that power was entirely wanting, and that in the second case it was considerable, although all the time we are dealing with the same organism—the identical ferment.

M. Schützenberger is astonished that fermentation can take place in the presence of free oxygen, if, as we suppose, the decomposition of the sugar is the consequence of the nutrition of the yeast, at the expense of the combined oxygen, which yields itself to the ferment. At all events, he argues, fermentation ought to be slower in the presence of free oxygen. But why should it be slower? We have proved that in the presence of oxygen the vital activity of the cells increases, so that, as far as rapidity of action is concerned, its power cannot be diminished. It might, nevertheless, be weakened as a ferment, and this is precisely what happens. Free oxygen imparts to the yeast an increased vital activity, but at the same time impairs rapidly its power as yeast—*quâ* yeast, inasmuch as under this condition it approaches the state in which it can carry on its vital processes after the manner of an ordinary fungus; the mode of life, that is, in which the ratio between the weight of sugar decomposed and the weight of the new cells produced will be the same as holds generally among organisms which are not ferments. In short, varying our form of expression a little, we may conclude with perfect truth, from the sum total of observed facts, that the yeast which lives in the presence of oxygen and can assimilate as much of that gas as is necessary to its perfect nutrition, ceases absolutely to be a ferment at all. Nevertheless, yeast formed under these conditions and subsequently brought into the presence of sugar, *out of the influence of air*, would decompose more *in a given time* than in any other of its states. The reason is that yeast which has formed in contact with air, having the maximum of free oxygen that it can assimilate, is fresher and possessed of greater vital activity than that which has been formed without air or with an insufficiency of air. M. Schützenberger would associate this activity with the notion of time in estimating the power of the ferment; but he forgets to notice that yeast can only manifest this maximum of energy under a radical change of its life-conditions; by having no more air at its disposal and breathing no more free oxygen. In other words, when its respiratory power becomes null, its fermentative power is at its greatest. M. Schützenberger asserts exactly the opposite (p. 151 of his work—Paris, 1875),* and so gratuitously places himself in opposition to facts.

In presence of abundant air-supply, yeast vegetates with

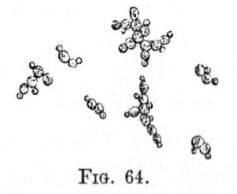

FIG. 64.

extraordinary activity. We see this in the weight of new yeast, comparatively large, that may be formed in the course

* Page 182, English edition.

of a few hours. The microscope still more clearly shows this activity in the rapidity of budding, and the fresh and active appearance of all the cells. Fig. 64 represents the yeast of our last experiment at the moment when we stopped the fermentation. Nothing has been taken from imagination, all the groups have been faithfully sketched as they were.*

In passing it is of interest to note how promptly the preceding results were turned to good account practically. In well-managed distilleries, the custom of aerating the wort and the juices, to render them more adapted to fermentation, has been introduced. The molasses, mixed with water, is permitted to run in thin threads through the air at the moment when the yeast is added. Manufactories have been erected, in which the manufacture of yeast is almost exclusively carried on. The saccharine worts, after the addition of yeast, are left to themselves, in contact with air, in shallow vats of large superficial area, realizing thus on an immense scale the conditions of the experiments which we undertook in 1861, and which we have already described in determining the rapid and easy multiplication of yeast in contact with air.

The next experiment attempted was to determine the volume of oxygen absorbed by a known quantity of yeast, the yeast living in contact with air, and under such conditions that the absorption of air was comparatively easy and abundant.

With this object we repeated the experiment that we performed with the large-bottomed flask (Fig. 62), employing

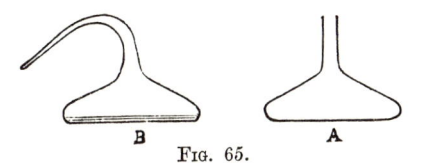

FIG. 65.

a vessel shaped like Fig. B. (Fig. 65), which is, in point of

* This figure is on a scale of 300 diameters, most of the figures in this work being of 400 diameters.

fact, the flask A with its neck drawn out and closed in a flame, after the introduction of a thin layer of some saccharine juice impregnated with a trace of pure yeast. The following are the data and results of an experiment of this kind.

We employed 60 c.c. (about 2 fluid ounces) of yeast-water, sweetened with 2 per cent. of sugar and impregnated with a trace of yeast. After having subjected our vessel to a temperature of 25° C. (77° F.) in an oven for fifteen hours, the drawn-out point was brought under an inverted jar filled with mercury and the point broken off. A portion of the gas escaped and was collected in the jar.

For 25 c.c. of this gas we found, after absorption by potash, 20·6, and after absorption by pyrogallic acid, 17·3. Taking into account the volume which remained free in the flask, which held 315 c.c., there was a total absorption of 14·5 c.c. (0·88 cub. in.) of oxygen.* The weight of yeast, in a state of dryness, was 0·035 gramme.

It follows that in the production of 35 milligrammes (0·524 grain) of yeast there was an absorption of 14 or 15 c.c. (about ⅞ cubic inch) of oxygen, even supposing that the yeast was formed entirely under the influence of that gas: this is equivalent to not less than 414 c.c. for 1 gramme of yeast (or about 33 cubic inches for every 20 grains).†

---

* [It may be useful for the non-scientific reader to put it thus:—that the 25 c.c. which escaped, being a fair sample of the whole gas in the flask, and containing (1) 25−20·6 = 4·4 c.c., absorbed by potash and therefore due to carbonic acid, and (2) 20·6−17·3 = 3·3 c.c., absorbed by pyrogallate, and therefore due to oxygen, and the remaining 17·3 c.c. being nitrogen, the whole gas in the flask, which has a capacity of 315 c.c., will contain oxygen in the above proportion, and therefore its amount may be determined, provided we know the total gas in the flask before opening. On the other hand, we know that air normally contains, approximately, ⅕th its volume of oxygen, the rest being nitrogen, so that, by ascertaining the diminution of the proportion in the flask, we can find how many cubic centimetres have been absorbed by the yeast. The author, however, has not given all the *data* necessary for accurate calculation.—D.C.R.]

† This number is probably too small; it is scarcely possible that the increase of weight in the yeast, even under the exceptional conditions of

Such is the large volume of oxygen necessary for the development of one gramme of yeast when the plant can assimilate this gas after the manner of an ordinary fungus.

Let us now return to the first experiment described in this paragraph (page 238), in which a flask of three litres capacity was filled with fermentable liquid, which, when caused to ferment, yielded 2·25 grammes of yeast, under circumstances where it could not obtain a greater supply of free oxygen than 16·5 c.c. (about one cubic inch). According to what we have just stated, if this 2·25 grammes (34 grains) of yeast had not been able to live without oxygen, in other words, if the original cells had been unable to multiply otherwise than by absorbing free oxygen, the amount of that gas required could not have been less than 2·25 × 414 c.c., that is, 931·5 c.c. (56·85 cubic inches). The greater part of the 2·25 grammes, therefore, had evidently been produced as the growth of an anaërobian plant.

Ordinary fungi likewise require large quantities of oxygen for their development, as we may easily prove by cultivating any mould in a closed vessel full of air, and then taking the weight of plant formed and measuring the volume of oxygen absorbed. To do this, we take a flask of the shape shown in Fig. 66, capable of holding about 300 c.c. (10½ fluid ounces), and containing a liquid adapted to the life of moulds. We boil this liquid and seal the drawn-out point, after the steam has expelled the air wholly or in part; we then open the flask in a garden or in a room. Should a fungus-spore enter the flask, as will invariably be the case in a certain number of flasks out of several used in the experiment, except under special circumstances, it will develop there and gradually absorb all the oxygen contained in the air of the flask. Measuring the

the experiment described, was not to some extent at least due to oxidation apart from free oxygen, inasmuch as some of the cells were covered by others. The increased weight of the yeast is always due to the action of two distinct modes of vital energy—activity, namely, in presence and activity in absence of air. We might endeavour to shorten the duration of the experiment still further, in which case we would still more assimilate the life of the yeast to that of ordinary moulds.

s

volume of this air, and weighing, after drying, the amount of plant formed, we find that for a certain quantity of oxygen absorbed we have a certain weight of mycelium, or of mycelium together with its organs of fructification. In an experiment of

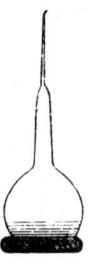

FIG. 66.

this kind, in which the plant was weighed a year after its development, we found for 0·008 gramme (0·123 grain) of *mycelium*, dried at 100° C. (212° F.), an absorption that amounted to not less than 43 c.c. (1·5 cubic inches) of oxygen, at 25°. These numbers, however, must vary sensibly with the nature of the mould employed, and also with the greater or less activity of its development, because the phenomenon is complicated by the presence of accessory oxidations, such as we find in the case of *mycoderma vini* and *aceti*, to which cause the large absorption of oxygen in our last experiment may doubtless be attributed.*

* In these experiments, in which the moulds remain for a long time in contact with a saccharine wort out of contact with oxygen—the oxygen being promptly absorbed by the vital action of the plant (see our *Mémoire sur les Générations dites Spontanées*, p. 54, note)—there is no doubt that an appreciable quantity of alcohol is formed because the plant does not immediately lose its vital activity, after the absorption of oxygen.

A 300-c.c. (10-oz.) flask, containing 100 c.c. of must, after the air in it had been expelled by boiling, was opened and immediately re-closed, on August 15th, 1873. A fungoid growth—a unique one, of greenish-grey colour—developed from spontaneous impregnation, and decolorized the liquid, which originally was of a yellowish-brown. Some large crystals, sparkling like diamonds, of neutral tartrate of lime, were precipitated. About a year afterwards, long after the death of the plant, we examined

The conclusions to be drawn from the whole of the preceding facts can scarcely admit of doubt. As for ourselves, we have no hesitation in finding in them the foundation of the true theory of fermentation. In the experiments which we have described, fermentation by yeast, that is to say, by the type of ferments properly so called, is presented to us, in a word, as the direct consequence of the processes of nutrition, assimilation, and life, when these are carried on without the agency of free oxygen. The heat required in the accomplishment of that work must necessarily have been borrowed from the decomposition of the fermentable matter, that is from the saccharine substance which, like other unstable substances, liberates heat in undergoing decomposition. Fermentation by means of yeast appears, therefore, to be essentially connected with the property possessed by this minute cellular plant of performing its respiratory functions, somehow or other, with oxygen existing combined in sugar. Its fermentative power—which power must not be confounded with the fermentative activity or the intensity of decomposition in a given time—varies considerably between two limits, fixed by the greatest and least possible access to free oxygen which the plant has in the process of nutrition. If we supply it with a sufficient quantity of free oxygen for the necessities of its life, nutrition, and respiratory combustions, in other words, if we cause it to live after the manner of a mould, properly so called, it ceases to be a ferment, that is, the ratio between the weight of the plant developed and that of the sugar decomposed, which forms its principal food, is similar in amount to that in the case of fungi.* On the other hand, if we deprive the yeast of air

this liquid. It contained 0·3 gramme (4·6 grains) of alcohol, and 0·053 gramme (0·8 grain) of vegetable matter, dried at 100° C. (212° F.). We ascertained that the spores of the fungus were dead at the moment when the flask was opened. When sown, they did not develop in the least degree.

* We find in M. Raulin's Note, already quoted, that "the minimum ratio between the weight of sugar and the weight of organized matter, that is, the weight of fungoid growth which it helps to form, may be

entirely, or cause it to develop in a saccharine medium deprived of free oxygen, it will multiply just as if air were present, although with less activity, and under these circumstances its fermentative character will be most marked; under these circumstances, moreover, we shall find the greatest disproportion, all other conditions being the same, between the weight of yeast formed and the weight of sugar decomposed. Lastly, if free oxygen occurs in varying quantities, the ferment-power of the yeast may pass through all the degrees comprehended between the two extreme limits of which we have just spoken. It seems to us that we could not have a better proof of the direct relation that fermentation bears to life, carried on in the absence of free oxygen, or with a quantity of that gas insufficient for all the acts of nutrition and assimilation.

Another equally striking proof of the truth of this theory is the fact, demonstrated in Chapter IV., that the ordinary moulds assume the character of a ferment when compelled to live without air, or with quantities of air too scant to permit of their organs having around them as much of that element as is necessary for their life as aërobian plants. Ferments, therefore, only possess in a higher degree a character which belongs to many common moulds, if not to all, and which they share, probably, more or less, with all living cells, namely the power of living either an aërobian or anaërobian life, according to the conditions under which they are placed.

It may be readily understood how, in their state of aërobian life, the alcoholic ferments have failed to attract attention. Those ferments are only cultivated out of contact with air, at the bottom of liquids which soon become saturated with carbonic acid gas. Air is only present in the earlier developments of their germs, and without attracting the attention of the operator, whilst in their state of anaërobian growth

expressed as $\frac{10}{3\cdot 2} = 3\cdot 1$." JULES RAULIN, *Études chimiques sur la végétation. Recherches sur le développement d'une mucédinée dans un milieu artificiel*, p. 192, Paris, 1870. We have seen, in the case of yeast, that this ratio may be as low as $\frac{4}{1}$.

their life and action are of prolonged duration. We must have recourse to special experimental apparatus to enable us to demonstrate the mode of life of alcoholic ferments under the influence of free oxygen; it is their state of existence apart from air, in the depths of liquids that attracts all our attention. The results of their action are, however, marvellous, if we regard the products resulting from them, in the important industries of which they are the life and soul. In the case of ordinary moulds, the opposite holds good. What we want to use special experimental apparatus for with them is to enable us to demonstrate the possibility of their continuing to live for a time out of contact with air, and all our attention, in their case, is attracted by the facility with which they develop under the influence of oxygen. Thus the decomposition of saccharine liquids, which is the consequence of the life of fungi without air, is scarcely perceptible, and so is of no practical importance. Their aerial life, on the other hand, in which they respire and accomplish their process of oxidation under the influence of free oxygen, is a normal phenomenon, and one of prolonged duration which cannot fail to strike the least thoughtful of observers. We are convinced that a day will come when moulds will be utilized in certain industrial operations, on account of their power of destroying organic matter. The conversion of alcohol into vinegar in the process of acetification, and the production of gallic acid by the action of fungi on wet gall-nuts, are already connected with this kind of phenomena.* On this last subject, the important

* We shall show, some day, that the processes of oxidation due to growth of fungi cause, in certain decompositions, liberation of ammonia to a considerable extent, and that by regulating their action we might cause them to extract the nitrogen from a host of organic *débris*, as also, by checking the production of such organisms, we might considerably increase the proportion of nitrates in the artificial nitrogenous substances. By cultivating various moulds on the surface of damp bread in a current of air, we have obtained an abundance of ammonia, derived from the decomposition of the albuminoids effected by the fungoid life. The decomposition of asparagus, and several other animal or vegetable substances, has given similar results.

work of M. Van Tieghem (*Annales Scientifiques de l'École Normale*, vol. vi.) may be consulted.

The possibility of living without oxygen, in the case of ordinary moulds, is connected with certain morphological modifications which are more marked in proportion as this faculty is itself more developed. These changes in the vegetative forms are scarcely perceptible in the case of *penicillium* and *mycoderma vini*, but they are very evident in the case of *aspergillus*, consisting of a marked tendency on the part of the submerged mycelial filaments to increase in diameter, and to develop cross partitions at short intervals, so that they sometimes bear a resemblance to chains of conidia. In *mucor*, again, they are very marked, the inflated filaments which, closely interwoven, present chains of cells which fall off and bud, gradually producing a mass of cells. If we consider the matter carefully, we shall see that yeast presents the same characteristics. For instance, what can more closely resemble the mucor of Plates V. and VI. than the *saccharomyces* of Figs. 33 and 37? Have we not in each case ramified chains of elongated cells or joints, more or less narrowed in the middle, and shorter segments or cells dropping off at the constrictions, and proceeding to bud in the liquid on their own account? Moreover, the less oxygen there is present, the more marked is the tendency to the formation of these budding cells, which isolate themselves and soon drop off. Who could ever imagine, in examining the ferment of *mucor* represented in Plate VI., that its first germ was the ordinary *mucor* that is found everywhere, with fine filaments, straight or ramified according to the variety, which send up aerial *hyphae*, terminating in little round heads bearing spores. So was it that in the ferment of Plate XI. we could scarcely recognize the ramified filaments of Figs. 33 and 37.

It is a great presumption in favour of the truth of theoretical ideas when the results of experiments undertaken on the strength of those ideas are confirmed by various facts more recently added to science, and when those ideas force themselves more and more on our minds, in spite of a *primâ facie* improbability. This is exactly the character of those ideas which we have just expounded. We propounded them in 1861, and not only have they remained unshaken since, but they have served to foreshadow new facts, so that it is much easier to defend them in the present day than it was to do so fifteen years ago. We first called attention to them in various notes, which we read before the Chemical Society of Paris, notably at its meetings of April 12th and June 28th, 1861, and in papers in the *Comptes rendus de l'Académie des Sciences*. It may be of some interest to quote here, in its entirety, our communication of June 28th, 1861, entitled, "Influences of Oxygen on the Development of Yeast and on Alcoholic Fermentation," which we extract from the *Bulletin de la Société Chimique de Paris* :—

"M. Pasteur gives the results of his researches on the fermentation of sugar and the development of yeast-cells, according as that fermentation takes place apart from the influence of free oxygen or in contact with that gas. His experiments, however, have nothing in common with those of Gay-Lussac, which were performed with the juice of grapes, crushed under conditions where they would not be affected by air, and then brought in contact with oxygen.

"Yeast, when perfectly developed, is able to bud and grow in a saccharine and albuminous liquid, in the complete absence of oxygen or air. In this case but little yeast is formed, and a comparatively large quantity of sugar disappears—sixty or eighty parts for one of yeast formed. Under these conditions fermentation is very sluggish.

"If the experiment is made in contact with the air, and with a great surface of liquid, fermentation is rapid. For the same quantity of sugar decomposed much more yeast is formed. The air with which the liquid is in contact is absorbed by the yeast. The yeast develops very actively, but its fermentative character tends to disappear under these conditions; we find, in fact, that for one part of yeast formed, not more than from four to ten parts of sugar are transformed. The fermentative character of this yeast, nevertheless, continues, and produces even increased effects, if it is made to act on sugar apart from the influence of free oxygen.

"It seems, therefore, natural to admit that when yeast functions as a ferment by living apart from the influence of air, it derives oxygen from the sugar, and that this is the origin of its fermentative character.

"M. Pasteur explains the fact of the immense activity at the commencement of fermentations by the influence of the oxygen of the air held in solution in the liquids, at the time when the action commences. The author has found, moreover, that the yeast of beer sown in an albuminous liquid, such as yeast-water, still multiplies, even when there is not a trace of sugar in the liquid, provided always that atmospheric oxygen is present in large quantities. When deprived of air, under these conditions, yeast does not germinate at all. The same experiments may be repeated with albuminous liquid, mixed with a solution of non-fermentable sugar, such as ordinary crystallized milk-sugar. The results are precisely the same.

"Yeast formed thus in the absence of sugar does not change its nature; it is still capable of causing sugar to ferment, if brought to bear upon that substance apart from air. It must be remarked, however, that the development of yeast is effected with great difficulty when it has not a fermentable substance for its food. In short, the yeast of beer acts in exactly the same manner as an ordinary plant, and the analogy would be complete if ordinary plants had such an affinity for oxygen as permitted them to breathe by appropriating this element from unstable compounds, in which case, according to M. Pasteur, they would appear as ferments for those substances.

"M. Pasteur declares that he hopes to be able to realize this result, that is to say, to discover the conditions under which certain inferior plants may live apart from air in the presence of sugar, causing that substance to ferment as the yeast of beer would do."

This summary and the preconceived views that it set forth

have lost nothing of their exactness; on the contrary, time has strengthened them. The surmises of the last two paragraphs have received a valuable confirmation from recent observations made by Messrs. Lechartier and Bellamy, as well as by ourselves, an account of which we must put before our readers. It is necessary, however, before touching upon this curious feature in connection with fermentations to insist on the accuracy of a passage in the preceding summary, the statement, namely, that yeast could multiply in an albuminous liquid, in which it found a non-fermentable sugar, milk-sugar for example. The following is an experiment on this point:—
On August 15th, 1875, we sowed a trace of yeast in 150 c.c. (rather more than 5 fluid ounces) of yeast-water, containing $2\frac{1}{2}$ per cent. of milk-sugar. The solution was prepared in one of our double-necked flasks, with the necessary precautions to secure absence of germs, and the yeast sown was itself perfectly pure. Three months afterwards, November 15th, 1875, we examined the liquid for alcohol; it contained only the smallest trace; as for the yeast, which had sensibly developed, collected and dried on a filter paper, it weighed 0·050 gramme (0·76 grain). In this case we have the yeast multiplying without giving rise to the least fermentation, like a fungoid growth, absorbing oxygen, and evolving carbonic acid, and there is no doubt that the cessation of its development in this experiment was due to the progressive deprivation of oxygen that occurred. As soon as the gaseous mixture in the flask consisted entirely of carbonic acid and nitrogen, the vitality of the yeast was dependent on, and in proportion to, the quantity of air which entered the flask in consequence of variations of temperature. The question now arose, was this yeast, which had developed wholly as an ordinary fungus, still capable of manifesting the character of a ferment? To settle this point we had taken the precaution, on August 15th, 1875, of preparing another flask, exactly similar to the preceding one in every respect, and which gave results identical with those described. We decanted this on November 15th,

pouring some wort on the deposit of the plant, which remained in the flask. In less than five hours from the time when we placed it in the oven, the plant had started fermentation in the wort, as we could see by the bubbles of gas rising to form patches on the surface of the liquid. We may add that yeast in the medium which we have been discussing will not develop at all without air.

The importance of these results can escape no one; they prove clearly that the fermentative character is not an invariable phenomenon of yeast-life, they show that yeast is a plant which does not differ from ordinary plants, and which manifests its fermentative power solely in consequence of particular conditions under which it is compelled to live. It may carry on its life as a ferment or not, and after having lived without manifesting the slightest symptom of fermentative character, it is quite ready to manifest that character when brought under suitable conditions. The fermentative property, therefore, is not a power peculiar to cells of a special nature. It is not a permanent character of a particular structure, like, for instance, the property of acidity or alkalinity. It is a peculiarity dependent on external circumstances and on the nutritive conditions of the organism.

§ II.— Fermentation in Saccharine Fruits Immersed in Carbonic Acid Gas.

The theory which we have, step by step, evolved, on the subject of the causes of the chemical phenomena of fermentation, may claim a character of simplicity and generality that is well worthy of attention. Fermentation is no longer one of those isolated and mysterious phenomena which do not admit of explanation. It is the consequence of a peculiar vital process of nutrition which occurs under certain conditions, differing from those which characterize the life of all ordinary beings, animal or vegetable, but by which the latter may be affected, more or less, in a way which brings them, to some extent, within the class of ferments, properly so called. We can even conceive that the fermentative character may belong to every organized form, to every animal or vegetable cell, on the sole condition that the chemico-vital acts of assimilation and excretion must be capable of taking place in that cell for a brief period, longer or shorter it may be, without the necessity for recourse to supplies of atmospheric oxygen; in other words, the cell must be able to derive its needful heat from the decomposition of some body which yields a surplus of heat in the process.

As a consequence of these conclusions it should be an easy matter to show, in the majority of living beings, the manifestation of the phenomena of fermentation; for there are, probably, none in which all chemical action entirely disappears, upon the sudden cessation of life. One day, when we were expressing these views in our laboratory, in the presence of M. Dumas, who seemed inclined to admit their truth, we added : " We would make a wager that if we were to plunge a bunch of grapes into carbonic acid gas, there would be immediately produced alcohol and carbonic acid, in consequence of a renewed action starting in the interior cells of the grapes, in such a way that these cells would assume the function of yeast-cells. We will make the experiment, and when you come to-morrow—it was our good fortune to have M. Dumas working in our laboratory at that time—we will give you an account of the result." Our predictions were realized. We then endeavoured to find, in the presence of M. Dumas, who assisted us in our endeavour, cells of yeast in the grapes; but it was quite impossible to discover any.*

* To determine the absence of cells of ferment in fruits that have been immersed in carbonic acid gas, we must first of all carefully raise the pellicle of the fruit, taking care that the subjacent parenchyma does not touch the surface of the pellicle, since the organized corpuscles existing on the exterior of the fruit might introduce an error into our microscopical observations. Experiments on grapes have given us an explanation of a fact generally known, the cause of which, however, had hitherto escaped our knowledge. We all know that the taste and aroma of the vintage, that is, of the grapes stripped from the bunches and thrown into

Encouraged by this result, we undertook fresh experiments on grapes, on a melon, on oranges, on plums, and on rhubarb leaves, gathered in the garden of the *École Normale*, and, in every case, our substance when immersed in carbonic acid gas, gave rise to the production of alcohol and carbonic acid. We obtained the following surprising results from some *prunes de Monsieur*[*] :—On July 31st, 1872, we placed twenty-four of these plums under a glass cylinder, which we immediately filled with carbonic acid gas. The plums had been gathered on the previous day. By the side of the cylinder we placed other twenty-four plums, which were left there uncovered. Eight days afterwards, in the course of which time there had been a considerable evolution of carbonic acid from the cylinder, we

tubs, where they get soaked in the juice that issues from wounded specimens, are very different from the taste and aroma of an uninjured bunch. Now grapes that have been immersed in an atmosphere of carbonic acid gas have exactly the flavour and smell of the vintage; the reason is that, in the vintage tub, the grapes are immediately surrounded by an atmosphere of carbonic acid gas, and undergo, in consequence, the fermentation peculiar to grapes that have been plunged in this gas. These facts deserve to be studied from a practical point of view. It would be interesting, for example, to learn what difference there would be in the quality of two wines, the grapes of which, in the one case, had been perfectly crushed, so as to cause as great a separation of the cells of the parenchyma as possible; in the other case, left, for the most part, whole, as in the case in the ordinary vintage. The first wine would be deprived of those fixed and fragrant principles produced by the fermentation of which we have just spoken, when the grapes are immersed in carbonic acid gas. By such a comparison as that which we suggest, we should be able to form an *à priori* judgment on the merits of the new system, which has not been carefully studied, although already widely adopted, of milled, cylindrical crushers, for pressing the vintage.

[*] We have sometimes found small quantities of alcohol in fruits and other vegetable organs, surrounded with ordinary air, but always in small proportion, and in a manner which suggested its accidental character. It is easy to understand how, in the thickness of certain fruits, certain parts of those fruits might be deprived of air, under which circumstance they would have been acting under conditions similar to those under which fruits act when wholly immersed in carbonic acid gas. Moreover it would be useful to determine whether alcohol is not a normal product of vegetation.

withdrew the plums and compared them with those which had been left exposed to the air. The difference was striking, almost incredible. Whilst the plums which had been surrounded with air (the experiments of Bérard have long since taught us that, under this latter condition, fruits absorb oxygen from the air and emit carbonic acid gas in almost equal volume) had become very soft and watery and sweet, the plums taken from under the jar had remained very firm and hard, the flesh was by no means watery, but they had lost much sugar. Lastly, when submitted to distillation, after crushing, they yielded 6·5 grammes (99·7 grains) of alcohol, more than 1 per cent. of the total weight of the plums. What better proof could we have than these facts of the existence of a considerable chemical action in the interior of fruit, an action which derives the heat necessary for its manifestation from the decomposition of the sugar present in the cells? Moreover, and this circumstance is especially worthy of our attention, in all these experiments we found that there was a liberation of heat, of which the fruits and other organs were the seat, as soon as they were plunged in the carbonic acid gas. This heat is so considerable that it may at times be detected by the hand, if the two sides of the cylinder, one of which is in contact with the objects, are touched alternately. It also makes itself evident in the formation of vapour, which condenses in little drops on those parts of the bell which are less directly exposed to the influence of the heat resulting from the decomposition of the sugar of the cells.*

* In these studies on plants living immersed in carbonic acid gas, we have come across a fact which corroborates those which we have already given in reference to the facility with which lactic and viscous ferments, and, generally speaking, those which we have termed the disease-ferments of beer, develop when deprived of air, and which shows, consequently, how very marked their aërobian character is. If we immerse beetroots or turnips in carbonic acid gas, we produce well-defined fermentations in those roots. Their whole surface readily permits the escape of the highly acid liquids, and they become filled with lactic, viscous, and other ferments. This shows us the great danger which may

In short, fermentation is a very general phenomenon. It is life without air, or life without free oxygen, or, more generally still, it is the result of a chemical process accomplished on a fermentable substance, *i.e.* a substance capable of producing heat by its decomposition, in which process the entire heat used up is derived from a part of the heat that the decomposition of the fermentable substance sets free. The class of fermentations, properly so called, is, however, restricted by the small number of substances capable of decomposing with the production of heat, and at the same time of serving for the nourishment of lower forms of life, when deprived of the presence and action of air. This, again, is a consequence of our theory, which is well worthy of notice.

The facts that we have just mentioned in reference to the formation of alcohol and carbonic acid in the substance of ripe fruits, under certain special conditions, and apart from the action of ferment, are already known to science. They were discovered in 1869 by M. Lechartier, formerly a pupil in the *École Normale Supérieure*, and his coadjutor, M. Bellamy.*
In 1821, in a very remarkable work, especially when we consider the period when it appeared, Bérard demonstrated several important propositions in connection with the maturation of fruits :—

I. All fruits, even those that are still green, and likewise even those that are exposed to the sun, absorb oxygen and set free an almost equal volume of carbonic acid gas. This is a condition of their proper ripening.

II. Ripe fruits placed in a limited atmosphere, after having absorbed all the oxygen and set free an almost equal volume of

result from the use of pits, in which the beetroots are preserved, when the air is not renewed, and that the original oxygen is expelled by the vital processes of fungi, or other deoxidizing chemical actions. We have directed the attention of the manufacturers of beetroot sugar to this point.

* LECHARTIER and BELLAMY, *Comptes rendus de l'Académie des Sciences*, vol. lxix., pp. 366 and 466, 1869.

carbonic acid, continue to emit that gas in notable quantity, even when no bruise is to be seen—"as though by a kind of fermentation," as Bérard actually observes — and lose their saccharine particles, a circumstance which causes the fruits to appear more acid, although the actual weight of their acid may undergo no augmentation whatever.

In this beautiful work, and in all subsequent ones of which the ripening of fruits has been the subject, two facts of great theoretical value have escaped the notice of the authors; these are the two facts which Messrs. Lechartier and Bellamy pointed out, for the first time, namely, the production of alcohol and the absence of cells of ferments. It is worthy of remark that these two facts, as we have shown above, were actually foreshadowed in the theory of fermentation that we advocated as far back as 1861, and we are happy to add that Messrs. Lechartier and Bellamy, who, at first, had prudently drawn no theoretical conclusions from their work, now entirely agree with the theory we have advanced.* Their mode of reasoning is very different from that of the savants with whom we discussed the subject before the Academy, on the occasion when the communication which we addressed to the Academy, in October, 1872, attracted attention once more to the remarkable

---

* Those gentlemen express themselves thus : " In a note presented to the Academy in November, 1872, we published certain experiments which showed that carbonic acid and alcohol may be produced in fruits kept in a closed vessel, out of contact with atmospheric oxygen, without our being able to discover alcoholic ferment in the interior of those fruits.

"M. Pasteur, as a logical deduction from the principles which he has established in connection with the theory of fermentation, considers that *the formation of alcohol may be attributed to the fact that the physical and chemical processes of life in the cells of fruit continue under new conditions, in a manner similar to those of the cells of ferment.* Experiments, continued during 1872, 1873, and 1874, on different fruits, have furnished results all of which seem to us to harmonize with this proposition, and to establish it on a firm basis of proof." *Comptes rendus*, t. lxxix., p. 949, 1874.

observations of Messrs. Lechartier and Bellamy.* M. Fremy, in particular, was desirous of finding in those observations a confirmation of his views on the subject of *hemi-organism*, and a condemnation of ours, notwithstanding the fact that the preceding explanations and, more particularly our Note of 1861, which we have quoted word for word in the last paragraph, furnish the most conclusive evidence in favour of those ideas which we advocate. Indeed, as far back as 1861 we pointed out very clearly that if we could find plants able to live when deprived of air, in the presence of sugar, they would bring about a fermentation of that substance, in the same manner as yeast does. Such is the case with the fungi already studied in Chapter IV.; such, too, is the case with the fruits employed in the experiments of Messrs. Lechartier and Bellamy, and in our own experiments, the results of which not only confirm those obtained by these gentlemen, but even extend them, in so far as we have shown that fruits, when surrounded with carbonic acid gas, immediately produce alcohol. When surrounded with air, they live in their aërobian state, and we have no fermentaction; immersed immediately afterwards in carbonic acid gas, they now assume their anaërobian state, and at once begin to act upon the sugar in the manner of ferments, and emit heat. As for seeing in these facts anything like a confirmation of the theory of hemi-organism, imagined by M. Fremy, the idea of such a thing is absurd. The following, for instance, is the theory of the fermentation of the vintage, according to M. Fremy.†

" To speak here of alcoholic fermentation alone," ‡ our

* PASTEUR, *Faites nouveaux pour servir à la connaissance de la théorie des fermentations proprement dites.* (*Comptes rendus de l'Académie des Sciences*, t. lxxv., p. 784). See, in the same volume, the discussion that followed; also, PASTEUR, *Note sur la production de l'alcool par les fruits*, same volume, p. 1054, in which we recount the observations anterior to our own, made by Messrs. Lechartier and Bellamy in 1869.

† *Comptes rendus*, meeting of January 15th, 1872.

‡ As a matter of fact, M. Fremy applies his theory of hemi-organism, not only to the alcoholic fermentation of grape juice, but to all other

author says, "I hold that in the production of wine it is the juice of the fruit itself that, in contact with air, produces grains of ferment, by the transformation of the albuminous matter; M. Pasteur, on the other hand, maintains that the fermentation is produced by germs existing outside the skin of the grapes."

Now what bearing on this purely imaginary theory can the fact have, that a whole fruit, immersed in carbonic acid gas, immediately produces alcohol and carbonic acid? In the preceding passage, which we have borrowed from M. Fremy, an indispensable condition of the transformation of the albuminous matter is the contact with air and the crushing of the grapes. Here, however, we are dealing with *uninjured fruits in contact with carbonic acid gas.* Our theory, on the other hand, which, we may repeat, we have advocated since 1861, maintains

fermentations. The following passage occurs in one of his Notes (*Comptes rendus de l'Académie*, t. lxxv., p. 979, October 28th, 1872):

"*Experiments on Germinated Barley.*—The object of these was to show that, when barley, left to itself in sweetened water, produces in succession alcoholic, lactic, butyric, and acetic fermentations, these modifications are brought about by ferments which are produced inside the grains themselves, and not by atmospheric germs. More than forty different experiments were devoted to this part of my work." Need we add that this assertion is based on no substantial foundation? The cells belonging to the grains of barley, or their albuminous contents, never do produce cells of alcoholic ferment, or of lactic ferment, or butyric vibrios. Whenever those ferments appear they may be traced to germs of those organisms, diffused throughout the interior of the grains, or adhering to their exterior surface, or existing in the water employed, or on the sides of the vessels used. There are many ways of demonstrating this, of which the following is one: since the results of our experiments have shown that sweetened water, phosphates, and chalk very readily give rise to lactic and butyric fermentations, what reason is there for supposing that if we substitute grains of barley for chalk, the lactic and butyric ferments will spring from those grains, in consequence of a transformation of their cells or albuminous substances? Surely, there is no ground for maintaining that they are produced by hemi-organism, since a medium composed of sugar, or chalk, or phosphates of ammonia, potash, or magnesia contains no albuminous substances. This is an indirect but irresistible argument against the hemi-organism theory.

T

that all cells become fermentative when their vital action is protracted in the absence of air, which are precisely the conditions that hold in the experiment on fruits immersed in carbonic acid gas. The vital energy is not immediately suspended in their cells, and the latter are deprived of air. Consequently, fermentation must result. Moreover, we may add, if we destroy the fruit, or crush it before immersing it in the gas, it no longer produces alcohol or fermentation of any kind, a circumstance that may be attributed to the fact of the destruction of vital action in the crushed fruit. On the other hand, in what way ought this crushing to affect the hypothesis of hemi-organism? The crushed fruit ought to act quite as well, or even better than that which is uncrushed. In short, nothing can be more directly opposed to the theory of the mode of manifestation of that hidden force to which the name of hemi-organism has been given, than the discovery of the production of these phenomena of fermentation in fruits surrounded with carbonic acid gas; whilst the theory, which sees in fermentation a consequence of vital energy in absence of air, finds in these facts the strictest confirmation of an express prediction, which from the first formed an integral part of its statement.

We should not be justified in devoting further time to opinions which are not supported by any serious experiment. Abroad, as well as in France, the theory of the transformation of albuminous substances into organized ferments had been advocated long before it was taken up by M. Fremy. It no longer commands the slightest credit, nor do any observers of note any longer give it the least attention; it might even be said that it has become a subject of ridicule.

An attempt has also been made to prove that we have contradicted ourselves, inasmuch as in 1860 we published our opinion that alcoholic fermentation can never occur without a simultaneous occurrence of organization, development, and multiplication of globules; or continued life, carried on from globules already formed.* Nothing, however, can be truer than that opinion, and at the present moment, after fifteen years of study devoted to the subject, since the publication to which we have referred, we need no longer say "we think," but instead, "we affirm" that it is correct. It is, as a matter of fact, to alcoholic fermentation, properly so called, that the charge to which we have referred relates—to that fermentation which yields, besides alcohol, carbonic acid, succinic acid, glycerine, volatile acids, and other products. This fermentation undoubtedly requires the presence of yeast-cells, under the conditions that we have named. Those who have contradicted us have fallen into the error of supposing that the fermentation

* PASTEUR, *Mémoire sur la fermentation alcoolique*, 1860; *Annales de Chimie et de Physique*. The word *globules* is here used for *cells*. In our researches we have always endeavoured to prevent any confusion of ideas. We stated at the beginning of our Memoir of 1860, that: "We apply the term *alcoholic* to that fermentation which sugar undergoes under the influence of the ferment known as *beer yeast*." This is the fermentation which produces wine and all alcoholic beverages. This, too, is regarded as the type for a host of similar phenomena, designated, by general usage, under the generic name of *fermentation*, and qualified by the name of one of the essential products of the special phenomenon under observation. Bearing in mind this fact in reference to the nomenclature that we have adopted, it will be seen that the expression *alcoholic fermentation* cannot be applied to every phenomenon of fermentation in which alcohol is produced, inasmuch as there may be a number of phenomena having this character in common. If we had not at starting defined that particular one amongst the number of very distinct phenomena, which, to the exclusion of the others, should bear the name *alcoholic fermentation*, we should inevitably have given rise to a confusion of language that would soon pass from words to ideas, and tend to introduce unnecessary complexity into researches which are already, in themselves, sufficiently complex to necessitate the adoption of scrupulous care to prevent their becoming still more involved. It seems to us that any further doubt as to the meaning of the words *alcoholic fermentation*, and the sense in which they are employed, is impossible, inasmuch as Lavoisier, Gay-Lussac, and Thénard have applied this term to the fermentation of sugar by means of beer yeast. It would be both dangerous and unprofitable to discard the example set by those illustrious masters, to whom we are indebted for our earliest knowledge of this subject.

of fruits is an ordinary alcoholic fermentation, identical with that produced by beer-yeast, and that, consequently, the cells of that yeast must, according to our own theory, be always present. There is not the least authority for such a supposition. When we come to exact quantitative estimations—and these are to be found in the figures supplied by Messrs. Lechartier and Bellamy—it will be seen that the proportions of alcohol and carbonic acid gas produced in the fermentation of fruits differ widely from those that we find in alcoholic fermentations, properly so called, as must necessarily be the case, since, in the former, the ferment-action is effected by the cells of a fruit, but in the latter by cells of ordinary alcoholic ferment. Indeed we have a strong conviction that each fruit would be found to give rise to a special action, the chemical equation of which would be different from that in the case of other fruits. As for the circumstance that the cells of these fruits cause fermentation, without multiplying, this comes under the kind of activity, which we have already distinguished by the expression *continuous life in cells already formed*.

We will conclude this paragraph with a few remarks on the subject of the equations of fermentations, which have been suggested to us principally in attempts to explain the results derived from the fermentation of fruits immersed in carbonic acid gas.

Originally, when fermentations were put amongst the class of decompositions by contact-action, it seemed probable, and, in fact, was believed, that every fermentation had its own well-defined equation, which never varied. In the present day, on the contrary, it must be borne in mind that the equation of a fermentation varies essentially with the conditions under which that fermentation is accomplished, and that a statement of this equation is a problem no less complicated than that in the case of the nutrition of a living being. To every fermentation may be assigned an equation in a general sort of way, an equation, however, which, in numerous points of detail, is liable to the thousand variations connected with the phenomena of life.

Moreover, there will be as many distinct fermentations brought about by one ferment as there are fermentable substances capable of supplying the carbon element of the food of that same ferment, in the same way that the equation of the nutrition of an animal will vary with the nature of the food which it consumes. As regards fermentation producing alcohol, which may be effected by several different ferments, there will be, in the case of a given sugar, as many general equations as there are ferments, whether they be ferment-cells, properly so called, or cells of the organs of living beings functioning as ferments. In the same way the equation of nutrition varies in the case of different animals nourished on the same food. And it is from the same reason that ordinary wort produces such a variety of beers when treated with the numerous alcoholic ferments which we have described. These remarks are applicable to all ferments alike; for instance, butyric ferment is capable of producing a host of distinct fermentations, in consequence of its ability to derive the carbonaceous part of its food from very different substances, from sugar, or lactic acid, or glycerine, or mannite, and many others.

When we say that every fermentation has its own peculiar ferment, it must be understood that we are speaking of the fermentation considered as a whole, including all the accessory products. We do not mean to imply that the ferment in question is not capable of acting on some other fermentable substance and giving rise to fermentation of a very different kind. Moreover, it is quite erroneous to suppose that the presence of a single one of the products of a fermentation implies the co-existence of a particular ferment. If, for example, we find alcohol among the products of a fermentation, or even alcohol and carbonic acid gas together, this does not prove that the ferment must be an alcoholic ferment, belonging to alcoholic fermentations, in the strict sense of the term. Nor, again, does the mere presence of lactic acid necessarily imply the presence of lactic ferment. As a matter of fact, different fermentations may give rise to one or even several identical products. We could not say with certainty, from a purely chemical point of view, that we were dealing, for example, with an alcoholic fermentation, properly so called, and that the yeast of beer must be present in it, if we had not first determined the presence of all the numerous products of that particular fermentation, and that they were present in those proportions, characteristic of that fermentation under conditions similar to those under which the fermentation in question had occurred. In works on fermentation, the reader will often find those confusions against which we are now attempting to guard him. It is precisely in consequence of not having had their attention drawn to such observations that some have imagined that the fermentation in fruits, immersed in carbonic acid gas, is in contradiction to the assertion which we originally made in our Memoir on alcoholic fermentation, published in 1860, the exact words of which we may here repeat:—"The chemical phenomena of fermentation are related essentially to a vital activity, beginning and ending with the latter; we believe that alcoholic fermentation never occurs"—we were discussing the question of ordinary alcoholic fermentation produced by the yeast of beer—" without the simultaneous occurrence of organization, development, and multiplication of globules, or continued life, carried on by means of globules already formed. The general results of the present Memoir seem to us to be in direct opposition to the opinions of MM. Liebig and Berzelius." These conclusions, we repeat, are as true now as they ever were, and are as applicable to the fermentation of fruits, of which nothing was known in 1860, as they are to the fermentation produced by means of yeast. Only, in the case of fruits, it is the cells of the parenchyma that function as ferment, *by a continuation of their vital activity in carbonic acid gas*, whilst in the other case the ferment consists of the cells of yeast.

There should be nothing very surprising in the fact that fermentation can originate in fruits and form alcohol, without the presence of yeast, if the fermentation of fruits were not confounded completely with ordinary alcoholic fermentation, yielding the same products and in the same proportions. It is through the misuse of words that the fermentation of fruits has been termed *alcoholic*, in a way which has misled many persons.* In this fermentation, neither alcohol nor carbonic acid gas exists in those proportions in which they are found in fermentations produced by yeast; and although we may determine in it the presence of succinic acid, glycerine, and a small quantity of volatile acids,† the relative proportions of these substances will be different from what they are in the case of alcoholic fermentation.

§ III.—Reply to certain Critical Observations of the German Naturalists, Oscar Brefeld and Moritz Traube.

The essential point of the theory of fermentation, which we have been concerned in proving in preceding paragraphs, may be briefly put in the statement that ferments, properly so called, constitute a class of beings possessing the faculty of living out of contact with free oxygen; or, more concisely still, we may say, fermentation is a result of life without air.

If our affirmation were inexact, if ferment-cells did require for their growth or for their increase in number or weight, as

* See, for example, the communications of MM. Colin and Poggiale, and the discussion on them, in the *Bulletin de l'Académie de Médicine*, March 2nd, 9th, and 30th, and February 16th and 23rd, 1875.

† We have elsewhere determined the formation of minute quantities of volatile acids in alcoholic fermentation. M. Béchamp, who studied these, recognized several belonging to the series of fatty acids, acetic acid, butyric acid, &c. "The presence of succinic acid is not accidental, but constant; if we put aside volatile acids that form in quantities which we may call infinitely small, we may say that succinic acid is the only normal acid of alcoholic fermentation." Pasteur, *Comptes rendus de l'Académie*, t. xlvii. p. 224, 1858

all other vegetable cells do, the presence of oxygen, whether gaseous or held in solution in liquids, this new theory would lose all value, its very *raison d'être* would be gone, at least as far as the most important part of fermentations is concerned. This is precisely what M. Oscar Brefeld has endeavoured to prove, in a Memoir read to the Physico-Medical Society of Wurzburg, on July 26th, 1873, in which, although we have ample evidence of the great experimental skill of its author, he has, nevertheless, in our opinion, arrived at conclusions entirely opposed to fact.

"From the experiments which I have just described," he says, "it follows, in the most indisputable manner, that *a ferment cannot increase without free oxygen*. Pasteur's supposition that a ferment, unlike all other living organisms, can live and increase at the expense of oxygen held in combination, is, consequently, altogether wanting in any solid basis of experimental proof. Moreover, since, according to the theory of Pasteur, it is precisely this faculty of living and increasing at the expense of the oxygen held in combination that constitutes the phenomenon of fermentation, it follows that the whole theory, commanding though it does such general assent, is shown to be untenable; it is simply inaccurate."

The experiments to which Dr. Brefeld alludes, consisted in keeping under continued study with the microscope, in a room specially prepared for the purpose, one or more cells of ferment in wort, in an atmosphere of carbonic acid gas, free from the least traces of free oxygen. We have, however, recognized the fact that the increase of a ferment out of contact with air is only possible in the case of a very young specimen; but our author employed brewer's yeast taken after fermentation, and to this fact we may attribute the non-success of his growths. Dr. Brefeld, without knowing it, operated on yeast in one of the states in which it requires gaseous oxygen to enable it to germinate again. A perusal of what we have previously written on the subject of the revival of yeast, according to its age, will show how widely the time required for such revival may vary in different cases. What may be perfectly true of the state of a yeast to-day may not be so to-morrow, since yeast is continually undergoing modifications. We have already shown the energy and activity with which a ferment can vegetate in the presence of free oxygen, and we have pointed out the great extent to which a very small quantity of oxygen held in solution in fermenting liquids can operate at the beginning of fermentation. It is this oxygen that produces revival in the cells of the ferment and enables them to resume the faculty of germinating and continuing their life, and of multiplying when deprived of air.

In our opinion, a simple reflection should have guarded Dr. Brefeld against the interpretation which he has attached to his observations. If a cell of ferment cannot bud or increase without absorbing oxygen, either free or held in solution in the liquid, the ratio between the weight of ferment formed during fermentation and that of oxygen used up must be constant. We had, however, clearly established, as far back as 1861, the fact that this ratio is extremely variable, a fact, moreover, which is placed beyond doubt by the experiments described in the preceding paragraph. Though but small quantities of oxygen are absorbed, a considerable weight of ferment may be generated; whilst if the ferment has abundance of oxygen at its disposal, it will absorb much, and the weight of yeast formed will be still greater. The ratio between the weight of ferment formed and that of sugar decomposed may pass through all stages between certain very wide limits, the variations depending on the greater or less absorption of free oxygen. And in this fact, we believe, lies one of the most essential supports of the theory which we advocate. In denouncing the impossibility, as he considered it, of a ferment living without air or oxygen, and so acting in defiance of that law which governs all living beings, animal or vegetable, Dr. Brefeld ought also to have borne in mind the fact which we have pointed out, that alcoholic yeast is not the only organized ferment which lives in an anaërobian state. It is really a small matter that one more ferment should be placed in a list of exceptions to the generality of living beings, for whom there is a rigid law in their vital economy which requires for continued life a continuous respiration, a continuous supply of free oxygen. Why, for instance, has Dr. Brefeld omitted the facts bearing on the life of the vibrios of butyric fermentation? Doubtless he thought we were equally mistaken in these: a few actual experiments would have put him right.

These remarks on the criticisms of Dr. Brefeld are also applicable to certain observations of M. Moritz Traube's, although, as regards the principal object of Dr. Brefeld's attack, we are indebted to M. Traube for our defence. This gentleman maintained the exactness of our results before the Chemical Society of Berlin, proving by fresh experiments that yeast is able to live and multiply without the intervention of oxygen. "My researches," he said, "confirm in an indisputable manner M. Pasteur's assertion that the multiplication of yeast can take place in media which contain no trace of free oxygen. . . . M. Brefeld's assertion to the contrary is erroneous." But, immediately afterwards, M. Traube adds: "Have we here a confirmation of Pasteur's theory? By no means. The results of my experiments demonstrate, on the contrary, that this theory has no sure foundation." What were these results? Whilst proving that yeast could live without air, M. Traube, as we ourselves did, found that it had great difficulty in living under these conditions; indeed he never succeeded in obtaining more than the first stages of true fermentation. This was doubtless for the two following reasons—first, in consequence of the accidental production of secondary and diseased fermentations, which frequently prevent the propagation of alcoholic ferment; and, secondly, in consequence of the original exhausted condition of the yeast employed. As long ago as 1861 we pointed out the slowness and difficulty of the vital action of yeast when deprived of air, and a little way back, in the preceding paragraph, we have called attention to certain fermentations that cannot be completed under such conditions without going into the causes of these peculiarities. M. Traube expresses himself thus: "Pasteur's conclusion, that yeast in the absence of air is able to derive the oxygen necessary for its development from sugar, is erroneous; its increase is arrested, even when the greater part of the sugar still remains undecomposed. *It is in a mixture of albuminous substances that yeast, when deprived of air, finds the materials for its development.*" This last assertion of M. Traube's is entirely disproved by those fermentation experiments in which, after suppressing the presence of albuminous substances, the action, nevertheless, went on in a purely inorganic medium, out of contact with air, a fact of which we shall give irrefutable proofs.*

* Traube's conceptions were governed by a theory of fermentation entirely his own, a hypothetical one, as he admits, of which the following is a brief summary: " We have no reason to doubt," Traube says, " that the protoplasm of vegetable cells is itself, or contains within it, a chemical ferment which causes the alcoholic fermentation of sugar; its efficacy seems closely connected with the presence of the cell, inasmuch as, up to the present time, we have discovered no means of isolating it from the cells with success. In the presence of air, this ferment oxidizes sugar, by bringing oxygen to bear upon it; in the absence of air it decomposes the sugar by taking away oxygen from one group of atoms of the molecule of sugar and bringing it to act upon other atoms; on the one hand yielding a product of alcohol by reduction, on the other hand a product of carbonic acid by oxidation.

Traube supposes that this chemical ferment exists in yeast and in all sweet fruits, but only when the cells are intact, for he has proved for himself that thoroughly crushed fruits give rise to no fermentation whatever in carbonic acid gas. In this respect this imaginary chemical ferment would differ entirely from those which we call *soluble ferments*, since diastase, emulsine, &c., may be easily isolated.

For a full account of the views of Brefeld and Traube, and the discussion which they carried on on the subject of the results of our experiments, our readers may consult the *Journal of the Chemical Society of Berlin*, vii. p. 872. The numbers for September and December, 1874, in the same volume, contain the replies of the two authors.

§ IV.—Fermentation of Dextro-Tartrate of Lime.*

Tartrate of lime, in spite of its insolubility in water, is capable of complete fermentation in a mineral medium.

If we put some pure tartrate of lime, in the form of a granulated, crystalline powder, into pure water, together with some sulphate of ammonia and phosphates of potassium and magnesium, in very small proportions, a spontaneous fermentation will take place in the deposit in the course of a few days, although no germs of ferment have been added. A living, organized ferment, of the vibrionic type, filiform, with tortuous motions, and often of immense length, forms spontaneously by the development of some germs derived in some way from the inevitable particles of dust floating in the air or resting on the surface of the vessels or materials which we employ. The germs of the vibrios concerned in putrefaction are diffused around us on every side, and, in all probability, it is one or more of these germs that develop in the medium in question. In this way they effect the decomposition of the tartrate, from which they must necessarily obtain the carbon of their food, without which they cannot exist, while the nitrogen is furnished by the ammonia of the ammoniacal salt, the mineral principles by the phosphate of potassium and magnesium, and the sulphur by the sulphate of ammonia. How strange to see organization, life, and motion originating under such conditions! Stranger still to think that this organization, life, and motion are effected without the participation of free oxygen. Once the germ gets a primary impulse on its living career by access of oxygen, it goes on reproducing indefinitely, absolutely without atmospheric air. Here then we have a fact which it is important to establish beyond the possibility of doubt, that we may prove that yeast is not the only organized ferment able to live and multiply when out of the influence of free oxygen.

* See Pasteur, *Comptes rendus de l'Académie des Sciences*, t. lvi. p. 416.

Into a flask, like that represented in Fig. 67, of 2·5 litres (about four pints) in capacity, we put:—

Pure, crystallized, neutral tartrate of lime	100 grammes.
Phosphate of ammonia	1 ,,
,, magnesium	1 ,,
,, potassium	0·5 ,,
Sulphate of ammonia..	0·5 ,,

(1 gramme=15·43 grains.)

To this we added pure distilled water, so as to entirely fill the flask.

In order to expel all the air dissolved in the water and adhering to the solid substances, we first placed our flask in a bath of chloride of calcium, in a large cylindrical white iron pot, set over a flame. The exit-tube of the flask was plunged in a test-tube of Bohemian glass three-quarters full of distilled water, and also heated by a flame. We boiled the liquids in the flask and test-tube for a sufficient time to expel all the air contained in them. We then withdrew the heat from under the test-tube, and immediately afterwards covered the water which it contained with a layer of oil, and then permitted the whole apparatus to cool down.

FIG. 67.

Next day we applied a finger to the open extremity of the exit-tube, which we then plunged in a vessel of mercury. In this particular experiment which we are describing, we permitted the flask to remain in this state for a fortnight. It might have remained for a century without ever manifesting the least sign of fermentation, the fermentation of the tartrate being a consequence of life, and life after the boiling no longer existed in the flask. When it was evident that the contents of the flask were perfectly inert, we impregnated them rapidly, as follows:—All the liquid contained in the exit-tube was removed by means of a fine caoutchouc tube, and replaced by about 1 c.c. (about 17 minims) of liquid and deposit from another flask, similar to the one we have described, but which had been fermenting spontaneously for twelve days; we lost no time in refilling completely the exit-tube with water which had been first boiled and then cooled down in carbonic acid gas. This operation lasted only a few minutes. The exit-tube was again plunged under mercury. Subsequently the tube was not moved from under the mercury, and as it formed part of the flask, and there was neither cork nor india-rubber, any introduction of air was consequently impossible. The small quantity of air introduced during the impregnation was insignificant, and it might even be shown that it injured rather than assisted the growth of the organisms, inasmuch as these consisted of adult individuals which had lived without air and might be liable to be damaged or even destroyed by it. Be this as it may, in a subsequent experiment we shall find the possibility removed of any aeration taking place in this way, however infinitesimal, so that no doubt may linger on this subject.

The following days the organisms multiplied, the deposit of tartrate gradually disappeared, and a sensible ferment action was manifest on the surface, and throughout the bulk of the liquid. The deposit seemed lifted up in places, and was covered with a layer of a dark-grey colour, puffed up, and having an organic and gelatinous appearance. For several days, in spite of this action in the deposit, we detected no disengagement of gas, except when the flask was slightly shaken, in which case rather large bubbles adhering to the deposit rose, carrying with them some solid particles, which quickly fell back again, whilst the bubbles diminished in size as they rose, from being partially taken into solution, in consequence of the liquid not being saturated. The smallest bubbles had even time to dissolve completely before they could reach the surface of the liquid. In course of time the liquid was saturated, and the tartrate was gradually displaced by mammillated crusts, or clear, transparent crystals of carbonate of lime at the bottom and on the sides of the vessel.

The impregnation took place on February 10th, and on March 15th the liquid was nearly saturated. The bubbles then began to lodge in the bent part of the exit-tube, at the top of the flask. A glass measuring-tube containing mercury was now placed with its open end over the point of the exit-tube under the mercury in the trough, so that no bubble might escape. A steady evolution of gas went on from the 17th to the 18th, 17·4 c.c. (1·06 cubic inches) having been collected. This was proved to be nearly absolutely pure carbonic acid, as indeed might have been suspected from the fact that the evolution did not begin before a distinct saturation of the liquid was observed.*

The liquid, which was turbid on the day after its impregnation, had, in spite of the liberation of gas, again become so transparent that we could read our handwriting through the body of the flask. Notwithstanding this, there was still a very active operation going on in the deposit, but it was confined to that spot. Indeed, the swarming vibrios were bound to remain there, the tartrate of lime being still more insoluble in water saturated with carbonate of lime than it is in pure water. A supply of carbonaceous food, at all events, was absolutely wanting in the bulk of the liquid. Every day we continued to collect and analyze the total amount of gas disengaged. To the very last, it was composed of pure carbonic acid gas. Only

* [Carbonic acid being considerably more soluble than other gases possible under the circumstances.—ED.]

during the first few days did the absorption by the concentrated potash leave a very minute residue. By April 26th all liberation of gas had ceased, the last bubbles having risen in the course of April 23rd. The flask had been all the time in the oven, at a temperature between 25° C. and 28° C. (77° F. and 83° F.). The total volume of gas collected was 2·135 litres (130·2 cubic inches). To obtain the whole volume of gas formed we had to add to this what was held in the liquid in the state of acid carbonate of lime. To determine this we poured a portion of the liquid from the flask into another flask of similar shape, but smaller, up to a gauge-mark on the neck.* This smaller flask had been previously filled with carbonic acid. The carbonic acid of the fermented liquid was then expelled by means of heat, and collected over mercury. In this way we found a volume of 8·322 litres (508 cubic inches) of gas in solution, which, added to 2·135 litres, gave a total of 10·457 litres (638·2 cubic inches) at 20° and 760, which calculated to 0° C. and 760 mm. atmospheric pressure (32° F. and 30 inches) gave a weight of 19·70 grammes (302·2 grains) of carbonic acid.

Exactly half of the lime of the tartrate employed got used up in the soluble salts formed during fermentation; the other half was partly precipitated in the form of carbonate of lime, partly dissolved in the liquid by the carbonic acid. The soluble salts seemed to us to be a mixture or combination of 1 equivalent of metacetate of lime, with 2 equivalents of the acetate, for every 10 equivalents of carbonic acid produced, the whole corresponding to the fermentation of 3 equivalents of neutral tartrate of lime.† This point, however, is worthy of being

* We had to avoid filling the small flask completely, for fear of causing some of the liquid to pass on to the surface of the mercury in the measuring tube. The liquid condensed by boiling forms pure water, the solvent affinity of which for carbonic acid, at the temperature we employ, is well known.

† The following is a curious consequence of these numbers and of the nature of the products of this fermentation. The carbonic acid liberated being quite pure, especially when the liquid has been boiled to expel all air from the flask, and capable of perfect solution, it follows that, the

studied with greater care: the present statement of the nature of the products formed is given with all reserve. For our point, indeed, the matter is of little importance, since the equation of the fermentation does not concern us.

After the completion of fermentation there was not a trace of tartrate of lime remaining at the bottom of the vessel: it had disappeared gradually as it got broken up into the different products of fermentation, and its place was taken by some crystallized carbonate of lime—the excess, namely, which had been unable to dissolve by the action of the carbonic acid. Associated, moreover, with this carbonate of lime there was a quantity of some kind of animal matter, which, under the microscope, appeared to be composed of masses of granules mixed with very fine filaments of varying lengths, studded with minute dots, and presenting all the characteristics of a nitrogenous organic substance.* That this was really the ferment is evident enough from all that we have already said. To convince ourselves more thoroughly of the fact, and at the same time to enable us to observe the mode of activity of the organism, we instituted the following supplementary observation. Side by side with the experiment just described, we

volume of liquid being sufficient and the weight of tartrate suitably chosen —we may set aside tartrate of lime in an insoluble, crystalline powder, along with phosphates at the bottom of a closed vessel full of water, and find soon afterwards in their place carbonate of lime, and, in the liquid, soluble salts of lime, with a mass of organic matter at the bottom, without any liberation of gas or appearance of fermentation ever taking place, except as far as the vital action and transformation in the tartrate are concerned. It is easy to calculate that a vessel or flask of five litres (rather more than a gallon) would be large enough for the accomplishment of this remarkable and singularly quiet transformation, in the case of fifty grammes (767 grains) of tartrate of lime.

* We treated the whole deposit with dilute hydrochloric acid, which dissolved the carbonate of lime, and the insoluble phosphates of calcium and magnesium; afterwards filtering the liquid through a weighed filter paper. Dried at 100° C. (212° F.), the weight of organic matter thus obtained was 0·54 gramme (8·3 grains), which was rather more than $\frac{1}{200}$th of the weight of fermentable matter.

290   STUDIES ON FERMENTATION.

conducted a similar one, which we intermitted after the fermentation was somewhat advanced, and about half of the tartrate dissolved. Breaking off, with a file, the exit tube at the point where the neck began to narrow off, we took some of the deposit from the bottom by means of a long, straight piece of tubing, in order to bring it under microscopical examination. We found it to consist of a host of long filaments of extreme tenuity, their diameter being about $\frac{1}{1000}$th of a millimetre (0·000039 in.); their length varied, in some cases being as

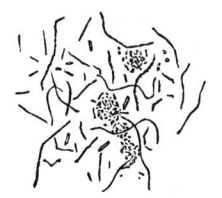

FIG. 68.

much as $\frac{1}{20}$th of a millimetre (0·0019 in.). A crowd of these long vibrios were to be seen creeping slowly along, with a sinuous movement, showing three, four, or even five flexures. The filaments that were at rest had the same aspect as these last, with the exception that they appeared punctate, as though composed of a series of granules arranged in irregular order. No doubt these were vibrios in which vital action had ceased, exhausted specimens which we may compare with the old granular ferment of beer, whilst those in motion may be compared with young and vigorous yeast. The absence of movement in the former seems to prove that this view is correct. Both kinds showed a tendency to form clusters, the compactness of which impeded the movements of those which were in motion. Moreover, it was noticeable that the masses of these latter rested on tartrate not yet dissolved, whilst the granular clusters of the others rested directly on the glass, at the bottom of the flask, as if, having decomposed the tartrate, the only carbonaceous food at their disposal, they had then died at the spot where we captured them from inability to escape, precisely in consequence of that state of entanglement which they combined to form, during the period of their active development. Besides these we observed vibrios of the same diameter, but of much smaller length, whirling round with great rapidity, and darting backwards and forwards; these were probably identical with the longer ones, and possessed greater freedom of movement, no doubt in consequence of their greater shortness. Not one of these vibrios could be found throughout the mass of the liquid.

We may remark that as there was a somewhat putrid odour from the deposit in which the vibrios swarmed, the action must have been one of reduction, and no doubt to this fact was due the greyish coloration of the deposit. We suppose that the substances employed, however pure, always contain some trace of iron, which becomes converted into the sulphide, the black colour of which would modify the originally white deposit of insoluble tartrate and phosphate.

But what is the nature of these vibrios? We have already said that we believe that they are nothing but the ordinary vibrios of putrefaction, reduced to a state of extreme tenuity by the special conditions of nutrition involved in the fermentable medium used; in a word, we think that the fermentation in question might be called putrefaction of tartrate of lime. It would be easy enough to determine this point by growing the vibrios of such a fermentation in media adapted to the production of the ordinary forms of vibrio; but this is an experiment which we have not ourselves tried.

One word more on the subject of these curious beings. In a great many of them there appears to be something like a clear spot, a kind of bead, at one of their extremities. This is an illusion arising from the fact that the extremity of these vibrios is curved, hanging downwards, thus causing a greater refraction at that particular point, and leading us to think that the diameter is greater at that extremity. We may easily undeceive ourselves if we watch the movements of the vibrio, when we will readily recognize the bend, especially as it is brought into the vertical plane passing over the rest of the filament. In this way we will see the bright spot, *the head* disappear, and then reappear.

The chief inference that it concerns us to draw from the preceding facts is one which cannot admit of doubt, and which we need not insist on any further—namely, that vibrios, as met with in the fermentation of neutral tartrate of lime, are able to live and multiply when entirely deprived of air.

§ V.—Another Example of Life Without Air— Fermentation of Lactate of Lime.

As another example of life without air, accompanied by fermentation properly so called, we may lastly cite the fermentation of lactate of lime in a mineral medium.

In the experiment described in the last paragraph, it will be remembered that the ferment-liquid and the germs employed in its impregnation came in contact with air, although only for a very brief time. Now, notwithstanding that we possess exact observations which prove that the diffusion of oxygen and nitrogen in a liquid absolutely deprived of air, so far from taking place rapidly, is, on the contrary, a very slow process indeed; yet we were anxious to guard the experiment that we are about to describe from the slightest possible trace of oxygen at the moment of impregnation.

We employed a liquid prepared as follows: Into from 9 to 10 litres (somewhat over 2 gallons) of pure water the following salts * were introduced successively, viz:—

---

* Should the solution of lactate of lime be turbid, it may be clarified by filtration, after previously adding a small quantity of phosphate of ammonia, which throws down phosphate of lime. It is only after this process of clarification and filtration that the phosphates of the formula are added. The solution soon becomes turbid, if left in contact with air, in consequence of the spontaneous formation of bacteria.

Pure lactate of lime .. .. .. 225 grammes
Phosphate of ammonia .. .. 0·75 ,,
Phosphate of potassium .. .. 0·4 ,,
Sulphate of magnesium .. .. 0·4 ,,
Sulphate of ammonia .. .. 0·2 ,,
[1 gramme=15·43 grains.]

On March 23rd, 1875, we filled a 6 litre (about 11 pints) flask, of the shape represented in Fig. 69, and placed it over a heater. Another flame was placed below a vessel containing the same liquid, into which the curved tube of the flask was

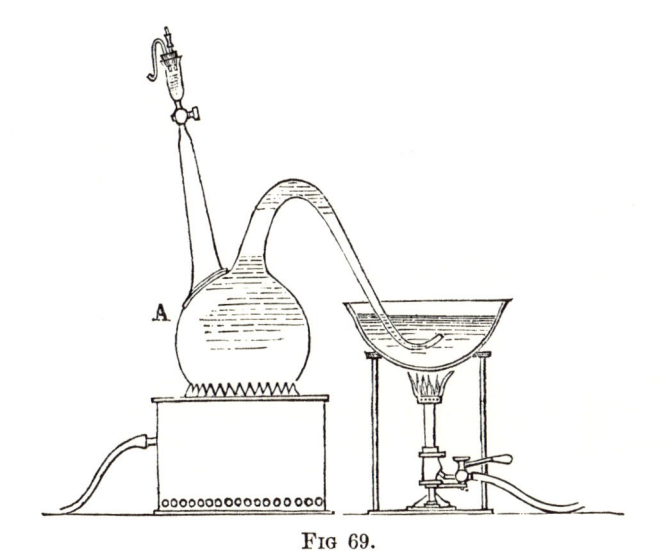

Fig 69.

plunged. The liquids in the flask and in the basin were raised to boiling together, and kept in this condition for more than half-an-hour, so as to expel all the air held in solution. The liquid was several times forced out of the flask by the steam, and sucked back again; but the portion which re-entered the flask was always boiling. On the following day, when the flask had cooled, we transferred the end of the delivery tube to a vessel full of mercury and placed the whole apparatus in an oven at a temperature varying between 25° C. and 30° C. (77° F. and 86° F.); then, after having refilled the small cylindrical tap-funnel with carbonic acid, we passed into it with all necessary precautions 10 c.c. (0·35 fl. oz.) of a liquid similar to that described, which had been already in active fermentation for several days out of contact with air and now swarmed with vibrios. We then turned the tap of the funnel, until only a small quantity of liquid was left, just enough to prevent the access of air. In this way the impregnation was accomplished without either the ferment-liquid or the ferment-germs having been brought in contact, even for the shortest space, with the external air. The fermentation, the occurrence of which at an earlier or later period depends for the most part on the condition of the impregnating germs, and the number introduced in the act, in this case began to manifest itself by the appearance of minute bubbles from March 29th. But not till April 9th did we observe bubbles of larger size rise to the surface. From that date onward they continued to come in increasing number, from certain points at the bottom of the flask, where a deposit of earthy phosphates existed; and at the same time the liquid, which for the first few days remained perfectly clear, began to grow turbid in consequence of the development of vibrios. It was on the same day that we first observed a deposit on the sides of carbonate of lime in crystals.

It is a matter of some interest to notice here that, in the mode of procedure adopted, everything combined to prevent the interference of air. A portion of the liquid expelled at the beginning of the experiment, partly because of the increased temperature in the oven and partly also by the force of the gas, as it began to be evolved from the fermentative action, reached the surface of the mercury, where, being the most suitable medium we know for the growth of bacteria, it speedily swarmed with these organisms.* In this way any passage of air, if such

* The naturalist Cohn, of Breslau, who published an excellent work on bacteria in 1872, described, after Mayer, the composition of a liquid

a thing were possible, between the mercury and the sides of the delivery-tube was altogether prevented, since the bacteria would consume every trace of oxygen which might be dissolved in the liquid lying on the surface of the mercury. Hence it is impossible to imagine that the slightest trace of oxygen could have got into the liquid in the flask.

Before passing on we may remark that in this ready absorption of oxygen by bacteria we have a means of depriving fermentable liquids of every trace of that gas with a facility and success equal or even greater than by the method of preliminary boiling. Such a solution as we have described, if kept at summer heat, without any previous boiling, becomes turbid in the course of twenty-four hours from a *spontaneous* development of bacteria; and it is easy to prove that they absorb all the oxygen held in solution.* If we completely fill a flask of a few litres capacity (about a gallon) (Fig. 67) with the liquid described, taking care to have the delivery-tube also filled, and its opening plunged under mercury, and, forty-eight hours afterwards, by means of a chloride of calcium bath, expel from the liquid on the surface of the mercury all the gas which it holds in solution, this gas, when analyzed, will be found to be composed of a mixture of nitrogen and carbonic acid gas, *without the least trace of oxygen.* Here, then, we have an excellent means of depriving the fermentable liquid of air; we have simply to

---

peculiarly adapted to the propagation of these organisms, which it would be well to compare for its utility in studies of this kind with our solution of lactate and phosphates. The following is Cohn's formula:—

Distilled water	.. .. ..	20 c.c. (0·7 fl. oz.)
Phosphate of potassium	.. ..	0·1 gramme (1·5 grains).
Sulphate of magnesium	.. ..	0·1 ,, ,,
Tribasic phosphate of lime..	..	0·01 ,, (0·15 grain).
Tartrate of ammonia	.. ..	0·2 ,, (3 grains).

This liquid, the author says, has a feeble acid reaction and forms a perfectly clear solution.

* On the rapid absorption of oxygen by bacteria, see also our *Mémoire* of 1872, *sur les Générations dites Spontanées*, especially the note on page 78.

completely fill a flask with the liquid, and place it in the oven, merely avoiding any addition of butyric vibrios before the lapse of two or three days. We may wait even longer; and then, if the liquid does not become impregnated spontaneously with vibrio germs, the liquid, which at first was turbid from the presence of bacteria, will become bright again, since the bacteria when deprived of life, or, at least, of the power of moving, after they have exhausted all the oxygen in solution, will fall inert to the bottom of the vessel. On several occasions, we have determined this interesting fact, which tends to prove that the butyric vibrios cannot be regarded as another form of bacteria, inasmuch as, on the hypothesis of an original relation between the two productions, butyric fermentation ought in every case to follow the growth of bacteria.

We may also call attention to another striking experiment, well suited to show the effect of differences in the composition of the medium upon the propagation of microscopic beings. The fermentation which we last described commenced on March 27th and continued until May 10th; that to which we are now to refer, however, was completed in four days, the liquid employed being similar in composition and quantity to that employed in the former experiment. On April 23rd, 1875, we filled a flask of the same shape as that represented in Fig. 69, and of similar capacity, viz., 6 litres, with a liquid composed as described at page 293. This liquid had been previously left to itself for five days in large open flasks, in consequence of which it had developed an abundant growth of bacteria. On the fifth day a few bubbles, rising from the bottom of the vessels, at long intervals, betokened the commencement of butyric fermentation, a fact, moreover, confirmed by the microscope, in the appearance of the vibrios of this fermentation in specimens of the liquid taken from the bottom of the vessels, the middle of its mass, and even in the layer on the surface that was swarming with bacteria. We transferred the liquid so prepared to the 6-litre flask arranged over the mercury. By evening a tolerably active fermentation had begun to manifest itself. On the 24th this fermentation was proceeding with astonishing rapidity, which continued during the 25th and 26th. During the evening of the 26th it slackened, and on the 27th all signs of fermentation had ceased. This was not, as might be supposed, a sudden stoppage, due to some unknown cause; the fermentation was actually completed, for when we examined the fermented liquid on the 28th we could not find the smallest quantity of lactate of lime. If the needs of industry should ever require the production of large quantities of butyric acid, there would, beyond doubt, be found in the preceding fact valuable information in devising an easy method of preparing that product in abundance.*

Before we go any further, let us devote some attention to the vibrios of the preceding fermentations.

On May 27th, 1862, we completely filled a flask, capable of holding 2·780 litres (about five pints), with the solution of lactate and phosphates.† We refrained from impregnating it with any germs. The liquid became turbid from a develop-

---

* In what way are we to account for so great a difference between the two fermentations that we have just described? Probably, it was owing to some modification effected in the medium by the previous life of the bacteria, or to the special character of the vibrios used in impregnation. Or, again, it might have been due to the action of the air, which, under the conditions of our second experiment, was not absolutely eliminated, since we took no precaution against its introduction at the moment of filling our flask, and this would tend to facilitate the multiplication of anaërobian vibrios, just as, under similar conditions, would have been the case if we had been dealing with a fermentation by ordinary yeast.

† In this case the liquid was composed as follows:—a saturated solution of lactate of lime, at a temperature of 25° C. (77° F.) was prepared, containing for every 100 c.c. (3½ fl. oz.) 25·65 grammes (394 grains) of the lactate, $C_6H_5O_5CaO$ [*new notation*, $C_6H_{10}CaO_6$]. This solution was rendered very clear by the addition of one gramme of phosphate of ammonia and subsequent filtration. For a volume of 8 litres (14 pints) of this clear, saturated solution, we used [1 gramme = 15·43 grains]:—

Phosphate of ammonia .. .. 2 grammes.
Phosphate of potassium .. .. 1 ,,
Phosphate of magnesium .. .. 1 ,,
Sulphate of ammonia .. .. 0·5 ,,

298   STUDIES ON FERMENTATION.

ment of bacteria, and then underwent butyric fermentation. By June 9th the fermentation had become sufficiently active to enable us to collect in the course of twenty-four hours, over mercury, as in all our experiments, about 100 cc. (about 6 cubic inches) of gas. By June 11th, judging from the volume of gas liberated in the course of twenty-four hours, the activity of the fermentation had doubled. We examined a drop of the turbid liquid. Here are the notes accompanying the sketch (Fig. 70) as they stand in our note-book :—"A swarm of vibrios, so active in their movements that the eye has great difficulty in following them. They may be seen in pairs throughout the

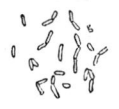

FIG. 70.

field, apparently making efforts to separate from each other. The connection would seem to be by some invisible, gelatinous thread, which yields so far to their efforts that they succeed in breaking away from actual contact, but yet are, for a while, so far restrained that the movements of one have a visible effect on those of the other. By and by, however, we see a complete separation effected, and each moves on its separate way with an activity still greater than it had before."

One of the best methods that can be employed for the microscopical examination of these vibrios, quite out of contact with air, is the following:—After butyric fermentation has been going on for several days in a flask, A (Fig. 71), we connect this flask by an india-rubber tube with one of the flattened bulbs previously described, page 156 (Fig. 31), which we then place on the stage of the microscope (Fig. 71). When we wish to make an observation we close, under the mercury, at the point b, the end of the drawn-out and bent delivery-tube. The continued evolution of gas soon exerts such a pressure within the flask, that when we open the tap r, the liquid is driven into the bulb *l l*, until it becomes quite full and the liquid flows over into the glass V. In this manner we may

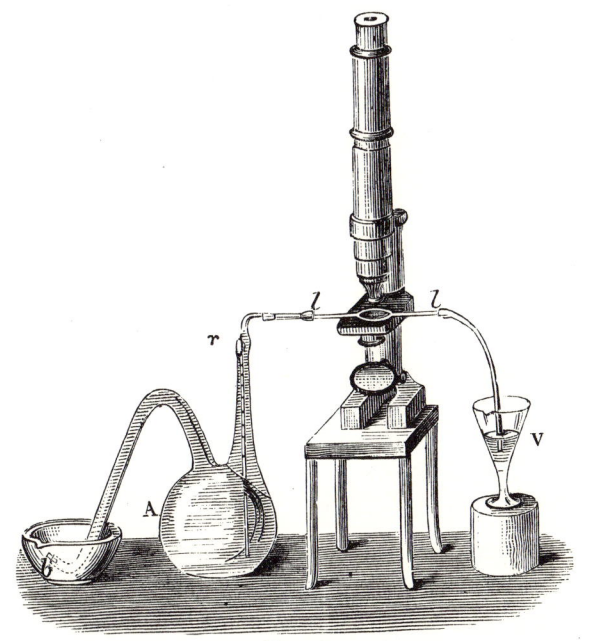

Fig. 71.

bring the vibrios under observation without their coming into contact with the least trace of air, and with as much success as if the bulb, which takes the place of an object glass, had been plunged into the very centre of the flask. The movements and fissiparous multiplication of the vibrios may thus be seen in all their beauty, and it is indeed a most interesting sight. The movements do not immediately cease when the temperature is suddenly lowered, even to a considerable extent, 15° C. (59° F.) for example; they are only slackened. Nevertheless, it is better to observe them at the temperatures most favourable to fermentation, even in the oven where the vessels employed in the experiment are kept at a temperature between 25° C. and 30° C. (77° F. and 86° F.).

We may now continue our account of the fermentation which we were studying when we made this last digression. On June 17th that fermentation produced three times as much gas as it did on June 11th, when the residue of hydrogen, after absorption by potash, was 72·6 per cent.; whilst on the 17th it was only 49·2 per cent. Let us again discuss the microscopic aspect of the turbid liquid at this stage. Appended is the sketch we made (Fig. 72) and our notes on it:—"A most beautiful object: vibrios all in motion, advancing or undulating. They have grown considerably in bulk and length since the 11th; many of them are joined together into long sinuous chains, very mobile at the articulations, visibly less active and more wavering in proportion to the number that go to form the chain, or the length of the individuals." This description is applicable to the majority of the vibrios which occur in cylindrical rods and are homogeneous in aspect. There are others, of rare occurrence in chains, which have a clear corpuscle, that is to say, a portion more refractive than the other parts of the segments, at one of their extremities.

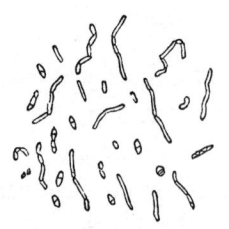

FIG. 72.

Sometimes the foremost segment has the corpuscle at one end, sometimes at the other. The long segments of the commoner kind attain a length of from 10 to 30 and even 45 thousandths of a millimetre. Their diameter is from $1\frac{1}{2}$ to 2, very rarely 3, thousandths of a millimetre.*

* [1 millimetre = 0·039 inch: hence the dimensions indicated will be— length, from 0·00039 to 0·00117, or even 0·00176 in.; diameter, from 0·000058 to 0·000078, rarely 0·000117 in.]

On June 28th, fermentation was quite finished; there was no longer any trace of gas, nor any lactate in solution. All the infusoria were lying motionless at the bottom of the flask. The liquid clarified by degrees, and in the course of a few days became quite bright. Here we may inquire, were these motionless infusoria, which from complete exhaustion of the lactate, the source of the carbonaceous part of their food, were now lying inert at the bottom of the fermenting vessel—were they dead beyond power of revival?* The following experiment leads us to believe that they were not perfectly lifeless, and that they behave in the same manner as the yeast of beer, which, after it has decomposed all the sugar in a fermentable liquid, is ready to revive and multiply in a fresh saccharine medium. On April 22nd, 1875, we left in the oven, at a temperature of 25° C. (77° F.), a fermentation of lactate of lime that had been completed. The delivery tube of the flask,

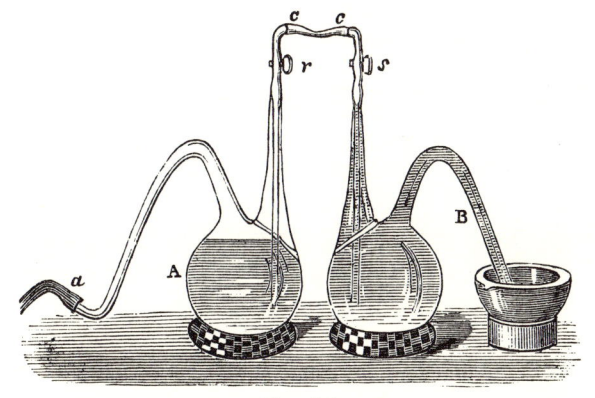

FIG. 73.

The carbonaceous supply, as we remarked, had failed them, and to this failure the absence of vital action, nutrition, and multiplication was attributable. The liquid, however, contained butyrate of lime, a salt possessing properties similar to those of the lactate. Why could not this salt equally well support the life of the vibrios? The explanation of the difficulty seems to us to lie simply in the fact that lactic acid produces heat by its decomposition, whilst butyric acid does not, and the vibrios seem to require heat during the chemical process of their nutrition.

A, (Fig. 73) in which it had taken place had never been withdrawn from under the mercury. We kept the liquid under observation daily, and saw it gradually become brighter; this went on for fifteen days. We then filled a similar flask, B, with the solution of lactate, which we boiled, not only to kill the germs of vibrios which the liquid might contain, but also to expel the air that it held in solution. When the flask, B, had cooled, we connected the two flasks, avoiding the introduction of air [*], after having slightly shaken the flask, A, to stir up the deposit at the bottom. There was then a pressure, due to carbonic acid at the end of the delivery tube of this latter flask, at the point a, so that on opening the taps r and s, the deposit at the bottom of flask A was driven over into flask B, which in consequence was impregnated with the deposit of a fermentation that had been completed fifteen days before. Two days after impregnation, the flask B began to show signs of fermentation. It follows, that the deposit of vibrios of a completed butyric fermentation may be kept, at least for a certain time, without losing the power of causing fermentation. It furnishes a butyric ferment, capable of revival and action in a suitable, fresh, fermentable medium.

The reader who has attentively studied the facts which we have placed before him cannot, in our opinion, entertain the least doubt on the subject of the possible multiplication of the vibrios of a fermentation of lactate of lime out of contact with atmospheric oxygen. If fresh proofs of this important proposition were necessary, they might be found in the following observations, from which it may be inferred that atmospheric oxygen is capable of suddenly checking a fermentation produced by butyric vibrios, and rendering them absolutely motionless, so that it cannot be necessary to enable them to live. On May 7th, 1862, we placed in the oven a flask holding 2·580 litres (4½ pints), and filled with the solution of

[*] To do this, it is sufficient first to fill the curved ends of the stopcocked tubes of the flasks, as well as the india-rubber tube $c\ c$, which connects them, with boiling water that contains no air.

lactate of lime and phosphates, which we had impregnated on the 9th with two drops of a liquid in butyric fermentation. In the course of a few days fermentation declared itself: on the 16th it was in progress, but feebly; on the 18th it was active; on the 30th it was very active. On June 1st it yielded hourly 35 c.c. (2·3 cubic inches) of gas, containing ten per cent. of hydrogen. On the 2nd we began the study of the action of air on the vibrios of this fermentation. To do this we cut off the delivery-tube on a level with its point of junction to the flask, then with a 50 c.c. pipette we took out that quantity (1¾ fl. oz.) of liquid which was, of course, replaced at once by air. We then reversed the flask with the opening under the mercury, and shook it every ten minutes for more than an hour. Wishing to make sure, to begin with, that the oxygen had been absorbed, we connected under the mercury the beak of the flask by means of a thin india-rubber tube filled with water, with a small flask, the neck of which had been drawn out, and was filled with water; we then raised the large flask with the smaller kept above it. A Mohr's clip, which closed the india-rubber tube, and which we then opened, permitted the water contained in the small flask to pass into the large one, whilst the gas, on the contrary, passed upwards from the large flask into the small one. We analyzed the gas immediately, and found that, allowing for carbonic acid and hydrogen, it did not contain more than 14·2 per cent. of oxygen, which corresponds to an absorption of 6·6 c.c., or of 3·3 c.c. (0·2 cubic inch) of oxygen for the 50 c.c. (3·05 cubic inches) of air employed. Lastly, we again established connection by an india-rubber tube between the flasks, after having seen by microscopical examination that the movements of the vibrios were very languid. Fermentation had become less vigorous without having actually ceased, no doubt because some portions of the liquid had not been brought into contact with the atmospheric oxygen, in spite of the prolonged shaking that the flask had undergone after the introduction of the air. Whatever the cause might have been, the significance of the phenomenon is not doubtful. To assure ourselves further of the effect of air on the vibrios, we half filled two test tubes with the fermenting liquid taken from another fermentation which had also attained its maximum of intensity, into one of which we passed a current of air, into the other carbonic acid gas. In the course of half an hour, all the vibrios in the aerated tube were dead, or at least motionless, and fermentation had ceased. In the other tube, after three hours' exposure to the effects of the carbonic acid gas, the vibrios were still very active, and fermentation was going on.

There is a most simple method of observing the deadly effect of atmospheric air upon vibrios. We have seen in the microscopical examination made by means of the apparatus represented in Fig. 71, how remarkable were the movements of the vibrios when absolutely deprived of air, and how easy it was to discern them. We will repeat this observation, and at the same time make a comparative study of the same liquid, under the microscope, in the ordinary way, that is to say, by placing a drop of the liquid on an object-glass, and covering it with a thin glass slip, a method which must necessarily bring the drop into contact with air, if only for a moment. It is surprising what a remarkable difference is observed immediately between the movements of the vibrios in the bulb and of those under the glass. In the case of the latter we generally see all movement at once cease near the edges of the glass, where the drop of liquid is in direct contact with the air; the movements continue for a longer or shorter time about the centre, in proportion as the air is more or less intercepted by the vibrios at the circumference of the liquid. It does not require much skill in experiments of this kind to enable one to see plainly that immediately after the glass has been placed on the drop, which has been affected all over by atmospheric air, the whole of the vibrios seem to languish and to manifest symptoms of illness— we can think of no better expression to explain what we see taking place—and that they gradually recover their activity about the centre, in proportion as they find themselves in part of the medium that is less affected by the presence of oxygen.

Some most curious facts are to be found in connection with an observation, the correlative and inverse of the foregoing, on the ordinary aërobian bacteria. If we examine below the microscope a drop of liquid full of these organisms under a coverslip, we very soon observe a cessation of motion in all the bacteria which lie in the central portion of the liquid, where the oxygen rapidly disappears to supply the necessities of the bacteria existing there; whilst, on the other hand, near the edges of the cover-glass the movements are very active, in consequence of the constant supply of air. In spite of the speedy death of the bacteria beneath the centre of the glass, we see life prolonged there if by chance a bubble of air has been enclosed. All round this bubble a vast number of bacteria collect in a thick, moving circle, but as soon as all the oxygen of the bubble has been absorbed they fall apparently lifeless, and are scattered by the movement of the liquid.*

We may here be permitted to add, as a purely historical matter, that it was these two observations just described, made successively one day in 1861, on vibrios and bacteria, that first suggested to us the idea of the possibility of life without air, and caused us to think that the vibrios which we met so frequently in our lactic fermentations must be the true butyric ferment.

We may pause a moment to consider an interesting question in reference to the two characters under which vibrios appear in butyric fermentations. What is the reason that some vibrios exhibit refractive corpuscles, generally of a lenticular form,

* We find this fact, which we published as long ago as 1863, confirmed in a work of H. Hoffmann's published in 1869, under the title *Mémoire sur les bactéries*, which has appeared in French (*Annales des Sciences naturelles*, 5th series, vol. xi.). On this subject we may cite an observation that has not yet been published. Aërobian bacteria lose all power of movement when suddenly plunged into carbonic acid gas; they recover it, however, as if they had only been suffering from anæsthesia, as soon as they are brought into the air again.

such as we see in Fig. 72? We are strongly inclined to believe that these corpuscles have to do with a special mode of reproduction in the vibrios, common alike to the anaërobian forms which we are studying, and the ordinary aërobian forms in which also the corpuscles of which we are speaking may occur. The explanation of the phenomenon, from our point of view, would be that, after a certain number of fissiparous generations, and under the influence of variations in the composition of the medium, which is constantly changing through fermentation as well as through the active life of the vibrios themselves, cysts, which are simply the refractive corpuscles, form along them at different points. From these gemmules we have ultimately produced vibrios, ready to reproduce others by the process of transverse division for a certain time, to be themselves encysted later on. Various observations incline us to believe that, in their ordinary form of minute, soft, exuberant rods, the vibrios perish when submitted to desiccation, but when they occur in the corpuscular or encysted form they possess unusual powers of resistance, and may be brought to the state of dry dust and be wafted about by winds. None of the matter which surrounds the corpuscle or cyst seems to take part in the preservation of the germ, when the cyst is formed, for it is all re-absorbed, gradually leaving the cyst bare. The cysts appear as masses of corpuscles, in which the most practised eye cannot detect anything of an organic nature, or anything to remind one of the vibrios which produced them; nevertheless, these minute bodies are endowed with a latent vital action, and only await favourable conditions to develop long rods of vibrios. We are not, it is true, in a position to adduce any very forcible proofs in support of these opinions. They have been suggested to us by experiments, none of which, however, have been absolutely decisive in their favour. We may cite one of our observations on this subject.

In a fermentation of glycerine in a mineral medium—the glycerine was fermenting under the influence of butyric vibrios—after we had determined the, we may say, exclusive presence of lenticular vibrios, with refractive corpuscles, we observed the fermentation, which, for some unknown reason, had been very languid, suddenly become extremely active, but now through the influence of ordinary vibrios. The gemmules with brilliant corpuscles had almost disappeared; we could see but very few, and those now consisted of the refractive bodies alone, the bulk of the vibrios accompanying them having undergone some process of re-absorption.

Another observation which still more closely accords with this hypothesis is given in our work on the silkworm disease (vol. i., page 256). We there demonstrate that, when we place in water some of the dust formed of desiccated vibrios, containing a host of these refractive corpuscles, in the course of a very few hours large vibrios appear, well-developed rods fully grown, in which the brilliant points are absent; whilst in the water no process of development from smaller vibrios is to be discerned, a fact which seems to show that the former had issued fully grown from the refractive corpuscles, just as we see *colpoda* issue with their adult aspect from the dust of their cysts. This observation, we may remark, furnishes one of the best proofs that can be adduced against the spontaneous generation of vibrios or bacteria, since it is probable that the same observation applies to bacteria. It is true that we cannot say of mere points of dust, examined under the microscope, that one particular germ belongs to vibrio, another to bacterium; but how is it possible to doubt that the vibrios issue, as we see them, from an ovum of some kind, a cyst, or germ, of determinate character, when, after having placed some of these indeterminate motes of dust into clean water, we suddenly see, after an interval of not more than one or two hours, an adult vibrio crossing the field of the microscope, without our having been able to detect any intermediate state between its birth and adolescence?

It is a question whether differences in the aspect and nature of vibrios, which depend upon their more or less advanced age, or are occasioned by the influence of certain conditions of the medium in which they propagate, do not bring about corresponding changes in the course of the fermentation and the nature of its products. Judging at least from the variations in the proportions of hydrogen and carbonic acid gas produced in butyric fermentations, we are inclined to think that this must be the case; nay, more, we find that hydrogen is not even a constant product in these fermentations. We have met with butyric fermentations of lactate of lime which did not yield the minutest trace of hydrogen, or anything besides carbonic acid. Fig. 74 represents the vibrios which we observed in a

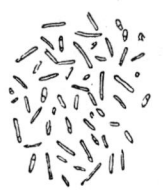

FIG. 74.

fermentation of this kind. They present no special features. Butyl alcohol is, according to our observations, an ordinary product, although it varies and is by no means a necessary concomitant of these fermentations. It might be supposed, since butylic alcohol may be produced, and hydrogen be in deficit, that the proportion of the former of these products would attain its maximum when the latter assumed a minimum. This, however, is by no means the case; even in those few fermentations that we have met with in which hydrogen was absent, there was no formation of butylic alcohol.

From a consideration of all the facts detailed in this paragraph we can have no hesitation in concluding that, on the one hand, in cases of butyric fermentation, the vibrios which abound in them and constitute their ferment, live without air or free oxygen; and that, on the other hand, the presence of gaseous oxygen operates prejudicially against the movements and activity of those vibrios. But now does it follow that the presence of minute quantities of air brought into contact with a liquid undergoing butyric fermentation would prevent the continuance of that fermentation, or even exercise any check upon it ? We have not made any direct experiments upon this subject; but we should not be surprised to find that, so far from hindering, air may, under such circumstances, facilitate the propagation of the vibrios and accelerate fermentation. This is exactly what happens in the case of yeast. But how could we reconcile this, supposing it were proved to be the case, with the fact just insisted on as to the danger of bringing the butyric vibrios into contact with air ? It may be possible that *life without air* results from habit, whilst *death through air* may be brought about by a sudden change in the conditions of the existence of the vibrios. The following remarkable experiment is well known : A bird is placed in a glass jar of one or two litres (60 to 120 cubic inches) in capacity, which is then closed. After a time the creature exhibits every sign of intense uneasiness and asphyxia long before it dies ; a similar bird of the same size is introduced into the jar; the death of the latter takes place instantaneously, whilst the life of the former may still be prolonged under these conditions for a considerable time, and there is no difficulty even in restoring the bird to perfect health by taking it out of the jar. It seems impossible to deny that we have here a case of the adaptation of an organism to the gradual contamination of the medium; and so it may likewise happen that the anaërobian vibrios of a butyric fermentation, which develop and multiply absolutely without free oxygen, perish immediately when suddenly taken out of their airless medium, and that the result might be different if they had been gradually brought under the action of air in small quantities at a time.

We are compelled here to admit that vibrios frequently abound in liquids exposed to the air, and that they appropriate the atmospheric oxygen, and could not withstand a sudden removal from its influence. Must we, then, believe that such vibrios are absolutely different from those of butyric fermentations? It would, perhaps, be more natural to admit that in the one case there is an adaptation to life with air, and in the other case an adaptation to life without air; each of these varieties perishing when suddenly transferred from its habitual condition to that of the other, whilst by a series of progressive changes one might be modified into the other.* We know that in the case of alcoholic ferments, although these can actually live without air, propagation is wonderfully assisted by the presence of minute quantities of air; and certain experiments, which we have not yet published, lead us to believe that, after having lived without air, they cannot be suddenly exposed with impunity to the influence of large quantities of oxygen.

We must not forget, however, that aërobian torulæ and anaërobian ferments present an example of organisms apparently identical, in which, however, we have not yet been able to discover any ties of a common origin. Hence we were forced to regard them as distinct species; and so it is possible that there may likewise be aërobian and anaërobian vibrios without any transformation of the one into the other.

The question has been raised whether vibrios, especially those which we have shown to be the ferment of butyric and many other fermentations, are, in their nature, animal or vegetable. M. Ch. Robin attaches great importance to the solution of this question, of which he speaks as follows†:—
"The determination of the nature, whether animal or vegetable, of organisms, either as a whole or in respect to their anatomical parts, assimilative or reproductive, is a problem which has been capable of solution for a quarter of a century. The method has been brought to a state of remarkable precision, experimentally, as well as in its theoretical aspects, since those who devote their attention to the organic sciences consider it indispensable in every observation and experiment

---

* These doubts might easily be removed by putting the matter to the test of direct experiment.

† ROBIN, Sur la nature des fermentations, &c. (Journal de l'Anatomie et de la Physiologie, July and August, 1875, p. 386).

to determine accurately, before anything else, whether the object of their study is animal or vegetable in its nature, whether adult or otherwise. To neglect this is as serious an omission for such students, as for chemists would be the neglecting to determine whether it is nitrogen or hydrogen, urea or stearine that has been extracted from a tissue, or which it is whose combinations they are studying in this or that chemical operation. Now, scarcely any one of those who study fermentations, properly so called, and putrefactions, ever pay attention to the preceding data. . . . . Among the observers to whom I allude even M. Pasteur is to be found, who, even in his most recent communications, omits to state definitely what is the nature of many of the ferments which he has studied, with the exception, however, of those which belong to the cryptogamic group called *torulaceæ*. Various passages in his works seem to show that he considers the cryptogamic organisms called *bacteria*, as well as those known as *vibrios*, as belonging to the animal kingdom (see *Bulletin de l'Académie de Médecine*, Paris, 1875, pp. 249, 251, especially 256, 266, 267, 289, and 290). These would be very different, at least physiologically, the former being *aërobian*, whilst the vibrios are *anaërobian*, that is to say, requiring no air to enable them to live, and being killed by oxygen, should it be dissolved in the liquid to any considerable extent."

We are unable to see the matter in the same light as our learned colleague does; to our thinking, we should be labouring under a great delusion were we to suppose " that it is quite as serious an omission not to determine the animal or vegetable nature of a ferment as it would be to confound nitrogen with hydrogen, or urea with stearine." The importance of the solutions of disputed questions often depends upon the point of view from which these are regarded. As far as the result of our labours is concerned, we devoted our attention to these two questions exclusively :—1. Is the ferment, in every fermentation properly so called, an organized being ? 2. Can this organized being live without air ? Now, what bearing can the question of the animal or vegetable nature of the ferment, of the organized being, have upon the investigation of these two problems? In studying butyric fermentation, for example, we endeavoured to establish these two fundamental points:—1. *The butyric ferment is a vibrio.* 2. *This vibrio may dispense with air in its life, and, as a matter of fact, does dispense with it in the act of producing butyric fermentation.* We did not consider it at all necessary to pronounce any opinion as to the animal or vegetable nature of this organism, and, even up to the present moment, the idea that vibrio is an animal and not a plant is, in our minds, a matter of sentiment rather than of conviction.

M. Robin, however, would have no difficulty in determining the limits of the two kingdoms. According to him, "every variety of cellulose is, we may say, insoluble in ammonia, as also are the reproductive elements of plants, whether male or female. Whatever phase of evolution the elements which reproduce a new individual may have reached, treatment with this reagent, either cold or raised to boiling, leaves them absolutely intact under the eyes of the observer, except that their contents, from being partially dissolved, become more transparent. Every vegetable, whether microscopic or not, every mycelium, and every spore thus preserves in its entirety its special characteristics of form, volume, and structural arrangements; whilst in the case of microscopic animals, or the ova and microscopic embryos of different members of the animal kingdom, the very opposite is the case."

We should be glad to learn that the employment of a drop of ammonia would enable us to pronounce an opinion, with this degree of confidence, on the nature of the lowest microscopic beings; but is M. Robin absolutely correct in his assumptions? That gentleman himself remarks that spermatozoa, which belong to animal organisms, are insoluble in ammonia, the effect of which is merely to make them paler. If a difference of action in certain reagents, in ammonia, for example, were sufficient to determine the limits of the animal and vegetable kingdoms, might we not argue that there must be a very great and natural difference between moulds and bacteria, inasmuch as the presence of a small quantity of acid in the nutritive medium facilitates the growth and propagation of the former, whilst it is able to prevent the life of bacteria and vibrios? Although, as is well known, movement is not an exclusive characteristic of animals, yet we have always been inclined to regard vibrios as animals, on account of the peculiar character of their movements. How greatly they differ in this respect from the diatomacæ, for example! When the vibrio encounters an obstacle it turns, or after having assured itself by some visual effort or other that it cannot overcome it, it retraces its steps. The colpoda—undoubted infusoria—behave in an exactly similar manner. It is true one may argue that the zoospores of certain cryptogamia exhibit similar movements; but do not these zoospores possess as much of an animal nature as do the spermatozoa? As far as bacteria are concerned, when, as already remarked, we see them crowd round a bubble of air in a liquid to prolong their life, oxygen having failed them everywhere else, how can we avoid believing that they are animated by an instinct for life, of the same kind as that which we find in animals. M. Robin seems to us to be wrong in supposing that it is possible to draw any absolute line of separation between the animal and vegetable kingdoms. The settlement of this line, however, we repeat again, no matter what it may be, has no serious bearing upon the questions that have been the subject of our researches.

In like manner the difficulty which M. Robin has raised in objecting to the employment of the word *germ*, when we cannot specify whether the nature of that germ is animal or vegetable, is in many respects an unnecessary one. In all the questions which we have discussed, whether we were speaking of fermentation or spontaneous generation, the word *germ* has been used in the sense of *origin of living organism*. If Liebig, for example, said of an albuminous substance that it gave birth to ferment, could we contradict him more plainly than by replying: "No; ferment is an organized being, the germ of which is always present, and the albuminous substance merely serves by its occurrence to nourish the germ and its successive generations."

In our Memoir of 1862, on so-called *spontaneous* generations, would it not have been an entire mistake to have attempted to assign specific names to the microscopic organisms which we met with in the course of our observations? Not only would we have met with extreme difficulty in the attempt, arising from the state of extreme confusion which even in the present day exists in the classification and nomenclature of these microscopic organisms, but we should have been forced to sacrifice clearness in our work besides; at all events, we should have wandered from our principal object, which was the determination of the presence or absence of life in general, and had nothing to do with the manifestation of a particular kind of life in this or that species, animal or vegetable. Thus we have systematically employed the vaguest nomenclature, such as *mucors, torulæ, bacteria*, and *vibrios*. There was nothing arbitrary in our doing this, whereas there is much that is arbitrary in adopting a definite system of nomenclature, and applying it to organisms but imperfectly known, the differences or resemblances between which are only recognizable through certain characteristics, the true signification of which is obscure. Take, for example, the extensive array of widely different systems that have been invented during the last few years for the species of the genera bacterium and vibrio in the works of Cohn, H. Hoffmann, Hallier, and Billroth. The confusion which prevails here is very great, although we do not of course by any means place these different works on the same footing as regards their respective merits.

M. Robin is, however, right in recognizing the impossibility of maintaining in the present day, as he formerly did, " that fermentation is an exterior phenomenon, going on outside cryptogamic cells, a phenomenon of contact. It is probably," he adds, " an interior and molecular action at work in the inmost recesses of the substance of each cell." From the day when we first proved that it is possible for all organized ferments, properly so called, to spring up and multiply from their respective germs, sown, whether consciously or by accident, in a mineral medium free from organic and nitrogenous matters other than ammonia, in which medium the fermentable matter alone is adapted to provide the ferment with whatever carbon enters into its composition, from that time forward the theories of Liebig, as well as that of Berzelius, which M. Robin formerly defended, have had to give place to others more in harmony with facts. We trust that the day will come when M. Robin will likewise acknowledge that he has been in error on the subject of the doctrine of spontaneous generation, which he continues to affirm, without adducing any direct proofs in support of it, at the end of the article to which we have been here replying.

We have devoted the greater part of this chapter to the establishing with all possible exactness the extremely important physiological fact of life without air, and its correlation to the phenomena of fermentations properly so called—that is to say, of those which are due to the presence of microscopic cellular organisms. This is the chief basis of the new theory that we propose for the explanation of these phenomena. The details into which we have entered were indispensable on account of the novelty of the subject no less than on account of the necessity we were under of combating the criticisms of the two German naturalists, Drs. Oscar Brefeld and Traube, whose works had cast some doubts on the correctness of the facts upon which we had based the preceding propositions. We have much pleasure in adding that at the very moment when we were revising the proofs of this chapter, we received from M. Brefeld an essay, dated from Berlin, January, 1876, in which, after describing his later experimental researches, he owns with praiseworthy frankness that Dr. Traube and he were both of them mistaken. Life without air is now a proposition which he accepts as perfectly demonstrated. He has witnessed it in the case of *mucor racemosus*, and has also verified it in the case of yeast. "If," he says, "after the results of my previous researches, which I conducted with all possible exactness, I was inclined to consider Pasteur's assertions as inaccurate, and to attack them, I have no hesitation now in recognizing them as true, and in proclaiming the service which Pasteur has rendered to science in being the first to indicate the exact relation of things in the phenomenon of fermentation." In his later researches, Dr. Brefeld has adopted the method which we have long employed for demonstrating the life and multiplication of butyric vibrios in the entire absence of air, as well as the method of conducting growths in mineral media associated with the fermentable substance. We need not pause to consider certain other secondary criticisms of Dr. Brefeld. A perusal of the present work will, we trust, convince him that they are based on no surer foundation than were his former criticisms.

To bring one's self to believe in a truth that has just dawned upon one is the first step towards progress; to persuade others is the second. There is a third step, less useful perhaps, but highly gratifying nevertheless, which is, to convince one's opponents.

We, therefore, have experienced great satisfaction in learning that we have won over to our ideas an observer of singular ability, on a subject which is of the utmost importance to the physiology of cells.

§ VI.—REPLY TO THE CRITICAL OBSERVATIONS OF LIEBIG, PUBLISHED IN 1870.*

In the Memoir which we published, in 1860, on alcoholic fermentation, and in several subsequent works, we were led to a different conclusion on the causes of this very remarkable phenomenon from that which Liebig had adopted. The opinions of Mitscherlich and Berzelius had ceased to be tenable in the presence of the new facts which we had brought to light. From

* LIEBIG, *Sur la fermentation et la source de la force musculaire* (*Annales de Chimie et de Physique*, 4th series, t. xxiii. p. 5, 1870.)

that time we felt sure that the celebrated chemist of Munich had adopted our conclusions, from the fact that he remained silent on this question for a long time, although it had been until then the constant subject of his study, as is shown by all his works. Suddenly there appeared in the *Annales de Chimie et de Physique* a long essay, reproduced from a lecture delivered by him before the Academy of Bavaria in 1868 and 1869. In this Liebig again maintained, not, however, without certain modifications, the views which he had expressed in his former publications, and disputed the correctness of the principal facts enunciated in our Memoir of 1860, on which were based the arguments against his theory.

"I had admitted," he says, "that the resolution of fermentable matter into compounds of a simpler kind must be traced to some process of decomposition taking place in the ferment, and that the action of this same ferment on the fermentable matter must continue or cease according to the prolongation or cessation of the alteration produced in the ferment. The molecular change in the sugar would, consequently, be brought about by the destruction or modification of one or more of the component parts of the ferment, and could only take place through the contact of the two substances. M. Pasteur regards fermentation in the following light:—The chemical action of fermentation is essentially a phenomenon correlative with a vital action, beginning and ending with it. He believes that alcoholic fermentation can never occur without the simultaneous occurrence of organization, development, and multiplication of globules, or continuous life, carried on from globules already formed. But the idea that the decomposition of sugar during fermentation is due to the development of the cellules of the ferment, is in contradiction with the fact that the ferment is able to bring about the fermentation of a pure solution of sugar. The greater part of the ferment is composed of a substance that is rich in nitrogen and contains sulphur. It contains, moreover, an appreciable quantity of phosphates, hence it is difficult to conceive how, in the absence of these elements in a pure solution of sugar undergoing fermentation, the number of cells is capable of any increase."

Notwithstanding Liebig's belief to the contrary, the idea that the decomposition of sugar during fermentation is intimately connected with a development of the cellules of the ferment, or a prolongation of the life of cellules already formed, is in no way opposed to the fact that the ferment is capable of bringing about the fermentation of a pure solution of sugar. It is manifest to any one who has studied such fermentation with the microscope, even in those cases where the sweetened water has been absolutely pure, that ferment-cells do multiply, the reason being that the cells carry with them all the food-supplies necessary for the life of the ferment. They may be observed budding, at least many of them, and there can be no doubt that those which do not bud still continue to live; life has other ways of manifesting itself besides development and cell-proliferation.

If we refer to the figures on page 81 of our Memoir of 1860, Experiments D, E, F, G, H, I, we shall see that the weight of yeast, in the case of the fermentation of a pure solution of sugar, undergoes a considerable increase, even without taking into account the fact that the sugared water gains from the yeast certain soluble parts, since, in the experiments just mentioned, the weights of solid yeast, washed and dried at 100° C. (212° F.), are much greater than those of the raw yeast employed, dried at the same temperature.

In these experiments we employed the following weights of yeast, expressed in grammes (1 gramme = 15·43 grains)—

2·313
2·626
1·198
0·699
0·326
0·476

which became after fermentation, we repeat, without taking

into account the matters which the sugared water gained from the yeast—

	grammes.	grains.
2·486	[Increase 0·173	= 2·65
2·963	,, 0·337	= 5·16
1·700	,, 0·502	= 7·7
0·712	,, 0·013	= 0·2
0·335	,, 0·009	= 0·14
0·590	,, 0·114	= 1·75

Have we not in this marked increase in weight a proof of life, or, to adopt an expression which may be preferred, a proof of a profound chemical work of nutrition and assimilation ?

We may cite on this subject one of our earlier experiments, which is to be found in the *Comptes rendus de l'Académie* for the year 1857, and which clearly shows the great influence exerted on fermentation by the soluble portion that the sugared water takes up from the globules of ferment :—

" We take two equal quantities of fresh yeast that have been washed very freely. One of these we cause to ferment in water containing nothing but sugar, and, after removing from the other all its soluble particles—by boiling it in an excess of water and then filtering it to separate the globules—we add to the filtered liquid as much sugar as was used in the first case along with a mere trace of fresh yeast, insufficient, as far as its weight is concerned, to affect the results of our experiment. The globules which we have sown bud, the liquid becomes turbid, a deposit of yeast gradually forms, and, side by side with these appearances, the decomposition of the sugar is effected, and in the course of a few hours manifests itself clearly. These results are such as we might have anticipated. The following fact, however, is of importance. In effecting by these means the organization into globules of the soluble part of the yeast that we used in the second case, we find that a considerable quantity of sugar is decomposed. The following are the results of our experiment : 5 grammes of yeast caused the fermentation of 12·9 grammes of sugar in six days, at the end of which time it was exhausted. The soluble portion of a like quantity of 5 grammes of the same yeast caused the fermentation of 10 grammes of sugar in nine days, after which the yeast developed by the sowing was likewise exhausted."

How is it possible to maintain that, in the fermentation of water containing nothing but sugar, the soluble portion of the yeast does not act, either in the production of new globules or the perfection of old ones, when we see, in the preceding experiment, that after this nitrogenous and mineral portion has been removed by boiling, it immediately serves for the production of new globules, which, under the influence of the sowing of a mere trace of globules, causes the fermentation of much sugar?*

In short, Liebig is not justified in saying that the solution of pure sugar, caused to ferment by means of yeast, contains none of the elements needed for the growth of yeast, neither nitrogen, sulphur, nor phosphorus, and that, consequently, it should not be possible, by our theory, for the sugar to ferment. On the contrary, the solution does contain all these elements, as a consequence of the introduction and presence of the yeast.

Let us proceed with our examination of Liebig's criticisms:—

"To this," he goes on to say, "must be added the decomposing action which yeast exercises on a great number of substances,

---

* It is important that we should here remark that, in the fermentation of pure solution of sugar by means of yeast, the oxygen originally dissolved in the water, as well as that appropriated by the globules of yeast in their contact with air, has a considerable effect on the activity of fermentation. As a matter of fact, if we pass a strong current of carbonic acid through the sugared water and the water in which the yeast has been treated, the fermentation will be rendered extremely sluggish, and the few new cells of yeast which form will assume strange and abnormal aspects. Indeed this might have been expected, for we have seen that yeast, when somewhat old, is incapable of development or of causing fermentation, even in a fermentable medium containing all the nutritive principles of yeast, if the liquid has been deprived of air; much more should we expect this to be the case in pure sugared water, likewise deprived of air.

and which resembles that which sugar undergoes. I have shown that malate of lime ferments readily enough through the action of yeast, and that it splits up into three other calcareous salts, namely, the acetate, the carbonate, and the succinate. If the action of yeast consists in its increase and multiplication, it is difficult to conceive this action in the case of malate of lime and other calcareous salts of vegetable acids."

This statement, with all due deference to the opinion of our illustrious critic, is by no means correct. Yeast has no action on malate of lime, or on other calcareous salts formed by vegetable acids. Liebig had previously, much to his own satisfaction, brought forward urea as being capable of transformation into carbonate of ammonia during alcoholic fermentation in contact with yeast. This has been proved by us to be erroneous. It is an error of the same kind that Liebig again brings forward here. In the fermentation of which he speaks (that of malate of lime), certain spontaneous ferments are produced, the germs of which are associated with the yeast, and develop in the mixture of yeast and malate. The yeast merely serves as a source of food for these new ferments without taking any direct part in the fermentations of which we are speaking. Our researches leave no doubt on this point, as is evident from the observations on the fermentations of tartrate of lime previously given.

It is true that there are circumstances under which yeast brings about modifications in different substances. Doebereiner and Mitscherlich, more especially, have shown that yeast imparts to water a soluble material, which liquefies cane-sugar and produces inversion in it by causing it to take up the elements of water, just as diastase behaves to starch or emulsin to amygdalin.

M. Berthelot also has shown that this substance may be isolated by precipitating it with alcohol, in the same way as diastase is precipitated from its solutions.* These are remark-

* DOEBEREINER, *Journal de Chimie de Schweigger*, vol. xii. p. 129, and *Journal de Pharmacie*, vol. i. p. 342.
MITSCHERLICH, *Monatsberichte d. Kön. Preuss. Akad. d. Wissen. zu Berlin,*

able facts, which are, however, at present but vaguely connected with the alcoholic fermentation of sugar by means of yeast. The researches in which we have proved the existence of special forms of living ferments in many fermentations, which one might have supposed to have been produced by simple contact action, had established beyond doubt the existence of profound differences between those fermentations, which we have dis-

and *Rapports annuels de Berzelius*, Paris, 1843, 3rd year. On the occasion of a communication on the inversion of cane sugar, by H. Rose, published in 1840, M. Mitscherlich observed: "The inversion of cane sugar in alcoholic fermentation is not due to the globules of yeast, but to a soluble matter in the water with which they mix. The liquid obtained by straining off the ferment on a filter paper, possesses the property of converting cane sugar into uncrystallizable sugar."

BERTHELOT, *Comptes rendus de l'Académie*. Meeting of May 28th, 1860. M. Berthelot confirms the preceding experiment of Mitscherlich, and proves, moreover, that the soluble matter of which that author speaks may be precipitated with alcohol without losing its invertive power.

M. Béchamp has applied Mitscherlich's observation, concerning the soluble fermentative part of yeast, to fungoid growths, and has made the interesting discovery that fungoid growths, like yeast, yield to water a substance that inverts sugar. When the production of fungoid growths is prevented by means of an antiseptic the inversion of sugar does not take place.

We may here say a few words respecting M. Béchamp's claim to priority of discovery. It is a well-known fact that we were the first to demonstrate that living ferments might be completely developed, if their germs were placed in pure water, together with sugar, ammonia, and phosphates. Relying on this established fact, that moulds are capable of development in sweetened water, in which, according to M. Béchamp, they invert the sugar, our author asserts that he has proved that, "living organized ferments may originate in media which contain no albuminous substances." (See *Comptes rendus*, vol. lxxv. p. 1519.) To be logical, M. Béchamp might say that he has proved that certain moulds originate in pure sweetened water, without nitrogen or phosphates or other mineral elements, for such a deduction might very well be drawn from his work, in which we do not find the least expression of astonishment at the possibility of moulds developing in pure water, containing nothing but sugar without other mineral or organic principles.

M. Béchamp's first Note on the inversion of sugar was published in 1855. In it we find nothing relating to the influence of moulds. His second, in which that influence is noticed, was published in January, tinguished as fermentations proper, and the phenomena connected with soluble substances. The more we advance, the more clearly we are able to detect these differences. M. Dumas has insisted on the fact that the ferments of fermentation proper multiply and reproduce themselves in the process, whilst the others are destroyed.* Still more recently M. Müntz has shown that chloroform prevents fermentations proper, but does not interfere with the action of diastase (*Comptes rendus*, 1875.) M. Bouchardat had already established the fact that "hydrocyanic acid, salts of mercury, ether, alcohol, creosote, and the oils of turpentine, lemon, cloves, and mustard destroy or check alcoholic fermentation, whilst in no way interfering with the glucoside fermentations (*Annales de Chimie et de Physique*, 3rd series, t. xiv., 1845.) We may add, in praise of M. Bouchardat's sagacity, that that skilful observer has always considered these results as a proof that alcoholic fermentation is dependent on the life of the yeast-cell, and that a distinction should be made between the two orders of fermentation.

M. Paul Bert, in his remarkable studies on the influence of

1858, that is, subsequently to our work on lactic fermentation, which appeared in November, 1857. In that work we established, for the first time, that the lactic ferment is a living organized being, that albuminous substances have no share in the production of fermentation, and that they only serve as the food of the ferment. M. Béchamp's Note was even subsequent to our first work on alcoholic fermentation, which appeared on December 21st, 1857. It is since the appearance of these two works of ours that the preponderating influence of the life of microscopic organisms, in the phenomena of fermentation, has been better understood. Immediately after their appearance M. Béchamp, who, from 1855, had made no observation on the action of fungoid growths on sugar, although he had remarked their presence, modified his former conclusions. (*Comptes rendus*, January 4th, 1858.)

* "There are two classes of ferments; the first, of which the yeast of beer may be taken as the type, perpetuate and renew themselves if they can find in the liquid in which they produce fermentation food enough for their wants; the second, of which diastase is the type, always sacrifice themselves in the exercise of their activity." (DUMAS, *Comptes rendus de l'Académie*, t. lxxv. p. 277, 1872.)

barometric pressure on the phenomena of life, has recognized the fact that compressed oxygen is fatal to certain ferments, whilst under similar conditions it does not interfere with the action of those substances classed under the name of *soluble ferments*, such as diastase (the ferment which inverts cane sugar) emulsin, and others. During their stay in compressed air, ferments proper ceased their activity, nor did they resume it, even after exposure to air at ordinary pressures, provided the access of germs was prevented.

We now come to Liebig's principal objection, with which he concludes his ingenious argument, and to which no less than eight or nine pages of the *Annales* are devoted.

Our author takes up the question of the possibility of causing yeast to grow in sweetened water, to which a salt of ammonia and some yeast-ash have been added—a fact which is evidently incompatible with his theory that a ferment is always an albuminous substance on its way to decomposition. In this case the albuminous substance does not exist; we have only the mineral substances which will serve to produce it. We know that Liebig regarded yeast, and, generally speaking, any ferment whatever, as being a nitrogenous, albuminous substance which, in the same way as emulsin, for example, possesses the power of bringing about certain chemical decompositions. He connected fermentation with the easy decomposition of that albuminous substance, and imagined that the phenomenon occurred in the following manner :—" The albuminous substance on its way to decomposition possesses the power of communicating to certain other bodies that same state of mobility by which its own atoms are already affected; and through its contact with other bodies it imparts to them the power of decomposing or of entering into other combinations." Here Liebig failed to perceive that the ferment, in its capacity of a living organism, had anything to do with the fermentation.

This theory dates back as far as 1843. In 1846 Messrs. Boutron and Fremy, in a Memoir on lactic fermentation, published in the *Annales de Chimie et de Physique*, strained the conclusions deducible from it to a most unjustifiable extent. They asserted that one and the same nitrogenous substance might undergo various modifications in contact with air, so as to become successively alcoholic, lactic, butyric, and other ferments. There is nothing more convenient than purely hypothetical theories, theories which are not the necessary consequences of facts; when fresh facts which cannot be reconciled with the original hypothesis are discovered, new hypotheses can be tacked on to the old ones. This is exactly what Liebig and Fremy have done, each in his turn, under the pressure of our studies, commenced in 1857. In 1864 Fremy devised the theory of *hemi-organism*, which meant nothing more than that he gave up Liebig's theory of 1843, together with the additions which Boutron and he had made to it in 1846; in other words, he abandoned the idea of albuminous substances being ferments, to take up another idea, that albuminous substances, in contact with air, are peculiarly adapted to undergo organization into new beings—that is, the living ferments which we had discovered—and that the ferments of beer and of the grape have a common origin.

This theory of hemi-organism was word for word the antiquated opinion of Turpin, as may be readily seen by referring to Chapter IV., section III. of the present work. The public, especially a certain section of the public, did not go very deeply into an examination of the subject. It was the period when the doctrine of spontaneous generation was being discussed with much warmth. The new word hemi-organism, which was the only novelty in M. Fremy's theory, deceived people. It was thought that M. Fremy had really discovered the solution of the question of the day. It is true that it was rather difficult to understand the process by which an albuminous substance could become all at once a living and budding cell. This difficulty was readily solved by M. Fremy, who declared that it was the result of some power that was not yet understood, the power of "organic impulse."[*]

[*] FREMY, *Comptes rendus de l'Académie*, vol. lviii. p. 1065, 1864.

Liebig, who, as well as M. Fremy, was compelled to renounce his original opinions concerning the nature of ferments, devised the following obscure theory (Memoir by Liebig, 1870, already cited) :—

"There seems to be no doubt as to the part which the vegetable organism plays in the phenomenon of fermentation. It is through it alone that an albuminous substance and sugar are enabled to unite and form this particular combination, this unstable form under which alone, as a component part of the mycoderm, they manifest an action on sugar. Should the mycoderm cease to grow, the bond which unites the constituent parts of the cellular contents is loosened, and it is through the motion produced therein that the cells of yeast bring about a disarrangement or separation of the elements of the sugar into other organic molecules."

One might easily believe that the translator for the *Annales* has made some mistake, so great is the obscurity of this passage.

Whether we take this new form of the theory or the old one, neither can be reconciled at all with the development of yeast and fermentation in a saccharine mineral medium, for in the latter experiment fermentation is correlative to the life of the ferment and to its nutrition, a constant change going on between the ferment and its food-matters, since all the carbon assimilated by the ferment is derived from sugar, its nitrogen from ammonia, and phosphorus from the phosphates in solution. And even all said, what purpose can be served by the gratuitous hypothesis of contact-action or communicated motion ? The experiment of which we are speaking is thus a fundamental one ; indeed, it is its possibility that constitutes the most effective point in the controversy. No doubt Liebig might say, " but it is the motion of life and of nutrition which constitutes your experiment, and this is the communicated motion that my theory requires." Curiously enough, Liebig does endeavour, as a matter of fact, to say this, but he does so timidly and incidentally : " From a chemical point of view, which point of view I would not willingly abandon, a *vital action* is a phenomenon of motion, and, in this double sense of *life* M. Pasteur's theory agrees with my own, and is not in contradiction with it (page 6)." This is true. Elsewhere Liebig says:—

"It is possible that the only correlation between the physiological act and the phenomenon of fermentation is the production, in the living cell, of the substance which, by some special property analogous to that by which emulsin exerts a decomposing action on salicin and amygdalin, may bring about the decomposition of sugar into other organic molecules; the physiological act, in this view, would be necessary for the production of this substance, but would have nothing else to do with the fermentation (page 10)." To this, again, we have no objection to raise.

Liebig, however, does not dwell upon these considerations, which he merely notices in passing, because he is well aware that, as far as the defence of his theory is concerned, they would be mere evasions. If he had insisted on them, or based his opposition solely upon them, our answer would have been simply this: "If you admit with us that fermentation *is* correlated with the life and nutrition of the ferment, we agree upon the principal point. So agreeing, let us examine, if you will, the actual cause of fermentation;—this is a second question, quite distinct from the first. Science is built up of successive solutions given to questions of ever-increasing subtlety, approaching nearer and nearer towards the very essence of phenomena. If we proceed to discuss together the question of how living, organized beings act in decomposing fermentable substances, we will be found to fall out once more on your hypothesis of communicated motion, since, according to our ideas, the actual cause of fermentation is to be sought, in most cases, in the fact of life without air, which is the characteristic of many ferments."

Let us briefly see what Liebig thinks of the experiment in which fermentation is produced by the impregnation of a saccharine mineral medium, a result so greatly at variance with his mode of viewing the question.* After deep consideration he pronounces this experiment to be inexact, and the result ill-founded. Liebig, however, was not one to reject a fact without grave reasons for his doing so, or with the sole object of evading a troublesome discussion. "I have repeated this experiment," he says, "a great number of times, with the greatest possible care, and have obtained the same results as M. Pasteur, excepting as regards the formation and increase of the ferment." It was, however, the formation and increase of the ferment that constituted the point of the experiment. Our discussion was, therefore, distinctly limited to this: Liebig denied that the ferment was capable of development in a saccharine mineral medium, whilst we asserted that this development did actually take place, and was comparatively easy to prove. In 1871 we replied to M. Liebig before the Paris Academy of Sciences in a Note, in which we offered to prepare in a mineral medium, in the presence of a commission to be chosen for the purpose, as great a weight of ferment as Liebig could reasonably demand.† We were bolder than we should, perhaps, have been in 1860; the reason was that our knowledge of the subject had been strengthened by ten years of renewed research. Liebig did not accept our proposal, nor did he even reply to our Note. Up to the time of his death, which took place on April 18th, 1873, he wrote nothing more on the subject.‡

* See our Memoir of 1860 (*Annales de Chimie et de Physique*, vol. lviii. p. 61, and following, and especially pp. 69 and 70, where the details of the experiment will be found.

† PASTEUR, *Comptes rendus de l'Académie des Sciences*, vol. lxxiii. p. 1419, 1871.

‡ In his Memoir of 1870, Liebig has made a remarkable admission: "My late friend Pelouze," he says, "had communicated to me, nine years ago, certain results of M. Pasteur's researches on fermentation. I told him that, just then, I was not disposed to alter my opinion on the cause of fermentation, and that if it were possible by means of ammonia to produce or multiply the yeast in fermenting liquors, industry would soon avail itself of the fact, and that I would wait to see if it did so; up to the present time, however, there has not been the least change in the manufacture of yeast." We do not know what M. Pelouze's reply was;

When we published, in 1860, the details of the experiment in question, we pointed out at some length the difficulties of conducting it successfully, and the possible causes of failure. We called attention particularly to the fact that saccharine mineral media are much more suited for the nutrition of bacteria, lactic ferment, and other lowly forms, than they are to that of yeast, and in consequence readily become filled with various organisms from the spontaneous growth of germs derived from the particles of dust floating in the atmosphere. The reason why we do not observe the growth of alcoholic ferments, especially at the commencement of the experiments, is because of the unsuitableness of those media for the life of yeast. The latter may, nevertheless, form in them subsequent to this development of other organized forms, by reason of the modification produced in the original mineral medium by the albuminous matters that they introduce into it. It is interesting to peruse, in our Memoir of 1860, certain facts of the same kind relating to fermentation by means of albumens—that of the blood, for example, from which, we may mention incidentally, we were led to infer the existence of several distinct albumens in the serum, a conclusion which, since then, has been confirmed by various observers, notably by M. Béchamp. Now, in his experiments on fermentation in sweetened water, with yeast-ash and a salt of ammonia, there is no doubt that Liebig had failed to avoid those difficulties which are entailed by the spontaneous growth of other organisms than yeast. Moreover, it is possible that, to have established the certainty of this result, Liebig should have had recourse to a closer microscopical observation than from certain passages in his Memoir he seems to have

but it is not difficult to conceive so sagacious an observer remarking to his illustrious friend, that the possibility of deriving pecuniary advantage from the wide application of a new scientific fact had never been regarded as the criterion of the exactness of that fact. We could prove, moreover, by the undoubted testimony of very distinguished practical men, notably by that of M. Pezeyre, director of distilleries, that upon this point also Liebig was mistaken.

adopted. We have little doubt that his pupils could tell us that Liebig did not even employ that instrument without which any exact study of fermentation is not merely difficult but well-nigh impossible. We ourselves, for the reasons mentioned, did not obtain a simple alcoholic fermentation any more than Liebig did. In that particular experiment, the details of which we gave in our Memoir of 1860, we obtained lactic and alcoholic fermentation together; an appreciable quantity of lactic acid formed and arrested the propagation of the lactic and alcoholic ferments, so that more than half of the sugar remained in the liquid without fermenting. This, however, in no way detracted from the correctness of the conclusion which we deduced from the experiment, and from other similar ones; it might even be said that, from a general and philosophical point of view—which is the only one of interest here—the result was doubly satisfactory, inasmuch as we demonstrated that mineral media were adapted to the simultaneous development of several organized ferments, instead of only one. The fortuitous association of different ferments could not invalidate the conclusion that all the nitrogen of the cells of the alcoholic and lactic ferments was derived from the nitrogen in the ammoniacal salts, and that all the carbon of those ferments was taken from the sugar, since, in the medium employed in our experiment, the sugar was the only substance that contained carbon. Liebig carefully abstained from noticing this fact, which would have been fatal to the very groundwork of his criticisms, and thought that he was keeping up the appearance of a grave contradiction by arguing that we had never obtained a simple alcoholic fermentation. It would be unprofitable to dwell longer upon the subject of the difficulties which the propagation of yeast in a saccharine mineral medium formerly presented. As a matter of fact, the progress of our studies has imparted to the question an aspect very different from that which it formerly wore; it was this circumstance which emboldened us to offer, in our reply to Liebig before the Academy of Sciences in 1871, to prepare, in a saccharine mineral medium, in the presence of a commission to be appointed by our opponent, any quantity of ferment that he might require, and to effect the fermentation of any weight of sugar whatsoever.

Our knowledge of the facts detailed in the preceding chapters concerning pure ferments and their manipulation in the presence of pure air, enables us to completely disregard those causes of embarrassment that result from the fortuitous occurrence of the germs of organisms, different in character from the ferments, introduced by the air or from the sides of vessels, or even by the ferment itself.

Let us once more take one of our double-necked flasks (Fig. 22, p. 110), which we will suppose is capable of containing three or four litres (six to eight pints).

Let us put into it the following :—

Pure distilled water.
Sugar candy .. .. 200 grammes.
Bitartrate of potassium .. 1·0 ,,
,, ,, ammonia .. 0·5 ,,
Sulphate of ammonia .. 1·5 ,,
Ash of yeast .. .. 1·5 ,,
[1 gramme = 15·43 grains.]

Let us boil the mixture, to destroy all germs of organisms that may exist in the air or liquid or on the sides of the flask, and then permit it to cool, after having placed, by way of extra precaution, a small quantity of asbestos in the end of the fine, curved tube. Let us next introduce a trace of ferment into the liquid, through the other neck, which, as we described, is terminated by a small piece of india-rubber tube closed with a glass stopper.

Here are the details of such an experiment :—

On December 9, 1873, we sowed some pure ferment—*saccharomyces pastorianus*. From December 11, that is, within so short a time as forty-eight hours after impregnation, we saw a multitude of extremely minute bubbles rising almost continuously from the bottom, indicating that at this point the fermentation had commenced. On the following days, several patches of froth appeared on the surface of the liquid. We left the flask undisturbed in the oven, at a temperature of 25° C. (77° F.). On April 24, 1874, we tested some of the liquid, obtained by means of the straight tube, to see if it still contained any sugar. We found that it contained less than two grammes, so that 198 grammes (4·2 oz. Troy) had already disappeared. Some time afterwards the fermentation came to an end; we carried on the experiment, nevertheless, until April 18, 1875.

There was no development of any organism absolutely foreign to the ferment, which was itself abundant, a circumstance that, added to the persistent vitality of the ferment, in spite of the unsuitableness of the medium for its nutrition, permitted the perfect completion of fermentation. There was not the minutest quantity of sugar remaining. The total weight of ferment, after washing and drying at 100° C. (212° F.), was 2·563 grammes (39·5 grains).

In experiments of this kind, in which the ferment has to be weighed, it is better not to use any yeast-ash that cannot be dissolved completely, so as to be capable of easy separation from the ferment formed. Raulin's liquid, the composition of which we have already given (p. 89, footnote), may be used in such cases with success.

All the alcoholic ferments are not capable to the same extent of development by means of phosphates, ammoniacal salts, and sugar. There are some whose development is arrested a longer or shorter time before the transformation of all the sugar. In a series of comparative experiments, 200 grammes of sugar-candy being used in each case, we found that whilst *saccharomyces pastorianus* effected a complete fermentation of the sugar, the caseous ferment did not decompose more than two-thirds, and the ferment which we have designated *new " high " ferment* not more than one-fifth: and keeping the flasks for a longer time in the oven had no effect in increasing the proportions of sugar fermented in these two last cases.

We conducted a great number of fermentations in mineral

media, in consequence of a circumstance which it may be interesting to mention here. A person who was working in our laboratory asserted that the success of our experiments depended upon the impurity of the sugar-candy which we employed, and that if this sugar had been pure—much purer than was the ordinary, white, commercial sugar-candy, which up to that time we had always used—the ferment could not have multiplied. The persistent objections of our friend, and our desire to convince him, caused us to repeat all our previous experiments on the subject, using sugar of great purity, which had been specially prepared for us, with the utmost care, by a skilful confectioner, Seugnot. The result only confirmed our former conclusions. Even this did not satisfy our obstinate friend, who went to the trouble of preparing some pure sugar for himself, in little crystals, by repeated crystallizations of carefully-selected commercial sugar-candy; he then repeated our experiments himself. This time all his doubts were overcome. It even happened that the fermentations with the perfectly pure sugar instead of being slow were very active, when compared with those which we had conducted with the commercial sugar-candy.

We may here add a few words on the non-transformation of yeast into *penicillium glaucum*.

If at any time during fermentation we pour off the fermenting liquid, the deposit of yeast remaining in the vessel may continue there, in contact with air, without our ever being able to discover the least formation of *penicillium glaucum* in it. We may keep a current of pure air constantly passing through the flask; the experiment will give the same result. Nevertheless, this is a medium peculiarly adapted to the development of this mould, inasmuch as if we introduce merely a few spores of *penicillium*, an abundant vegetation of that growth will afterwards appear on the deposit. The descriptions of Messrs. Turpin, Hoffmann, and Trécul have, therefore, been based on one of these illusions which we meet with so frequently in microscopical observations.

When we laid these facts before the Academy,* M. Trécul professed his inability to comprehend them : †

"According to M. Pasteur," he said, "the yeast of beer is *anaërobian*, that is to say, it lives in a liquid deprived of free oxygen; and to become *mycoderma* or *penicillium* it is above all things necessary that it should be placed in air, since, without this, as the name signifies, an aërobian being cannot exist. To bring about the transformation of the yeast of beer into *mycoderma cerevisiæ* or into *penicillium glaucum*, we must accept the conditions under which these two forms are obtained. If M. Pasteur will persist in keeping his yeast in media which are incompatible with the desired modification, it is clear that the results which he obtains must be always negative."

Contrary to this perfectly gratuitous assertion of M. Trécul's, we do not keep our yeast in media which are calculated to prevent its transformation into *penicillium*. As we have just seen, the principal aim and object of our experiment was to bring this minute plant into contact with air, and under conditions that would allow the *penicillium* to develop with perfect freedom. We conducted our experiments exactly as Turpin and Hoffmann conducted theirs, and exactly as they stipulate that such experiments should be conducted—with the one sole difference, indispensable to the correctness of our observations, that we carefully guarded ourselves against those causes of error which they did not take the least trouble to avoid. It is possible to produce a ready entrance and escape of pure air in the case of the double-necked flasks which we have so often employed in the course of this work, without having recourse to the continuous passage of a current of air. Having made a file-mark on the thin curved neck at a distance of two or three centimetres (an inch) from the flask, we must cut round the neck at this point with a glazier's diamond, and then remove it, taking care to cover the opening immediately with a sheet of paper

---

* PASTEUR, *Comptes rendus de l'Académie*, vol. lxxviii. pp. 213-216.
† TRÉCUL, *Comptes rendus de l'Académie*, vol. lxxviii. pp. 217, 218.

which has been passed through the flame, and which we must fasten with a thread round the part of the neck still left. In this manner we may increase or prolong the fructification of fungoid growths, or the life of aërobian ferments in our flasks.

What we have said of *penicillium glaucum* will apply equally to *mycoderma cerevisiæ*. Notwithstanding what Turpin and Trécul may assert to the contrary, yeast, in contact with air as it was under the conditions of the experiment just described, will not yield *mycoderma vini* or *mycoderma cerevisiæ* any more than it will *penicillium*.

The experiments described in the preceding paragraphs on the increase of organized ferments in mineral media of the composition described, are of great physiological interest. Amongst other results, they show that all the proteic matter of ferments may be produced by the vital activity of the cells, which, apart altogether from the influence of light or free oxygen (unless, indeed, we are dealing with aërobian moulds which require free oxygen), have the power of developing a chemical activity between carbo-hydrates, ammoniacal salts, phosphates and sulphates of potassium and magnesium. It may be admitted with truth that a similar effect obtains in the case of the higher plants, so that in the existing state of science we fail to conceive what serious reason can be urged against our considering this effect as general. It would be perfectly logical to extend the results of which we are speaking to all plants, and to believe that the proteic matter of vegetables, and perhaps of animals also, is formed exclusively by the activity of the cells operating upon the ammoniacal and other mineral salts of the sap or plasma of the blood, and the carbo-hydrates, the formation of which, in the case of the higher plants, requires only the concurrence of the chemical impulse of green light.

Viewed in this manner, the formation of the proteic substances would be independent of the great act of reduction of carbonic acid gas under the influence of light. These substances would not be built up from the elements of water, ammonia, and carbonic acid gas, after the decomposition of this last; they would be formed where they are found in the cells themselves, by some process of union between the carbo-hydrates imported by the sap, and the phosphates of potassium and magnesium and salts of ammonia. Lastly, in vegetable growth, by means of a carbo-hydrate and a mineral medium, since the carbo-hydrate is capable of many variations, and it would be difficult to understand how it could be split up into its elements before serving to constitute the proteic substances, we may hope to obtain as many distinct proteic substances, and even cellulose substances, as there are carbo-hydrates. We have commenced certain studies in this direction.

If solar radiation is indispensable to the decomposition of carbonic acid and the building up of the primary substances in the case of higher vegetable life, it is still possible that certain inferior organisms may do without it and nevertheless yield the most complex substances, fatty or carbo-hydrate, such as cellulose, various organic acids, and proteic matter; not, however, by borrowing their carbon from the carbonic acid which is saturated with oxygen, but from other matters still capable of acquiring oxygen, and so of yielding heat in the process, such as alcohol and acetic acid, for example, to cite merely carbon compounds most removed from organization. As these last compounds, and a host of others equally adapted to serve as the carbonaceous food of *mycoderms* and the mucedines, may be produced synthetically by means of carbon and the vapour of water, after the methods that science owes to Berthelot, it follows that, in the case of certain inferior beings, life would be possible even if it should be that the solar light was extinguished.*

---

* See on this subject the verbal observations which we addressed to the Academy of Sciences, at its meetings of April 10th and 24th, 1876.

CHAPTER VII.

New Process for the Manufacture of Beer.

THE principles established in the course of this work implicitly involve the conditions of a new process of manufacture, the essential feature of which would consist in the production of a beer of excellent keeping qualities, we might even say a beer that could not undergo alteration. It will not be difficult now to make ourselves clear on the point.

We have shown in the first place, that the changes which take place in the ferment, the wort, and the beer itself, are due to the presence of microscopic organisms of an entirely different character to that of the ferment-cells properly so called, which organisms, by simultaneously giving rise, in the course of their multiplication in the wort, ferment, or beer, to other products, make the materials difficult to keep or effect their deterioration. Again, we have seen that these change-producing organisms, the ferments of disease, never arise spontaneously in the wort or beer, but, whenever they make their appearance in these fluids, have been imported from without, either in company with the yeast, or from accession of atmospheric dust, or from contact with the vessels, or from the materials themselves which the brewer uses in his manufacture. Moreover, we know that these disease-ferments, or their germs, are destroyed when the wort has its temperature raised to the boiling-point. And, following up the inferences from such facts, we have seen that wort exposed to pure air, after having

z

been heated to boiling, remains absolutely free of any sort of fermentation.

Inasmuch then as the disease-germs of wort and beer are destroyed in the copper in which the wort is boiled, and as, by employing a perfectly pure ferment, we guard against the admission of any foreign ferment of an evil character, we have it in our power to prepare a beer which shall be incapable of undergoing any pernicious fermentation whatsoever. This we shall have effected provided we can take the wort as run off from the coppers, cool and manipulate it out of contact with ordinary air or in contact with pure air, charge it with a pure yeast, and, lastly, store the beer when the fermentation is complete in vessels thoroughly purified from disease-ferments.*

§ I.—PRELIMINARY EXPERIMENTS.

We may readily satisfy ourselves as to the truth of these inferences. The following is one of the earliest experiments which I devised with a view to establish their certainty. Into a flask with a straight neck of about a litre ($1\frac{3}{4}$ pints) capacity, a quantity of wort from a brewery was introduced and there raised to boiling, and whilst the vapour still issued from the neck of the flask, connection was made with a two-necked flask in which the cultivation of pure yeast had been carried on.

* M. Galland, a brewer in Maxéville, near Nancy, published with his name, in November, 1875, a pamphlet, which was reproduced in the brewing journals of that date, bearing the title, *It is said,* "*the air being impure, let us exclude it ;*" *I say,* "*The air being impure, let us purify it.*" These two aphorisms, together or apart, constitute the essential novelty of my researches on beer, and M. Galland is mistaken in attempting to appropriate the merit of the second alternative (see my note in the *Comptes rendus* of the 17th November, 1873, and the text of the letters-patent obtained 13th March of that year). M. Galland has devised some arrangements for putting the latter of these two schemes into practice; but it is possible, of course, to effect this in a variety of ways. M. Velten, a brewer in Marseilles, had already accomplished this in his efforts to carry out practically the procedure advocated in the present work.

The cork and glass tube used for this purpose had previously been treated with boiling water.

When the wort had cooled down in the flask and matters were arranged as represented in Fig. 75, I raised the two-necked flask so as to cause a little of the liquid and yeast to flow into the wort. Thereupon fermentation was set up, and the resulting carbonic acid gas made its escape by the drawn-out end of the doubled-necked flask. The entire arrangement with

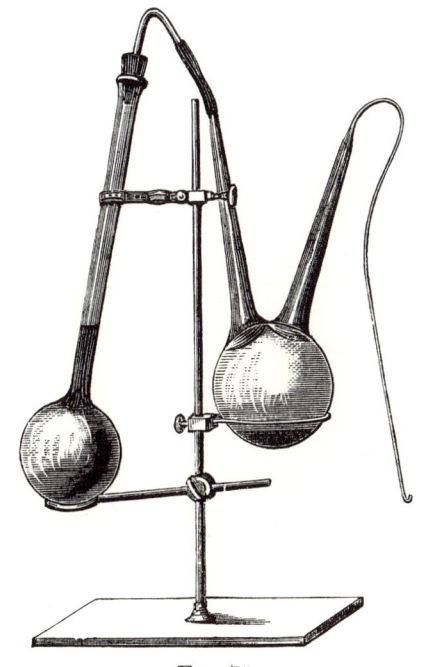

FIG. 75.

its supporting stand remained in this connection for eighteen months, sometimes on a stove, sometimes in the laboratory, exposed to all the variations of external temperature. At the end of that time I tasted the beer in the flask; it was perfectly sound, and the ferment, submitted to the microscope, showed not the slightest trace of any foreign ferments: and, doubtless, the

340   STUDIES ON FERMENTATION.

experiment might have been protracted over any number of years with the same result.

The only change that occurs in course of time is the appearance in the neck of the flask at the surface of the beer of a deposit of small prominences resembling a crystallization, but which really consists of those forms of ferment to which in Chapter V. I attached the name of *aërobian ferment*. The beer, after being transferred to a bottle that had been washed with hot water, was kept for several months in the heat of summer, without exhibiting the slightest trace of deterioration.

The essential conditions of the preceding experiment can

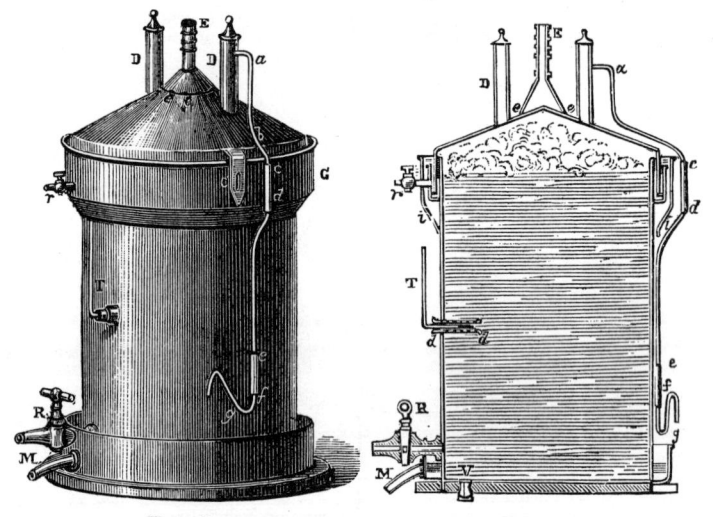

FIG. 76.   FIG. 77.

readily be realized on the large scale. For this purpose we may employ the apparatus in the above sketch (Figs. 76 and 77) constructed of tin or tinned copper. As appears from the sketch, this consists of a cylindrical tub resting on a support, and closed at the top by a cover, whose lower edge fits into a gutter containing water. The wort prepared in the copper is led into the cylinder, a process which does not materially lower its temperature. Now we know that wort in breweries which has been cooled in contact with the air, and so got charged with disease-germs, will, nevertheless, recover its faculty of keeping for any length of time in pure air, if we again raise its temperature to 80° C. (176° F.) or even 70° or 75° C. (158°, 167° F.) Having filled the tub with the hot wort and put on the lid, we then connect, by means of a caoutchouc tube $c\,d$, the metal tube $a\,c$ (which opens into one of the tubulures projecting above the lid) with the system of tubes $d\,e, f\,g$, of which $d\,e$ is fixed to the cylinder; ef is a caoutchouc junction connecting e with the bent glass tube g. We then dash over the apparatus, lid, tubulures, and their corks a quantity of boiling water. This collects in the gutter in which the lid rests, and any excess overflows into a second gutter outside the first, where, however, it cannot remain, but passes away by means of a ring of small holes between the base of the outer trough $i\,i$ and the cylinder. The overflow is collected in a third trough at the bottom, whence it can be removed by a pipe M. T is a bent thermometer to indicate the temperature of the wort; its bulb is protected by an inlet socket $d\,d$, pierced with holes; r is a stopcock for discharging the water in the gutter, which serves as a hydraulic junction between the cylinder and its lid; R, V, are stopcocks, or openings for the discharge of the liquid in the cylinder and its deposit. The next process is to cool the vessel, which may be done either by leaving it to itself, or by introducing a current of cold water through the tubulure E, soldered on to the lid. This tubulure is of the form of an inverted funnel, and is pierced at the bottom with a close row of holes, through which the cold water issues in a sheet over the surface of the cover. In whichever way the cooling is effected, the external air continues all the time to enter the vessel beneath the lid by way of the long, narrow passage $g, f\,e\,d\,c\,a$, and must necessarily get purified by depositing in its course all fungoid-germs, just as happened in the case of the two-necked flask of air experiments. This, however, may be still further secured by introducing a small plug of cotton wool, or asbestos, into the end of the tube g.

The experiments which we have carried out with this apparatus have proved that, by adopting such an arrangement, beer, a liquid peculiarly liable to change, may be kept as long as we wish, for weeks or months, in contact with air, since the tube g is open, without evincing the least symptom of disease. It matters little whether the leaves and strobiles of the hops are introduced with the hot wort or strained off; the result is the same. On the other hand, a leak in the apparatus from which the wort gets mixed with ordinary water from outside during cooling, will speedily effect a change in the wort and cause it to swarm with vibrios, or butyric ferment, lactic ferment, and other germs of disease, whilst its taste will be rendered extremely nauseous. It can only be through one's own fault, that is, from want of skill in carrying out the operation, that any change can be brought about by the water in the gutter not being kept out of the fermenting vessel. That water may even become putrid without the organisms contained in it being able to reach the wort in the fermenting vessel. The apparatus may be of any size whatever; we have worked with vessels containing 12 hectolitres with as much ease and certainty as when we used an apparatus of 1 hectolitre (22 gallons).

It is easy to carry out the process of cooling in the presence of carbonic acid gas if we fit a bent tube, similar to $a\,c\,d\,e\,f\,g$, to the second tubulure D. Through this tube, or its companion, the gas can be passed as it issues from an apparatus in which it is generated, or from a gasometer filled with it, or from a vessel of beer undergoing fermentation.

However, there is no necessity that the cooling should take place in the fermenting vessel. It may be effected separately, in vessels of greater or less depth, in spiral coils surrounded with cold water, or in any kind of refrigerator, provided always that the conditions of purity are satisfied, and that the flow of the cooled wort takes place under the same conditions. Jets of steam, which are already extensively used for the cleansing of pipes in breweries, may be employed here with great advantage.

The pitching may be effected in various ways. A two-necked

flask of a capacity of from 200 to 300 cc. (about 7 to 10 fl. ozs.), in which not more than 100 cc. (3½ fl. ozs.) of wort has been fermented, will be sufficient for an apparatus of 1 hectolitre (22 gallons), although the flask may not contain more than 1 or 2 decigrammes (1½ to 3 grains) of yeast. In the manufacture of beer, as at present conducted, the employment of so minute a quantity of yeast would lead to most disastrous results. The fermentation would unfailingly become lactic and butyric, since the foreign germs with which commercial worts and yeasts are always contaminated would have ample time to develop during the first twenty-four or forty-eight hours, whilst the small quantity of yeast used in the pitching could scarcely do more than begin to develop during that time. It is simply with the object of avoiding these secondary fermentations that the brewer uses large quantities of yeast for pitching. After the wort and yeast have been *pulled up*,* a process which every practical brewer adopts after pitching, every part of the liquid is occupied by a multitude of yeast-cells, which seize upon the oxygen in solution, germinate with activity, turn to their own account the food-supplies most easily assimilated, and prevent the growth of the germs of disease-ferments. In the new process which we are now explaining, things happen quite differently. Our wort is pure, and our yeast is pure, and if only a single cell of yeast were introduced into the wort, the vital activity of this would be sufficient to bring about alcoholic fermentation, and to transform the wort into beer, without our having the least reason to apprehend the simultaneous development of any other organisms whatsoever. In short, the new process enables us to pitch with as small a quantity of yeast as we like. It is, nevertheless, inexpedient to employ too minute a quantity, since by doing so we should retard the commencement of fermentation.

In the case of an apparatus of 5 hectolitres (110 gallons) or double that capacity, the pitching may be accomplished by means

* [Non-technically, stirred about.—ED.]

of flasks holding from 4 to 9 litres (from 7 to 10 or 11 pints), (Fig. 79), or copper cans, tinned inside, holding from 10 to 15

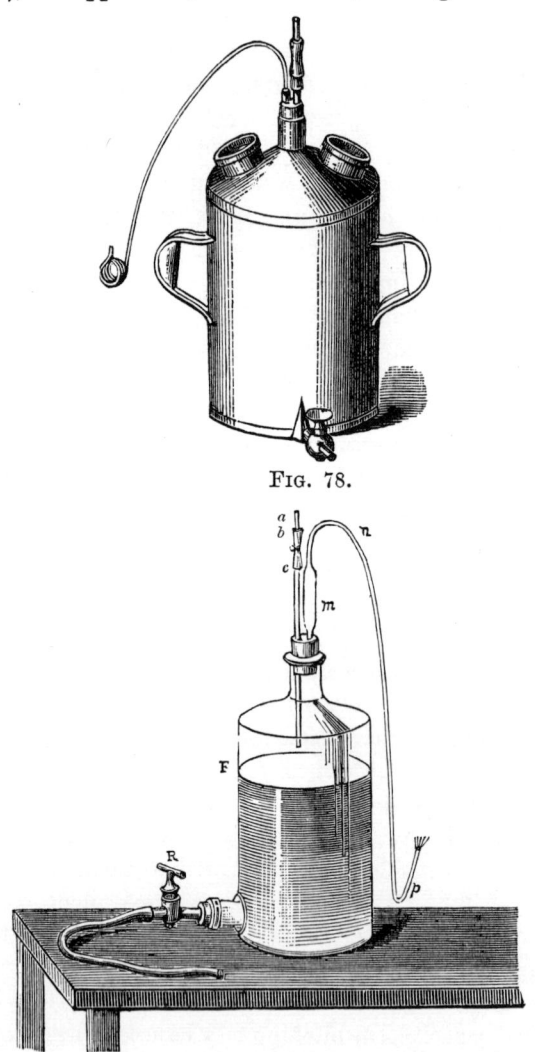

FIG. 78.

FIG. 79.

litres (2¼ to 3¼ gallons), and provided at the upper conical end with glass tubes (Fig. 78). The vessel must be half or two-thirds filled with wort. For this purpose it will be well always to employ wort that has been preserved in bottles by Appert's process. We must use a stopper provided with tubes, as represented in Fig. 79 : ab is a glass stopper which closes the india-rubber tube bc; mnp is a fine glass tube, or, better still, made of copper.

The tap R being closed, a long india-rubber tube is attached to the extremity of the curved tube, and the flask is completely immersed in a hot-water bath; the india-rubber tube projects from the bath and keeps the interior of the vessel in communication with the external atmosphere. If the tube mnp is of copper, we may avail ourselves of its flexibility and bend it upwards, so as to place its open extremity outside the bath. The water in the bath is then gradually raised to a temperature of 100° C. (212° F.), at which it is kept for a quarter or half an hour. In the case of copper cans, it is more convenient to place them over a gas-heater. They may be treated in the same manner as the flasks with curved necks. Vessels prepared in this manner may remain in a laboratory, or in any part of a brewery, for an indefinite time, without the wort in them undergoing the least change. It gradually darkens in colour through a direct oxidation of a purely chemical nature, but no tendency to disease will manifest itself.

Some days before we require to pitch an apparatus of several hectolitres, we impregnate one of these flasks or cans.* For this purpose we pass the flame of a spirit lamp over the tubes cba and mnp, to destroy the particles of dust that might pass inside at the moment when the stopper ab is taken out, and then by means of a long, straight glass tube we take some of

* As stated in the paragraph on aërobian ferments, in Chapter V., "low" yeasts, to be preserved in their state of "lowness," must be submitted to often-repeated growths—every fifteen days in winter and every ten days in summer, that is to say, they must be grown afresh after each of these intervals. If this is done, there will be no reason to apprehend the formation of aërobian ferments, which, as we have stated before, may embarrass us by transforming our "low" yeasts into "high" yeasts.

the liquid from a flask or vessel containing pure beer in a state of fermentation, and let a few drops of this, with the yeast that it holds in suspension, fall into the flask or can ; the stopper $a\ b$ is once more passed through the flame and then replaced ; generally in the course of one or two days the yeast develops in the flask sufficiently for the fermentation to show itself. We may shorten the operation still further by emptying into the can the contents of one of those double-necked flasks. To do this, we have simply to attach the straight tube of the flask to the india-rubber $b\ c$, and pour the liquid in. In a similar manner we introduce, through one of the tubulures surmounting the lid of the fermenting apparatus, the contents of the flasks or cans, either whilst they are still in active fermentation, or after fermentation is over. For this purpose, the tap R is connected by means of an india-rubber tube (Fig. 79), with a tube passing through a cork fixed in one of the tubulures of the large apparatus. All this may be done in considerably less time than we have taken to describe it ; and the operation may be performed accurately and safely by any one who has witnessed it a few times, even though he may not be skilled in chemical manipulations, especially if he takes care to bear in mind the very simple principles which we have explained.

Since certain parts of the apparatus—the outer opening of the tap, or the india-rubber tubing, for example—may contract particles of dust from the air, those parts, before being used, must be boiled in water, or washed with boiling water, or passed through the flame of a spirit lamp, to destroy the germs mixed with the particles of dust that settle upon them.

The method of cooling the wort in contact with carbonic acid prevents access of oxygen to the latter up to the time of pitching, so that the development of the yeast takes place apart from the influence of oxygen. Now, we know that these conditions necessitate the employment of a very young yeast— a yeast that is in course of active germination, such as may be taken from an incipient preparatory fermentation. Nevertheless, even with this, the development of the yeast under such conditions is extremely slow, and the fermentation takes from fifteen to twenty-five days; whilst, under the same circumstances, but with an aerated wort, it would be finished in from eight to twelve days. This is a considerable drawback, but, perhaps, a still more serious inconvenience is that the beer takes much longer to clarify, and does so with greater difficulty than those beers which are made with aerated worts. At the same time, this is largely compensated by the superior quality of the beer, which is stronger and has greater fulness on the palate, whilst the aroma of the hops is preserved to an extent never found in beers brewed by the ordinary process. Besides this, the yeast deposited at the bottom of the fermenting vessel is much less active, and, being of an older type, is revived with greater difficulty than that which forms in aerated worts. This, which might be considered a disadvantage, if we had to employ the yeast afterwards for pitching, has the great advantage of giving a beer which, when racked, undergoes its secondary fermentation only slowly, and with difficulty.* A beer of this kind is better adapted than ordinary beer to stand a long journey without developing great pressure inside the casks, and, if bottled, it will contain very little deposit, and will not froth violently when uncorked. The reason is, that a yeast is the more active, the more ready to multiply rapidly, and to work vigorously the more highly aerated the wort was in which it was grown. On the other hand, a yeast formed apart from air readily gets exhausted, and may even perish in the liquid in which it ferments, when that is kept out of contact with air; in other words, the vital action of yeast is more restricted when

* It has been observed by brewers that, sometimes, without any apparent cause, a yeast suddenly becomes inactive and fermentation ceases. Accidents of this kind may probably be explained in the same manner as the facts of which we are speaking. If a wort has not been aerated, or if it has been deprived of oxygen by a commencing development of microscopic organisms, the yeast formed in it will be very inferior, and the fermentation may stop at its commencement or soon afterwards. In such a case, an aeration of the yeast and wort would be the best remedy.

it has not been subjected to the action of oxygen during its formation.

If a great depth of wort, the surface of which alone is in contact with atmospheric air, is left to cool down, it will act in almost exactly the same manner as that which is cooled under an atmosphere of carbonic acid gas, because the oxygen of the air is very slow in pervading wort that is undisturbed. The gas will be taken into solution by the upper layer only, whilst the bulk of the liquid will remain unaffected by it. In some experiments which we conducted in a vessel which contained wort to a depth of 70 centimetres (27·5 inches), and which was provided with a tap that enabled us to draw off some of the liquid every day, until we had reduced the depth to 35 centimetres, we found, at the end of eight days, that there was not a trace of oxygen in solution at the latter depth. It is even probable that, considering the slow diffusion of the oxygen, on the one hand, and the combination that may take place between it and certain components of the malt, on the other hand, it would take a long time for all the wort, if undisturbed and of a certain depth, to become saturated with oxygen. In the vessel represented in Figs. 76 and 77 there is a considerable depth of wort to cool down. Nevertheless, the mere fact of the possibility of an aeration from the surface, whilst the wort is cooling down in contact with pure air, is enough to account for a certain effect that is produced on the yeast, later on, for the more youthful appearance of the yeast of the deposit, compared with that which we find in the case of wort cooled in the presence of carbonic acid gas. The difference between the results is particularly striking if, in both cases, we follow up microscopically the development of the yeast during the first few days succeeding the pitching.

The influence of the air on fermentation is considerable. In the ordinary process of brewing, fermentations would be almost impossible, and in every case most defective, if the wort, before being run into the fermenting vessels, were not aerated by its passage over the "coolers," where the aeration is more or less effective, according as the liquid is more or less shallow. Worts and yeasts being impure, that is containing the germs of foreign ferments, those germs would have time to germinate in the fermenting vessels during the delay that the want of aeration in the wort would cause in the development of the yeast. We are aware that several inventions have been proposed to do away with the coolers, and we feel convinced that the object has been to remedy irregularities in fermentation. Considering the facts which we have published[*] on the development of yeast in the presence of air, and its inactivity in non-aerated media, such inventions ought to be supplemented by some means of further aeration for the prevention of the mischief that they must otherwise cause. In the existing process of brewing, the employment of coolers is a necessity.

The influence of the air on the vital action of the yeast may be proved in ways innumerable. The following is an experiment which we have often carried out with surprising results. A fermentation is going on; we draw off the liquid as rapidly as we please, and pour it back again into the vessel immediately. Within an hour we find a marked increase in the fermentation, evidenced by the liberation of a greater quantity of carbonic acid gas. This experiment may be performed with especial ease if we use the fermenting apparatus that we have described, for, by fitting a gas measurer to the escape tube $a\ b\ c\ d\ e\ f\ g$, the number of litres produced before the drawing off of the liquid may be compared with those obtained after. The least physical change in the running of the fermenting liquid whilst it is being drawn off, modifies the effect in question; such as change in the diameter of the stream, the height from which it falls, its greater or less scattering in falling, all influence it. Again, as might be expected from such results, corresponding modifications take place in the cells of yeast which come under the influence of the air. They become firmer in aspect and outline, their plasma becomes fuller, assumes a younger and more

[*] PASTEUR, *Comptes rendus de l'Académie des Sciences*, vol. lii. p. 1260, and *Études sur le Vin*, 2nd Edition, p. 277.

transparent aspect, and the vacuoles disappear. The molecular granulations, too, are less apparent. At a certain focus they disappear; at another they reappear, not as black spots, however, but as brilliant points so small as to be scarcely perceptible. If germination has been suspended it is resumed; in short, everything tends to prove—and having the yeast actually under our eyes we cannot doubt the fact—that the life of the cells is more decided, and the work of nutrition more active after they have been brought into contact with the oxygen of the air, and have absorbed a greater or less quantity of that gas.

Under the ordinary conditions of brewing, the atmospheric air is present in very varying quantities, whether introduced by the wort which holds more or less in solution, or by diffusion over the surface of the vessels, so that the same cells of yeast live by turns without air and with air. At first they absorb all the oxygen held in solution, and multiply under the influence of this absorption. Afterwards, when the supply has been exhausted, and various assimilations have resulted from it, they are deprived of it. Their life continues apart from oxygen, and if the vessel were closed, fermentation would be accomplished under these conditions, although more slowly. The vessel being open, a small quantity of air diffuses continuously through the layer of carbonic acid gas on the surface, and supports the vitality of the cells.

It is interesting to observe that, in the working of breweries, there are several empirical practices the explanation of which is to be found wholly in the fact that the aeration of wort or beer exercises a great influence on fermentation. In many breweries we have seen the pitching performed in the following manner: the brewer, having mixed his yeast in many times its volume of wort, pours all the thick liquid from a height from one bucket into another, and from that back again into the first, and so on a great many times, until the two buckets are filled with the froth enclosing air. In certain London breweries we have seen a bucket suspended by a pulley over the fermenting tun, which is 3 or 4 metres (10 or 12 feet) in depth ; this the brewer, by means of a cord, can lower into the tun and pull up again at will, giving it a kind of see-saw movement which agitates the surface of the liquid and aerates it. The use of the fermenting tun itself and the racking of the wort from that tun into casks have the effect of aerating the beer and the yeast, and imparting to the latter a greater vigour and activity.

The resumption of fermentation in cask, after the beer has been run out of the tuns in "low" fermentation breweries is, in our opinion, principally due to the aeration of the beer at the moment when it is racked. The brewer ought to bear in mind that, during racking, every detail is of importance ; it makes a great difference whether when the beer is run into the casks it falls from a height or is conducted by a tube to the bottom of the casks, whether it passes directly into the casks, or is poured into them from buckets, and whether it runs in a stream of small or large diameter, since these different methods cause the introduction of corresponding different quantities of air into the beer.

We have devised a simple arrangement for bringing the fermenting liquid into contact with various proportions of atmospheric air. Appended is a sketch of this apparatus (Fig. 80). Instead of one tube serving alike for the entrance and escape of gas, there are two similar ones, each of which opens into one of the tubulures on the cover. Round the other end of one of the tubes is fitted a kind of muff or bag, composed of a cylindrical cage of metallic gauze, over which a layer of well-combed cotton wool is placed, the whole being covered with a muslin bag. The object of this arrangement is to act as an air-filter for retaining the particles of dust. When fermentation has commenced in the apparatus, we have simply to press momentarily the india-rubber connection between the tube from the lid and the tube with the bag. This will at once cause a regular stream of carbonic acid to issue from the end of the uncovered tube, whilst the air will enter by the filtering tube to take its place ; and this arrangement will be maintained throughout the whole course of the fermentation, even if we omit the precaution of increasing the power of the syphon by making the tube for the escape of this gas longer than the other one.*

It will be readily understood how, whether by this last method, or by the diameter of the tubes, we may vary the

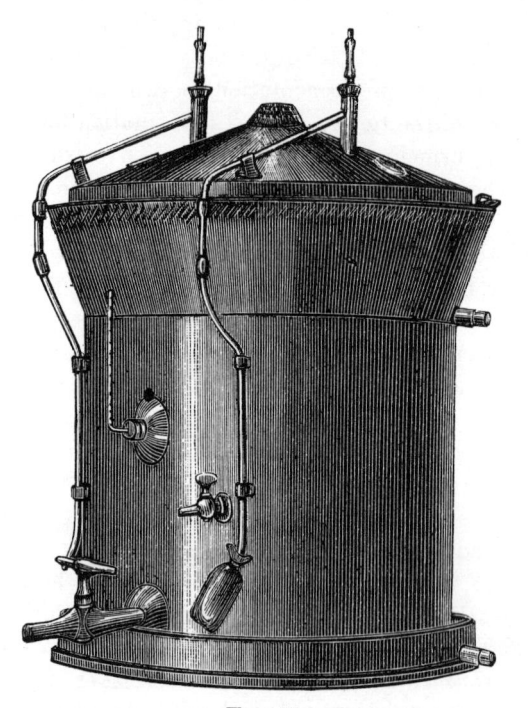

FIG. 80.

conditions of this circulation of air in the apparatus, on the surface of the beer.

* We may here remark that the system of gutters in the above apparatus is much simpler than that described in connection with Figs. 76 and 77. The water which falls on the cover is carried off, when the gutter is full, by a circle of grooves, inclined so that the streams running from them meet and form more readily a sheet of water, which flows over the exterior surface of the cylindrical vessel.

§ II.—Method of Estimating the Oxygen held in Solution in Wort.

The use of carbonic acid gas and the cooling of the wort, in contact with that gas or in contact with very limited quantities of pure air, are by no means necessary to the application of the new process. There is only one thing that is absolutely essential—which is, the *purity* of the gases in the presence of which the wort is cooled and treated. If, therefore, it is well to aerate our wort, either before or during fermentation, this may be done, on the sole condition that the air employed does not introduce any germs of disease that are likely to develop in the beer during fermentation or afterwards. The question of aerating the wort is not, however, so simple a matter as it seems at first sight. A very simple observation will show that wort cannot be safely oxygenated by exposure, without precaution, to the air, even leaving out of account the germs of disease which that air may contain. It is easy to show that finished wort has a decided flavour and aroma of hops, as well as a sweet taste, and that it leaves a certain pleasant, bitter after-taste on the palate. When we taste it in this condition we cannot help thinking that a liquor of the kind, after fermentation, ought to constitute a very valuable beverage, as wholesome as it is pleasant. Now all this pleasant and refreshing sensation that the wort leaves on the palate, which is due as much to the aroma as to the bitterness of the hop, disappears absolutely, we may say, if the wort is left exposed to contact with air for a sufficient time, and that whether the air be warm or cold. We may easily perform the experiment in one of our two-necked flasks, in which we can preserve the wort, in contact with pure air, without any fear of change. The oxygen of the air enters into combination with the substances that the hop introduces into the wort, and the wort, in consequence of this oxidation, gradually becomes transformed into a saccharine decoction, without odour, in which even the bitter flavour is destroyed or hidden. In other words, the wort grows weak and flat, in just the same way that beer and wine do, as well as all the various natural or artificial worts which serve to produce them. Thus it is evident that considerable care is necessary in subjecting wort and beer, whether in course of manufacture or finished, to the action of atmospheric air. If, therefore, it is a good thing to supply wort with oxygen, as we have already pointed out, in order to facilitate the fermentation and nourish the yeast, it is, on the other hand, important that the quantity supplied to it should not be too great, otherwise we may injure the quality of the beer, and particularly its fulness on the palate, that is its apparent strength, which has very little to do with the proportion of alcohol in it. The strength of a beer is intimately connected with those substances introduced by the hops into the wort and thus into the beer, to which we previously alluded, and of which too little is known; their properties and the palatableness resulting from them are very readily affected by the oxygen of the air.*

We have, therefore, to ascertain the measure in which air occurs during the process of brewing, and whether, in the actual process, there may not be too great a proportion of active oxygen present. The study of this subject requires that we should know what quantities of oxygen may be held in solution in the wort or absorbed by direct combination. Fortunately this has been rendered a comparatively easy matter by a rapid method of estimating the oxygen held in solution in liquids of various kinds, devised by M. Schützenberger in 1872. As soon as this method was made known, we requested M. Raulin, who was attached to our laboratory as assistant-director, to apply it to the determination of oxygen in wort. This he did with his accustomed skill, devising certain alterations of details

* [It will be well for the reader to bear in mind, that the word "strength," used by Pasteur many times in this chapter, has a different meaning to that which attaches to it in the minds of English brewers, who in nearly every case use it in reference to *original gravity*, while the author employs it, in this chapter, at any rate, to denote the *palate characteristic of strength*, in other words *palate-fulness*. For this reason we have thought it best in many cases to actually substitute the term " palate-fulness," or " body," for the literal translation of the French word "force."—F. F.]

which rendered the method at the same time surer and more expeditious.

The principal feature in M. Schützenberger's process consists in the employment of a salt, the properties of which that chemist was the first to recognize; he has named it *hydrosulphite of soda*, and it is obtained by the action of zinc filings on a solution of bisulphite of soda, out of contact with air.

Hydrosulphite of soda S^2O^2,NaO,HO, which is isomeric with hyposulphite of soda, only differs from the bisulphite by two equivalents of oxygen.* When brought into contact with free oxygen, it absorbs that gas instantaneously and becomes converted into bisulphite; similarly when mixed with water, it immediately absorbs the oxygen held in solution. Again there are colouring matters, such as M. Coupier's soluble aniline blue, that are instantaneously decolourized by hydrosulphite of soda, whilst they resist the action of the bisulphite. If, taking care to avoid the access of air, we add hydrosulphite of soda to a certain volume of water—a litre, for example—that has been deprived of air and faintly coloured with Coupier's blue, we shall see that a few drops will be sufficient to effect the decoloration. If, on the contrary, the water is aerated, the decoloration will not be effected before a sufficient quantity of the hydrosulphite has

---

* [As some confusion has existed in the nomenclature of these salts, it may be as well to offer some explanation.

The salt here used for absorbing oxygen was discovered by Schützenberger, and named by him *hydrosulphite of soda*. It no longer now goes by that name, being called *hyposulphite of soda*, $NaHSO_2$.

The salts formerly known as *hyposulphites* are now called *thiosulphates*, as $Na_2S_2O_3$.

Thus to put them together we have:—

Hyposulphite (Hydrosulphite)	..	..	$NaHSO_2$
Bisulphite	..	..	$NaHSO_3$
Thiosulphate (Hyposulphite)	..	..	$Na_2S_2O_3$

The thiosulphates were formerly regarded as containing the elements of water in their composition, thus:—$Na_2H_2S_2O_4$, which being halved would give $NaHSO_2$, isomeric with hyposulphite, as Pasteur says. It is further to be observed that Pasteur uses the old notation, in which the number of atoms of sulphur and oxygen are the double of what they are in the new.—D. C. R.]

been added to absorb the oxygen in solution, and the volume of the reagent required is in proportion to the quantity of oxygen in solution in the water. To render the process sensitive, we must dilute the hydrosulphite to such an extent that 10 c.c., for example, may correspond very nearly with 1 c.c. of oxygen. If the reagent would keep we should only have to determine directly, once for all, the volume of oxygen that a known volume of the liquid could absorb; but, in consequence of its extreme liability to change through contact with air, it is necessary to titrate the liquid every time before using it. This is easily done in the following manner:—

According to the observations of Messrs. Schützenberger and Lalande, the hydrosulphite decolourizes an ammoniacal solution of sulphate of copper, reducing the copper to a lower state of oxidation; the sulphite and bisulphite having no action as long as there is an excess of ammonia. We prepare a strongly ammoniacal solution of sulphate of copper, containing such a quantity of copper that 10 c.c. of the liquid will correspond, as far as action on the hydrosulphite is concerned, with 1 c.c. of oxygen. Calculation by equivalents gives us the correct value verified by direct experiment.[*]

The object of the modification which M. Raulin has introduced, is to avoid the loss of time thus occasioned by the changes which take place in the titrated liquids by long keeping, as well as certain errors which may arise from the acidity of the wort. On this latter point M. Schützenberger has remarked that the quantities of hydrosulphite of soda corresponding with one and the same volume of oxygen vary with the acidity of the liquid operated upon, a phenomenon which that skilful chemist explains by the formation of oxygenated water, of varying stability in media of different acidity.

Instead of determining the strength of the titrated solution of hydrosulphite before each operation, we take the solution as it happens to be, and determine its strength by causing it to

[*] SCHÜTZENBERGER, *Comptes rendus de l'Académie des Sciences*, vol. lxxv., p. 880.

act on a known volume of pure water saturated with oxygen at a certain temperature. The tables of solubility of oxygen in water give the exact volume of oxygen on which the measured volume of hydrosulphite used has acted. According to Bunsen, about one minute's brisk shaking in a closed bottle, with excess of air, will be sufficient to effect the maximum saturation of the water at the temperature at which we operate.

For experiments on wort we require:—

1. A 2-litre (3½ pints) flask, A, containing *saturated* hydrosulphite of soda,* of such strength that 2·5 c.c. will be sufficient to absorb almost all the oxygen in 50 c.c. of water saturated with air at the ordinary temperature (that is, 1 volume of hyposulphite must equal 20 volumes of water).

2. A 2-litre flask, B, containing a solution of indigo-carmine, 50 c.c. of which will be decolourized by about 20 c.c. of the hydrosulphite. This solution contains about 20 grammes (30·7 grains) of commercial indigo-carmine per litre (1·76 pints).

3. An apparatus, C, for the production of hydrogen.

4. An experimental apparatus composed of a burette, D, graduated in tenths of a cubic centimetre, and a three-necked Wolff's bottle, E.

5. A flask, F, holding about 100 c.c. provided with a straight tube divided into tenths of a cubic centimetre, and containing a

---

* M. Schützenberger applies the term *saturated* to a solution of hydrosulphite prepared thus, or very nearly so: a current of sulphurous acid is passed through a solution of commercial bisulphite of soda, to excess; 100 c.c. (3½ fl. oz.) of this solution and 30 grammes (46 grains) of zinc filings are put into a small flask, so as to completely fill it; the bottle is corked up and the mixture is shaken briskly for about a quarter of an hour. Lastly, the contents of this flask are poured into a large 2-litre flask, with water and containing milk of lime, prepared by mixing 100 grammes (3·2 troy oz.) of quicklime in the water just before it is used. The whole is shaken briskly for some minutes and then left to settle. The supernatant liquid soon becomes bright. This is the hydrosulphite; but in this state it is too concentrated; and should be syphoned into another 2-litre flask half full of water. In the alkaline condition this salt absorbs gaseous oxygen much less rapidly than in the acid, so that the liquids will retain their strength much longer, if they are kept in well-corked bottles.

solution of ammonia of such strength that about ten drops of it will neutralize the acidity in 50 c.c. (1·76 fl. oz.) of wort.

To perform the operation we shake about 150 c.c. (5·3 fl. oz.) of distilled water, at the existing temperature, in a 1-litre flask for a minute or so; this saturates it with air, and we must at the same time note the temperature. To be extremely precise, we should note also the barometrical pressure.

Into the bottle E we introduce about 50 c.c. of the indigo solution, and 200 c.c. of water at about 60° C. (140° F.), and

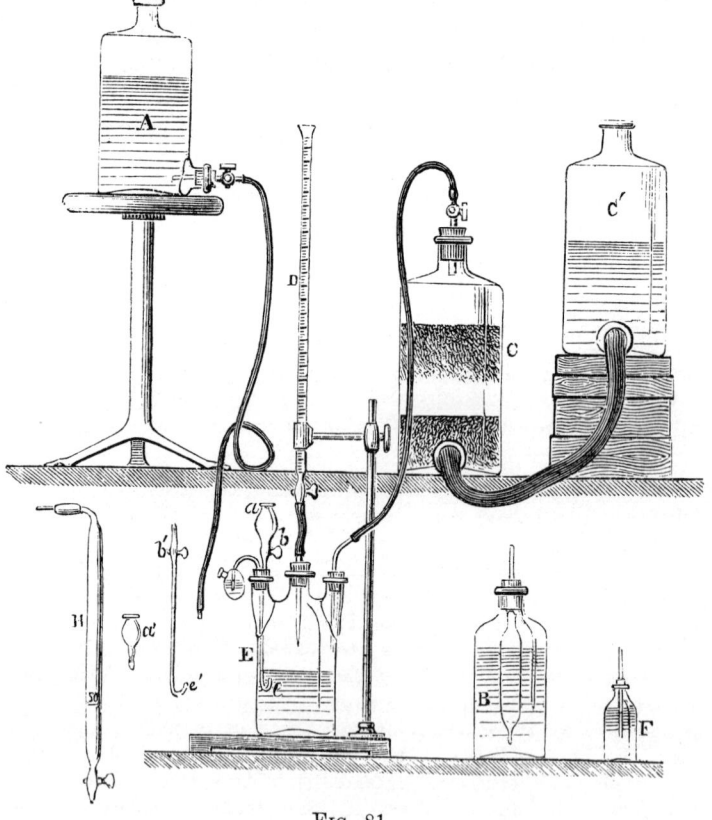

FIG. 81.

fill the tube e to the point b with water saturated with air; we then expel the air from the bottle E by a current of hydrogen.

The blue colour of the liquid in the bottle is then very carefully brought to a yellow tint, by running in, drop by drop, the hydrosulphite with which the burette D is filled.

We next pour 50 c.c. of distilled water saturated with air into the funnel a, and pass it into the flask; the blue colour reappears. We must then bring back the colour to exactly the same tint of yellow. Let n represent the number of divisions on the burette denoting the volume of hydrosulphite employed for this purpose.

We repeat this last operation immediately, taking 50 c.c. of the wort, the oxygen of which we wish to determine, having first introduced into the funnel a a sufficient number of drops of the ammoniacal solution to neutralize the acidity of the wort. Let n' represent the number of divisions of hydrosulphite employed to restore the yellow tint in the case of the wort.

We once more perform the experiment with 50 c.c. of saturated water; let n'' be the number found.*

The ratio which the quantity of oxygen held in solution in the wort bears to the quantity of oxygen contained in the same volume of water saturated with air, at the temperature t, and under the pressure H, will be $\dfrac{n'}{\frac{n+n''}{2}}$; it will be sufficient in most cases to bear in mind this ratio.

When we want to deduce the absolute quantity of oxygen held in solution in a volume V of the wort, we have merely to multiply this ratio by the quantity of oxygen contained in the same volume of water saturated with air, at the temperature t and under the pressure H, a very simple problem if we know the coefficients of the solubility of oxygen in water at different temperatures. These coefficients are given for ordinary temperatures in the following table, which was compiled by Bunsen. We have restricted the numbers to three places of decimals:—

* The numbers n and n'' will vary as the wort, or liquid which we have to test, is perfectly neutral or otherwise. Should it be acid $n'' \angle n$, should it be alkaline $n \angle n''$. This would be a very exact method of estimating the acidity or alkalinity of any coloured liquid.

Temperatures.	Coefficients.	Temperatures.	Coefficients.
0° C. (32° F.)	0·040	11° C. (51·8° F.)	0·032
1° C. (33·8° F.)	0·040	12° C. (53·6° F.)	0·031
2° C. (35·6° F.)	0·039	13° C. (55·4° F.)	0·031
3° C. (37·4° F.)	0·038	14° C. (57·2° F.)	0·030
4° C. (39·2° F.)	0·037	15° C. (59·0° F.)	0·030
5° C. (41·0° F.)	0·036	16° C. (60·8° F.)	0·029
6° C. (42·8° F.)	0·035	17° C. (62·4° F.)	0·029
7° C. (44·6° F.)	0·035	18° C. (64·4° F.)	0·029
8° C. (46·4° F.)	0·034	19° C. (66·2° F.)	0·028
9° C. (48·2° F.)	0·033	20° C. (68·0° F.)	0·028
10° C. (50·0° F.)	0·033		

The primary condition which enables us to rely on the exactness of this method is the fact which we have mentioned above, that a liquid if shaken up with air for one minute will become perfectly saturated with oxygen. Substantially this is the case. In estimating the oxygen in different parts of a liquid treated thus, we have invariably obtained the same figures to within about $\frac{1}{50}$th.

It is true that the variable quantity of the oxygen held in solution in the liquid contained in the part of the tube *eb*, as well as the oxygen absorbed during the treatment of the liquid in contact with air, constitute causes of error. Experience, however, proves that these causes of error are insignificant, as long as we have to deal with a liquid the aeration of which is not very far removed from the point of saturation, and whose solubility-coefficient for oxygen is not widely different from that of water for the same gas. Under such conditions we have always found a constant ratio, to within about $\frac{1}{40}$th, between the same liquid and air-saturated distilled water, placed under the same circumstances.

If, on the other hand, we have to deal with a liquid which holds but a minute quantity of oxygen in solution, the causes of error mentioned may very seriously affect our results, and it will be absolutely necessary to avoid them. The liquid experimented on must be treated out of contact with air, by aspirating it directly from the vessel that contains it into the pipette H, which is graduated for 50 c.c., and causing it to pass thence into the flask E, by substituting the pipette for the funnel a. Finally, before arranging the pipette, we cause a small quantity of the liquid in the flask, which has been previously brought to the exact yellow tint, to pass, by pressure, through the tube eb, so as to avoid the cause of error that is likely to result from the air held in solution in the liquid of that tube.

The liquid, the oxygen of which has to be determined, may also be passed directly from the vessel containing it into the flask E; the rest of the operation being performed as already described.

It was by this method that the oxygen held in saturate solution in wort was determined. The following are the principal results obtained by M. Raulin:—

1. At different pressures the ratio between the quantities of oxygen held in solution in water and in wort is, all other conditions being similar, constant. This ratio has been found equal to 1·20 in the case of wort and water saturated with air at the ordinary pressure, and 1·24 in the case of wort and water saturated with pure oxygen.

2. The ratio between the coefficient of the solubility of oxygen in water and that of its solubility in wort is very nearly constant at different temperatures, increasing, however, slightly as the temperature diminishes.

This ratio has been found to be—

Temperatures.
26° C. (78·8° F.) .. .. .. 1·20
19·5° C. (67·1° F.) .. .. .. 1·25
4° C. (39·2° F.) .. .. .. 1·37

Another wort gave the following results:—

Temperatures.
9° C. (48·2° F.) .. .. .. 1·15
21° C. (69·8° F.) .. .. .. 1·10
25° C. (77·0° F.) .. .. .. 1·07

3. The ratio between the quantities of oxygen held in solution in water and those held in solution in wort increases with the concentration of the wort. By evaporating the same wort to different degrees of concentration, and afterwards saturating it with air, at the same temperature, we obtained the following figures for the ratio in question:—

Weak wort	..	..	..	1·06
The same evaporated to half	..	..	..	1·15
,, ,, ,, $\frac{2}{5}$	..	..	..	1·27
,, ,, ,, $\frac{3}{10}$	..	..	..	1·45
,, ,, ,, $\frac{1}{6}$	..	..	..	1·96

4. Worts of different origin, but of the same density and temperature, when saturated with oxygen, always contain very nearly the same quantity of that gas.

Two portions of the same wort, shaken up with air, one being hot the other cold, then left to themselves for some time, and afterwards saturated with air, at the same temperature, gave the figures 1·22 for the ratio between the oxygen in the water and that in the wort.

Different worts of the same density, saturated at a temperature of 15° C. (59° F.), gave the following ratios:—

Wort kept in a bottle with air for 19 months	1·140
Wort recently prepared	1·142
Wort kept in a bottle without air for 20 months, aerated for 18 days	1·142
Wort evaporated to dryness and made up with water..	1·126

5. The solubility of oxygen in wort differs very little from the solubility of oxygen in sweetened water of the same density.

An experiment was made with a solution of sugar on the one hand, and with wort more or less diluted with water on the other hand, at the same temperature of 11° C. (51·8° F.). The following figures were obtained for the ratios of solubility:—

	Solution of Sugar.	Wort.
Marking 17·9° Balling*	1·278	1·27
,, 14·0° ,,	1·190	1·15
,, 7·0° ,,	1·092	1·06

6. From the preceding results it is easy to deduce a general formula which shall give the coefficient of solubility of oxygen in any wort, marking B° by *Balling*, and at temperature $t°$.

From the figures of (2) it follows that above and below the temperature of 15° C. (59° F.), the ratio which the coefficient of solubility of oxygen in water bears to that of the solubility of the same gas in wort varies about 0·006 for each degree of the thermometer. From the figures of (3) it follows that the same ratio varies about 0·002 for each degree of *Balling* above and below the 15th degree on the instrument.

By taking c for the coefficient of solubility of oxygen in water at $t°$ C., and c' for that of oxygen in wort also at $t°$ C., and having a density B, by *Balling* at 15° C.; and taking X for the ratio $\frac{c}{c'}$ at 15° C. and 15° *Balling*, we shall have

$$\frac{c}{c'} = X + (B-15)\ 0·022 - (t-15)\ 0·006.$$

By carefully ascertaining the ratio $\frac{c}{c'}$ for different worts, and adopting the preceding formula, we have found for X a mean value of 1·16.

* [The Balling saccharometer being almost unknown in England, we may explain that its indications are for percentages of sugar in saccharine solutions, or of extract in worts; 17·9° Balling, therefore, means 17·9 per cent. of sugar or extract in the respective liquids.—F. F.]

The definitive formula, therefore, is:

(1) $\dfrac{c}{c} = 1\cdot 16 + (B-15)\ 0\cdot 022 - (t-15)\ 0\cdot 006,$

or again,

(2) $\dfrac{c'}{c} = 0\cdot 86 - (B-15)\ 0\cdot 016 + (t-15)\ 0\cdot 004.$

The coefficient c of the solubility of oxygen in water will be found in the table given a few pages back.

§ III.—On the Quantity of Oxygen existing in a state of Solution in Brewers' Worts.[*]

The wort, when it comes from the copper in which it is boiled with the hops, remains exposed upon the coolers for a time, the length of which varies according to circumstances, the most important of which is the exterior temperature. The average time is from seven to eight hours, during which the volume of the wort diminishes, whilst its density increases; at the same time, it deposits its proteinaceous matters and absorbs oxygen from the air, either by way of solution or of combination.

In the present paragraph we shall confine ourselves to the uncombined oxygen held in a state of solution in wort, recognizable by the change of colour produced by its action on white indigo.

The use of the coolers enables the brewer to obtain his wort in two distinct states of limpidity—filtered wort and unfiltered wort. At the same time there is a further difference between these worts, namely, in the quantity of oxygen held in solution. The unfiltered wort comes direct from the coolers; the wort to be filtered, mixed with a part of the deposit, is run into a special vessel, from which it is distributed over the filtering surfaces, which are generally of felt; filtered bright, it is then received in a reservoir, from which it is distributed amongst special fermenting vessels. Falling through the air in a thin stream of drops, it must necessarily have become charged with

[*] Experiments made, at our request, by MM. Calmettes and Grenet, at Tantonville, in Tourtel's brewery.

a greater quantity of oxygen than ordinary wort. In good breweries it is put apart by itself to ferment, and the yeast which it yields is firmer and deposits more easily than that of unfiltered wort. As for the fermentation, it is, under similar conditions, quicker by a day or a day and a half than in the case of ordinary wort. The difference in the quantity of oxygen held in solution in the two kinds of wort is greater in proportion as the external temperature is lower; in winter it may be twice as great as in summer. The reason is that in summer a boiling wort does not obtain a minimum temperature of 20° C. (68° F.), on the best coolers, in less than six or seven hours. After leaving the coolers it is passed over a refrigerator. In winter it attains that temperature in about three hours, or less, which then goes on sinking on the coolers. During the last two or three hours which are employed in bringing the temperature still lower, as also during the running off, the wort absorbs an appreciable quantity of oxygen. In other words, wort in winter remains for a longer time at low temperatures, in free contact with air.

Another circumstance unites with this exposure upon the coolers to increase the aeration of the wort; the wort is run into the fermenting tuns through pipes of large sectional area, more or less bent, and carries with it by suction considerable quantities of air, which, from the continual agitation, gets well mixed with it. The effect of this mixing in the pipes is to considerably increase the proportion of air in solution in the wort, especially in winter, when the temperature of the wort is lower; and from the figures given below we may, although it is very variable, put the average increase at a quarter of the whole amount. The calculation has been made by comparing the quantities of air held in solution in two samples of the same wort, one of which was taken from the coolers at the moment of "turning out,"* and the other from the fermenting vessel after it was filled.

* See foot-note, page 367.

Let us call the ratio between the quantity of oxygen held in solution by a wort, and that which the same wort would hold in solution if saturated at the same temperature, the *degree of saturation* of that wort at the temperature t.

The determination of degrees of saturation is reduced to a comparison of the number of divisions of hydrosulphite n which satisfies the wort in the first case, with the number n' corresponding with the same wort saturated at the same temperature. The ratio $\dfrac{n}{n'}$ gives the degree of saturation at the temperature t.

In experiments made with a wort at 14·5° *Balling* as mean density, we found the following results:—

In summer, in the case of worts reduced to the temperature of 5° C. (41° F.) by a refrigerator, the degrees of saturation may be set down as—

> For unfiltered worts .. .. 0·500
> For filtered worts .. .. .. 0·800

In winter, in the case of some worts which were racked at a temperature of from 3° to 4° C. (37·4° to 39·2° F.), without the use of a refrigerator, we found the saturation complete in both worts. In the case of a very low external temperature, however (—10° C., 14° F.), we have failed to determine the saturation in an unfiltered wort. As regards the mean winter figures, in the case of worts racked at a temperature of 5° C. (41° F.), they may be fixed at these:—

> For unfiltered wort .. .. .. 0·850
> For filtered wort .. .. .. 0·950

In autumn and spring we find the mean figures to be intermediate between those given above:—

> For unfiltered wort .. .. 0·500 to 0·850
> For filtered wort .. .. 0·800 to 0·950

From these ratios it is easy to find the quantity of oxygen contained in brewers' worts, if we also refer to Bunsen's Tables

STUDIES ON FERMENTATION. 367

and the formula (2) given in the preceding section. At the temperature of 5° C. (41° F.), at which the above worts were "gathered,"* and not taking into account the very small correction that should be made for the difference of half a degree on Balling, we find, by this formula, as the ratio of the coefficients of the solubility of oxygen in saturated wort and in water—

$$\frac{c'}{c} = 0\cdot82$$

Now, at the temperature of 5° C., the quantity of oxygen held in solution in 1 litre of water is, according to Bunsen, 0·036 litre, at the atmospheric pressure, and therefore at the pressure of $\frac{1}{5}$th atmosphere, which is that of the oxygen in atmospheric air, it will be—

$$\frac{0\cdot036}{5} \text{ litre} = 7\cdot2 \text{ c.c.—[that is, 2 cubic inches per gallon.]}$$

And, consequently, in the case of saturated wort, it will be—

7·2 c.c. × 0·82 = 5·904 c.c.—[that is, 1·62 cub. inches per gall.]

Multiplying this last number of c.c. by the different *degrees of saturation* found, we shall obtain the volumes of oxygen held in solution in 1 litre of different worts :—

Summer worts { Unfiltered 0·500 × 5·904 c.c. = 2·952 c.c.
              { Filtered   0·800 × 5·904 „ = 4·723 „

Winter worts { Unfiltered 0·850 × 5·904 „ = 5·018 „
             { Filtered   0·950 × 5·904 „ = 5·609 „

It is important to notice that we are here dealing with wort taken from the fermenting vessel just before it was pitched;

* [For non-technical readers we may explain the expressions "gathered," here used, and "turning out," used on page 365. "Turning out" describes the operation of emptying the *copper* contents into the *hop-back*, or the *hop-back* contents on to the *coolers*. "Gathering" refers to the time when the worts are finally intermixed and *weighed*, prior to the commencement of vinous fermentation.—F. F.]

that is to say, when the quantity of oxygen held in solution was as large as the treatment to which it had been subjected allowed of its being. The mode of taking it for examination is as follows:—A burette, H (Fig. 81), is plunged into the fermenting vessel, the temperature of which at the time is ascertained very exactly, the upper part of the burette being fitted with an india-rubber tube, $a\,b$, longer than itself. The liquid is then sucked up the tube, and soon completely fills the apparatus and runs out at b (Fig. 82). By lowering the tube the whole arrangement thus forms a syphon, and enables us to let the wort that we are experimenting on flow for some minutes; when every trace of air has been thus expelled, the lower tap is closed and the liquid is introduced into Schützenberger's apparatus.

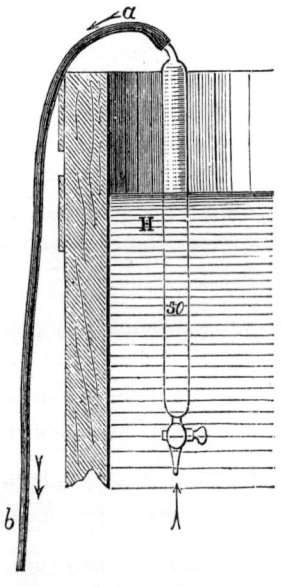

FIG. 82.

As for the saturated wort, the value of which in oxygen serves to determine one of the elements of the degree of saturation, it is readily obtained by introducing a volume of from 100 c.c. to 150 c.c. of wort into a 2-litre or 3-litre flask, and shaking it briskly so as to saturate it with air; it is then poured into a settling-glass, to separate it from the great quantity of froth formed in the shaking, and then, by means of a graduated pipette, 50 c.c. is taken for examination.

We have spoken of the influence that oxygen has on the activity of yeast, on its development and, consequently, on the progress of fermentation. Moreover, we know, from experiments already mentioned, which we communicated to the Academy and the Chemical Society in 1861, that the rapid development of yeast in contact with air is in reciprocal relation to the disappearance of the oxygen from the air. Knowing the conditions of the aeration of wort from the moment when it arrives on the coolers until the moment when, in the fermenting tun, it is about to be pitched, it would be interesting to ascertain what happens to the oxygen dissolved in the wort at the moment of pitching, how yeast is affected when suddenly brought into contact with that oxygen; what part, in short, that gas plays in fermentation.

Let us therefore follow up, hour by hour, the degree of saturation after pitching, in Tourtel's brewery. On November 4th, 1875, some wort at 14° Balling was pumped on to the coolers at 7 p.m., and at 4 a.m. went down to a 32-hectolitre (700 gallons) tun, its temperature then being 6° C. (42·8° F.) The pitching, in which about 100 grammes (3·2 oz. troy) of pressed yeast was used per hectolitre (22 gallons), took place at 5 a.m. The following is the curve of the degrees of saturation of the oxygen, as drawn by Messrs. Calmettes and Grenet.

The abscissæ represent the time expressed in hours, and the ordinates give the degrees of saturation of the wort with oxygen. It will be seen that about twelve hours after the pitching, and at a temperature of 6° C., all the oxygen had disappeared, absorbed by the yeast. We shall find that wort by itself, unassociated with yeast, would also have combined with oxygen; but in the course of twelve hours, at 6° C., this combination would have been scarcely appreciable in absence of yeast. It follows, therefore, that the oxygen in solution is taken up by the yeast, under the conditions of which we are speaking. This has been proved directly by an experiment.

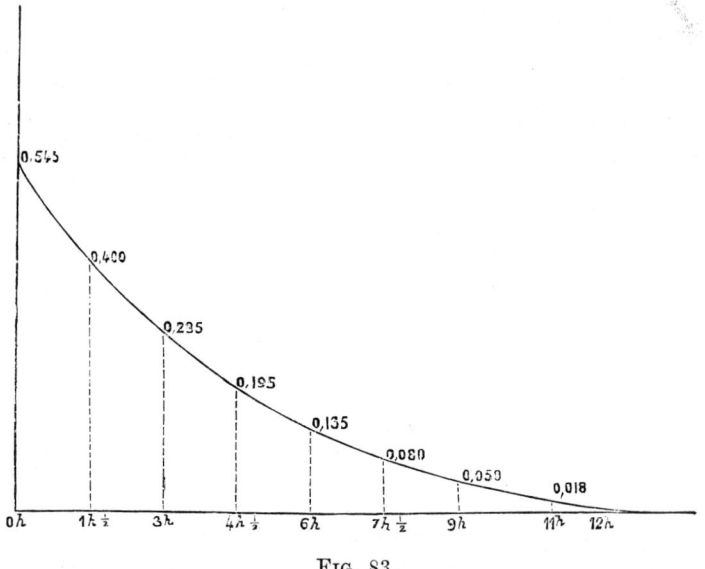

FIG. 83.

A double quantity of yeast was employed for a tun similar to the preceding one, and it was found that the oxygen in solution disappeared completely in less than half the time that it took to disappear in the first case.* It is very important to notice that in our 32-hectolitre tun, at the moment when we determined the complete disappearance of the oxygen in solution, the cells of yeast had assumed a younger and fuller appearance than they had at first; but they had not multiplied at all up to

* We know also from the direct experiments of M. Schützenberger, performed on aerated water with which yeast had been mixed, that yeast causes all the oxygen in solution to disappear very quickly, so that hydrosulphite gives no evidence of a trace. (See SCHÜTZENBERGER, *Revue scientifique*, vol. iii. (2), April, 1874).

that time, nor were there even any buds then visible on them. The oxygen, therefore, must be stored up somehow in the cells, taken up by their oxidizable matters to be brought into work subsequently, or to act as a *primum movens* of life and nutrition, spreading its influence over several successive generations of cells.

§ IV.—ON THE COMBINATION OF OXYGEN WITH WORT.

The atmospheric oxygen is not merely taken into solution by wort; it also combines with it, as a very simple experiment will suffice to show. If we place in a tinned iron vessel some boiling wort, separated from the hops in the copper, and cool it suddenly by plunging it into iced water, and after having cooled it down in this manner to 15° or 20° C. (59° or 68° F.), saturate it with oxygen, by shaking it briskly in a large flask, and then completely fill a vessel with it and close it up for twelve hours, we shall find at the end of that time, if we test it with the hydrosulphite of soda, as we have described in § II., that it does not contain a trace of free oxygen. The whole of the gas which was originally held in solution will have entered into combination, that is to say, the liquid, first coloured blue with the indigo-carmine, and then brought to a yellow tint by means of the hydrosulphite of soda, will not regain its original blue colour through the action of this wort. The following experiments were undertaken with the object of studying this property of wort, and in order that we might form some idea of its importance, and of the total quantity of oxygen that wort can absorb under certain special circumstances. The experiments were performed in our own laboratory on wort from Tourtel's brewery, which M. Calmettes had forwarded to us in bottles prepared in the brewery at Tantonville, in the following manner: Each bottle was filled with boiling wort taken from the copper and closed with a bored cork, through which the neck of a funnel passed; the funnel also was filled with the wort, and the whole preserved from contact with air by a layer of oil. The next day the bottles were corked full by the help of a bottling needle,* previously heated, with perfect corks that had been passed through the flame. The bottles arrived in Paris in very good condition, quite full of the liquid up to the corks. They were left undisturbed for one or two days at the same temperature as that to which they had been exposed during the corking and the journey. The object of this was to afford time for a deposit of the wort to form at the bottom of each bottle. As a matter of fact, we know that wort boiling in the copper is charged with proteinaceous matters and other floating and insoluble substances. The wort above the deposit was turbid and opaline; it was in this state when we used it for our experiments. It may be taken for granted, without risk of appreciable error, that the wort had been absolutely deprived of oxygen in solution, inasmuch as it had been bottled when boiling, and had cooled down out of contact with air. As for the quantity of oxygen that it might have held in combination, this must have been insignificant, although there must have been some, since the wort had been exposed to the air in the copper; the oxygen in combination, however, could have had no appreciable influence on the results which we obtained. Let us call this wort *boiled wort*.

First Experiment.—Into a straight-necked flask we introduced a certain measured quantity of this wort by means of a syphon, taking care that the syphon should only act on the opaque wort, and should not reach the deposit at the bottom of the bottle. We then drew out the neck to a fine tube in the flame and

[* The bottling needle (*foret à aiguille*) is a contrivance for permitting a cork to be driven into a bottle completely filled with liquid, without bursting the bottle. It consists of a slightly-tapering iron pin about $\frac{1}{5}$th inch in diameter and 2 inches in length, somewhat flattened, and slightly curved throughout its entire length, with a groove running down one side from end to end, the pin being jointed with a ring, like a common ring cork-screw. In using it the pin is driven into the bottle alongside the cork, thus allowing the excess of liquid to escape as the cork advances. When the cork is completely home, the needle is withdrawn, and the elasticity of the cork enables it to fill up the space left, so that we have the bottle corked air-tight, and no air left between the cork and liquid.—D. C. R.]

boiled the wort; and during ebullition we sealed the end of the fine tube. After it had cooled, we arranged that pure air should enter the flask. To do this we made a file mark near the fine closed point of the flask, and connected the point by a piece of india-rubber tubing with a glass tube containing a column of asbestos, which we heated. We then broke off the point of the flask inside the india-rubber tube, so that the air entered the flask after being filtered through the asbestos. We removed the india-rubber tube and sealed up once more the fine end of the neck at the point where we had broken it off. Finally, to aerate the wort to saturation, we shook the flask briskly for some minutes, and then placed it in a hot-water bath, where we left it for about a quarter of an hour. We afterwards removed it to an oven at 25° (77° F.). We repeated the same operation next day and the four succeeding days.

The wort, which at first was scarcely coloured, gradually assumed a reddish-brown tint, and deposited an amorphous matter, but without brightening. It became clear, however, when filtered, which was not the case with the turbid, opaline wort in the bottles when they arrived.

The following is an analysis of the air in the flask, made immediately after a renewed and vigorous shaking, the object of which was to saturate the wort with air before analyzing the supernatant air:—

November 29th.
    Temperature at which
    the flask was refilled
    with air .. .. ..   4° C. (29·2° F.)
    Atmospheric pressure. 751 mm. (29·6 ins.)
    Total volume of flask .. .. 333 c.c. (20·32 cub. in.)
    Volume occupied by the wort .. .. 120 ,, (7·32 ,,)

December 8th.
    Volume of gas analyzed 27·6 c.c. (1·68 cub. ins.)
    After treatment with potash .. .. .. 27·4 c.c. (1·67 ,,)
    ,,   ,, pyrogallol .. .. 22·4 ,, (1·36 ,,)

          Oxygen .. . .. 5·0 c.c. (0·305 cub. in.)

Composition of the gas :— Per cent.
Oxygen .. .. 18·25
Nitrogen .. .. 81·57

The formula which we deduced above (§ II.) allows us to conclude that at the temperature of 8° C. (46·4° F.), which was the temperature at which the wort was saturated before the analysis given above, the quantity of oxygen in solution in the 120 c.c. (4·2 fl. oz.) of wort was 0·84 c.c. (0·051 cub. in.).

At the moment when the flask was closed, the total volume of oxygen, calculated to zero and 760 mm. (30 in.) pressure, was 44·73 c.c. (2·729 cub. in.).

At the moment when the analysis was finished, the volume of oxygen was calculated to the same conditions of temperature and pressure, 38·86 c.c. (2·355 cub. in.) ; 5·87 c.c. (0·374 cub. in.) has, therefore, disappeared. Now, as there is 0·84 c.c. (0·051 cub. in.) in solution, there has, consequently, been an absorption, by combination with 120 c.c. of wort, of 5·03 c.c. (0·32 cub. in.) of oxygen, or 41·7 c.c. per litre (11·6 cub. ins. per gallon).

Second Experiment.—In a similar experiment, in which, however, the flask was kept for five days at a rigorously constant temperature of 55° C. (131° F.), day and night, and in which the supernatant air was not shaken up with the wort, we found—

Volume of gas analyzed .. 28·5
After treatment with potash .. .. 28·3
  ,,   ,,   ,, pyrogallol .. .. 23·0
                                   ———
Oxygen .. .. 5·3

Composition of the gas :— Per cent.
Oxygen .. .. 18·6
Nitrogen .. .. 81·4

STUDIES ON FERMENTATION.

	cc.
Total oxygen at first	29·40
,, ,, remaining	26·04
,, ,, that has disappeared	3·36
,, ,, in solution	0·54
,, ,, in combination	2·82

Or per litre, 35·2 c.c. (9·8 cub. ins. per gallon).

The colour of the wort in this experiment had become sensibly similar to that of the wort in the preceding experiment.

Third Experiment.—In another experiment we left the flask, for the same length of time again, after it had been refilled with air and reclosed, at a temperature which varied between 2° and 4° C. (35·6° and 39·2° F.). In this case we found—

Volume of air analyzed	27·8
After the action of potash	27·8
After pyrogallic acid	22·3
Oxygen	5·5

Composition of the gas:—	Per cent.
Oxygen	19·7
Nitrogen	80·3

	c.c.
Total oxygen at first	29·40
,, ,, remaining	27·58
,, ,, that has disappeared	1·82
,, ,, in solution	0·44
,, ,, in combination	1·38

Or per litre, 17·20 c.c. (4·8 cub. ins. per gallon).

In this last experiment the wort was scarcely darker in

colour. Its colour, compared with that of wort cooled on the coolers in the brewery, was slightly darker; but the difference, although it existed, was scarcely appreciable. We shall revert to this fact, which is of importance, presently.

Fourth Experiment.—The following series of experiments were undertaken to enable us to form some idea of the rapidity with which oxygen is absorbed by wort.

We employed three flasks, A, B, C, of the following capacities:—

$$A = 234$$
$$B = 214$$
$$C = 203$$

into which we introduced the following quantities of wort (boiled wort, without air):—

Into A	96 c.c.
,, B	84 ,,
,, C	84 ,,

The necks of the flasks were then drawn out and sealed in a flame, the liquid being at a temperature of 5° C. (41° F.). The flasks were then placed in a hot-water bath and kept at 100° C. (212° F.) for a quarter of an hour. The flask A was repeatedly shaken during cooling, as also was the flask B, this being omitted in the case of the flask C.

The contents of flask A were submitted to analysis as soon as it was quite cooled—that is to say, in about three hours. The analysis of contents of B and C was delayed for about twenty-four hours. We took the precaution of not commencing the analysis before we had shaken the flasks for a few minutes, so that the wort in all of them might be saturated at a fixed temperature, and thus enable us to ascertain the exact quantity of oxygen in solution.

The analyses showed that the worts in the three flasks contained :—

Flask A, oxygen in combination, per litre   20   c.c.
  „   B,   „   „   „   21·4 c.c.
  „   C,   „   „   „   16·8 c.c.

Several facts may be deduced from these experiments: the shaking up of the wort with air has a marked effect on the absorption; a very appreciable absorption immediately follows the shaking up of the wort when warm; whereas, in the case of cold wort that has remained undisturbed, the absorption takes place slowly.

The results of the preceding experiments plainly show that the wort, which is very hot when it comes on to the coolers, where it remains for several hours, must absorb an appreciable quantity of oxygen by combination; but these same experiments teach us nothing definite concerning the volume of oxygen that is actually absorbed. We can only gather from the remark which concludes the third experiment given above, that the total quantity of oxygen absorbed by the wort in Tourtel's brewery, during the time that it remains on the coolers, must be less than 17 c.c. per litre (4·7 cubic inches per gallon), inasmuch as the coloration effected by combined oxygen in the proportion of 17 c.c. per litre was considerably greater than that of the wort taken from the backs in the brewery.

If we knew the curve of cooling on the Tourtonville coolers we might easily, in experiments conducted in our laboratory, assimilate the conditions of our experiments to those of the oxidation of the wort in the brewery, by exposing wort in contact with air in closed flasks to temperatures varying according to the indications of the curve in question. For this purpose, we induced M. Calmettes to study the process of cooling upon the coolers at Tantonville. In Fig. 84 the figures found in one of that gentleman's experiments are given.

378   STUDIES ON FERMENTATION.

The abscissæ represent the time expressed in hours; the ordinates, the degrees of temperature. The exterior temperature was 0° C. (32° F.); the atmosphere was calm. The wort was pumped on to the coolers at 5.20 p.m., its temperature then being 85° C. (185° F.), and the operation of pumping lasted from 5.20 to 5.30 p.m. The first determination was made at 5.30 p.m., and was repeated every ten minutes until 7.30 p.m.

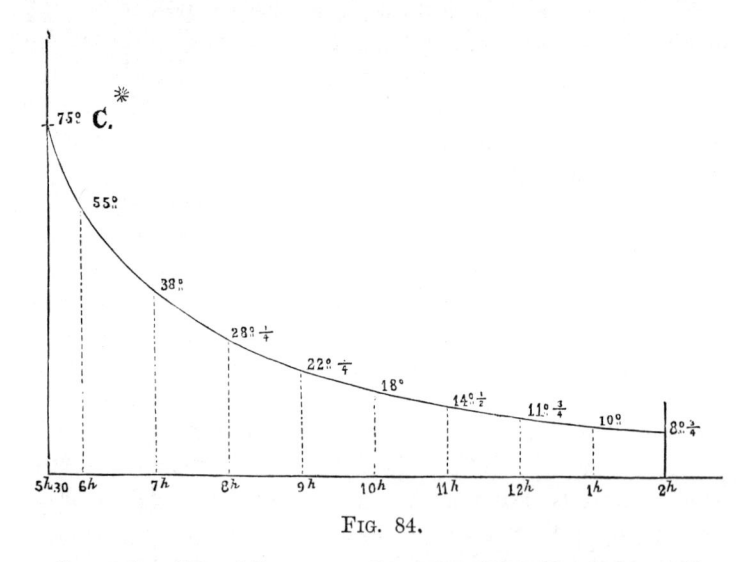

FIG. 84.

Curve of cooling of the wort on the coolers (December 18th, 1875).

Between 7.30 and 8.30 p.m. it was repeated every twenty minutes; after that, it was repeated every half-hour until 2 a.m., when the wort went down to the fermenting vessels. The mean depth of the wort was 8·5 centimetres (3·1 inches).

Having determined the rate of cooling in the brewery, we made the following experiment: a known quantity of wort from the copper—deprived, consequently, of oxygen—in the

[* The corresponding Fahrenheit degrees are, proceeding from 5ʰ·30 downwards to 2ʰ, 167°, 131°, 100·4°, 82·8°, 72°, 64·4°, 58·1°, 53·1°, 50°, 47·7°.—D. C. R.]

same condition as when it comes on the coolers, was put into a graduated, cylindrical vessel, which was then closed with an india-rubber cork, and placed immediately, without being shaken, in a hot water bath at 85° C. (185° F.). Another vessel similar to the preceding one, and having a thermometer passed through the cork, and immersed in the wort, enabled us to observe the temperature. The temperature was gradually reduced, in exact accordance with the data of the preceding curve, until the water, in the course of eight hours and a half, was brought down to 10° C. (50° F.). It is true, that we cannot pretend to have realized all the conditions of the coolers, in this manner, but we approached them very nearly; moreover, it was an approximation rather than a rigorous determination that we desired to obtain. We then collected over mercury the air which remained in the flask, and analyzed it very carefully; at the same time, with Schützenberger's apparatus, we determined the oxygen held in solution in the wort so treated. From the results thus obtained we easily found the quantity of oxygen that had disappeared—that is, the oxygen which the wort had acquired from the atmosphere of the flask, and which had combined with the oxidizable matters of the wort.

The volume of the flask being 815 c.c., that of the wort 391 c.c., and the depth of the liquid 8 cm., we found an absorption by combination of 9·49 c.c. of oxygen per litre of wort (2·63 cub. ins. per gallon). Another flask treated in the same manner gave us similar results.

As the oxygen in solution has so great an influence on fermentation, it is important that we should, likewise, know the effect produced by the oxygen in combination. The following considerations and experiments may throw some light on this subject:—

We have already remarked that natural saccharine worts oxidize, and acquire colour in contact with air, and that this coloration disappears when these worts are caused to ferment. This furnishes one presumption, that the oxygen in combination disappears then, from being abstracted by the ferment. A similar phenomenon is observable in the case of wort. After having acquired a marked dark shade by remaining in contact with pure air, it loses this colour very appreciably during fermentation; and if the wort does not quite regain the colour which it originally had when it came from the copper, this circumstance is probably owing to the fact that the quantity of oxygen in combination with the wort is larger than that which is abstracted by the yeast. We have seen that yeast absorbs oxygen, since, in the case of a saccharine wort, more or less saturated with oxygen in solution, when fermentation commences, the first effect of the ferment is to cause that oxygen to combine with its own substance. We should, therefore, expect to find the oxygen in combination, as well as that held in solution, in wort, abstracted by the yeast and contributing to the activity of fermentation. As a matter of fact, this is proved by direct experiments, for the fermentation of a wort that has oxidized in contact with air, or of one from which all the oxygen that was held in solution in it has disappeared by direct combination, is much more easy, rapid, and complete than the fermentation of the same wort when it contains no oxygen, whether free or combined. These experiments were as follows: we boiled some *copper wort* in a large double-necked flask, like those shown in Fig. 73; all the air being expelled, pure air was allowed to enter the flask; and when the wort was cool it was saturated with this air, by being shaken briskly for a quarter of an hour. The wort was then forced by a pressure of air, applied to the extremity of the S-shaped tube, into smaller flasks, similar to the preceding ones; these we filled completely, and then plunged the end of their sinuous tubes under mercury. After waiting for two or three days, a longer time than was required for the oxygen in solution to enter into combination—a fact which we confirmed by means of a similar flask, which served as a standard—we caused the wort, so prepared, to ferment in the flasks, and side by side, for the sake of comparison, some *copper wort* that contained no air in solution or combination.

In other experiments we operated on pure wort, saturated

with oxygen in combination, by being allowed to remain for one year in an open flask in contact with pure air. This wort was deprived of air in solution by a protracted boiling over mercury. It was then pitched, out of contact of air, with an old yeast. The yeast underwent no development at all, a proof that oxygen in combination cannot act like oxygen that is free, or simply in solution, in effecting the revival of the yeast; nevertheless, after the revival has been once started by means of a small quantity of air, fermentation declares itself with much greater facility than in the case of copper wort, placed under the same conditions, but deprived of oxygen in combination.

§ V. On the Influence of Oxygen in Combination on the Clarification of Wort.

Oxygen in combination has another effect which it is essentially important to point out, for it concerns the clarification of beer. One of the most valued properties of this beverage is its limpidity and brilliancy. We know from the results of the fourth experiment in the preceding paragraph that in the case of a wort shaken up when hot with air, and examined as soon as cold, that is, after an interval of only three hours, we find a notable volume of oxygen to have been absorbed by combination; in the experiment to which we allude, this volume was not less than 20 c.c. of oxygen per litre of wort. The shaking up of the wort when cold with air saturated it with oxygen in solution, but the quantity of oxygen which under these conditions entered into combination, in the course of three hours, is insignificant, although saturation by solution may be attained in the course of one minute's shaking. If two samples of the same wort are shaken up with air, one of them being hot and the other cold, and both filtered after having been left undisturbed for twenty-four hours, or even immediately after the agitation, we cannot fail to be struck with the great difference that they will present in point of brightness. The wort that was shaken up hot will have more colour, and will be brilliant; the other will be turbid, and will not become clear for five or six days, when left to itself in contact with air and filtered again. This explains a fact that may be easily verified in practice: Boiled wort, if cooled down suddenly, or slowly but out of contact with air, or shaken up cold in contact with air, is opaque when filtered; whilst the same wort, cooled down on the coolers where it has taken a certain quantity of oxygen into combination, generally passes through the filter very bright. The intelligent brewer is uneasy when this is not the case, for it cannot be denied that the easy clarification of wort has a favourable influence on the easy clarification of beer.

It would, nevertheless, be a grave error to suppose that the clarification of beer must necessarily follow that of wort, and we may be permitted to make a digression here on the subject, to prove this statement.

On February 3rd, 1874, we brewed 2 hectolitres (44 gallons) of beer. The boiling wort, hops and all, was run into a vessel like that represented in Fig. 80, but provided in addition with a false bottom, pierced with holes and fixed at 1 centimetre (0·39 inch) above the true bottom of the vessel; this was meant to retain the spent hops. The temperature of the wort in the vessel after it was filled, February 3rd, 4 p.m., was 90° C. (194° F.), that of the room was 10° C. (50° F.). We permitted the wort to cool down gently, without running cold water over the vessel. The wort indicated a density of 14° Balling.

The following temperatures were taken:—

	Temperature of Wort.	Temperature of Room.
Feb. 4, 11 a.m.	38° C. (100·4° F.)	9° C. (48·2° F.)
7 p.m.	30° C. (86° F.)	9° C. (48·2° F.)
11.30 p.m.	26·3° C. (79·3° F.)	9° C. (48·2° F.)

	Temperature of Wort.	Temperature of Room.
Feb. 5, 9 a.m. ...	21° C. (69·8° F.)	8° C. (46·4° F.)
12 a.m. ...	19·75° C. (66·6° F.)	8° C. (46·4° F.)
4 p.m. ...	18° C. (64·4° F.)	8·5° C. (47·3° F.)
Feb. 6, 11 a.m. ...	14° C. (57·2° F.)	8° C. (46·4° F.)
Feb. 7, 2 p.m. ...	11° C. (51·8° F.)	7° C. (44·6° F.)

At the end of this time the wort drawn from the smaller tap half-way up the vessel had already become very bright, although it was taken from the bulk of the liquid above the deposit of hops.

On February 8th the temperature of the wort was 9·5° C. (49·1° F.), and that of the room 5° C. (41° F.); the wort was again very bright. Taken from the small tap and tested by Schützenberger's process it gave no evidence of free oxygen in solution, although its surface was in contact with air. It continued absolutely pure, the arrangements of our vessel, as we have already explained, allowing only such air to enter as was first deprived of its disturbing germs.

Not till February 12th, after we had again determined the purity and brilliant clearness of the wort, a brilliancy which we can compare with nothing so well as Cognac, without the faintest trace of cloudiness, did we set it to ferment in a vessel similar to that in which it had cooled, but without the false bottom. In the process of transfer we effected its aeration by causing it to fall on a small inverted tinned iron capsule some 4 or 5 centimetres (1½ to 2 inches) in diameter. By this arrangement the wort took up air to the extent of rather more than a third of its saturate capacity, that is to say, by spreading over the capsule, and falling from it in a kind of sheet, it absorbed a volume of oxygen more than a third of the total amount of oxygen which it was capable of absorbing at the existing temperature; this was 12° C. (53·6° F.) at the moment when the wort was drawn off. The pitching was accomplished with a 6-litre flask containing about 4 litres (7·04 pints) of beer that had been in "low" fermentation from February 3rd. The beer was cleansed on February 24th, and had a density of $5\tfrac{1}{4}°$ Balling. We collected 2·345 kilos (75·39 oz. troy) of yeast, containing 56 per cent., that is, 1·313 kilos (42·21 oz. troy) of pressed yeast, containing 36·7 per cent. of yeast dried at 100° C. (212° F.), that is 482 grammes (15·49 oz. troy) for the brew, which would give 241 grammes (7·748 oz. troy) of yeast formed per hectolitre (22 gallons).

The beer was turbid when drawn off, and the small glassful that we removed did not brighten in twenty-four or even forty-eight hours. The samples for some days previously had been in the same condition. The yeast existed as a fine deposit without any straggling yeast about the sides. The want of brightness was dependent rather on spurious colour than on any actual turbidity. We may here remark that if in the preceding experiment the wort had taken up oxygen into combination as well as into solution at the time that it was aerated, the other conditions being the same, the beer would have been bright and better.

It follows from this experiment that a wort may be *perfectly bright* at the moment when it is pitched, yet fail to produce a beer which shall be bright when racked, or one that will brighten subsequently otherwise than with great difficulty. We may add that when we repeated this same experiment, cooling the wort, however, as rapidly as the conditions of our apparatus permitted, and employing iced water, the beer appeared very nearly bright when it was racked, and brightened pretty quickly in cask and in bottle. The total duration of cooling was not longer than two hours.

The question here arises what part does the oxygen combined with wort play in the clarification of the latter, or in the clarification of beer? Although it may be difficult to give a definite answer to this question, we must bear in mind that in cases where the beer brightens best, if we examine it under the microscope during fermentation, we see, besides the clusters of yeast-cells, floating amorphous particles, which are larger and more compact than those to which the turbidity of worts and muddy beers is due, a circumstance which should lead us to suppose that the oxygen in combination with the wort has the effect of modifying the nature of the amorphous deposit which is produced during the fermentation of the wort. During boiling, the hop yields to the wort a variety of resinous, odorous, and astringent substances, which, for the most part, are held in solution by the presence of sugar and dextrin. At the moment when, under the influence of the yeast, which is itself more or less oxidized, the sugar becomes transformed into alcohol and carbonic acid, a portion of the bitter and resinous matters of the hop becomes insoluble and remains in a state of suspension in the liquid. It is very probable that at this point it is when the combined oxygen assumes its function of modifying the physical structure of these insoluble particles, agglomerating them, so that they become more easily deposited.*

Moreover, oxidation tends to form a special precipitate in the wort, which precipitate contributes towards the collection and deposition of the very fine particles suspended in the wort, by a

---

* We have remarked in our observations on No. 6 of Plate I. (p. 6) that amongst the amorphous granular deposits of wort and beer we often find minute balls of resinous and colouring matter, perfectly spherical and very dense, which if the liquids be shaken up will render them very turbid, but which readily and rapidly deposit again, without remaining in suspension in the least. Such then is the form in which the deposits of wort in course of fermentation are precipitated, when the wort has been freely exposed to oxygen. One day in the laboratory we were desirous of starting a fermentation in a vessel capable of holding 12 hectolitres (264 gallons). But as we only had at our disposal a copper capable of holding $2\frac{1}{2}$ hectolitres, we procured the wort from a neighbouring brewery in two barrels of 6 hectolitres each. This wort we re-heated, in portions, in our $2\frac{1}{2}$ hectolitre copper, a treatment which had the effect of oxidizing the wort more than it would have been in the brewery. In this case the beer fell remarkably bright, and the cells of yeast were accompanied by the deposit of minute agglomerations sketched in Plate I, No. 6. We have repeated this experiment on a smaller scale and have obtained the same result.

mechanical action, similar to that which we notice in fining operations. On the coolers an effect of this kind is produced. The wort in the copper contains insoluble matters which pass on to the coolers. Very bright when boiling, it grows turbid as it cools, and then contains two kinds of insoluble substances: 1. Substances insoluble alike in the hot and cold liquid, some of which even, as we have just seen, are formed under the influence of heat and air: all these substances precipitating rapidly to the bottom of the vessels. 2. Very fine particles insoluble in the cold, but soluble in the hot liquid, appearing as the wort cools down, and giving it a milky appearance. If the air does not come into play they remain in suspension for an indefinite time, so to say. Wort taken boiling from the copper and cooled down, therefore, forms a considerable deposit at the bottom of the bottles. Now, if we put this wort into bottles without filling them, putting into some only the milky wort from above the deposit, and into others the same wort along with some of the deposit, then raise it to 100° C. (212° F.), and before it has time to cool down shake it up with air a good many times, it will be readily seen that the wort in the bottles containing the deposit will brighten more rapidly and satisfactorily than those in the bottles without the deposit. The deposits which are insoluble in the copper have, therefore, an influence on the clarification. We must add, however, that this influence cannot be compared with that of direct oxidation.

The "turning out" of the wort and its stay upon the coolers to a certain extent exhibit the different conditions which take part in its clarification, inasmuch as the wort charged with its insoluble matters is run off very hot, and with more or less violence against the external air.

§ VI.—Application of the Principles of the New Process of Brewing with the Use of Limited Quantities of Air.

We have now an idea of the quantities of oxygen which occur, free or combined, in the actual processes of manufacture. We know, moreover, that an excess of air may be injurious, especially to the aroma of the beer, and to that quality which consumers prize so highly, which goes by the name of *bouche*. It must, therefore, be important to ascertain whether in existing processes the proportion of active oxygen may not be excessive. The best practical means of determining this would consist in comparing the products of different processes with progressively increasing access of air, starting from none at all, as in the case of cooling in the presence of an atmosphere of carbonic acid gas. The following arrangement (Fig. 85) permits us to realize these conditions :—

The wort brought to a temperature between 75° and 80° C. (167° and 176° F.) in the double-bottomed vessel C, passes by the tube *a b* into a refrigerator, such as Baudelot's, for example, but acting in an inverse manner to the ordinary mode of using Baudelot's ; that is to say, the wort is made to circulate inside the tubes, whilst the cold water plays on the outside.* The

* It is evident that this arrangement may be modified in many ways. Any of the ordinary worms, or, generally speaking, any of the more modern refrigerators invented during the last few years, may be adopted. The only point that is of importance is the preservation of the purity of the wort during cooling.

The Baudelot refrigerator is extensively adopted in France; for this reason we used it in our experiments at Tantonville. We might equally well, by enclosing the worm in a casing of sheet iron or tinned copper, pass our wort over the exterior of the tubes, the cold water passing through them. The wort would cool quicker in this way than with the arrangement described in the text, and if we arrange to admit only pure air into the case, always under conditions of purity. The aeration, moreover, could be made as much as we wished.

388   STUDIES ON FERMENTATION.

wort when cooled, its temperature being indicated by a ther-

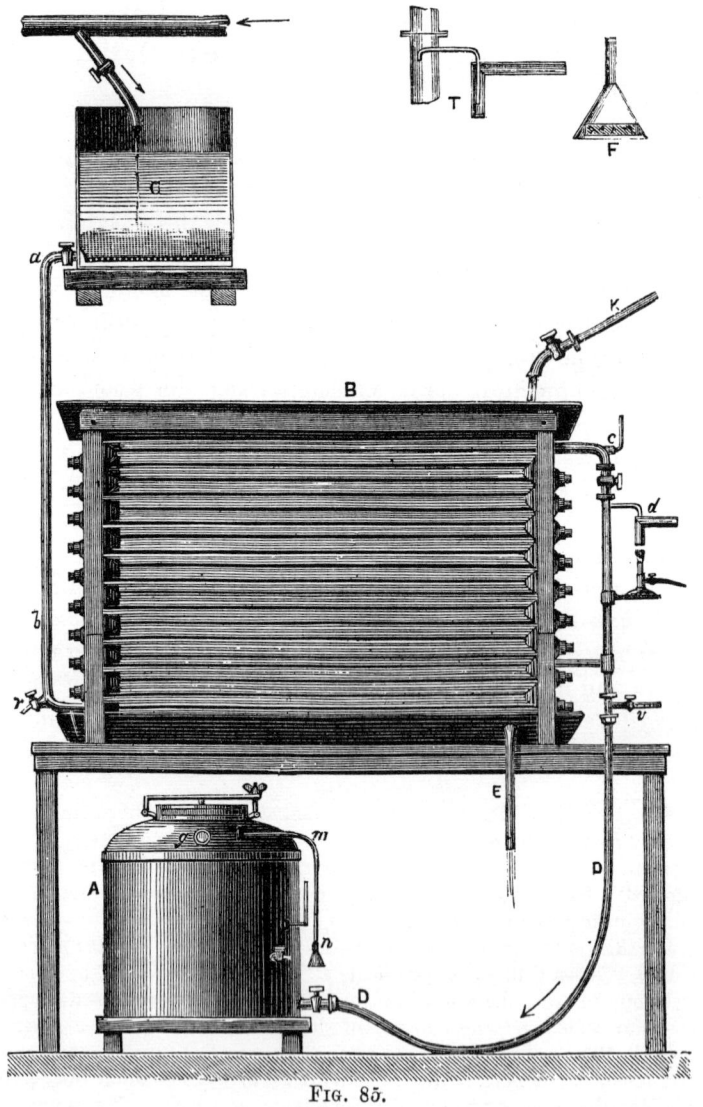

FIG. 85.

mometer *c*, passes down by the tube *c*DD to fill the fermenting vessel A. This vessel is made of tinned iron, or, better still, tinned copper, and has a cover provided with a man-hole and eye-hole; *m n* is one of the tubes for the circulation of air during fermentation; its connecting-tube is not represented, it would be behind the vessel.

At the point *d* there is a pipe for admission of pure air; this is represented on a larger scale at T. The wort, as it runs through the large tube, carries with it air from outside, and this air is calcined on its way in by means of a flame which plays on the copper tube through which it passes. This arrangement supplies a third or more of the total quantity of oxygen that the wort is capable of acquiring by solution at the temperature at which we work.

F represents the arrangement of the reversed funnel in which the tube *m n* terminates. Its mouth is closed with cotton-wool held in place between two pieces of wire gauze, for the purpose of purifying the air that enters by it into the fermenting vessel during fermentation.

v is an entrance tap for steam, by means of which the vessel and refrigerator are cleansed from all extraneous germs before each fermentation, and before the wort passes into the refrigerator.

When the fermenting vessel A is at work, we may start a fermentation in a second vessel in the following manner: opening a small tap situated at about a third of the height of the vessel, we pass a few litres of the fermenting beer into a can of tinned copper, previously purified by a current of steam, and filled with pure air. This can is then emptied into the fresh vessel, an operation of no difficulty, since we have merely to connect the tap of the can with the small tap of the vessel, and lastly, the vessel is filled with wort, which then mixes with the fermenting liquid. These various manipulations, it is evident, are performed under conditions of complete purity, without the slightest contact of the liquids either with the exterior air or with utensils contaminated by disturbing germs.*

* This arrangement limits the proportion of oxygen that may be introduced into the wort by direct oxidation. But it would be easy to

It is seldom that an industry adopts at once in their entirety new practices which would necessitate a re-arrangement of plant, and the process of which we are speaking would require such re-arrangement, as far as the fermenting vessels and the method of cooling the wort are concerned. The new process would, however, be of great value if once introduced, simply for the manufacture of pure ferment and pure wort, or even for that of pure ferment alone. In other words, we might retain the ordinary methods employed in low fermentation, use the same method of cooling or the new one, the same fermenting vessels, and the process of fermentation at low temperatures; the yeast, however, would be prepared in a state of purity in the closed vessel which we have described, collected in those vessels, aerated, and then employed after the old-established custom; better still, the pitching might be performed with beer in the act of undergoing pure fermentation.

Above the fermenting-stage there might be arranged a room for the vessels used in the new process, from which the pure beer could be run for pitching purposes into the large tuns in the brewery below. It is true that beer prepared in this manner would not be perfectly pure, but from the results which have

increase this at will, by causing the wort as it comes from the copper and the hop-back to pass into a cylinder turning horizontally on its axis and furnished with blades fixed inside, so as to divide the wort and bring it better into contact with the air in the cylinder. Instead of a revolving cylinder we might use a fixed vessel, in which the wort could be stirred up by some arrangement outside. In either case we should have to take care that the air was pure when it came into contact with the wort, but this would be a matter of no difficulty; we would simply have to make communication with the outer air by means of a tube filled with cotton wool. Any air that might be in the vessel at the moment when the wort was introduced would be purified by the high temperature of the wort coming from the copper. We should, moreover, gain the great advantage of being able to bring oxygen to bear on our wort in determinate amounts. From this vessel it would pass on to the refrigerator. We might again raise the wort oxidized on the coolers to a temperature of 75° C. (167° F.), to recool it in this manner and aerate it by means of the pure-air pipe.

been obtained by working on this system, there is no doubt that it would possess keeping qualities far superior to those of beer made with ordinary yeast, even supposing that beer to have been treated with every possible precaution, and to be as pure as any produced in the best regulated breweries.

In the month of September, 1874, we conducted an experiment at Tantonville, in a closed vessel capable of holding 6 hectolitres (132 gallons). The deposit of yeast served to pitch an open vessel, the wort of which had, moreover, been cooled under conditions of purity. The cooling had been effected by means of the Baudelot refrigerator, represented in Fig. 85, the wort in the closed vessel having been similarly treated. For shortness sake, we may designate the closed vessel and its beer by the letter K, and use the letter M for the open vessel and its beer, and T for the corresponding beer of the brewery. The vessel K was pitched on September 4th, and racked on September 17th, the beer then showing a density of 5·5° Balling.

The beers K and M were sent to Paris at the same time as some barrels of the beer T, brewed by the ordinary process; and samples of these different beers, which arrived on October 22nd, were procured from five different cafés for purposes of examination.

The beer M did not suffer by comparison with the beer T. The similarity between the flavours of these two was so close as to puzzle even experienced judges. In both cases the beer was brilliantly clear. In two cafés the beer M was even preferred to T, being considered softer on the palate (*moelleuse*) and of more decided character (*corsée*) than T, a circumstance which may be explained by the fact that its wort had been less aerated.

The beer K, although very clear and bright, was considered inferior to M, but the sole reason of this was that at the date when it was tasted—November 3rd—it did not froth. As we have already remarked, a peculiarity of the beers made in closed vessels is that their secondary fermentation takes a longer time to develop. The yeast held in suspension in the beer, at the moment when it is drawn off, is, in the case of all beers, the yeast of a supplementary fermentation, if we may use that expression. In the ordinary process of brewing, this yeast, in consequence of the greater aeration of the wort at the commencement of fermentation, is more active, or, rather, more ready to revive and multiply than is that which develops in closed vessels. If the barrels of the K beer had been tapped on the 12th or 15th of November, instead of on the 3rd, it is probable that they would have contained as much carbonic acid gas as the beer M contained at the earlier date. This delay in the resumption of fermentation, which characterizes beer made in closed vessels, is an advantage, inasmuch as it facilitates the transmission of the beer to long distances, besides giving us the smallest deposits of yeast in cask or bottle, as we have already pointed out.

In comparing the keeping qualities of the beer M and the beer T (the latter being the brewery beer), we made the following observations:—*

On November 25th we began to detect in the brewery beer an unsound flavour; a large deposit, too, had formed; the beer had lost its brilliancy, and frothed enormously. The deposit swarmed with diseased ferments, especially those represented in Nos. 1 and 7 of Plate I. The beer M, on the contrary, was in brilliant condition, with an insignificant deposit, and an ordinary froth, if anything, rather small, and beautifully bright.

On December 3rd the beer M was still good, very clear, and in excellent preservation; it was considered by professional brewers as remarkably sound.

December 22nd, the same beer M was still very bright and good.

January 20th, the beer was still bright; for the first time, however, we detected in the deposit in the bottles, which was still small, the filaments of turned beer. This unsoundness was

---

* One of the barrels of the brewery beer was bottled about the end of October, at the same time that a barrel of M was.

STUDIES ON FERMENTATION.   393

in its earliest stage. Now, comparing the relative unsoundness of the two beers, we see that M kept at least two months longer than the corresponding brewery beer. This example shows us that as far as the keeping powers and the quality of beer are concerned, the existing process would gain considerably by the employment of pure wort and pure ferment; and, indeed, it seems likely that the new process may be introduced into breweries with this object in view.

In the course of the summer of 1875 we made the following observations on the keeping qualities of a beer brewed on the new system, all the details of which had been rigorously carried out. The beer brewed at Tantonville during the months of June and July, at a temperature of 13° C. (55·4° F.), in 50-litre and 80-litre casks (11 and 18-gallon), had been sent by slow trains to Arbois (Jura), where we were staying for a time. The temperature of the wine cellars in which these barrels were stored was, on June 1st, 12·5° C. (54·5° F.); this rose gradually until September 1st, when it attained 18° C. (64·4° F.). In this cellar the brewery beer, brewed in the ordinary way, underwent change in the course of fifteen days or three weeks, whilst the beer brewed on the new system remained sound for several months. It is true that some of the barrels lost their frothiness, and that the beer in them underwent a peculiar vinous change, but these effects in no way depend on the conditions peculiar to the new process.

Comparing the beers K, M, T, of which we have been speaking, we see that, however useful the aeration and oxidation of the wort may be in quickening fermentation and facilitating clarification, yet it is by no means indispensable to the success of our operations that we should introduce into our worts large quantities of oxygen, whether by solution or combination. Beyond a certain limit—a limit which is undoubtedly overstepped in the existing process—oxygen is injurious to the palate characteristics and aroma of beer.

These comparisons have proved to us that the new process can be applied to wort aerated to the third of its saturate-capacity for oxygen, and pitched with a good " low " yeast, taken from the fermentation of a wort aerated in the same way, and that the beers thus obtained not only possess vastly superior keeping properties, but are equal in quality and superior in palate-fulness to beers brewed with the same wort on the existing system. We should be perfectly justified in forming this conclusion as to the *strength* * of the beer furnished by the new process, even if on tasting it we found that the new beer M was merely equal in strength to Tourtel's beer brewed in the ordinary manner, since the wort in the new process, other conditions being the same, is weaker than the same wort treated in the usual way, from not having undergone that evaporation on the coolers which concentrates it. If we were to restore to the concentrated wort of ordinary brewing all the water lost by it through evaporation, the beer that we should obtain would be sensibly weakened.†

One thing, however, is that we must employ good varieties of " low " yeast. We have seen how the employment of certain forms of yeast renders the clarification of beers difficult, as well as extremely slow, and almost prevents their falling bright at the end of fermentation. These yeasts, moreover, frequently impart to beer a peculiar yeast-bitten flavour, which does not disappear even after a prolonged stay in cask. Even repeated growth of these yeasts, whether in closed or in open vessels, and no matter what quantity of air we may supply them with

* Refer foot-note, page 354.
† The evaporation on the coolers varies according to the arrangements in different breweries; but in no case is it less than several hundredths of the total volume. One special advantage of the new process is that it gives us, *ceteris paribus*, a volume of beer that is 5, 6, or 7 per cent. greater than that which we should obtain by the old process, without in any way affecting the strength of the beer. It is easy to ascertain the quantity that evaporates on the coolers, by determining the quantity of water that must be added to a known volume of wort coming from the coolers to bring its density back exactly to that of the original wort, both being calculated to the same temperature. Bate's English saccharometer, which shows differences of nearly $\frac{1}{1000}$th in density, may be employed with advantage in this determination.

before fermentation, seems to have no effect in changing their character. The only thing we can do with these varieties of yeast is to get rid of them with all speed, and to replace them with others.

Notwithstanding the comparative success that has attended various trials of the new process on the commercial scale, that process has not yet been practically adopted: and here we must bear in mind that we have not to deal with any casual invention or mechanical improvement that could be introduced all at once into the working of a brewery; we are dealing with operations of considerable delicacy, which necessitate the adoption of a special plant to carry them out. Under such conditions time and labour are required to effect a change in the established processes of a great industry. This, however, cannot diminish the confidence that we have in the future of our process, and it is our hope that the same confidence will be shared in by all those who may give this work an attentive perusal.

APPENDIX.

Whilst this work was passing through the press there appeared two small works on the subject of the generation of inferior organisms.

One of them was by M. Fremy. The author's object seems to have been merely to give an account, under a new form, of the part which he took in the discussion on the origin of ferments that was carried on before the Academy of Sciences in 1871–1872. In the course of that discussion M. Fremy had announced his intention of publishing an extensive Memoir, full of facts, bearing on the subject. The perusal of the promised work gave us much disappointment. Not only were our experiments, and the conclusions which we drew from them, given there, for the most part in a manner which we could not possibly accept, but, moreover, M. Fremy had confined himself to deducing, by the help of his favourite hypothesis, a series of *à priori* opinions based on half-finished experiments, not one of which, in our opinion, had been brought to the state of demonstration. To tell the truth, his work was the romance of hemi-organism, just as M. Pouchet's work of an earlier date was the romance of heterogenesis. And yet, what could be clearer than the subject under discussion? We maintain, adducing incontestable experimental evidence in support of our theory, that

APPENDIX. 397

living, organized ferments spring only from similar organisms likewise endowed with life; and that the germs of these ferments exist in a state of suspension in the air, or on the exterior surface of objects. M. Fremy asserts that these ferments are formed by the force of hemi-organism acting on albuminous substances, in contact with air. We may put the matter more precisely by two examples:—

Wine is produced by a ferment, that is to say, by minute, vegetative cells which multiply by budding. According to us, the germs of these cells abound in autumn on the surface of grapes and the woody parts of their bunches; and the proofs which we have given of this fact are as clear as any evidence can be. According to M. Fremy, the cells of ferment are produced by spontaneous generation, that is to say, by the transformation of nitrogenous substances contained in the juice of the grape, as soon as that juice is brought into contact with air.

Again, blood flows from a vein; it putrefies, and in a very short time swarms with bacteria or vibrios. According to us the germs of these bacteria and vibrios have been introduced by particles of dust floating in the air or derived from the surface of objects, possibly the body of the wounded animal, or the vessels employed, or a variety of other objects. M. Fremy, on the other hand, asserts that these bacteria or vibrios are produced spontaneously, because the albumen, and the fibrin of the blood themselves possess a semi-organization, which causes them, when in contact with air, to change spontaneously into these marvellously active minute beings.

Has M. Fremy given any proof of the truth of his theory? By no manner of means; he confines himself to asserting that things are as he says they are. He is constantly speaking of hemi-organism and its effects, but we do not find his affirmations supported by a single experimental proof. There is, nevertheless, a very simple means of testing the truth of the theory of hemi-organism; and on this point M. Fremy and ourselves are quite at one. This means consists in taking a quantity of grape juice, blood, wine, &c., from the very interior of the organs which contain those liquids, with the necessary precautions to avoid contact with the particles of dust in suspension in the air or spread over objects. According to the hypothesis of M. Fremy, these liquids must of necessity ferment in the presence of pure air. According to us, the very opposite of this must be the case. Here, then, is a crucial experiment of the most decisive kind for determining the merits of the rival theories, a criterion, moreover, which M. Fremy perfectly admits. In 1863, and again in 1872, we published the earliest experiments that were made in accordance with this decisive method. The result was as follows:—The grape juice did not ferment in vessels full of air, air deprived of its particles of dust—that is to say, it did not produce any of the ferments of wine; the blood did not putrefy—that is to say, it yielded neither bacteria nor vibrios; urine did not become ammoniacal—that is to say, it did not give rise to any organism; in a word the origin of life manifested itself in no single instance.

In the presence of arguments so irresistible as these, M. Fremy, throughout the 250 pages of his work, continues to repeat that these results, which, he admits, seem subversive of his theory, are, nevertheless, explicable by the circumstance that the air in our vessels, although pure at first, underwent a sudden chemical change when it came in contact with the blood, or urine, or grape juice; that the oxygen became converted into carbonic acid gas, and that, in consequence, hemi-organism could no longer exercise its force. We are astonished at this assertion, for M. Fremy must be aware that, since 1863, we have given analyses of the air in our vessels after they had remained sterile for several days—for ten, twenty, thirty, or forty days—at the highest atmospheric temperatures, and that oxygen was still present, often even in proportions almost identical with those to be found in atmospheric air.* Why has M. Fremy made no allusion to these analyses? This was the chief, the essential

* See *Comptes rendus*, vol. lxi., p. 734, 1863.

APPENDIX. 399

point in question. Besides, if M. Fremy had wished to test the truth of his explanation, there was a very simple means of restoring the purity of the air in contact with the liquids open to him ; he might have passed through his vessels a slow and continuous current of pure air, day and night. We have done this a hundred times, and we have always found that the sterility of the putrescible or fermentable liquids remained unaffected.

The hemi-organism hypothesis is, therefore, absolutely untenable, and we have no doubt that our learned friend will eventually declare as much before the Academy, since he has more than once publicly expressed his readiness to do so as soon as our demonstrations appear convincing to him. How can he resist the evidence of such facts and proofs ? Persistence in such a course can benefit nobody, but it may depreciate the dignity of science in general esteem. It would gratify us extremely to find the rigorous exactness of our studies on this subject acknowledged by M. Fremy, and regarded by that gentleman with the same favour bestowed upon it everywhere abroad. It may be doubted if there exists at the present day a single person beyond the Rhine who believes in the correctness of Liebig's theory, of which M. Fremy's hemi-organism is merely a variation. If M. Fremy still hesitates to accept our demonstrations, the observations of Mr. Tyndall may effect his conversion.

The other publication to which we alluded was the work of the celebrated English physicist, John Tyndall. It was read before the Royal Society of London, at a meeting held on January 13, 1876.

The following letter explains how the illustrious successor of Faraday at the Royal Institution came to undertake these researches :—

" London, February 16, 1876.

" Dear Mr. Pasteur,—

" In the course of the last few years a number of works

bearing such titles as "The Beginnings of Life"; "Evolution and the Origin of Life," &c., have been published in England by a young physician, Dr. Bastian. The same author has also published a considerable number of articles in different reviews and journals. The very circumstantial manner in which he describes his experiments, and the tone of assurance with which he advances his conclusions, have produced an immense impression on the English as well as the American public. But what is more serious still, from a practical point of view, is the influence that these writings have exercised on the medical world. He has attacked your works with great vigour, and, although he has made but slight impression on those who know them thoroughly, yet he has succeeded in producing a very great and, I may add, a very pernicious one on others.

"The state of confusion and uncertainty had come to be so great that, about six months ago, I thought that I should be rendering a service to science, and at the same time performing an act of justice to yourself, in submitting the question to a fresh investigation. Putting into execution an idea which I had entertained for some six years, the details of which were set forth in an article in the *British Medical Journal*, which I had the pleasure of sending you, I have gone over a great deal of the ground on which Dr. Bastian had taken his stand, and, I believe, refuted many of the errors by which the public had been misled.

"The change which has taken place since then in the tone of the English medical journals is quite remarkable, and I am inclined to think that the general confidence of the public in the exactness of Dr. Bastian's experiments has been considerably shaken.

"In taking up these researches again, I have had occasion to refresh my memory by another perusal of your works; they have revived in me all the admiration which I experienced when I first read them. It is my intention now to pursue these researches until I have dissipated any doubts that may be entertained in respect to the unassailable exactness of your conclusions.

"For the first time in the history of science, we are justified in cherishing confidently the hope that, as far as epidemic diseases are concerned, medicine will soon be delivered from empiricism, and placed on a real scientific basis; when that great day shall come, humanity will, in my opinion, recognise the fact that the greatest part of its gratitude will be due to you.

"Believe me, ever very faithfully yours,

"JOHN TYNDALL."

We need scarcely say that we read this letter with the liveliest gratification, and were delighted to learn that our studies had received the support of one renowned in the scientific world alike for the rigorous accuracy of his experiments as for the lucid and picturesque clearness of all his writings. The reward as well as the ambition of the man of science consists in earning the approbation of his fellow-workers, or that of those whom he esteems as masters.

Mr. Tyndall has observed this remarkable fact, that in a box, the sides of which are coated with glycerine, and the dimensions of which may be variable and of considerable size, all the particles of dust floating in the air inside fall and adhere to the glycerine in the course of a few days. The air in the case is then as pure as that in our double-necked flasks. Moreover, a transmitted ray of light will tell us the moment when this purity is obtained. Mr. Tyndall has proved, in fact, that to an eye rendered sensitive by remaining in darkness for a little, the course of the ray is visible as long as there are any floating particles of dust capable of reflecting or diffusing light, and that, on the other hand, it becomes quite obscure and invisible to the same eye as soon as the air has deposited all its solid particles. When it has done this, which it will do very quickly

—in two or three days, if we employ one of the boxes used by Mr. Tyndall—it has been proved that any organic infusions whatever may be preserved in the case without undergoing the least putrefactive change, and without producing bacteria.

On the other hand, bacteria will swarm in similar infusions, after an interval of from two to four days, if the vessels which contain them are exposed to the air by which the cases are surrounded. Mr. Tyndall can drop into his boxes, at any time he wishes, some blood from a vein or an artery of an animal, and show conclusively that such blood will not, under these circumstances, undergo any putrefactive change.

Mr. Tyndall concludes his work with a consideration of the probable application of the results given in his paper to the etiology of contagious diseases. We share his views on this subject entirely, and we are obliged to him for having recalled to mind the following statement from our *Studies on the Silkworm Disease*:—"Man has it in his power to cause parasitic diseases to disappear off the surface of the globe, if, as we firmly believe, the doctrine of spontaneous generation is a chimera."

THE END.

INDEX.

A

Absorption of gases by air-free liquids, 292
 oxygen by blood, 50; by urine, 50
 from solutions by *bacteria*, 295
Acidity, natural, of wine a preservative, 2, and footnote
 of beer heated, 20
 action on ferments, 35
Acetate of lime from fermentation of tartrate, 288
Acid, sulphuric, facilitating filtration, 250
Acid, carbonic, *v.* carbonic acid
Adaptability of liquids to certain growths, 36, 73, 85
 (supposed) of vibrios to aërobian or anaërobian conditions, 309, 310
Aeration, reviving influence of, 138
 adoption by brewers of, 253
 tardy, of wort in deep vessels, 348
 on "coolers," its importance, 348, 349
Aeration-conditions in ordinary brewing process, 350, 351, 364, 365
Aeration of wort, apparatus for regulating, 352

Aeration, influence on clarification of worts, 381
 experiments on its influence on growth, 107, 130
Aërobian, definition, 116
 ferment, growth of, 208, 209
 ferments, general characteristics, 210; origin of, 210 (footnote); cultivation of, 211; aspects of, 212—217; distinguishing features of, 218
 life in ferments overlooked, 260
"Age," as applied to a ferment, 169
Age of cells, 246
Aged aspect of exhausted cells, 133, 147
Air, influence on ferment-life, 242
 renewal of, in brewers' yeast, 246, 247
 mode of expulsion from growing media, 285
 unnecessary to life of *vibrios*, 292
 injurious to life of *vibrios*, 304
Air, compressed, and ferment-life, 324
 composition unaffected by contact with blood, &c., 398
Albumen-transformation theory of fermentation, 273
Albuminous liquids, growth of yeast in, 265

D D 2

INDEX.

Alcohol, percentage in heated beer, 20
Alcoholic ferment, minute species of, 71
Alcohol, detection in minute quantity, 78, 79 (footnote)
    produced by *penicillium*, 99, and following pages
    by *aspergillus glaucus*, 101, and following pages
    by *mycoderma vini*, 111, 113
    explanation of, 114
Alcoholic fermentation, general explanation of, 114, 115
Alcohol, proportion of, to mucor forming it, 134, and following pages
Alcohol produced by moulds, 258 (footnote)
    production of, within fruits, 267
Alcoholic fermentation, restricted meaning, 275 (footnote)
    necessary relation with yeast-cells, 275
Alternaria tenuis, 157
Ammonia, a test for vegetable organisms (Robin), 312
Ammoniacal urine, 45, 46
Anaërobian, definition, 116
    growth of yeast, 239, and following pages
    precautions to be observed in, 248
    life of fruit-cells, 272
    growth of *vibrios*, 302
Animal or vegetable nature of organisms, 312, and following pages
Anti-ferments, 45
Apparatus for sterilizing liquids, 27
    for producing pure beer, 340, &c.
    for pure pitching, 344
    for pure aeration, 352
    for cooling beer with regulated supply of pure air, 388, 389
Appert's experiment, 62
Aroma of beer destroyed by excess of air, 353
Asbestos, useful plug, 27, and footnote, 30
Ascospores of yeast, 150 (footnote)
Aspect of yeast variable, 37

Aspergillus glaucus, functioning as ferment, 101, and following pages
    different aspects of, 105
Atmospheric germs, 6, 26, 38
    variety of, 39, 76, 87 (footnote)
Autonomy of organisms, 84 (footnote)

B

Bacteria, 35, 36; medium for growth of, 294; absorption of air from solutions by, 295
Bacteria and butyric vibrios, how related, 296
    influence of oxygen upon, 305
Bail mentioned, 92, 93, 127
Balling saccharometer explained, 363 (footnote)
Barley-wine, 1 (footnote), 230
Barley decoctions, experiments on development of ferments in, (Fremy) 273 (footnote)
Bary, De, mentioned, 92; on relations of yeast to other organisms, 180, 181
Bastian's experiments, 403
Baudelot refrigerator, 387 (footnote)
Bavarian beer, 10
Béchamp's *microzyma* theory, 121
    influence of air on fermentation, 178 (footnote)
Beer, definition, 1; difference between it and wine, 1
    changeable nature of: effects upon brewing purposes, 2, 3
    two kinds only, "high" and "low:" difference, 7
    samples of bottled, examined, 222
    general precautions for pure manufacture of, 338
    improved apparatus for commercial production, 340, and following pages
Beet root preservation in pits, 269 (footnote)
Berkeley mentioned, 92

INDEX. 405

Bellamy's researches on fermentation in fruits, 270
Berard on fermentation of fruits, 270, 271
Berthelot's mode of isolating inverting constituent of yeast, 322 (footnote)
Bert, action of compressed air on ferments, 324
Birds, experiment upon, described, 309
Bistournage, 43 (footnote)
Bisulphite of lime used by bottlers, 15
Blood, study of sterilized, 49, 50
Blood-crystals, 50 (footnote)
Boiling sterilizes liquids, 34
Bottling needle, 372 (footnote)
Bottled beer, treatment of, 16
Bouche influenced by presence of oxygen, 387
Bouchardat, 323
Brefeld, strictures on Pasteur's theory criticised, 280
convinced of truth of Pasteur's theory, 315, 316
Breweries, statistics of, 10
Brewing, change in processes of, 7
practices largely empirical, 222
Brewing processes under conditions of purity, 390
Budding, rate of, experiment on, 145
process of, 146
Buffon's hypothesis mentioned, 121
Bulbs, glass, for study of growths, 156 (footnote)
for vibrios, 298
Bunsen, tables of solubility of oxygen in water, 360
Butyric vibrios in must, 65; in wort, 70
Butyric acid from fermentation of lactates, 297
not a suitable food for vibrios, why? 301 (footnote)
Butyric fermentations yield variable products, 308

C

Cagniard Latour, on cause of fermentation, 60
Calmettes, M., 369, 371; experiments on the curve of cooling of wort, 377, 378
Carbolic acid for purifying yeasts, 232
Carbonate of lime crystals formed in fermentation of lactate, 294
Carbonic acid, influence on preservation and fermentation of fruits, 268
evolution from fermentation of tartrate of lime by vibrios, 287
amount of evolution, 288
mode of collection of, 288
influence on bacteria, 305 (footnote)
Caseous ferment, occurrence, 200; aspect, 201; endurance of heat, 203 (footnote); meaning of title, 202; origin of in brewers' high yeast, 203, 204; origin of in English pale ale, 204, 224; aërobian form of, 215
Cells, power of endurance, 134
aspect of dead, 139 (footnote)
Cells, glass, for study of growths, 155 (footnote)
Cells, probable function in elaborating proteic matter, 335
Cellulose, not soluble in ammonia (Robin), 312
Change of yeast, usual remedy for disease, 22
Chauveau on castration, 43
Circumstances modifying nature of germs present in atmosphere, 73, 87 (footnote)
Cladosporium, 55 (footnote)
Clarification of liquids by fungi, 66 (footnote)
of wort, 381, and following pages
of a wort and its beer not always correlated, 382, 383
Cohn's medium for growth of vibrios, 294 (footnote)

Colour darkened by oxidation in pure liquids, 57
Coloration of vibrio-fermented liquors, 291
Colpoda, 39, 40
Composition of medium, influence on life, 296
Conidia, definition, 137
Conditions affecting the ferment character of cells, 266
Consumption of beer in France, statistics, 17 (footnote)
Contagion and ferments, 41, and following pages
Continuity, non-, of germs in air, 62
Continuous vital activity of cells, 278
Contact-action, theory of, 326
"Coolers," importance in aeration of wort, 348, 349
  influence on worts, 364
Cooling of wort must be rapid in ordinary brewing, 2
  artificial of "low" beers, 12
Cooling of wort in presence of carbonic acid, 342; difficulties of the process, 346, and following pages
Corpuscles on grapes and stalks, 54
Corpuscles refractive in bodies of vibrios, 300, v. also cysts
Correlation of special germs with special fruits, 61
  of special ferment and fermentation product, 277
Cotze and Feltz, 43
Crushers for the vintage, 268 (footnote)
Cream of tartar, v. tartrate
Cultivation of yeast under conditions of purity, 29—32
  of pure penicillium, mode of, 88, and following pages
  of aërobian ferments, 211, and following pages
Cysts of vibrios, 306, 307

D

Davainne, on splenic fever, &c., 42

Daughter-cells, 146
Dead cells, aspect of, 139 (footnote)
Declat's treatment of infectious diseases, 44
Dematium, 167; resemblance to *Saccharomyces pastorianus*, 179, 180, 181, 214
  resemblance to "caseous" yeast, 201
Degrees, Balling, v. Balling
Deposits, amorphous, of wort, 6, 193, 385, and footnote
Deterioration of beer correlated with presence of foreign organisms, 26, 32
Differential vitality, a means of separating ferments, 226
Difficulty of experiments on growths, 63, 85
Disease-ferments, what they are, why so called, 4
  classification and account of, 5, 6
  origin of, 6
  inactive at low temperatures, 14
  often found only in deposits, 24
  not everywhere in atmosphere, 31
Disease-germs usually latent, 220
  development in bottled beer, 222
Diseases of wort and beer, meaning of, 19
  mode of proving the cause of, 19, 20
Diseased beer always result of disease ferments, 26
Distribution of germs limited, 61
Division, fissiparous, of vibrios, 299
Dried yeast, 81
Dryness decreases sensitiveness of moulds to heat, 35
Dumas, distinction between organized and unorganized ferments, 323
Dust, atmospheric, contains disease-germs, 6, 26
  on fruits, experiments with, 153, and following pages
  when fertile, 157, and following pages
Dutch yeast, 200

Duval, Jules, experiments on transformation of ferments illusory, 37

E

Efflorescence of fermented liquors, 108, 117
Egg-albumen, experiments on, 51
Egypt, beer first brewed in, 17
Empiricism in ordinary brewing, 222
Energy stored by cells, 133, 134
Endogenous sporulation of yeast, 150 (footnote), 172
English beers all "high," 7
 temperatures and yeast employed, 8 (footnote)
 breweries, usages of, 8 (footnote), 14
Errors, causes of, *v.* experimental errors
Equations of fermentations variable, 276, 277
Examination of deposits, mode of, 21 (footnote)
Exhaustion, definition of, 171 (footnote)
Exhausted vibrios, 290
Experimental errors, 63, 85, 92
 avoided by use of double-necked flasks, 120
Experiments, exactness of Pasteur's, 95 (footnote)
 to prove connection between quality of ferment and quality of beer, 26, and following pages
 on living fluids, 47, and following pages
 comparative, on pure must and must with corpuscles boiled and unboiled, 54, and following pages
 by Gay-Lussac on must, 62, 63
 by Pasteur after Gay-Lussac, 64
 on distribution of ferments, 65, and following pages
 on distribution of fungus-spores, 68

Experiments in wide shallow dishes, 69, and following pages
 comparative on germs in air, 72, and following pages
 with non-fermentative species of *torula*, 78
 on spontaneous impregnations, 65, 66, 69, 73, 79, 87 (footnote)
 on spontaneous fermentation, 184
 on dried yeast, 81, and following pages
 on influence of aeration on growths, 107
 on aeration and its absence, 130, and following pages
 on function of oxygen on ferment-life, 238, and following pages
 on the capacity of yeast for oxygen, 255
 on influence of carbonic acid on fruits, 268
 on growth of vibrios apart from air, 285
 on fermentation of lactate of lime apart from air, 292, and following pages
 on influence of air on vibrio-life, 303, 304
 on influence of air on bacterium-life, 305
 on gradual adaptability of organisms to adverse life-conditions, 309
 on influence of air on fermentation, 349
 on solubility-coefficients of wort for oxygen, 361—3
 of brewers' worts, 366, and following pages
 on combination of oxygen with worts, 371, and following pages
 on the rapidity of the combination, 376
 on amount of combination, 379
 on non-transformation of *mycoderma vini*, 110, and following pages, 113 (footnote)

Experiments on non-transformation of *mycoderma aceti*, 124, and following pages
   of *mucor racemosus*, 128, and following pages
   on non-transformation of yeast into penicillium, 333—335
   on cultivating pure *penicillium*, 88, and following pages
   on its transformation into yeast, 91
   transformation, Trécul's, details of, 98
   with submerged *aspergillus*, 101, and following pages
   penicillium, 99
   in disproof of the *hemi-organism* theory, 273 (footnote)
   on growth of mixed moulds, 112
   on purification of mixed ferments, 226, and following pages
   on growth of *mucor mucedo*, 140, 141
   on proportion between weights of mucor and alcohol formed, 134, and following pages
   on the anaërobian cultivation of yeast, 239, and following pages
   on variation of proportion of sugar used to yeast formed, 249
   on growth of yeast in sugar solutions, 318, and following pages, 331—333
   on dust on fruits, 153, and following pages
   on seasonal influences on fertility of dust-germs, 157, and following pages
   on exhaustion of yeast, 169, and following pages
   of "high" yeast, 189, 190
   on revival of yeast, 207, 208
   on cultivation of aërobian ferment, 211, and following pages
   on gradual *senescence* of yeast, 245
   on production of a pure beer, 338, and following pages
   on clarification of worts and beers, 382, and following pages

Experiments, comparative, on the qualities of beers brewed by different processes, 391
   on rate of budding, 145
Exportation of "high" beers unsatisfactory, 16

F

Ferment, *v.* also yeast
Ferments of disease, *v.* disease-ferments
Ferments, special, 14, 15
Ferments and animal diseases, 41, and following pages
   butyric, lactic, alcoholic, 72
   moulds functioning as, 100, 101, and following pages, 111, 113, 129, 133
   general character of a, 115
   of grape, varieties, origin, 150, and following pages
   alcoholic, summary of, 196
   intermixture of, 224, 225
   mode of separation of mixed, 226 and following pages
   succession of, in must, 227
   exceptional vital processes of, 236, 237
Ferment power in relation to time discussed, 252
   character, how related to heat, 270
   and fermentation correlated, 277
   a chemical substance existing in cells (Traube), 283 (footnote)
   of tartrate of lime, 290
Ferments, two classes, distinctive characteristics, 323
Fermentation, rapid, inexpedient, 3
   spontaneous, in case of must, 4
   "top" and "bottom," *v.* "high" and "low"
   masked by moulds in shallow vessels, 75 (footnote)
   by *penicillium* (Trécul) 94
   by *mycoderma vini*, 111, 113
   by *mucor racemosus*, 129, 139
   alcoholic, general explanation of, 114, 115

Fermentation, conditions of, in sweetened mineral liquids, 211
without air, 242
with and without air, results compared, 243, 244
a cell-life without air, 259
a general phenomenon, 266, 267
of fruits not truly "alcoholic," 276
not definable, according to Brefeld, as life without air, 280
of lactate of lime, 294
Fermentative energy, 252
character dependent on conditions, 266
Filamentous tissue (Turpin), 123
Fitz on fermentation, 142
Fissiparous division of vibrios, 299
Flask sterilizing, 27, 29
Flasks with double necks, advantage of, 120
Fluid, Raulin's, 88 (footnote)
Flavour dependent on ferment species, 230
Foreign organisms correlated with unsound beer, 26, 32
greatly promoted by adaptability of liquids, 36
Formula for solubility-coefficient of any wort for oxygen, 364
Fremy's statement of *hemi-organism*, 52
answer to Pasteur's facts, 58
explanation of vintage fermentation, 272
"organic impulse," 325
latest assertions, 396—399
Fruits, ferment organisms on surface of, 153, and following pages
internal fermentation of, 267, and following pages
yeast cells not present within, 267 (footnote)
influence of carbonic acid gas on preservation of, 268
respiratory processes of, according to Bérard, 270
fermentation within, Lechartier and Bellamy, 270

Fruits, crushed and uncrushed, fermentation of, 274
Fruit-cells, anaërobian life of, 272
Fungi, wide distribution of spores, 68
absorption of oxygen by, 257
production of alcohol by, 258 (footnote)
Fungoid manner of growth of well-aerated yeast, 251

G

Galland's claims of priority, 338 (footnote)
Gay-Lussac's experiments on grape-juice, 59, 60
Gayon's experiments on egg-albumen, 51
"Gathered," 367 (footnote)
Generation, theories of, contrasted, 397
Germs of ferments in air, &c., 6, 26, 38
brought by other matters, 38
absent from fruits, when? 58, 59, 157, and following pages
not universally distributed, 61, 63, 181 (footnote)
distribution experiments, 65, and following pages, 87 (footnote)
and their correlated fruits, 61
of disease latent, 220
Germ, use of term by Pasteur, 313
Germ theory of disease discussed, 46, 47
Globuline tissue (Turpin), 123
Globulines, punctiform, 121, and following pages
Globules, 275 (footnote)
Glycerine, fermentation of, by vibrios, 306, 307
Gosselin, M., report, 44
and Robin on ammoniacal urine, 45
Gramme, value in grains, 135 (footnote)
Granules in wort, explanation of, 95
Graham's, Dr., criticisms of Pasteur, 13 (footnote), 196 (footnote)

Graham, Dr., on aspect of bottom yeast, 194 (footnote)
Grape juice, experiments on, 57, 59
Grape-ferments, *v.* ferments
Grapes, do they contain cells of yeast? 267
Greasiness of *mycoderma vini*, 80, and footnote

H

Hallier mentioned, 92
Hard water, influence on aspect of yeast, 194 (footnote)
Head of vibrio, 292
Heating sufficient as preventing deterioration of liquids, 20
    influence on beer, 20
Heat, production of, its relation to ferment-power, 270
Hemi-organism, chimerical, 53, 162, 399, 273 (footnote)
    latest assertions by Fremy on subject of, 396—399
    theory of vintage-fermentation, 272, 273
Heterogenesis, facts against, 51
"High" fermentation, meaning of, 8, 9
    beers, disadvantages of, 12, 13
    ferment, aspect of, 188, 189
    characteristics of, summary, 191
    ferment (new), occurrence, 198
    aspect and characteristics of, 199
    aërobian form of, 216
High yeast, aërobian form, aspect of, 214
Hoffmann, H., transformation of ferment, 92, 93
Hop-oil as a beer-antiseptic, 16, and footnote
Hopping influence on growths *quâ* temperature, 96
Hot countries, absence of breweries in, 16
Hydrogen from vibrionic life, 300

Hydrogen, occasional absence in butyric fermentations, 308
Hydrosulphite of soda, composition, use in determinations of oxygen, 355, and footnote
    preparation of *saturated* solution, 357 (footnote)
    alterability of solutions of, 356
    improved method of M. Raulin, 356, and following pages

I

Ice, quantities consumed in "low" breweries, 11
Illusions as to absence of foreign organisms, 36, 85, 92
Impregnations, spontaneous, 65, 66, 69, 73, 79
Impregnation, mode of (*penicillium glaucum*), 86
Impurity of ferments, source of experimental errors, 37
    of yeast masked for a time, 220
Increase of yeast disproportionate to sugar used, 237
Infusions, nature of organisms in, 39
Infusoria, 35
Insoluble substances in wort, 386
Inverting constituent of yeast, 321, and footnote
Isolation of ferment, 77

L

Lactic ferments, 5, 36
    transformation from and into other ferments (Duval), 37
Lactate of lime, fermentation of, 292
Lechartier and Bellamy, researches on fermentation in fruits, 270
Leptothrix, 36
Liebig's views of fermentation, 317, and following pages
    on fermentation of malate of lime, 321
    definition of a ferment, 324

INDEX. 411

Liebig's modified theory, 326 ; answer to, by Pasteur, 326, 327
neglect of microscopical observations, 329, 330
Lime, bisulphite, use of, by bottlers, 15
carbonate sterilized, use of in growths, 126
dextro-tartrate, 284
acetate and metacetate, 288
lactate, fermentation of, 292
Lister's, Prof., letter on germ-theory, 43
London breweries, usages of, 8 (footnote)
Pasteur's visit to, 22—24
"Low" fermentation, meaning of, 9, 10 ; advantages, 12
beer breweries, statistics of, 10
properties of, according to Dr. Graham, 13
yeast and "high" yeast distinct, 192, 193
yeast, aspect of, 193 ; characteristics, 195
aërobian form of, 215
Low temperatures prejudicial to disease-ferments, 14

M

Malignant pustule, 42
Mashings, 3
Medium, mineral, for growing lactic vibrios, 293, 297 (footnote)
Cohn's formula, 294 (footnote)
for growth of bacteria, 294
Medium, composition of, influence on life, 296
Microscopical study of yeast important, 23
formerly neglected in English breweries, 22—24
Microscopical examination of vibrios, 298, 299
Microzyma, 121 ; source of *mycoderma aceti* according to Béchamp, 124

Milk, temperature of sterilization of, 34
Milk-sugar, growth of yeast in, 265
Mother of vinegar, v. mycoderma aceti
Moulds thrive in acid liquors, 36
functioning as ferments, 100, 101, and following pages, 111, 113, 129, 133
growth of, and production of alcohol, 257, 258 (footnote)
suggested employment of, industrially, 261
Mucedines, 36, 40
Mucor mucedo and *racemosus* on must, 66
Mucor racemosus, different aspects of, 105
pure growth of, 128, and following pages
Mucor normal, growth of, 132
weight of to alcohol formed, 134, and following pages
morphology of abnormal growth, 137
Mucor mucedo distinguished from *racemosus*, 140
growth in double-necked flasks, 140, 141
Müntz, 323
Must, fermentation of, always regular, 3
pure fermentation of, 54, and following pages
succession of ferments in, 227, 228
Mycelium and *mycoderma vini* on wine, 56, 65
Mycoderma in wort experiments, 70
Mycoderma vini, arborescent form of, 77
growth of pure, experiments on, 110, and following pages, 120
growth with *penicillium*, 112
with *mucor*, 112
endogenous sporulation, 151 (footnote)
Mycoderma aceti transformations (Béchamp), 124
pure growth of, 124, and following pages

N

Nageurs used in low fermentation, 9
Nature of liquids, influence on growths, 36, 73, 85
Natural liquids for pure growths, use of, 40, 41
  experiments on, 47, and following pages
Neutrality, conditions of, as affecting sterilization of liquids, 34; explanation of fact, 35
Neutralization of acidity in pure growths, mode of, 126
New high ferment, *v.* high
New process of brewing, 391—393
Nitrogenous soluble parts of yeast, 319, 320
Nomenclature used by Pasteur purposely vague, 314
Normal growth of mucor, 132

O

Organic substances, have they any tendency to become organized? 33
Organic liquids sterilized by boiling, 34
Organizable globulines (Turpin), 123
Organisms and animal diseases, 42
Ouillage, 2
Oxidation of germ-free liquids, 57
  processes of fungi, 261, and footnote
  of wort, excessive, injurious, 353, 354
Oxygen absorbed by blood, 50
  by urine, 50
  and fermentation, according to Gay-Lussac, 60
  store-energy imparted to cells by, 134
  no influence upon fermentation, (Béchamp), 178 (footnote)
  function in fermentation, experiments on, 238, and following pages

Oxygen, influence on fermentation (Schützenberger and Pasteur), 253, 254
  amount absorbable by yeast, 255
  deficiency of, function in fermentation, 259
  influence on products, 100, 108, 113
  influence on morphology of moulds and ferments, 105, 106, 133, 137, 262
  necessity of, to growth of yeast discussed, 280
  unnecessary and adverse to vibrionic life, 284, and following pages
  necessary to bacterial life, 305
  removal from solutions by bacteria, 295
  growth of vibrios apart from, 302
  compressed, influence on ferment life, 324
  determination of, in worts (Schützenberger), 355, and following pages
  solubility-coefficients in water (Bunsen), 360
  usual amounts in solution in brewers' worts, 366, 367
  changes in amounts during brewing processes, 369, 370
  combination of, with hopped wort, 371, and following pages
  experiments on rapidity of combination, 376
  on amount of, under brewing conditions, 379
  in combination with wort not available for yeast, 380, 381
  clarification of wort by, 385

P

Palate-fulness definition, 354, and footnote
  impaired by oxidation, 354
Parasites and their germs, 40
  influence on animal diseases, 41

INDEX. 413

Pasteur's repetition of Trécul's experiments, 98, 99
   subject of his inquiries stated, 311
   experiments, exactness of, 95 (footnote)
Pasteurization, meaning and use, 15 (footnote)
Patches of froth in growth of pure yeast, 31
Penicillium glaucum on must, 66
   growth of pure, 86, and following pages
   precaution, 89
   transformed into ferment (Trécul), 94
   spores, varieties of, 97
   production of alcohol by, 99, and following pages
   transformation into mycoderma, 109
Phenol for purifying yeasts, 232
Pitching, mode of, for pure beer, 342, and following pages
   flasks, 344
   peculiar in London breweries, explanation, 350, 351
Plaster of Paris and yeast powder, 81, and following pages
Ploussard grapes, experiments on, 161
Polymorphism of organisms, 84 (footnote), also v. transformation
Precautions for pure fermentation of must, 64
   brewers', to check disease-germs, 220, and following pages
   for pure anaërobian growth of yeast, 248
Preservation of yeast, 207
Preoccupation of liquids by organisms, 36, 109, 220
Products of fermentation variable, 276, 277
Price of beer as affected by losses from disease, 24
Proliferous pellicles, 121
Proportions of alcoholic products variable, 276, 277

Proportions of products diagnostic of the fermentation, 279
Proteic matter elaborated by cells, 335
"Pulling up," 343
Pure growth of yeast, precautions for, 29—32
   growths in natural liquids, 40, 41
   wort and ferment, advantages of, 391—393
Purification of mixed ferments, 226, and following pages
   practical methods, growth in sweetened water, 230
   shallow basins, 231
   in acid and alcoholic liquids, 231
   with aid of carbolic acid, 232
Putrid wort, ferments of, 5
Putrefaction prevented by use of sterilizing flask, 27
   of yeast, cause of, 221
   of tartrate of lime, 291

Q

Qualities of "high" and "low" beers, 12, 13, 19, 196
Quality of beer dependent on kind of ferment, 26, and following pages

R

Racking, 222
   precautions necessary in, 351
Raulin's fluid, 88 (footnote)
   improvement on Schützenberger's oxygen process, 356, and following pages
   experiments on solubility of oxygen in worts, 361—363
Rayer on splenic fever, &c., 42
Reducing action of vibrios, 291
Rees, Dr., 150 (footnote)
Refrigerator, Baudelot's, 387 (footnote)

Revival of mould-cells by aeration, 130, 131 (footnote), 138
Revival of starved yeast, 148, 208
vibrios, 301, 302
Ripening of fruits, 270, 271
Robin, Ch., mentioned, 93; strictures on Pasteur, 310, 311
recantation of views on ferment-action, 314

S

Saccharomyces apiculatus, 71, and footnote, 150
exiguus, 185, *ellipsoideus*, 165
pastorianus, 151; mode of growth of, 167
two aspects, globular and filamentous, 168, 169
exhaustion and revival of, aspects, 172, and following pages
occurrence as impurity in most ferments, 225
most suitable for growth experiments in sugar solutions, 332
Saccharomyces pastorianus, *ellipsoideus*, *apiculatus* in must, 227, and following pages
Sang de rate, 43
Schützenberger on budding of yeast, 146, and footnote
Schützenberger's strictures on Pasteur's views answered, 252, and following pages
process for determining oxygen in solutions, 355
Seasons, influence on success in brewing, 25
at which germs are absent on fruits, 58, 59
Secondary fermentation in English beers, 224.
Senescence of yeast cells, 208
gradual of yeast cells, experiments on, 245
Shallow basins for purification of yeasts, 231

Sodium hydrosulphite, *v.* hydrosulphite
Solubility-coefficients of oxygen in water (Bunsen), 360
in worts (Raulin), 361—363
Sour beer, ferments of, 5
Soundness of beer always dependent on purity of yeast, 26, 32
Specialization of ferment-variations, 197
Specimens, necessary precautions for taking, 126 (footnote)
Splenic fever, 42
Spontaneous fermentation used in must, not in beer, 4
fermentation or putrefaction prevented by use of sterilizing flask, 28
ferment, definition of, 182; experiment on, 184
generation, facts against, 51, 52, 57
supported by experimental errors, 62, 63
(Trécul's theory of), 94, 95
impregnations, 65, 66, 69, 73, 79
use in isolating ferments, 77
Spores on grapes, gooseberries, &c., 54
of fungi widely distributed, 68
Statistics of breweries, 10
of French beer consumption, 17 (footnote)
Starved yeast, appearance of, 148
Stability of sterilized liquids, 286
Stemphylium spores, 55 (footnote)
Sterilizing apparatus, 27, 29, 285
flask, 28
Sterilization-temperature of various liquids, 34
Stock beer, 223
Store beer, must be surrounded by ice, 16
Straw wine, peculiar fermentation of, 166
Strength, Pasteur's use of word, 354
saving by the new process, 394
Submerged *penicillium*, 99
aspergillus, 101, and following pages
mycoderma, 111, 113, and following pages
mucor, 129, and following pages, 133

INDEX. 415

Submerging growths, precautions for, 91 (footnote)
Succession of transformations (Trécul's scheme), 93, 94
Sugar decomposition by submerged cells, 114
    different modes of, by different cells, 115
    decomposed disproportionate to yeast formed, 237, and following pages
    variation of disproportion in different cases, 249
    amount decomposed in a given time, as an index of fermentative energy (Schützenberger's views), 252
    solutions pure with mineral salts, growth of yeast in, 317, and following pages
    denial of the fact by Liebig and reply by Pasteur, 328, 329
Surface growth of yeast in pure culture, 31
Sweetened water for exhausting yeast, 169, 170, 190
    for purification of yeasts, 230

T

Tartrate-acid of potash for purifying yeasts, 231
    -dextro of lime, fermentation of, 284, and following pages
    products of, 288
    ferment of, 290
Temperatures in use in London breweries, 8 (footnote)
    high, prejudicial to quality of "low" beer, 19
    at which disease-ferments perish, 20; differs in different liquids, 34, 96
    influence on fermentation, 129

Temperatures suitable for "high" or "low" yeasts respectively, 192
    influence of on mixed "high" and "caseous" yeasts, 203
    for observing active vibrios, 299
Theories of generation opposite stated, 397
Tieghem, Van, on ammoniacal urine, 45
Torula, sense in which used, 73 (footnote)
    varieties of, 77
    non-fermentative species, 78
Transformation of ferments, according to Duval, 37
    of non-fermentative to fermentative impracticable, 80
    of *penicillium* into yeast impracticable, 91
    of ferment into moulds (Hoffmann), 92
    series, Trécul's scheme of, 93, 94
    of *penicillium* to *mycoderma* (Ch. Robin), 109 (footnote)
    of *mycoderma vini* refuted, 113 (footnote)
    Turpin's system of, 122, and following pages
    of *mycoderma aceti* (Béchamp), 124
    historical account of views on, 128 (footnote)
    of *mucor* (Bail), 127
    of filamentous into globular yeast, 169
    of yeast into *penicillium*, &c., impracticable, 333—335
    mutual of low and high yeast, discussed, 192, 193
    of "high" yeast into "caseous" ferment illusory, 203
    of albumen, theory of the vintage, 272, 273
    theory disproved generally, 273 (footnote)
Traube, Dr., on ammoniacal urine, 46

Traube, Dr., researches on fermentation, 282
theory of fermentation, 283 (footnote)
Trécul and Fremy, *v.* Fremy
Trécul's theory of successive transformations, 93, 94
    details of transformation experiments, 98
    theory refuted, 99
Trousseau grapes, experiments on, 162
"Turned" beer, ferments of, 5; filaments of, 23
"Turning out," 367 (footnote)
Turpin, M., mentioned, 92
Turpin's system of transformations, 122, and following pages, 113 (footnote)
Tyndall, letter to Pasteur, 399—401

U

Unsoundness of beer correlated with disease-organisms, 26, 32
Urea-ferment, the transformation of (Duval), 37
Urine, ammoniacal, 45, 46
Urine, sterilized, study of, 49, 50

V

Variability of fermentation products, 277
Variations of ferment strengthened and established, 197
Varieties of yeast, 149, and following pages
Vaureal, De, budding of yeast, 146 (footnote)
Vegetable distinguished from animal organisms by ammonia (Robin), 312
Vesicular tissue (Turpin), 123

Vibrio, 36; butyric, 65, 70
    also an example of anäerobian life, 282, 284
    active and exhausted, 290
    reducing action of, 291
Vibrionic ferment of tartrate of lime, 290
Vibrios, *head* of, 292; supposed reproductive corpuscles, 306
    growth of, in lactate media, 293
    medium for growth of, according to Cohn, 294 (footnote)
    not genetically related to bacteria, 296
    of butyric fermentation, description of, 298, 300
    mode of examining microscopically, 298
    fissiparous division of, 299
    measurements of, 300
    cannot live on butyrates, 301 (footnote)
    revival of, 301, 302; anaërobian growth of, 302
    life of, destroyed by oxygen, 303, 304
Vigour of ordinary brewer's yeast, 246
Vin de paille, 166
Vinegar, temperature at which it is sterilized, 34
Vinous flavour in stock beer, 224
Vintage, varied conditions of, 268 (footnote)
    fermentation, theory of, according to Fremy, 272, and following pages
Viscous wort, ferments of, 5
Visit to London brewery by Pasteur, 22—24
Vital processes of ferment exceptional, 237
    activity of yeast apart from air, 259
    potential in cells, 278
Vitiation of experiments, causes of, 63, 85, 92

W

Wad-dressing, antiseptic, 44
Water, hard, influence on aspect of yeast, 194 (footnote)
Weights of *mucor* and alcohol, proportion of, 134, and following pages
Weight of yeast grown, what due to, 257 (footnote)
Wide dishes, experiments on fermentation in, 69, 70
favourable to mould developments, 75 (footnote)
Wine, less liable to deteriorate than beer, 2
temperature of sterilization, 34
Wort, definition, 2; cooling of, 3, 4
temperature of sterilization, 34
solubility of oxygen in, 361, and following pages
formula for solubility in any wort, 364
Worts, brewers', usual amounts of oxygen in solution, 366, 367
experiments on amounts, 379
Wort, hopped, its affinity for oxygen, 371, and following pages
mode of transmitting it free of oxygen, 371, 372
insoluble substances in, 386

Y

Yeast, v. also ferment, germs, torulæ
nature and properties of, 143, and following pages
starved and well-nourished, appearances contrasted, 147, 148
varieties of, 149, and following pages
commercial origin of, where? 187
relations to other organisms, 180, 181

Yeast, commercial mixtures, 224, 225
practical purification of, 230-233
impurities in masked for a time, 220
exceptional characteristics of, 237
growth of in sterilizing flasks, 29—32
not transformable into any other organism, 37
aspect may change under modified circumstances, 37
non-transformation of *mycoderma vini* into, 120
mucor into, 132
non-fermentative species of, 79, 80, 206, 207
"high," characteristic aspect of, 188—192
well aerated, fungoid mode of growth, 251
anaërobian growth, cause of fermentation, 259
growth of, in solutions of sugar, 318, and following pages
growth in relation to proportion of sugar used, 237, and following pages
difficult propagation in saccharine mineral media, 329, 330
growth of, without producing alcohol, 265
capacity of absorbing oxygen, 255
necessity of oxygen for its growth discussed, 280
incapable of using oxygen in combination in worts, 380, 381
soluble nitrogenous part of, 320, 321, 79 (footnote)
dried into dust still active, 81, and following pages
does not perish at temperatures at which disease-ferments do, 20
sudden inactivity of, cause and cure, 347 footnote)

Yeast, change of, a trade custom, 22
   reason of addition of yeast to wort, 3
   proportion commonly added, 3
   reason of the large proportion used, 343
Yeast-cells abundant in brewing laboratories, 75
   gradual senescence of, 245

Yeast-cells, mode of examining fruits for, 267 (footnote)
   necessary relation to "alcoholic fermentation," 275
Yeast-water, definition, 79 (footnote)
   exhaustion of yeast by, 171
   use of in pure growths (*penicillium*), 88
"Youth" of cells, 246